DISTANT DRUMS

THE ROLE OF COLONIES IN BRITISH
IMPERIAL WARFARE

This book is dedicated to
my three brothers,
David Lawrence Jackson, Matthew John Jackson,
and Paul Daniel Jackson,
boys from Bodmin Moor

DISTANT DRUMS

THE ROLE OF COLONIES IN BRITISH IMPERIAL WARFARE

ASHLEY JACKSON

sussex
ACADEMIC
PRESS
Brighton • Portland • Toronto

2 4 6 8 10 9 7 5 3

First published in hardcover 2010, reprinted in paperback 2012, by
SUSSEX ACADEMIC PRESS
PO Box 139
Eastbourne BN24 9BP

and in the United States of America by
SUSSEX ACADEMIC PRESS
920 NE 58th Ave   Suite 300
Portland, Oregon 97213-3786

and in Canada by
SUSSEX ACADEMIC PRESS (CANADA)
8000 Bathurst Street, Unit 1, PO Box 30010, Vaughan, Ontario L4J 0C6

British Library Cataloguing in Publication Data
A CIP catalogue record for this book is available from the British Library.

Library of Congress Cataloging-in-Publication Data
Jackson, Ashley.
Distant drums : the role of colonies in British imperial warfare / Ashley Jackson.
    p. cm.
Includes bibliographical references and index.
ISBN 978-1-84519-349-2 (hbk. : acid-free paper)
ISBN 978-1-84519-438-3 (pbk. : acid-free paper)
    1. Great Britain—Colonies—History. 2. Great Britain—Colonies—History, Military. 3. Great Britain—Colonies—History, Naval. 4. Great Britain—History, Military. 5. Great Britain—History, Naval. 6. Great Britain—Colonies—Defenses. I. Title.
DA16.J24 2010
355.009171′241—dc22

2009018794

Mixed Sources
Product group from well-managed forests and other controlled sources
www.fsc.org Cert no. SGS-COC-2482
© 1996 Forest Stewardship Council

Typeset and designed by Sussex Academic Press, Brighton & Eastbourne.
Printed by TJ International, Padstow, Cornwall.

Contents

List of Illustrations

*Cover illustration*s: front, top, Nigerian troops, 1915; middle, a recruitment poster that uses Ceylonese national sentiment — an appeal to the Lion of Lanka and the need to defend the homeland (SLNA); bottom, Sikhs on the march in France, 1916; back, Air Vice Marshal Sir Keith Park climbs away from Malta in his Spitfire, seen off by Mauritian and Basotho troops (IWM).

Illustrations are placed after page 172.

The author and publisher are grateful to Sri Lanka National Archives in Colombo (SLNA) and the Imperial War Museum, London (IWM), and their respective liaison personnel, for permission to reproduce the above photographs.

Preface

Distant Drums contributes to several distinct fields of imperial, military, naval, and regional history. It is a book about the history of imperial warfare, the history of the Indian Ocean, and individual countries in Africa and Asia, which deepens our understanding of the metropolitan and peripheral connections that bound the Empire together all along the chain of imperial command — from Whitehall to Pretoria to Mafeking and Serowe, and from the Admiralty Building to river gunboats on the Yangtze. It is argued in this book that the colonial empire was in fact at the very heart of imperial defence for a number of reasons, despite the common focus on the defence deliberations and capabilities of Britain, the Dominions, and India. It is also argued that the role of colonies in imperial defence needs to be far better integrated with the history of the British military, the history of world wars, and the national histories of dozens of former colonies. *Distant Drums* thus seeks to tie a grand strategic awareness of imperial warfare to the minutiae of war in distant places and the role played by seemingly irrelevant people and locations. Too often, still, distant colonies and their people are non-existent in general constructions of Britain and its modern wars and the system of imperial defence.

Distant Drums shows how colonies were central to the defence of the British Empire in the twentieth century. It explains the system of imperial defence, and, using specialist knowledge of the war in a number of African and Asian colonies, examines the manner in which colonial societies were mobilized during periods of global conflict. After examining the role of colonies in the growth of the Empire and its defensive arrangements in chapters 1 and 2, *Distant Drums* considers the First World War as an imperial conflict. It then looks in detail at the Second World War, documenting the recruitment of colonial soldiers, their manifold roles in British military formations, and the impact of war upon the colonial home front. It assesses the problems associated with the use of colonial troops far from home, and the networks used to achieve the mobilization of a global empire.

Distant Drums reveals the role of colonies in imperial warfare and

ix

argues that the colonial empire has played second fiddle to the 'white' Dominions and India in studies of imperial defence and warfare. It examines the major contours of imperial defence and the role played by colonies in imperial warfare (chapters 1 and 2). The colony of Ceylon is then used to demonstrate the martial role of colonies (chapter 3). Its history as a military base, strategic asset and contributor of resources to Britain's world wars is described, chronicling an association that began in the mid-eighteenth century and lasted for over 200 years. The book then turns to the significance of the Indian Ocean in the First World War and the nature of the conflict in the east of Suez region and its impact upon colonies (chapter 4). The war experience of the African territory of Bechuanaland is then reconstructed, providing a detailed example of the contribution made by a distant, apparently insignificant, colony during the First World War (chapter 5). *Distant Drums* then turns to the role of colonies during the Second World War. Using the High Commission Territories in Southern Africa as examples, the manner in which colonies were mobilized for war and men recruited to serve in the British Army are considered (chapter 6), as are the important tasks that they performed whilst serving with British and imperial forces in the Middle East and Southern Europe (chapter 7). Two chapters then analyse the problems that could attend the utilization of colonial soldiers if they weren't properly treated or were employed for the wrong reasons, again illustrating the levels of imperial authority linking ministries in London to governors in the colonies, regional military commanders, and district officials and chiefs on the ground (chapters 8 and 9). The importance of the Indian Ocean during the Second World War is then examined, as is the role of the Indian Ocean colonies of Ceylon and Mauritius (chapter 10). The book closes with two chapters that describe the networks of imperial authority that brought the Empire to war, particularly the role played by colonial governors (chapters 11 and 12). The conclusion highlights the role played by colonies in Britain's wars and in defining Britain's strategic posture in the post-Second World War decades (characterized by counterinsurgency, strategic colonial bases, and the Falklands conflict), arguing that, even in the early twenty-first-century, colonies remain a key part of the defence mission of the British armed forces and continue to offer facilities that enhance Britain's strategic reach.

Distant Drums is an important contribution to our understanding of the role of British colonies in twentieth-century warfare and offers valuable insights into the way in which imperial networks were employed to connect imperial resources to Britain's strategic needs. It is based upon archival research in Britain and overseas and draws upon the author's expertise in the history of colonies such as Basotuland, Bechuanaland, Ceylon, Mauritius, and Swaziland. Five of the book's chapters have been especially written for this book, the others are previously published articles that have been substantially revised.

Acknowledgements

I would like to thank Anthony Grahame of Sussex Academic Press for all of his help in the preparation of this study. The Imperial War Museum kindly gave permission to use images, as did the Director of the Sri Lanka National Archives. The British Academy and the University of Oxford supported research trips to Botswana, Mauritius, and Sri Lanka. Some of the chapters are revised and rewritten versions of journal articles published in the *Journal of Southern African Studies*, *African Affairs*, *The Journal of Military History*, *War and Society*, *Royal United Services Institute for Defence Studies Journal* and chapters from Andrew Stewart and Chris Baxter (eds), *Diplomacy at War* (Leiden: Brill, 2008) and Greg Kennedy (ed.), *Imperial Defence: The Old World Order, 1856–1956* (London: Routledge, 2008).

Thanks, as always, are also due to my wife, my parents, and my grandmother for their support and enthusiasm for my work.

Glossary

9th Foot British line (infantry) regiment stationed in Ceylon between 1796 and 1820, also known as the Green Howards after an early colonel commandant. Raised in 1688 it became the 19th in 1751 and in 1782 had a county appellation attached to become the 1st North Riding of Yorkshire Regiment of Foot. In 1795 the title Princess of Wales's Own was added. In 1881 numerical appellations were dropped throughout the British Army's line regiments, and it became the Princess of Wales's Own Yorkshire Regiment. Now a part of the Yorkshire Regiment.

Admiralty British office of state responsible for the Royal Navy.

AAPC Auxiliary African Pioneer Corps ('Auxiliary' subsequently dropped).

ABDA American–British–Dutch–Australian Command, the Second World War's first joint allied command, with General Sir Archibald Wavell as Supreme Commander.

Adjutant General's Department Army department responsible for military administration, personnel, and discipline.

Age-regiment In many African societies youths were initiated into age-regiments, a process designed to teach them lessons about adulthood and the lore and custom of their people, and often involving circumcision. Age-regiments were used for communal labour tasks and could be mobilized in times of war.

Anzac Name for Australian and New Zealand soldiers, from the First World War acronym ANZAC, Australia and New Zealand Army Corps.

ANZUK Force Australia, New Zealand, United Kingdom Force, a joint military presence in Singapore from 1971 to 1975 comprising frigates, a submarine, ANZUK Brigade, and an air force presence at Butterworth in Malaysia.

APC African Pioneer Corps, a Second World War force under the British Army's Royal Pioneer Corps.

ARP   Air Raid Precautions.

Askari   An East African soldier of the King's African Rifles, recruited from Kenya, Nyasaland, Tanganyika, and Uganda, often a term used to describe any African soldier.

ATS   Auxiliary Territorial Service.

Bechuanaland Protectorate Police   The paramilitary mounted police force established in 1902–3 and ending the anomaly of the British South Africa Police having a hand in the administration of this British protectorate.

British South Africa Company   Company founded by Cecil Rhodes and granted a Royal Charter in 1889. It was responsible for administering Southern and Northern Rhodesia, ruling both colonies until 1923 when they became responsibilities of the British government.

British South Africa Police   The paramilitary force established to pursue the British South Africa Company's policies in the Rhodesias.

Caprivi Strip   The narrow stretch of land linking South West Africa to the Zambezi, running along the northern border of Bechuanaland. Given to the Germans by the British and named after Bismarck's successor as Chancellor, Georg Graf von Caprivi.

Carrier Corps   The First World War labour force in East Africa, started in Kenya and ultimately recruiting over 400,000 Africans to support the British campaign against German forces led by Colonel Paul von Lettow-Vorbeck.

Central Mediterranean Forces   Name for 15th Army Group, the Allied formation responsible for operations in Sicily and Italy. 15th Army Group was renamed Allied Forces Italy in January 1944, then Allied Central Mediterranean Forces in the same month, and finally Allied Armies Italy in March 1944.

Ceylon Defence Force   From 1910, the umbrella organization for all locally-raised military forces in Ceylon, including light infantry, mounted rifles, planters' rifles, artillery, and signals.

Ceylon Light Infantry   Founded in 1881 as the Ceylon Light Infantry Volunteers (the 'Volunteers' was dropped in 1910), the CLI saw service in the Boer War, the First World War, and the Second World War.

Ceylon Mounted Infantry Part of the Ceylon Volunteers founded in 1892.

Ceylon Planters Rifle Corps Volunteer regiment recruited from among Ceylon's European community (1900–1949). It saw service in the Boer War and the First World War, and during the Second World War provided over 700 officer recruits for the British and Indian armies.

Ceylon Regiment Regiment comprising African, Indian, Malay, and Sinhalese battalions founded soon after the British take over of Ceylon.

Chief A common designation for indigenous rulers, especially in Africa, that became a formalized title within the imperial chain of authority.

China Station The Royal Navy's permanent establishment in Far Eastern waters, with headquarters at Hong Kong, Shanghai, and Singapore and facilities at Tientsin and Wei-Hai-Wei. Responsible for British interests in the South China Sea, the lower Yangtze, the Western Pacific, and the Dutch East Indies. Merged in December 1941 with the East Indies Station to form the Eastern Fleet.

CO Commanding Officer

Colonial empire The general term for the British Empire territories administered by the Colonial Office, therefore excluding the Dominions and India.

Colonial Office British office of state responsible for the affairs of the colonial empire.

Company A military unit; three companies (usually) form one battalion. In the African Pioneer Corps, a company comprised 365 officers and men.

CSM Company Sergeant Major.

Dikgotla plural of *kgotla*, the traditional centre of political discussion and decision-making among Batswana communities.

District Commissioner Member of the Colonial Administrative Service (from 1954 Her Majesty's Overseas Civil Service) responsible for the administrative affairs of a district, one of the administrative divisions into which British colonies were divided. Also known as District Officer, in other parts of the Empire as Residents or Political Agents.

Dominions Office   British office of state responsible for British relations with the self-governing Dominions, and for the High Commission Territories in Southern Africa.

Dominion   A political term within the British Empire applied to the self-governing territories.

East Africa campaign   Campaign fought during the First World War and lasting from 1914 until 1918, and also a campaign during the Second World War lasting from 1940 until 1941 when British forces achieved the total defeat of Italian forces in the region.

East Africa Command   British Army command structure with headquarters in Nairobi, subordinate to Middle East Command in Cairo.

East India Company   The chartered company founded in 1600 and granted a Royal charter, responsible for trade with India and increasingly for ruling, administering, and defending British India. In 1858 its administrative responsibilities were taken over by the British government.

East Indies Station   The Royal Navy's permanent establishment in the Indian Ocean region, with headquarters in Colombo and shore bases in Africa, the Red Sea, and the Persian Gulf. During the First World War it was combined with forces in the Mediterranean and known as the East Indies and Egypt Station.

Fleet Air Arm   The air force of the Royal Navy, run by the Royal Air Force until 1939.

German Pacific Squadron   Commanded by Admiral Graf von Spee, this was the German navy's fleet stationed in eastern waters, with headquarters at Tsingtao.

Governor   Common term for the lead of the British administration in a Crown colony, appointed by the monarch to represent him/her.

Government Secretary   The second in command to the governor in a British Crown colony, sometimes known as the Chief Secretary.

Guerre de course   A form of naval warfare that aims to interdict the enemy's supply lines and force him to disperse his resources in order to hunt for raiders and protect convoys. Also known as commerce raiding.

HAA   Heavy Anti-Aircraft guns.

High Seas Fleet   The German navy's major fleet, stationed in Germany and intended to match the Royal Navy's Grand Fleet.

High Commissioner Overseas representative of the British monarch in the Dominions.

High Commission Territories (HCT) Basutoland, Bechuanaland, and Swaziland, three southern African territories ruled through the office of the High Commissioner to South Africa on behalf of the Dominions Office, staffed by members of the Colonial Administrative Service.

High Commission Territories Corps Pioneer labour force which served in the Middle East between 1946 and 1949.

HMSO His/Her Majesty's Stationery Office. Now The Stationery Office.

Imperial defence a general term referring to the methods by which the collective defence of the Empire was planned for at the level of British and Dominions' governments and military policy-makers, and the academic study of such.

Imperial troops British imperial forces available for service anywhere in the world.

Indian Ocean region The Indian Ocean and its annexes, the Red Sea, Persian Gulf, Arabian Sea, Bay of Bengal, and Southern Ocean, viewed by British military planners as a strategic whole, known to the Admiralty as the Indian Ocean Region.

Indian Ocean rim The land surrounding the Indian Ocean, most of which formed part of the British Empire, from the Swahili Coast and Red Sea, the Arabian peninsula and Persian Gulf, India, Burma, Malaya, and Singapore.

King's African Rifles Imperial service infantry unit recruited from British colonies in east and central Africa. Formed in 1902 through union of the Central African Rifles, East African Rifles and Uganda Rifles.

Kgotla Administrative and political centre of Batswana tribal life, the *kgotla* was the central meeting place where the chief and his headmen, and male members of the tribe, discussed affairs of tribal importance, with offices for clerks and police attached.

Locally-raised troops Troops, part time or full time, recruited for service within their colonies of origin. Performing internal security tasks and for use to defend the colony in times of general war.

London Missionary Society Non denominational missionary society founded in 1795 and active in Africa and the Pacific.

Mandate   German and Ottoman colonies conquered by the Allies in the First World War became mandates of the newly-formed League of Nations, administered under in trust by colonial powers such as Britain and France. Among others, British mandates included Iraq, Palestine, South West Africa, Trans-Jordan, and Tanganyika.

Mauritius Defence Force   Home guard formation

Mauritius Regiment   The name given to the Mauritius Territorial Force when it became an imperial formation liable for active service beyond Mauritius and its dependencies.

Mauritius Territorial Force   Locally-raised military unit formed in 1935 for internal security and local defence duties.

Mauritius Volunteer Force   First World War military force recruited to relieve imperial troops of duties in Mauritius.

Middle East Command   With headquarters in Cairo, Middle East Command was responsible for British military interests in the Mediterranean, North Africa, East Africa, and the Middle East. In September 1941 East Africa Command was formed as a subordinate command, and in August 1942 the creation of a new Persia and Iraq Command relieved MEC of responsibility for those parts of the Middle East.

Native Military Corps   A labour force of the Union Defence Force.

NATO   North Atlantic Treaty Organization, founded in 1949.

NCO   Non Commissioned Officer

Other Ranks   Soldiers other than officers

Pax Britannica   The 'peace of Britain'. A term describing the world order established after the Revolutionary and Napoleonic Wars in which Britain's industrial and military power underpinned world peace.

Pitso   A tribal gathering at the local or national level in Basutoland.

Protectorate   A legal definition of a colonial territory in which the British protected inhabitants from external aggression whilst allowing indigenous political authorities to continue to rule their people.

Red Sea Patrol   A division of the East Indies Station responsible for security in the Red Sea, a major sea line of communication and known for its piracy and smuggling activities.

Regular Army   The permanent peacetime establishment of the British Army, distinguishing it from hostilities-only soldiers and conscripts.

Reserve   British colonies in Africa were divided into reserves, administrative units usually conforming to the territory of a particular tribe and chiefdom.

Resident Commissioner   The title of the leading British administrator in a colony or protectorate where a High Commissioner sat at the level above and was responsible for relations with Whitehall. Thus in most territories, there was a Governor with direct relations to Whitehall. In some territories, however, a High Commissioner oversaw those relations. This was the case in the Pacific and in Southern Africa.

Resident Magistrate   Before the 1930s, a common name for District Commissioners.

RPC   Royal Pioneer Corps

RSM   Regimental Sergeant Major

SEAC   South East Asia Command

Sepoy   A soldier of the Indian Army

Shore base   A Royal Navy land establishment.

SOE   Special Operations Executive

South African Native Labour Contingent   Contingent of over 20,000 Africans recruited from Basutoland, Bechuanaland, South Africa, and Swaziland for service in Europe in 1917.

Strategic Defence Review   A British government policy document (Command 5566) published in 1998 at the behest of the incoming Labour administration, setting out Britain's strategic vision and its defence policy.

Union of South Africa   The Act of Union (1909) created the modern state of South Africa, formally uniting British colonies (Cape Colony and Natal) and the former Boer republics (Orange Free State and the Transvaal).

Viceroy   The monarch's representative in India, head of the Government of India.

War Office   (WO) The British office of state responsible for the British Army.

WRNS   Women's Royal Naval Service.

1

The British Colonial Empire and Imperial Warfare

Then the marching began, the solemn convolutions of armed men, a khaki-coloured ballet of stiff arms and stiff legs. It was a scene beloved of the British, stamped out over half the world for two centuries and more. Men and arms, moving to orders, under a blue foreign sky.

Square-bashing in Hong Kong colony. From Leslie Thomas, *Onward Virgin Soldiers* (1971)

The British Empire was a sprawling mass of territories acquired over a period of four centuries. Despite the uniformity suggested by the famous map of the world showing all British possessions shaded red, the Empire was extremely diverse and few people ever had an intimate knowledge of all of it. The British public were notoriously uninformed about the colonies. As Alfred Lyttelton, Secretary of State for the Colonies, quipped at the Corona Club dinner in June 1905, the British people are ignorant of many things, but 'there are few things of which they are so ignorant as the Crown Colonies'. It was almost *de riguer* for newly-appointed members of the Colonial Administrative Service to require the assistance of an atlas upon first hearing the name of the colony in which they were to begin their careers as administrators. The politicians in charge of the affairs of the Empire at the highest level could be similarly nonplussed when it came to the bewildering diversity and sheer size of the colonial empire — even so fervent an imperialist as Joseph Chamberlain. Chamberlain, one of the most powerful politicians of his day, had deliberately chosen the Colonial Office in 1895 as opposed to one of the more important ministries open to him (the Home Office and the Treasury) because he strongly believed that Britain's imperial estate needed far more

1

prominence in the nation's affairs. Illustrating his sketchy knowledge of the gallimaufry of colonies over which he presided, the Zionist leader Theodor Herzl made a memorable diary entry after meeting Chamberlain in October 1902 to try and find a location for Jewish settlement, possibly in the colony of Cyprus:

> The most striking thing about the interview was that Chamberlain didn't have a very detailed knowledge of the British possessions which undoubtedly are at his command. It was like a big junk shop whose manager isn't quite sure whether some unusual article is in the stock room. I need a place for the Jewish people to assemble. He's going to have a look and see if England happens to have something like that in stock.[1]

Despite this lack of knowledge, the colonies were all part of a system of effective global governance, with an effective system of imperial defence protecting them. Every one of the fifty or so possessions that made up the colonial empire, from Aden and Antigua to Uganda and Zanzibar, had a role to play in British imperial defence calculations, and was mobilized to an amazing extent during the world wars of the twentieth century. Even long before the struggles of 1914–18 and 1939–45, Britain's global wars with European rivals had witnessed the superpower of the day using colonies all over the world as tools of war. In the era of the Seven Years War and the Revolutionary and Napoleonic Wars, for example, Britain seized enemy colonies from the West Indies to the East Indies with abandon. It sent thousands of troops and protecting fleets to conquer Mediterranean strongholds and sack enemy redoubts such as Madeira, Minorca and Manila, and used captured colonies as bargaining counters at subsequent peace treaties, retaining the choicest strategic locations for its own burgeoning colonial collection.

The colonial empire was made up of the fifty or so territories that were ruled through the Colonial Office, as distinct a branch of the imperial tree as were the 'white' Dominions or the India Raj. It was in many ways the British Empire 'proper', for it was the part that the British government most thoroughly ruled; as the twentieth century dawned the Dominions were increasingly autonomous and had to be 'consulted' on most matters of Empire-wide significance, and the growth of a sophisticated and articulate nationalist movement in India meant that the Raj had increasingly to be handled as a Dominion-in-waiting. The Colonial Office had a major role in numerous territories that were *not* officially British colonies or protectorates. These included the Mandates established in the Middle East, Africa, and the Pacific following the First World War, as well as the Southern African High Commission Territories (transferred from the Colonial Office to the Dominions Office in 1925, though they continued to be staffed by the Colonial Office). The Colonial Office was also involved in the administration of the privately-ruled Sarawak (handed over to the Colonial Office by its white Rajah in 1946), countries enjoying a 'special relationship' with Britain, such as Tonga, and areas of 'informal empire' such as Shanghai and the Trucial states of the Persian Gulf. Britain's colonies were to be found in the West Indies, Central America, the Atlantic, and the Mediterranean; in sub-Saharan Africa; and east of Suez from Aden across the islands of the Indian Ocean to Ceylon, Malaya, Hong Kong, and the islands of the Pacific.

The role of colonies in imperial warfare has been consistently under-valued and their histories less well developed than those of the former 'white' Dominions and India. Colonies were woven into the tapestry of British warfare and Britain's presence on the world stage as the foremost power. Yet the military history of the colonial empire has been over-looked, the breathtaking spectacle of the recruitment of massive armies to serve British causes taken for granted, and too little thought afforded the extraordinary feats of mobilization required to bring a vast empire to war. Colonial mobilization was an incredible phenomenon that should to this day elicit gratitude from Britain and a less blinkered view of history in former colonies themselves, where the desire to emphasize national (and often nationalist) history and to expunge empire from the historical record has sometimes led to a failure to appreciate how important even small colonies were in the most momentous wars in history. Many countries have failed to adequately connect their own history to an important aspect of modern international history.

The fact is that whatever the inequities of colonial rule and no matter how unpalatable the memory, dozens of colonies participated in defeating Napoleon, Kaiser Wilhelm, Hitler, Mussolini, and Hirohito. Whilst colonies might not have asked to become part of the British Empire (though the leaders of some did), they helped win the world wars, laurels that are surely worth claiming. What is more, the 'it wasn't our war' lament is only true up to a point; throughout history, there have always been some parts of the world that were victim to the intrusions of more powerful outsiders. Such was the colonial world, and if Britain had lost either of the world wars of the twentieth-century, these colonies would not have entered a nirvana of freedom, economic prosperity, and political significance on the world stage. Rather, they would have entered

3

a new age of colonial rule, and one dominated by powers with far less benign colonial intentions and methods than Britain.

The role of colonies in defending Britain and the Empire was better acknowledged at the time than it has been in subsequent historical memory. At Queen Victoria's Diamond Jubilee in 1897, for example, colonial military formations featured prominently in the procession through London that accompanied the Queen's carriage. There were, of course, plenty of representatives from the 'white' Dominions and India. From the subcontinent came a deputation of officers from the Imperial Service Troops, a force of 20,000 men raised by India's princes to commemorate the 1887 jubilee. There were cavalry contingents from Canada and Natal, and mounted infantry units from Cape Town, New South Wales, Queensland, South Australia, and Victoria. The procession included representatives of the 48th Canadian Highlanders and the Royal Canadian Mounted Police, as well as the Perth (West Australia) Artillery Volunteers. But interspersed among these Indian and Dominions units, in all their elaborate regimental splendour, there were plenty of men from the colonial empire. Colonial units involved in the great procession at the heart of this imperial jamboree were the Trinidad Mounted Rifles and the Cypriot Zaptiehs, a military police unit of 670 men. The 1,100-strong Malta Militia was represented as was the Royal Malta Artillery, a 460-strong regular corps of the British Army recruited in Malta. There was also the Trinidad Field Artillery, the West African Infantry, the Trinidad Infantry, Dyak Police of the British North Borneo Company, the Jamaica Artillery, the Sierra Leone Artillery, the Sierra Leone Force, Hausa soldiers, the British Guiana Police, the Ceylon Light Infantry, the Ceylon Artillery Volunteers, and soldiers from Hong Kong and the Straits Settlement.

In marked contrast to the First World War, popular memory of the Second World War to a large extent left the Empire out of the equation. 'Whereas the paradigmatic image of Britain in the first war was Sir Bernard Partridge's lion surrounded by her cubs snarling defiance under a flapping Union Jack, that of the second is Low's British Tommy challenging the storm-clouds with the cry, "Very well then: alone!". The fact that Britain could command the resources of a quarter of the globe containing some 500 million inhabitants received little emphasis at the time, and even less since.'[2] Whereas Sir Charles Lucas's official history of the colonial empire between 1914 and 1918 was published by Oxford University Press in five large volumes, Sir John Shuckburgh's official history of the colonies in the Second World War remained unpublished. The British Empire, and in particular the colonies, were being written out of the memory of how Britain fought wars and the imperial nature of Britain's defensive responsibilities and dispositions.

The military contribution of colonies and the role of military labour

So the war contribution of Britain's colonial empire has received limited attention from imperial historians and — perhaps more surprisingly — the significance of this contribution to the logistical support of the British Empire's fighting formations has been similarly overlooked by *military* historians. An older historiography construed 'imperial defence' as a rather exclusive branch of imperial history in which Britain and the Dominions argued at imperial conferences about contributions to Empire-wide defence provision but achieved a degree of inter-operability as Dominions units were able to slot into British formations, connected as they were by shared training, shared weaponry, the habit of appointing British officers, and the procurement of British-built ships, aircraft, and vehicles. The story of the development of imperial defence highlighted the Dominions' increasing preoccupation with their own regional defence, and their marked reluctance to contribute financially to the cause of imperial defence beyond the security of their own borders, a point of view that always exasperated British politicians and officials.

The increasing emphasis of the Dominions on defence within their own regions, as opposed to contributing willy-nilly to British-led imperial ventures in distant places, worked against Britain's centripetal defence tendencies. Britain sought to centralize command to the greatest extent possible whilst getting the Dominions to increase their financial and military contributions to imperial defence, which meant stumping up cash for Britain to buy the hardware and train the men, or providing their own forces that could serve in the Mediterranean and Atlantic, not just their own coastal waters. But imperial defence, the Dominions argued, was an *imperial* responsibility, and thus a burden for the hard-pressed British taxpayer to bear. The British in turn argued that imperial defence was everyone's responsibility, and that it was just as relevant for Australians to serve in the Mediterranean as the Pacific; imperial defence was one and indivisible. Though some progress was made, the fully integrated system of imperial defence dreamed of by British officials and by those advocating ever closer imperial federation was not to be. Today, 'imperial defence' demands a much wider academic construction than this traditional field of study with its heavy focus on the relationships

5

between Britain and the Dominions, not just because colonial resources were always so important for imperial defence, but also because the colonies *came to supplant* India and the Dominions in the imperial defence equation during the twentieth-century. For whilst India and the Dominions were moving towards legal independence within the Empire-Commonwealth, and away from military integration with Britain, the colonial empire *was becoming increasingly enmeshed within Britain's imperial defence system.*

In contrast to the French, the British did not maintain a large army drawn from the colonial empire as a permanent supplement to the Regular Army, though the idea had received some consideration. Though there was nothing to compare to France's large Afrrican army, the British Empire could boast a number of permanent (i.e. maintained in peace-time) colonial military formations that were designated *imperial* troops and liable therefore, like the Indian Army, for overseas service. In this category were units such as the King's African Rifles and the Royal West African Frontier Force. In addition there were *locally-raised* units that were not imperial, but recruited to fulfil a military or paramilitary role in their home colonies and immediate areas, like the Somali Camel Corps, the Transjordan Frontier Force, and the Mauritius Territorial Force. This was all part of a logical system of imperial defence that also involved colonies as providers of major base facilities for imperial forces, such as Malta's role as headquarters of the Mediterranean Fleet and Singapore's role as the guardian of the Eastern empire.

A remarkable role performed by colonies during imperial wars was the recruitment of hundreds of thousands of raw recruits, often into military units created entirely from scratch. The fact that these soldiers were effective in their various roles, with no higher incidence of mutiny or inefficiency than regular British soldiers, is to the great credit of the men themselves and the authorities that recruited them. New formations hastily created during times of imperial danger had no peace-time military tradition to draw upon, and no time in which to build the unique regimental loyalties that are the bedrock of the British Army. Unlike existing imperial and Indian Army formations — such as the King's African Rifles and the Gurkhas — in which the welfare of the soldier and his family was well catered for according to long-established principles, the raw recruit from the colonies faced many uncertainties concerning his terms of service and his family's welfare. Yet these large-scale colonial formations served Britain effectively in all of its world wars.

The imperial nature of twentieth-century world wars

The First World War was a global struggle in the tradition of the Seven Years War and the Revolutionary and Napoleonic Wars, yet more far reaching and destructive. The entire Empire was called upon to participate. Colonies in the Indian Ocean region were affected by the fighting in Africa and the Middle East, and the Indian Ocean sea lanes were vital for the transit of troops and their supplies, including those deployed to Africa and Mesopotamia and those journeying from Australia and New Zealand to fight in Europe and the Middle East. Among other labour units sent to France were a Fijian Labour Detachment, a Chinese Labour Corps (numbering 140,000), and the South African Native Labour Contingent, which included men from Basutoland, Bechuanaland, and Swaziland. An Egyptian Labour Corps (numbering 300,000) served in the Sinai theatre, as did smaller units, like the 1,700 men of the Mauritius Labour Battalion sent to work on the inland waterways of Mesopotamia, and the Ceylonese men of the Royal Army Service Corps also enduring the inhospitable climate of that treacherous theatre of war.

The British Cabinet and the General Staff never lost sight of the imperial implications of the war, despite the intense national focus on the situation in Europe. By the outbreak of war a Committee of Imperial Defence existed, and the Dominions had access to the *imperi arcana* and the portals of Whitehall decision-making. As in previous imperial wars, it was not long before cavalry and infantry regiments, as well as warships, were leaving Dominion ports for fighting fronts thousands of miles away. This unparalleled essay in global consultation and governance, an expression of the unity of the British world in the face of adversity, was most visibly symbolized by Lloyd George's creation of an Imperial War Cabinet in 1917.

Buttressing the imperial view of the war at the grand strategic level was the presence in the British government of a number of renowned imperialists. Lloyd George and Churchill were noted for their interest in Britain's imperial status, as were men such as Leopold Amery, Arthur Balfour, Lionel Curtis, George Curzon, and Alfred Milner. These men were determined that the 'southern world' would be secured as a result of the war, which meant Britain conquering German colonies in the Pacific, East Africa, and Southern Africa, dominating the land bridge between Europe and India following the collapse of the Ottoman Empire, eradicating German influence in the greater Middle East, and securing the oil reserves of the Gulf once and for all. The destruction of the German and Ottoman empires would quite naturally lead to much more red on the map as the premier Allied power staked the victor's claim, even if American influence meant that some of the new territories were to appear in atlases and gazetteers as League of Nations 'mandates', which nevertheless, denoting their true status, became responsibilities of the Colonial Office.

The ways and the places in which Britain fought the First World War — as well as the strategic aims of the British and Dominions governments in its prosecution — bore the unmistakable hallmarks of Britain's imperial lineage. Infantry slogging matches in the shadow of Mount Kilimanjaro, or dusty campaigning in the land of Lawrence of Arabia, were far more than exotic sideshows to slaughter on a European centre stage. Similarly, the naval war was a global vigil involving patrol and convoy escort work as well as gun duels, though the common image of the Grand Fleet and the High Seas Fleet scowling at each other across the North Sea before and after the brief orgy of violence at Jutland reinforces the focus on the European theatre. In the First World War, unlike the Second, the control of the seas upon which *Pax Britannica* and imperial security rested held firm, despite the challenge of the German navy. Yet this control was still tested in the Atlantic, the Indian Ocean, and the Pacific — and the territories within them over which the Union Flag flew. Those territories, in turn, were called upon to support the Empire's war. Variations on Kitchener's famous poster calling Britons to arms appeared around the world, as colonial governors sought to mobilize their territories for war on the home front and for the recruitment of labour and fighting battalions for service overseas.

As in 1914–18, the war that started on 3 September 1939 was deeply marked by Britain's imperial status and again witnessed the participation of all its colonies. This time, however, their involvement was even more profound, and the security of the colonial empire more seriously threatened. 'Never in our peacetime travels had we imagined that war could ever reach the enormous empty solitudes of the inner desert, walled off by sheer distance, lack of water, and impassable seas of sand dunes.' Thus wrote Major R. A. Bagnold, desert traveller and founder of the Long Range Desert Group. The wars of the twentieth century were distinguished by their capacity to affect the parts of the world that other wars simply couldn't reach, bringing brief and intense fire-fights to the most inhospitable parts of the Libyan Desert, traumatic occupation to colonies in the Central Pacific and South-east Asia, communal war cultivation to the Kalahari, and army recruitment drives and Spitfire squadrons to the islands and atolls of the Indian Ocean. Forgotten Addu Atoll in the Maldives became a naval base of great importance when the Japanese onslaught threatened; the Cocos-Keeling Islands played host to Liberators and Spitfires as the war in the East reached its climax; and the Bahamas, governed by the Duke of Windsor, witnessed the opening of American bases and an RAF training school, the arrival of Cameron Highlanders and Canadians, as well as inflation, labour emigration to America, and riots in Nassau caused by wage differentials between locals and American contract labourers.

The forces of the British Empire were shunted around the world to defend its key strategic points and even its tiny outposts, and to defend Britain itself: Canadians flocked to Britain in the first winter of the war and entered Hong Kong weeks before its surrender; New Zealanders sailed across the Indian Ocean bound for Egypt and Palestine; Ceylonese artillerymen were dispatched to guard cable and wireless stations in the Cocos-Keeling Islands and the Seychelles; Pioneers from Basutoland and Swaziland supported the Eighth Army in Italy and Libya; Trinidadians joined the RAF as Caymanians joined the navy; Fijians fought alongside American troops in the Central Pacific; South African airmen flew over Ethiopia and Madagascar; and Indian Army battalions torched the oil wells and put up a spirited defence of Borneo when the Japanese landed.

The British war effort was a breathtaking example of overseas power projection and what today would be termed 'coalition warfare', as the phenomenon that was the British Empire turned its sprawling mass to martial endeavour. Hundreds of years of British imperial history and tradition and the networks, infrastructure, indigenous alliances, and institutions that it had forged were called to life by the decision of the imperial government in London to send an ultimatum to Germany demanding the withdrawal of German troops from Poland. Germany's failure to respond to that ultimatum, and the state of war that subsequently came about, announced to the world in Neville Chamberlain's doleful broadcast, sent a current running throughout the overseas power centres of Empire from Cairo to Colombo to Canberra, and they sprang to life alongside the imperial metropole and mobilized their respective regions for war.

The Second World War, therefore, was intensely imperial in nature. There was, for example, a shared experience on the home front whether people lived in Britain, Jamaica, Nigeria, Mauritius, Malaya, or Hong Kong — food shortages and ration books, air raid shelters, blackouts, profiteering, inflation, war savings schemes, recruitment into civil defence and military units, the requisitioning of public buildings, and the construction of all manner of military facilities. This shared experience can also be seen in the multinational nature of almost all 'British' armies, fleets, and air squadrons around the world. The infrastructure provided by colonies was more important than ever. A key feature was the use of existing and ad hoc economic structures to aid the Allied war effort; the tea planters association in Assam turned its resources to the construction of military roads, executives from Far Eastern merchant houses such as Jardine and Matheson joined the covert war behind enemy lines, and inventions like the Middle East Supply Centre and the West African Supply Board ensured that regional economic needs were met and impe-rial raw materials were efficiently linked to consumer ministries in London and Washington. During the war the strategic mineral, raw material, and food resources of the colonial empire were crucial to the British war effort, but because they were 'ours' as opposed to Australian or Canadian, they have seldom been acknowledged as a distinct contri-bution from overseas dependent territories.

For most of the conflict Britain hardly fought a European war at all, and even the Battle of the Atlantic, which provided Britain with its food and armaments lifeline and the wherewithal to become a *place d'armes* ready for D-Day and the assault on Fortress Europe, was testa-ment to Britain's historic links to the non-European world. Confined in Europe by German power and the defeat of its principal ally, for Britain the Eastern war became a primary focus. For the British impe-rial state, survival depended upon control of the sea lanes, not only of the Atlantic but also of the Indian Ocean, as well as victory in the lands on that ocean's rim where 'sideshow' campaigns proliferated — in Burma, East Africa, Iran, Iraq, Java, Madagascar, Malaya, and Sumatra. The Indian Ocean sea lanes and bases connected imperial fighting fronts in Africa, the Middle East, Asia, and South-east Asia and the war efforts of all the major belligerent nations, as well as carrying the trade that kept the Empire from starvation. Whilst well remembered, the war in the Mediterranean and the Middle East suffers from the skewed logic that fails to associate the British war experience adequately with Britain's imperial heritage and the need to defend a global estate. The 'Mediterranean strategy', and the drama of the defence of Malta and the battles against Rommel, was all about the defence of imperial commu-nications and imperial oil and the sea route connecting Britain and Europe to Asia and the East; the fact that it was also a point from which to threaten the 'soft underbelly' of Axis Europe was a geographical by-product of this fundamental fact. Finally, the British Empire has been largely written out of the Pacific theatre and the war against Japan,

Singapore marking an historical full stop and the Burma struggle divorced from its strategic context.

Colonies played a much more significant role in the world wars than is acknowledged, as providers of military infrastructure, manpower, and resources. Having argued that the world wars of the twentieth-century were intensely imperial affairs, and that the role of colonies in the provision of imperial defence has been largely unacknowledged, the following chapter considers the role played by colonies in modern warfare and British strategic calculations.

2

The Role of Colonies in Imperial Defence

The ship was filled mostly with Service families heading for Egypt, India, and the Far East . . . The *Kaisar-i-Hind* dropped anchor in the deep blue Grand Harbour of Valetta just as the sun was setting and it was an unforgettable sight, tier upon tier of honey-coloured houses rising on one side and Fort Ricasoli, built in 1400 by the Knights of Malta, brooding benevolently on the other. In between lay the leviathans of the greatest navy in the world. 'Retreat' was being sounded by the massed bands of the Royal Marines on the Flight Deck of the giant carrier *Eagle*, whilst astern of her lay three more — *Furious*, *Argus*, and *Ark Royal*. Ahead there was a line of huge battleships and beyond them again, the tall rather old-fashioned looking County class cruisers . . . the light cruiser squadrons, the destroyer and submarine flotillas . . . Pinnaces, Admirals' barges and shore boats slashed the blue water with white . . . As the final plaintive note of the 'Retreat' floated out from *Eagle*, the sinking sun kissed the topmost houses and churches of Valetta with gold and all over the Grand Harbour as signal lights winked from a hundred mastheads, the White Ensign and Union Jacks of the Royal Navy were lowered.

> David Niven, subaltern in the Highland Light Infantry, arriving in
> Malta in 1930 to join his battalion as part of the colony's garrison.[3]

The term 'imperial defence' describes a distinct branch of historical and military studies, and the strategic planning of the British government until at least the 1950s when it was the responsibility of London to defend hundreds of millions of people overseas. The use of the term 'imperial defence' was commonplace in Whitehall and among those interested in military and strategic affairs. There was a Cabinet Committee of Imperial Defence; books on 'imperial military geography' appeared in regular

12

editions until the 1960s; and even in the late twentieth century, university courses offered papers examining the genesis of 'imperial defence' and its central tenets. The constituent elements of imperial defence were several. The foundation stone was British sea power. Resting on it were the twin pillars of the British Army and the Indian Army. In the classic formulation of imperial defence the Royal Navy and Britain's two imperial armies were supplemented by the naval and military forces of the 'white' Dominions. But even this wide-ranging construction of imperial defence was often too narrowly construed, because the role of the *rest* of the British Empire — the mass of colonies, protectorates, and protected states sprawling across the globe from the Caribbean to the South Pacific — was peripheralized, if acknowledged at all.

It is argued in this book that the colonial empire was in fact at the very heart of imperial defence for a number of reasons, despite the common focus on the defence deliberations and capabilities of Britain, the Dominions, and India. It is also argued that the role of colonies in imperial defence needs to be far better integrated with the history of the British military, the history of world wars, and the national histories of dozens of former colonies. This chapter examines the reasons why the colonies were central to imperial defence. First, it was because imperial defence was all about defending colonies (as well as Britain, the Dominions, India, and the interconnecting sea routes), and many colonies had been gained precisely because of their imperial defence utility. 'Small' wars on the colonial frontier were the meat and drink of the British military (particularly the Army, and later the RAF), throughout most of the nineteenth and twentieth centuries, irrespective of the amount of time spent planning for a pan-imperial response to the challenge of great power rivals. Beyond the wars fought against European rivals (and once against Japan) that occurred roughly every half century from the Seven Years War of 1756–63 until the Second World War, most British fighting took place in colonial or semi-colonial regions of the world.

Another reason why colonies were central to imperial defence was because they contributed a huge amount to defending the Empire — most notably through the provision of military and civilian manpower, base infrastructure, and industrial and primary resources needed to support the British war economy and ensure imperial economic survival. The colonial empire supplied more troops to the imperial cause during the Second World War than all of the Dominions combined and loaned £48,846,000 to the British government and gave £24,014,948 as an outright gift. The defence of the British Empire always relied on a network of fortress colonies — places such as Bermuda, Ceylon,

Gibraltar, Malta, Mauritius, and Singapore. The base infrastructure furnished by colonies, from early stone forts to ports protected by anti-torpedo booms and anti-aircraft guns, sophisticated electronic listening stations, and aerodromes, was essential to the functioning of the British military system. Colonies acted as bases for the armed forces charged with the manifold tasks that went into making imperial defence a reality, and acted as regional power centres for the garrisons, air squadrons, and naval units charged with the task of projecting British power and influence. Without the base infrastructure provided by the colonial empire, the sea routes that connected it could not have been defended, and Australia, India, and New Zealand would have been marooned. Simply put, without colonies the British Empire could not have existed in the form that it did because it could not have been defended from external aggressors or internal rebels.

As providers of military labour the colonies were a godsend for the British government, and deserve as much recognition for this as Anzacs or the sepoys receive for their feats of arms at Gallipoli and Imphal. As well as furnishing the Empire with fighting units (over 80,000 Africans fought in Burma during the Second World War, and the East Africa campaign was dominated by African infantrymen), the colonies provided the 100,000-strong logistical support army upon which the Eighth Army depended. The colonies and regions of semi-colonial penetration were particularly prized as a source of military labour: slaves provided a ready source of military manpower and Britain's presence in China secured the transit of thousands of Chinese to work in South Africa at the time of the Anglo-Boer War of 1899–1902. During the First World War the British Empire really showed its capacity to move people. Over 140,000 Chinese were taken to the Western Front as labourers and hundreds of thousands of Arabs, recruited mainly from Egypt, were employed as labourers in the Sinai campaign. Still in an era of human porterage, the East Africa campaign employed hundreds of thousands of African labourers, and over 30,000 Southern Africans joined the South African Native Labour Contingent for service in France. At Gallipoli the 29th British Division was supported by a military labourer battalion comprising Palestinian Jews, and men of the Ceylon Planters Rifles Corps guarded the Anzac commander's headquarters at Gallipoli whilst other Ceylonese men served with the British Army's Sanitary Corps in Mesopotamia.

Policing the internal frontiers and the idea of imperial protection

Studies of imperial defence traditionally focus upon the Empire's capacity to pool resources and withstand an attack from a major industrialized power. But imperial defence wasn't all about using imperial resources to ward off the threat of Germany, Italy, or Japan. It was also a ceaseless quest to suppress internal dissent and indigenous challenges to British colonial rule, and studies of imperial defence need therefore to encompass both the external and internal frontiers. The defence of the British Empire's internal frontiers was a great training ground for the British Army and the multifarious non-British military formations that were a feature of the Empire's military power.

In fighting colonial campaigns, tactical, logistical, and organizational skills were honed. From the 1860s on 'firepower and organizational ability allied with technology to give the Europeans the advantage' in their wars of empire and colonial campaigning demonstrated the innovative use of firearms and other technology, military animals, river transit, railways, and infantry and cavalry tactics. Examples are to be found in the British campaign in the Sudan in the 1890s and the Indian Army's expedition to Abyssinia under Lieutenant-General Sir Robert Napier in 1868. The Ashanti campaign of 1873–74 was noted for the successful partnership of the Snider rifle, the seven-pounder field gun, and Sir Garnet Wolseley's leadership, while the Zulu War of 1879 is remembered for military incompetence leading to disaster, despite the successful conclusion of the campaign shortly after the battle of Isandhlwana. Five years later Major-General Sir Charles Warren led 5,000 men in a bloodless expedition to claim Bechuanaland for the British Empire, accompanied by an array of modern weapons and military technology. These types of campaigns were *legion* during the days of imperial growth in the eighteenth and nineteenth centuries and surprisingly common during the years of imperial decline in the twentieth century, when colonies formed the backdrop of numerous counterinsurgency campaigns.

Given the constitutional and political realities of imperial rule, British subjects in the colonies had no representation at anything above the local level. They could justifiably claim therefore to depend upon British protection against external aggression, for, unlike the Dominions, they had no political autonomy, and so the 'self government begets self defence' aphorism did not apply. Thus a fundamental feature of the nexus between Britain and its colonial subjects was the provision of security

15

from external aggression, as well as the maintenance of internal law and order ('security of the Overseas Territories' — Britain's remaining colonies — is second on the list of 'Defence Missions and Tasks' in the government's 1998 *Strategic Defence Review*). This was a core contract in the relationship between Britain and its imperial territories and their indigenous rulers, and therefore a central plank of imperial defence. Thus in November 1939 the British Consul at Muscat asked the Sultan of Muscat and Oman for new air and naval facilities as the British sought to expand their reach given the war against Germany, and re-affirmed His Majesty's Government's 'readiness to protect Your Highness's territories including Gwadar from any external aggression . . . while in the event of internal disturbances they are prepared to give Your Highness such assistance as may be possible'. The very term 'protectorate', a recognized status in international law under which many parts of the world had become part of Britain's colonial empire, implied the duty of Britain to protect the inhabitants.

Imperial defence, therefore, meant protecting colonial subjects from the attentions of foreign powers, maintaining internal law and order, and engaging indigenous societies in the defence project. It was the *breach* of this all-important imperial contract to defend colonies from external aggression that did so much damage to Britain's reputation, and the legitimacy of Britain's continued rule, when millions of colonial subjects found themselves at the mercy of the Imperial Japanese Army in December 1941 as British forces surrendered in Borneo, Burma, Hong Kong, Malaya, Sarawak, Shanghai, and Singapore. The shock of these lightning defeats, and the manner of British surrender or retreat, stunned the watching world and spelt tragedy for those caught up in the fighting. The collapse of the vaunted Singapore strategy and deflation of the Royal Navy's invincibility myth when HMS *Prince of Wales* and *Repulse* were sunk were hammer blows to the imperial defence system as it had for a century and a half been conceived.

Quite apart from protection against external aggression, another dimension of this particular aspect of imperial defence was the imperial power's pledge to bring internal law and order. This was the reason why the British were always so anxious to destroy internal rebellions and challenges to colonial authority, be they in the form of hut tax rebellions in Sierra Leone, millenarian movements such as the Chilembwe uprising in Nyasaland in 1915, the Watchtower movement in inter-war Northern Rhodesia, or post-Second World War insurgencies in colonies such as Aden, Cyprus, Kenya, and Malaya. Internal rebellions challenged colonial authority and made a mockery of its claim to political control and possession of a monopoly of lethal force, in the process tarnishing imperial prestige, that ineffable yet indispensable buttress of imperial authority. Bringing internal peace was also one of the great foundation and justification myths of British imperialism, and it was therefore exceedingly embarrassing if a colony was in the grip of violent rebellion, prey to cattle-raiders, or home to an underground politico-religious movement beyond the ken of colonial intelligence and police services. Colonial control, and a monopoly of lethal force, was vital to imperial defence.

This provision of defence from external aggression entailed an obligation in the other direction; when the needs of imperial defence demanded, colonial subjects were expected to rally to the colours. Thus in August 1914 the Resident Commissioner of Bechuanaland, Colonel Frederick Panzera, told the Protectorate's chiefs, assembled at his Mafeking headquarters, that their support was required in the coming struggle with Germany. Since becoming the colonial power in 1885, declared Panzera, a 'selfless' Britain 'had done so much for them, by spending money for years without return, and by finding men for their protection [principally against the expansionist tendencies of neighbouring Boers], and to preserve intact for them and their children the land held by their fathers'. It was now time to call in the favour. Similarly, in 1942 the Governor of Mauritius fell out with the War Office when he tried to get his colony released from an obligation to contribute to the maintenance of the British garrison on the island. As a fortress colony, Mauritius had since the nineteenth century contributed to its own defence in this way (five-and-a-half percent of revenue). From the mid-1930s the Government of Mauritius was also paying for the locally-recruited Mauritius Territorial Force. This led the Government of Mauritius to reason that, as the imperial garrison was there for imperial purposes, Mauritius should be let off the imperial commitment and concentrate on paying for its new local defence force. A nitpicking dispute between London and Port Louis arose over where 'local' defence stopped and 'imperial' defence began. With a world war in progress and defence costs rising alarmingly, the Governor argued that the imperial government should take over the entire defence burden, especially given his government's maintenance of local defence forces. London's response was lukewarm. It referred to the great burden already being born by the British taxpayer because of the war, and pointed out that Mauritius made no contribution to the Royal Navy even though it was 'almost entirely dependent on Naval Defence'. Sharpening the knife, the Colonial Office also suggested that there was 'a good deal of evidence that the Mauritius Defence measures locally taken are bad value for money'.

'Small' wars: Core imperial defence business

The British Army soldiered throughout the colonial empire for most of the nineteenth and twentieth centuries, fighting campaigns that came to shape its identity as a 'small war' force. There is a direct line running from the 'pacification' operations of the nineteenth century to the era of 'imperial policing' after the First World War and onto the era of classic 'counterinsurgency' warfare that followed the Second World War in numerous parts of the colonial empire. Some might choose to see a further continuation, to the current period of 'peace support' and 'stabilization' operations still being conducted by the British military in parts of Africa and Asia.

'Small' colonial wars they might have been when compared to clashes between major industrialized powers, though they were not so small when one considers the financial and logistical support required to maintain a couple of thousand men in a distant part of the world, or the casualties that could ensue; at Isandlwana in South Africa in 1879 over 1,300 imperial soldiers were lost in a single battle; at Maiwand in Afghanistan in the following year nearly a thousand were killed in just a few hours; and as late as the 1930s, thousands of British and Indian servicemen perished 'on the grim', campaigning against the Fakir of Ipi in Waziristan. Also, as Iain Smith reminds us, 'small wars are big wars to those that lose them'. Furthermore, these wars were certainly not small by today's standards, in terms of the numbers of troops and ancillary supporters deployed, the sea lift required to convey, protect, and supply them, and the casualties sustained. But, although 'small wars' could be 'big box office' because of the Victorian media's relish for heroic campaigns in which redcoats dished natives under tropical suns, these wars usually remained 'small' in the British mind because the British Army had the habit of being continuously on campaign; during the period of Queen Victoria's (and indeed Queen Elizabeth's) 'little wars', there were often many expeditions involving hundreds or thousands of men being conducted simultaneously. 'Small wars' in the colonies or on the colonial periphery shaped the organization and identity of the British Army, and preserved the RAF's independence in the years immediately following the First World War. It is amazing to contemplate the extent to which Britain's imperial history involved fighting, either against imperial rivals at the regional and international levels, or against internal opponents of British rule. Even before a territory became red on the map, there was often a lengthy period during which British military forces were involved, in exploratory expeditions or as protection for British political and commercial enclaves as British rule was made good and 'effective occupation' established (many of the nineteenth century's great explorers, such as John Hanning Speke and Richard Burton, were Indian Army officers, and the Royal Navy led the world in polar exploration).

Colonial wars were also considered 'small' in the minds of the British public because actual British losses were usually small, more men dying through disease on overseas service than from wounds sustained in battle. Most importantly, they remained 'small' because the much greater loss of non-white lives barely registered in the public imagination because they were considered to be of far less value than white lives, and because the 'big' logistical effort involved in putting redcoats into battle — usually involving large numbers of indigenous labourers — was seldom acknowledged. The Anglo-Zanzibar war of August 1896, which lasted for all of forty minutes, left 500 Zanzibaris dead and wounded in exchange for one wounded British sailor. Colonial wars were also 'small' because the role of logistics attracted and continues to attract less attention than it warrants. Logistics, the art of supplying war, of labouring in order to bring arms to bear on the enemy, has never attracted much attention, though by definition feats of arms conducted thousands of miles from home were all about the logistical tail, just as much as the pointed teeth of infantry squares and Gatling guns. The Royal Engineers, indeed, achieved prominence because they supplied so many of the commanders of Britain's manifold imperial ventures.

In making British rule a reality in colonial territories, and then in providing for their security, indigenous manpower was essential.* Thus British rule had gradually been extended in what became the colony of Kenya by a series of actions in which British forces acted alongside Maasai warriors, as for a decade the interests of the two parties aligned before the 1904 Maasai moves which saw them ejected from their lands for the purposes of white settlement. In Southern Africa, the people of the Bakgatla tribe in the Bechuanaland Protectorate were involved in the Anglo-Boer War of 1899–1902, and provide a good example of the use of indigenous resources in times of imperial warfare. The Transvaal-Bechuanaland border ran through the Bakgatla Reserve, and the Bakgatla people harboured animosity towards the Boers because of their mistreatment of Africans and desire for their land and cattle. The tribe had also to contend with the territorial ambitions of the British South Africa Company. The Bakgatla were well armed with rifles bought

---

* In nineteenth-century warfare colonial troops were often crucial because of their resistance to diseases that killed Europeans more readily.

from the proceeds of age-regiments sent to work in the Johannesburg mines.

Realizing, like other Bechuanaland chiefs, that greater evils than British rule beset his kingdom, Chief Lentshwe reconciled himself to British rule and accepted the imposition of hut tax, which he had at first resisted. The first hostile act of the Boer War took place in Bechuanaland when Boers sabotaged the Cape–Rhodesia cable south of Mahalapye on 12 October 1899; between 12 and 15 October Boer raiders also cut the Mafeking–Gaberones rail and telegraph lines at Ootse. On 26 October the British asked Chief Lentshwe to stand by to repel invaders. Ammunition was sent to Lentshwe, who was at first reluctant to get involved. But events forced his hand, as the British evacuated the Gaberones–Mochudi region and the Boers crossed the border and looted Mochudi, the Bakgatla capital. Bakgatla forces engaged a small Boer raiding party at Molotwana north of Mochudi. There followed a British–Bakgatla raid on Deerdepoort and its commando camp late in November, which led to Boer reprisals. In 1900 there was a major Bakgatla raid into the Transvaal, which enabled the tribe to replenish cattle stocks depleted by the recent rinderpest epidemic. Thus from its inception the Bakgatla took part in the Boer War on Britain's side, a colonial people sucked into the security equations that attended the march of empire, both for their own reasons and for those of their colonial masters.

Imperial wars and the role of colonies in protecting the empire

Imperial warfare required huge amounts of manpower to support British forces, and the colonies were a prime source of manpower for military labour and fighting units; as will be seen in the following chapters, colonies such as Bechuanaland, Ceylon, Mauritius, and Swaziland were called upon to provide soldiers and labourers for service in distant war theatres, particularly, though not exclusively, during times of world war. From the Malays recruited from captured Dutch colonies and the African slaves employed in fighting the kingdom of Kandy in the early nineteenth century, to the soldiers from Indian Ocean and Southern African colonies employed in Egypt and Libya until the 1950s, colonial manpower was essential to British military endeavour.[1] The initial conquest of colonies often involved the investment of large scale military resources, including colonial troops or porters. Over 1,800 Anglo-Dutch marines seized Gibraltar in 1704 during the War of the Spanish Succession. The British conquest of Minorca in 1798 involved 3,000 men and a sizeable invasion fleet. The three wars fought against the kingdom of Kandy involved British and native armies of up to 6,000 men. The conquest of Mauritius, Réunion, and Rodrigues in 1809–10 required a sizeable naval force drawn from the Royal Navy and the Honourable East India Company Marine to protect the sixty flat-bottomed troop-carrying vessels that ferried an army of over 10,000 men from the Cape and India to the Mascarenes. And in the 1880s Major-General Sir Charles Warren led a force of nearly 5,000 British and South Africa men to declare Bechuanaland a British territory.

In world wars, and therefore in the very *performance* of imperial defence, using one's own colonies and conquering the enemies' colonies was standard practice. In the 1930s and 1940s Britain used the prospect of colonies and colonial base rights in its diplomatic dealings with both Germany and America, seeking to appease the former with the offer of colonies (preferably French ones) and to involve the latter in the war and gain valuable military resources by offering extensive base rights in the West Indies. In world wars, colonies were seized for their strategic value, but also for their utility as bargaining counters at peace treaties.

The conquest of the French Indian Ocean colonies of Mauritius, Réunion, and Rodrigues serves as an example. In 1795 Britain 'initiated a policy of depriving France of her colonies, or "filching sugar islands" as Sheridan put it'.[4] Apart from the sugar — not a factor in the strategic decision-making of the British government at the time — the reason for taking these colonies was their use as bases from which French forces attacked British shipping and launched operations in India. On Mauritius, many French settlers were prepared to sever ties with France rather than emancipate their slaves, though a flavour of contemporary metropolitan occurrences reached them in the form of Revolutionary administrators and a guillotine, tested on an unfortunate goat. The British were threatened not only by French warships preying on their India trade from their bases in the Mascerenes, but by the prospect of French activity in Egypt and Persia, requiring a naval squadron in the Red Sea and orders to the Bombay government to seize the island of Perim.

In charge of Britain's campaign to rid the Indian Ocean of French colonies was a general with decades of imperial experience behind him: Sir John Abercromby. Before arriving in Bombay as commander-in-chief and being ordered to conquer the French colonies, he had had a classic military career, involving service in Europe and the colonies. As a young man he had travelled with his father, Lieutenant-General Sir Ralph Abercromby, and 15,000 men to the West Indies where he saw fighting in St Lucia, Demerara, and St Vincent. At a time of unrelenting global warfare, Abercromby next found himself stationed in Ireland, before again serving under his father as part of an army of 10,000 men sent to Helder in Holland. In 1800 he washed up in the Mediterranean as a colonel and was part of the army that took Malta and then landed at Aboukir Bay in order to eject Napoleon from Egypt. Travelling in Europe on the renewal of hostilities in 1803, Abercromby was imprisoned at Verdun, promoted major-general in absentia, and exchanged in 1808 for a French general captured by the British. In 1809 he became Commander-in-Chief of the Bombay Presidency, and his association with the island colonies of the Indian Ocean began.

Shortly after arriving at Bombay, Abercromby was directed by the Governor-General, Lord Minto, to commence operations against the Isle de France (Mauritius). The French fortress island was being used as a base for operations against India and the merchant shipping of the British Empire; between 1793 and 1802 Mauritius-based ships had seized 119 British prizes. The campaign began when Lieutenant Colonel Henry Keating landed with 1,800 European and 1,850 Indian troops and occupied the French island of Rodrigues on 20 June 1809. This island was then used as a platform for British operations against Réunion, which fell to the British on 8 July. With Réunion and Rodrigues in the bag, the British closed in on the major prize, Mauritius. Keating sought, with the cooperation of the local naval commander, Commodore Josias Rowley, to secure a British foothold in the small islets north and east of the main island prior to a land attack. The capture of the Ile de la Passe at the entrance to Grand Port led to a significant naval encounter fought between 20 and 27 August 1810 — the Battle of Grand Port — in which the British lost all four frigates engaged, the French two frigates, a corvette, and an Eastindiaman. It was the most serious setback suffered by the Royal Navy during the Napoleonic Wars, and is recorded on the Arc de Triomphe in Paris.

Bound for the islands from Madras aboard HMS *Ceylon*, Abercromby's progress was temporarily halted when in the Action of 18 September the frigate was captured by the French ship *Venus*. The timely arrival of Commodore Rowley in HMS *Boadicea* retrieved the situation: *Ceylon* was recaptured and *Venus* became a British warship. But the Battle of Grand Port had major strategic implications for the Indian Ocean, tilting the balance in favour of the French, and leaving the French commander, Commodore Jacques Hamelin, free to hunt British shipping to and from India and the Far East. It took over three months for the balance of naval power in the Indian Ocean to tip back in Britain's favour.

This occurred when Admiral Albemarle Bertie arrived with a powerful battle squadron in December. This enabled the invasion of Mauritius to go ahead. The invasion required substantial forces, assembled from British possessions across the Indian Ocean region. As Abercromby wrote on 12 October to Robert Dundas, President of Board of Control for the affairs of India, 'the Force to be employed on the attack is to be drawn from Bengal, Madras, Bombay, Bourbon [Réunion] and the Cape, and when united at Rodriguez, will, I hope, not be less than 7,000 European and 3,000 Native Infantry'. The invasion went in successfully, and on 3 December 1810 Abercromby was able to write to Lord Minto: 'I have the satisfaction to acquaint Your Lordship that this Island was ceded to His Britannic Majesty by capitulation which was signed at an early hour this morning'. Events at the subsequent peace treaty reveal the strategic logic of capturing colonies in times of imperial warfare. Réunion was handed back to the French, Mauritius ceded to Britain. This was simply because the latter possessed ports from which French warships could interdict British trade, and the former did not. Until the capture of Mauritius, all British trade east of the Cape had required the protection of armed convoys.

The colonial empire, as demonstrated, had always been central to imperial defence, because it required defending and because it was, in turn, responsible for helping defend and police the imperial estate. In 1801 the War Department became the War and Colonies Department to reflect the importance of the colonies to British warfare (in 1854 two separate ministries were established). It was as a platform for force projection that the colonies contributed most consistently to imperial defence. Colonies provided barracks for the army and ports for the navy. They provided watering holes, repair yards, recreational retreats, ammunition dumps, fuel reservoirs, sheltered harbours, naval shore bases, aerodromes, administrative centres, internment centres, cable and wireless installations, and flying boat anchorages. They also acted as prison camps for thousands of men captured during imperial wars — Boers, Germans, and Italians were dispersed as prisoners of war all over the Empire — and for individual leaders who needed to be kept under arrest. Arabi Pasha of Egypt, Archbishop Makarois of Cyprus, Napoleon Bonaparte, Cetshwayo of the Zulus, the Kabaka of Buganda, and the Shah of Iran were among the numerous dignitaries confined to British colonies, usually island colonies, as prisoners. From the early twentieth century intelligence-gathering facilities linked to Bletchley Park and then GCHQ were located in colonies such as Bermuda, Ceylon, Cyprus, Hong Kong, Kenya, Mauritius, and Singapore.

The colonies were pivotal to the imperial defence calculations of British governments because they provided strategically located bases in an age where power projection relied upon local concentrations of troops and ports of call for warships guarding the Empire's sea routes. The extension of Britain's protective shield to distant Dominions — the heart of imperial defence no less — *depended upon colonial bases*. Whilst Australia and New Zealand, for example, might have military and naval forces of their own, these were never sufficient to withstand the hostile attentions of a great power enemy and were integrated with and dependent upon the military and naval forces of Britain. So the security of these two Dominions rested ultimately upon the British Army and, in particular, the Royal Navy. In order to get to the antipodes should an attack ever come, the army and navy (and later the air force) depended upon British domination of sea routes and air routes, and regional power points along the way. Colonial bases performed this vital function, without which the Australasian Dominions would have been marooned. By the 1930s, for example, the air reinforcement route to Australia ran from Britain to Victoria Point in Singapore via Gibraltar, Malta, Egypt, Habbaniyah, Basra, Sharjah, Karachi, Allahabad, Calcutta, and Mingaladon near Rangoon. The navy continued to depend on colonial strongholds that stretched from the Mediterranean across the Indian Ocean and through the Straits of Malacca eastwards to the Pacific and the South China Sea.

Colonial bases were indispensable to the British Army, which required 'prepositioned' forces all over the world in order to react to local crises. The British Army was designed for service overseas, most line regiments consisting of two battalions, one usually stationed overseas, the other remaining at home, enabling rotation and reinforcement. In 1842 British regiments (excluding those in Britain, the Dominions, and India) were stationed in Antigua, Barbados, Bermuda, Ceylon, Gibraltar, Jamaica, Malta, Mauritius, St Helena, Sierra Leone, and Trinidad. In 1881 British troops (excluding those in Britain, the Dominions, and India) were stationed in Barbados (813 troops), Bermuda (2,200), Bahamas (101), British Guiana (246), British Honduras (247), Ceylon (1,224), Cyprus (420), Gibraltar (4,158), the Gold Coast (191), Hong Kong (1,167), Jamaica (778), Malta (5,626), Mauritius (355), St Helena (210), Sierra Leone (441), the Straits Settlements (1,028), and Trinidad (121). The system remained the same in 1939. On the day that the Second World War broke out the British Army was still portioned out around the world. British Army battalions and even brigades were stationed in Burma Egypt, Palestine, Shanghai, the Sudan, and Tientsin. In the colonial empire, there were British Army infantry battalions (and artillery, engineers, and signals units) in Aden, Bermuda, Cyprus, Gibraltar, Hong Kong, Jamaica, Malta, Malacca, Palestine, and Singapore. Many other colonies, such as Ceylon and Mauritius, were home to other British Army units, most commonly drawn from the Royal Artillery, the Royal Corps of Signals, and the Royal Engineers.

Locally-raised military forces:
National armies in waiting

Colonies were central to imperial defence because they were responsible for their own internal security and that of their borders. By maintaining police and volunteer military formations to achieve this, colonial governments reduced the workload of the Regular Army, a factor that contributed to its ability to retain a small peacetime structure. Internal colonial security required the maintenance of military formations and police forces. Most colonies had a volunteer defence force and many maintained full-time military units, often supporting, or actually a part of, British forces. In 1948 there were forty-three separate colonial police forces. Colonial military and paramilitary formations were formed primarily to defend their own borders and to prevent internal unrest, though a tradition soon developed of expanding these forces in times of general war for service elsewhere in the Empire or in order to allow the release of British troops from garrison duties.

In extending its writ around the world, the British Army always made extensive and effective use of these locally-recruited formations. They performed three functions: overseeing a colony's internal security; helping secure it from external threats by forming coastal artillery units or infantry companies to defend strategic points should an attack ever come; and providing units for service overseas during periods of imperial warfare. The growth of colonial military forces went hand in hand with British expansion, and the formation of a regiment was at the top of the list when the British arrived on a distant shore, along with the creation of a school, a racecourse, a club, and a church. Thus when British sovereignty came to Fiji in 1874, it wasn't long before the Fiji Armed Constabulary was formed, and in 1898 its commander, Colonel Claude Francis, organized the Fiji Volunteer Corps. This force, dedicated to internal security, soon proved its value when the Empire needed manpower overseas. In the First World War Fiji sent labourers to France, and in the Second World War the Fiji Military Forces played an important role in defending the colony, and served alongside American and New Zealand forces fighting in other Pacific islands.

All colonies had some kind of defence force, such as the Newfoundland Militia, the Barbados Volunteer Force, the St Kitts and Nevis Defence Force, the British Guiana Militia, the Straits Settlement Volunteer Force, the Sarawak Rangers, the Transjordan Frontier Force, and the Fiji Defence Force Signals. Some colonies, such as Ceylon and particularly those in Africa, maintained professional full-time fighting units. Colonial Africa was home to numerous military formations, highly valued by imperial military and political leaders. They were usually raised in the name of the Crown, most famously the King's African Rifles and the Royal West African Frontier Force. The Central Africa Rifles had been established in 1891 around a nucleus of Sikhs, and was renamed the King's African Rifles in 1902. These imperial forces provided a bank of experience and organizational continuity that could be readily expanded during times of world war. In the First World War, for example, the King's African Rifles' strength rose to twenty-two battalions, falling back in the 1930s to about 3,000 men. The Second World War brought further expansion as the King's African Rifles climbed to forty-three battalions. The West African Frontier Force (it became 'Royal' in 1925 when the King became its Colonel-in-Chief) was formed at the behest of Colonial Secretary Joseph Chamberlain in 1897 to provide Britain with a more robust presence in the face of French expansion in the region. The Royal West African Frontier Force served in East Africa in both world wars and in Burma during the Second World War, even contributing a brigade to Orde Wingate's Chindits fighting behind Japanese lines.

Other long-standing African military units included the Somaliland Camel Corps, raised in 1912 to check inter-tribal fighting, and the Northern Rhodesia Regiment (both Somali and Northern Rhodesian units served in Burma in the Second World War). Other parts of the colonial empire followed the same pattern. The West India Regiment was actually part of the British Regular Army. Raised in 1795 and recruited from freed slaves, it saw service in the Napoleonic Wars, including participation in the attack on New Orleans in 1800. At its largest, the Regiment contained twelve battalion-strength regiments. It served in the West Indies as well as West Africa during the nineteenth century, and in the Middle East during the First World War, before being disbanded in 1927. Most other colonies boasted their own military formations. The Mauritius Territorial Force was formed in the 1930s to supplement the British garrison on the island, manning coastal defence artillery and forming an infantry unit to repel enemy attack. During the Second World War it became The Mauritius Regiment, and one of its battalions joined the garrison established in Madagascar after the British invasion of May 1942. If the men of the Colonial Administrative Service were the 'steel frame' around which the British colonial empire was built, these locally-recruited military units, alongside the British and Indian armies, provided the cold steel that buttressed it.

Colonies as naval and air bases

As well as being garrison centres for the British Army, colonies provided the Royal Navy with the bases upon which it depended for its global reach. They provided infrastructure without which the navy could not have sustained its presence around the world, be it performing anti-slaving patrols off the east and west coasts of Africa, hunting pirates in the Indonesian archipelago, or searching for German U-boats in the Mediterranean. By 1914 overseas shore bases included HMS *Cormorant* at Gibraltar, headquarters of the East Atlantic Station, as well as the submarine base HMS *Rapid*. HMS *St Angelo* and *Egmont* were shore bases in Malta. HMS *Alert* was the depot ship in the Persian Gulf, and HMS *Tamar* the naval headquarters of the China Station in Hong Kong (as she was until British withdrawal in 1997). The North America and West Indies Station was served by HMS *Terror* on Bermuda along with bases in Canada and Newfoundland, and HMS *Pursuivant* in the Falklands served the South East Coast Station.

Some colonies served as headquarters for important Royal Navy fleets. Thus Bermuda was home to the North America and West Indies Station, Malta to the Mediterranean Fleet, Hong Kong to the China Station, and Ceylon to the East Indies Station. The East Indies Station, responsible for policing the vast Indian Ocean region from the Bay of Bengal and Sunda Straits as far afield as the Swahili coast, the Arabian Sea, the Persian Gulf, and the Red Sea, provides a good example of the work of overseas naval formations. Until the Station's closure in 1958 its warships continued to undertake East African and Persian Gulf cruises, showing the flag on land, playing cricket and rugby with expatriate and indigenous teams, putting the Marines ashore to entertain the locals with martial music or to quell disturbances, performing gunnery demonstrations, and holding 'harbour lights' events and hosting cocktail parties.

Naval visits were used as an opportunity to exercise colonial garrisons. In May 1939, for example, the East Indies Station cruiser HMS *Liverpool* took part in the Navy's annual visit to Mauritius. This always provided an opportunity for ceremonial events and military exercises. *Liverpool* put a raiding party of Marines ashore, ordered to take certain key points on the island which were to be defended by the Mauritius Territorial Force. The ship's captain, meanwhile, paid courtesy calls, the Royal Marines band entertained the locals, and tours were conducted around the ship, which was floodlit at night as it lay at anchor in Port Louis harbour. Also in 1939, the Commander-in-Chief of the East Indies Station issues forth from his headquarters in Colombo to visit the many colonies across the Indian Ocean that fell under his command. He arrived in Mauritius aboard the cruiser HMS *Gloucester*. A garden party for 1,400 people was held at Government House, at which the guest of honour was the governor of the neighbouring French colony of Réunion. These visits were all part of maintaining the system of imperial defence; reassuring colonies that they were protected and that the ubiquity and power of the Royal Navy was real, whilst exercising locally-recruited defence forces alongside those of the imperial fighting services.

In the same way that the British Army received assistance from locally-raised forces, so too did the navy. Colonies such as Ceylon, Kenya, Tanganyika, and Trinidad had their own naval forces for operations in territorial waters, and during the Second World War they were able to assume responsibility for local convoy escort work as well as mine clearance, relieving the Royal Navy of duties and allowing it to concentrate stretched resources in other areas. Colonies operated as key links on the sea routes that ensured imperial trade and security; places such as Ceylon, Gibraltar, and Sierra Leone forming vital points in the Empire's convoy network. Locally-recruited naval forces also helped man coastal batteries and the Port War Signals Stations that supervised the security of imperial ports. The RAF recruited local formations to perform essential duties on their colonial air stations, such as the Aden Protectorate Levies and the Mauritius (Marine Crafts) Section, which supported RAF flying boat anchorages around the island.

Another colony that served as headquarters to one of the navy's major overseas fleets was Hong Kong. The China Station had its home in Hong Kong (with other main bases including Hankow, Shanghai, Tientsin, and Wei-Hei-Wei), and was responsible for maritime security in the South China Sea and on China's great rivers, particularly the Yangtze and the West River. The China Station was also intended to check Russian naval power in northern East Asia. The station's strength usually comprised a number of destroyers and sloops and a squadron of elderly cruisers with a more modern cruiser as flagship. Inland work was the preserve of the quaint but proven shallow draft river gunboats (with splendid names such as HMS *Aphis, Bee, Dragonfly, Glowworm, Ladybird, Moorhen, Petrel,* and *Widgeon*). Weighing up to 645 tons, river gunboats looked like Mississippi steamers but packed an array of weapons — twelve-pounders, three-inch anti-aircraft guns, Lewis guns, and even six-inch guns. Some of the earlier gunboats had originally been built for service with Kitchener on the Nile, others for action on the Danube during the First World War. The job of these gunboats in eastern waters, from the end of the nineteenth century until the very day of Japan's assault on Britain's eastern empire in December 1941, was to patrol the inland waterways protecting British interests and providing the general security essential for the continuance of trading activities. The China Station also provided important force projection ashore, for example contributing significantly to the relief of the European legations in Peking during the Boxer Rebellion of 1900. In the 1930s the China Station's work was increasingly overshadowed by the prospect of war with Japan, and by the time war came, the Station had virtually ceased to exist, its ships having been transferred to other theatres rather than face embarrassment and pointless sacrifice when the Japanese struck with far superior forces. The China Station was merged with the East Indies Station to form the Eastern Fleet, based at Singapore and, when it surrendered in February 1942, in Ceylon.

The colonial empire also provided bases for the projection of air power and the development of rapid imperial communications (pioneered by Imperial Airways). From the 1920s Aden (a Crown colony from 1937 after its transfer from Indian administration) became headquarters for the RAF in Arabia, supported by airfields in Oman, bases in Aden itself such as RAF Sheikh Othman and RAF Khormaksar, and facilities on offshore islands such as Masirah and Sharjah. The Aden Protectorate Levies were raised to help the RAF guard their Arabian bases. Ceylon was home to the RAF's 222 (General Reconnaissance) Group responsible for air patrols across the Indian Ocean region, and the China Bay Royal Naval Air Station on the island hosted a total of forty-four squadrons during the Second World War. The Cocos-Keeling Islands, Diego Garcia, Mauritius, the Seychelles, and Madagascar all developed air facilities in order to extend the RAF's coverage of the region.

Another important air route dependent upon colonial bases crossed Africa from the Gold Coast and Nigeria to the Sudan and Egypt, and delivered thousands of aircraft to Middle East Command and Asia. It was supported by aerodromes in numerous British and Free French colonies.

On their journey to Africa, over 20,000 aircraft from America halted in mid-Atlantic to refuel on the British colony of Ascension (as aircraft and warships were to do decades later during the Falklands conflict). Ascension had a lengthy history as a martial colony. When Napoleon was exiled to St Helena in 1815 a British garrison took possession of Ascension so as to forestall its use in a rescue attempt. It also acted as a sanatorium for Royal Navy ships on anti-slavery patrols off the West African coast, and from 1823 until 1922 was under the control of the Admiralty, listed as a 'sloop of war'.

Gaining colonies to stop the enemy using them

Such colonies, if not British, could be employed by Britain's enemies in times of war. Thus British colonies contributed to imperial defence by the very fact of being British, because any colony possessed by a rival or enemy power was a potential point of strength from which to harry British shipping, threaten British interests, or transmit wireless messages to hostile vessels. Many British colonies had been gained purely because of their strategic significance, and because of the danger that they would present to British interests if in the hands of an enemy. Gibraltar was taken from the Spanish for this reason, Ceylon from the Dutch, and Mauritius from the French during the Napoleonic Wars. Numerous Caribbean islands were gained during European struggles in the seventeenth and eighteenth centuries, and enjoyed a strategic recrudescence years later when base rights were granted to the Americans as they sought to shore up the 'Caribbean Sea Frontier' in the face of the German submarine threat. Moreover, even the most remote colonies could become militarily important during wartime; in 1942 the German pocket battleship *Graf Spee* was spotted from the remote South Atlantic island of Tristan da Cunha. Soon thereafter it was taken over by the Admiralty as HMS *Atlantic Isle*, a radio station was constructed to monitor U-boat movements and a meteorological station established, manned by a Royal Navy personnel and the newly-created Tristan Defence Volunteers.

The policy of colonial acquisition prompted by the need to prevent potential rivals or actual enemies gaining useful bases meant that 'East of the Cape of Good Hope after 1824 there was no foreign port from which an enemy squadron could effectively challenge British command of the Indian Ocean'.[5] Colonies such as the Cape, Ceylon, Java, and Mauritius were taken because they were too dangerous left in enemy hands, as had been the case with Gibraltar and Minorca in an earlier period of European warfare. This compulsion to acquire colonies because of defensive requirements included control of seemingly unimportant territories (though they often acquired strategic significance later), such as the Cocos-Keeling Islands, Diego Garcia, and the Maldives. Aden was claimed by British and Indian forces because of its strategic location and its suitability as a refuelling point. The outpost was used as a base for Indian Army intervention in Abyssinia in 1868, and again in 1940–41 when British Somaliland was evacuated, and then retaken, in the struggle against Italy. Labuan was bagged by the Admiralty in 1846 because of its convenient location on a key shipping route between Singapore and China (closing a 1,500-mile gap in the chain of harbours circling the world), and Penang was claimed by the East India Company in the 1780s as a base from which piracy could be suppressed and maritime traffic protected. In 1878 Cyprus was prised from the Ottoman sultan as the British took steps to ensure a firm territorial base in a region threatened by Russia's march towards Constantinople and the Dardanelles (Cyprus remains an important British military base, recently used during Operation Highbrow in 2006, which saw the evacuation of over 4,500 British and other personnel from Lebanon). During both of the twentieth centuries' world wars enemy colonies were taken in order to neutralize the military threat that they posed. Italian possessions in Africa had to be conquered, Vichy French colonies such as Madagascar could not be permitted to remain unsecured, and in the First World War German colonies in Africa harboured wireless transmitters that directed warships against British shipping.

Some colonies took great pride in their importance as 'fortress' colonies, ideally placed because of their proximity to important sea routes or rivals' interests, or because of their suitability as naval bases or troop concentration points. These included Bermuda, Gibraltar, Malta, Mauritius, and Singapore. Some, such as Gibraltar and Malta, maintained the practice of appointing a military, as opposed to a civilian, governor. From 1905 the crest of Mauritius incorporated the phrase '*Stella Clavisque Maris Indici*' ('Star and Key of the Indian Ocean'), reflecting pride in the island's pivotal strategic importance in an earlier phase of global warfare. Mauritius, and numerous other British possessions across the Indian Ocean and on its rim, ensured that the world's third largest ocean remained a 'British lake' into the post-war period.

Singapore, Southern Rhodesia, Malta, and the Falkland Islands

Singapore presents a classic case of the colonial empire's role in imperial defence. At first, when Stamford Raffles ran up the flag in 1819, the island's purpose was to serve as a defensive hub for the activities of the East India Company. Soon, however, it became an indispensable feature on the Admiralty's 'Route to the East' given its commanding position on the Straits of Malacca. Singapore's stock rose even higher in the early 1920s as it became Britain's primary eastern naval stronghold with the investment of millions of pounds, intended to deter Japan from disturbing the imperial equilibrium east of Suez, and the hinge upon which the defence of Hong Kong, Malaya, Burma, Borneo, French-Indo China, the Dutch East Indies, and the Pacific Dominions and colonies hung. During the decolonization years Aden and Singapore emerged as the two major overseas bases that guaranteed Britain's continued global military reach.

The rhetoric of imperial loyalty and the display of Union Flags and bunting were features of life in Jamaica and the Seychelles as much as in Canada or New Zealand. Southern Rhodesians, displaying Union Flags from all major buildings in the capital Salisbury in 1914, worried about how their war effort compared to that of the Dominions, until two drafts of the Rhodesia Regiment joined regiments in Britain and cast the colony's ratio of soldiers-to-settlers in a very favourable light (this wasn't just imperial loyalty; the Southern Rhodesian settlers dream was to be granted the self-government enjoyed by the Dominions, and wanted therefore to show how well they measured up). Southern Rhodesia relied for its local security on the paramilitary forces of a private company, the British South Africa Company. Its British South Africa Police (BSAP) had been created to accompany Cecil Rhodes' Pioneer Column into Mashonaland in 1890. In 1908 it numbered 450 Europeans and 530 Africans, backed up by a Southern Rhodesian Volunteer force of 2,000. Until the early 1920s Southern Rhodesia was ruled by the chartered company and its military and paramilitary formations. The BSAP took part in the Matabele war of 1893, the suppression of the Ndebele and Shona rebellions of 1896, and the Anglo-Boer War. During the First World War the BSAP served with distinction in the East Africa campaign, and in 1914 captured Schuckmannsburg in German South-West Africa. In the early 1920s Southern Rhodesia became a self-governing colony, entrenching the authority of the settlers and their military formations. In the inter-war period Southern Rhodesia continued to provide Britain with a political and military presence in Central Africa, considered an important counterweight to South African influence in the region. During the Second World War Southern Rhodesian forces played an important role in the East Africa campaign, contributing much needed mechanized, transport, and air power units to the imperial force deployed. Southern Rhodesian units, famously its armoured car brigade, then went on to form part of the South African Division in North Africa and the Middle East. Distinct Southern Rhodesian squadrons became part of the RAF in Britain, and the colony trained over 7,000 airmen for the RAF as part of the British Empire Air Training Scheme. The Rhodesia African Rifles fought in Burma, and Southern Rhodesians were prominent in the Long Range Desert Group, a behind-enemy-lines formation that fought in the Western Desert that later became part of the SAS.

By any index Malta, like Singapore, was one of the most important colonies in the imperial defence matrix. Britain was invited to take over the island by the local notables in 1798 in order to end the French occupation, and Nelson duly achieved this transfer of authority by besieging Valetta in the following year. Malta thereafter became a Crown colony and began its life as a British strategic jewel. The island was used to check the ambitions of regional rulers such as Mehmet Ali of Egypt, and for concentrating troops in order to curb Russia's Mediterranean ambitions (it was also the departure point for the armada that sailed to Egypt during the 1956 Suez Crisis). First and foremost, Malta was home to the Mediterranean Fleet, the potent force behind Britain's claim to be mistress of the Mediterranean Sea. In the 1920s Malta's importance as a nodal point in the imperial defence system was heightened when it became the main base for the fleet that would be sent east should Japanese expansionism require naval deterrence. Malta was ten days sailing closer than British ports, and there was at the time no port east of Suez that could accommodate modern battleships (until the completion of Singapore's facilities in the 1930s). Malta's major defence assets from a British point of view, therefore, were the two main harbours at Valetta, which after expansion could accommodate the strengthened Mediterranean Fleet and its support vessels. The naval base featured extensive repair and storage facilities, and employed 14,000 Maltese workers.

The colony was also home to an army garrison, which in 1925 consisted of two battalions of British troops, with artillery and engineers support, supplemented by the locally-raised King's Own Malta

Regiment and the Royal Malta Artillery. A seaplane base had been established during the First World War at Kalafrana, and a landing ground developed at Hal Far for the Fleet Air Arm. Malta's finest hour as an imperial defence asset came during the Second World War, when it acted as a base for submarines and surface vessels attacking Axis trans-Mediterranean shipping, for hundreds of aircraft attacking Axis ports and ships and flying reconnaissance missions (including those which located the Italian battlefleet anchored at Taranto), and as a staging post for aircraft travelling to the Middle East and Far East. Britain could not have waged war in the eastern Mediterranean in the manner that it did without this vital strategic asset, a fact underlined by the massive risks taken by the British government in committing precious resources to the famous Malta convoys.

Even distant imperial outposts had a role to play as links in the imperial defence chain. The Falkland Islands depended for their defence upon the naval shield, and were duly threatened by the fact that powerful German warships were at large in the early months of the First World War. With *Scharnhorst* and *Gneisenau* in the vicinity, women and children were evacuated to outlying farms and shepherds' houses, and the Falkland Islands Volunteer Force was placed on alert. The islands acted as a link in the Royal Navys' wireless network that spanned the globe, and a minefield was laid at Port William. Before the Battle of the Falklands HMS *Canopus* was positioned at the east end of Stanley harbour, settling on low water mud, with her 12-inch main armament directed by an observation post on Sapper Hill connected to the ship by telephone. On 6 December 1914 HMS *Invincible, Carnarvon, Inflexible, Kent, Cornwall, Glasgow, Bristol,* and *Macedonia* arrived. Two days later the islands' signal station received a report of a four-funnel and two-funnel man-of-war sighted from Sapper Hill, steering northwards. In the famous battle that followed Vice-Admiral Graf von Spee's squadron was all but annihilated by Vice-Admiral Sir Doveton Sturdee's battlecruisers. Over 2,200 Germans perished on that day (which is still a public holiday in the colony). This one-sided encounter avenged the defeat at the Battle of Coronel fought in the Pacific on 1 November, when von Spee's ships had bested Vice-Admiral Sir Percy Cradock's squadron and sunk HMS *Monmouth* and *Good Hope* with all hands.

Following the Battle of the Falklands the islands were reinforced, demonstrating Britain's commitment to defending the colonial empire. In May 1915 SS *Ismailia* and *Freshfield* arrived at Port Stanley with materials and staff for the erection of a high-power naval wireless station. In September 1915 a submarine cable was laid connecting the Falklands to

Montevideo. In January 1916 HMS *Lancaster* arrived and began positioning heavy guns around Stanley, and parties of Royal Marines were left ashore to man them. The Falklands were again touched by world war between 1939 and 1945, as Britain took measures to see off German threats in the Antarctic region, and stake its claim to British Antarctic Territory in the face of the ambitions of both enemies and allies alike. For a period the Falklands were garrisoned by a British infantry battalion, for fear that German forces — or those of a German-influenced South American republic — would seek to take them. British wounded from the Battle of the River Plate were landed at Port Stanley for hospital treatment; over 150 Falkland Islanders' served in imperial military forces; and ten aircraft were bought for the RAF with funds raised by the islanders. To borrow the title of John Harris's novel about Sierra Leone during the 1939–45 conflict, it was 'a funny place to hold a war', but that was the nature of imperial defence during times of global conflict.

The martial character of colonies

The extent of military activity in the colonial empire — the recruitment of local forces, visits of imperial forces, the presence of garrisons and naval stations, the regularity of ceremonial events involving marching men and military music — meant that colonies were marked by the martial traditions of empire that were a characteristic of British society. Though only a few colonies had substantial white populations, all had a white community, and the governor and his district officers ensured that the great anniversaries of British military endeavour were celebrated, and that the locals knew all about the military prowess that underpinned Britain's dominion over palm and pine. Empire Day, Royal milestones such as coronations and jubilees, Empire Tour visits — all presented a chance for martial display and the gathering of a colony's European and non-European ex-servicemen. In 1937, for example, Edward Twining organized Uganda's coronation celebrations. There was a military tattoo and fireworks display, during the course of which the Governor set off fifty rockets. A bugler sounded the Retreat into the darkness and then forty spotlights, floodlights, and footlights illuminated the scene. Schoolboys then performed the 'Parade of the Toy Soldiers' wearing red tunics and white pillbox hats, and 120 warriors in leopard skins and ostrich feathers, wielding spears and shields, performed a war dance. There was then a showing of a film called *From Savage to Soldier*. The central event, and the sensation of the evening, was a radio relay of the voice of the new King-Emperor, broadcast through concealed loud-speakers.

Amongst the Europeans in the colonies — administrators, settlers, missionaries, traders, and the like — were a fair sprinkling of former military men, many of whom maintained a state of readiness should the colours ever call for a final flourish in order to quell a 'native uprising' or fight the king's enemies overseas. White communities throughout the colonial world, no matter how small, displayed the same imperial patriotism common in Britain and the settler territories, a patriotism more zealous the smaller the settler community and the greater the distance from the mother country. Imperial wars also led to more colonial settlement, as colonies and Dominions offered ex-servicemen generous terms in order to entice them to start new lives in places such as Kenya and Southern Rhodesia.

Colonial rule meant the importation of a decidedly martial tone into a territory. In addition to locally-raised army units, most colonies had other forms of military and paramilitary organizations on the books. In the mid-1920s the Gold Coast, for example, had a range of forces at its disposal in addition to the Gold Coast Regiment (part of the Royal West African Frontier Force). There was a military reserve of ex-servicemen that could be mobilized quickly, and a territorial defence force with a European and an African section, the former including machine-gun companies. In addition to the general police there was a paramilitary Northern Territories Constabulary, recruited mainly from ex-military circles; an Escort Police; separate mine, railway, and marine police branches; and an armed Preventive Force serving on the frontiers as part of the customs service. Many of the Europeans in the colony possessed firearms and practiced in rifle clubs supported by government funds.

A colony's involvement in local and imperial military operations left its mark on the built environment. In the Matopos Hills south of Bulawayo, alongside the graves of Cecil Rhodes and Leander Starr Jameson at World's End, is a grand frieze set in marble depicting the Shangani Patrol, a column of Rhodesian settlers killed in battle by the Ndebele in 1893. The city of Hobart in the former colony of Tasmania nestles beneath mounts Wellington and Nelson. In a further echo of the Napoleonic Wars, the quayside neighbourhood of Salamanca is named after Wellington's triumphant battle of 1812. Elsewhere in the city, a pith-helmeted statue commemorating Tasmania's participation in the Anglo-Boer War stands near Government House and the Cenotaph, and in Bellerive an ornamental lamppost commemorates a soldier who lost his life in the Boer War. Echoing the significance of imperial wars and its history as a garrison colony, the map of Mauritius features names such as Arsenal, Balaclava, Sebastopol, Gunners Quoin, and Signal Mountain. The Falkland Islanders erected a memorial to the men who died at the Battle of the Falklands, and the Governor of Ceylon, Brigadier-General Sir William Henry Manning, unveiled the Cenotaph War Memorial on Galle Face Green, Colombo, in 1923. It was moved further inland during the Second World War, to Victoria Park, for fear that its prominent seafront position might make an irresistible target for Japanese gunners. There are military cemeteries all over the island, such as the Colombo Cemetery containing 628 graves of servicemen from Bengal, Britain, Ceylon, Cochin, East Africa, Holland, Italy, Madras, Nepal, Northern Rhodesia, and Southern Rhodesia, and other military cemeteries in places such as Kandy and Trincomalee. On Kenyatta Avenue in Nairobi, the War Memorial bears a dedication to the Carrier Corps who laboured across East Africa. In Iraq, the Basra War Memorial was moved in the late 1990s towards Nasariyah. It commemorates 40,500 Commonwealth soldiers who lost their lives in operations in Mesopotamia between 1914 and 1921.

Reasons for the marginalization of the role of colonies in imperial defence

Given the importance of colonies in the system of imperial defence as described in this chapter, the extent to which the colonial empire has played second fiddle to the Dominions and India in studies of imperial defence is surprising. The reasons for this, however, are not difficult to discern. The Dominions and India provided the Empire with its main non–British defence assets that could be utilized for *imperial* purposes. No colonies maintained their own major warships or air squadrons; colonial military formations, whilst extensive, were relatively small during peacetime; and, with the exception of units like the King's African Rifles, they were intended primarily for internal policing duties rather than external warfighting. In the parlance of the time, they tended to be *locally raised* units for local defence and security tasks, rather than *imperial* units. One of the main roles performed by colonies during imperial wars — providing essential military labour to support fighting fronts the world over — belongs to a branch of military affairs that has had a Cinderella career. This is the role of logistics, the art of 'supplying war' that is so vital though so easily overshadowed by the role played by military formations directly involved in actual *fighting*. Thus whilst colonies contributed

hundreds of thousands of men to the army and to 'home front' formations such as home guards and civil labour corps', their contribution was
unlikely to be recognized by a world that was much more interested in
acts of gallantry on the battlefield.

The common omission of the colonial empire from imperial defence
deliberations and subsequent studies also reflects the fact that the colonies
were voiceless compared to the more 'mature' parts of the Empire; the
Dominions were self-governing, autonomous, virtually independent
and, as the twentieth century progressed, increasingly involved in central
imperial defence decision-making, and able to say 'no' to London (as
during the Chanak crisis of 1922). Some Dominion prime ministers sat
on the Imperial War Cabinet and they sent representatives to the
Versailles Peace Conference as part of the British Empire Delegation.
India, whilst ruled autocratically at the highest levels by British authorities, had always been represented in imperial defence counsels by the
Viceroy, the Secretary of State for India, and the Commander-in-Chief
India, and the Raj had gathered to itself a huge network of influence and
imperial defence responsibilities throughout the Indian Ocean region and
Middle East. Whilst the teeming millions in India had little say in the
decisions of their rulers, those rulers did have a say in the defence deliberations of the British Empire at the highest level because of the size of
the subcontinent's military resources and the tradition of autonomy
grown up since the days of the East India Company. Furthermore, the
Indian Civil Service and Indian Army's officer corps was becoming
increasingly Indianized, a phenomenon that did not occur to anything
like the same extent in the colonies.

In contrast to the Dominions and India, the colonies were ruled
directly from London through the Colonial Office, and did as they were
bid. Though all colonies possessed local political authorities through
whom the British worked — the African chiefs of the High Commission
Territories and proto-parliamentary bodies such as the Basutoland
National Council, the Bechuanaland African Advisory Council, the
Council of Government in Mauritius, and the State Council in Ceylon
— in most parts of the colonial empire the common people were without
political influence or control over their own lives, subjects of the King-
Emperor rather than citizens. Governors had little say in the Empire's
defence deliberations, and the Colonial Office was a relatively puny beast
in the Whitehall jungle.

The peripheralization of the colonies in imperial defence has been
little remedied by the passage of time, whatever the self-congratulatory
predilections of a 'post-colonial' and 'post-modern' society that likes to

think that it has rectified the attitudes to non-whites and the non-Western world that afflicted past generations. On the contrary, the 'enormous condescension of posterity', to pilfer E. P. Thompson's brilliant phrase, remains much in evidence. Montgomery continues to have triumphed in the Western Desert with his army of Australians, Britons, Frenchmen, Indians, New Zealanders, Poles, South Africans, and Southern Rhodesians, but *without* the 100,000 colonial men supporting these fighting units who came from places such as Bechuanaland, Ceylon, Cyprus, Mauritius, Palestine, Rodrigues, and Swaziland. Similarly, whilst the First World War's East Africa campaign remains peripheral it is not entirely obscured from vision, though the tens of thousands of Africans who died there, carrying guns and ammunition for imperial infantrymen, are lost without trace in popular memory, as are the tens of thousands of Chinese men working for, and in many cases burying, their white superiors on the Western Front.

The colonial empire's poor billing in studies of imperial defence also stems from the fact that colonies were considered, erroneously but typically, to be consumers of imperial defence rather than contributors, though the amount of sterling that the colonial empire was to donate to the Empire's major wars (and the relatively paltry sums that the Dominions were prepared to commit in peacetime), makes this a questionable assumption, as does the essential nature of the base role performed by colonies and their substantial manpower contribution to imperial defence. But the truth is that the colonial empire was always taken for granted; officials in Whitehall were more likely to see a colony as a drain on imperial defence resources rather than as a contributor, and the fact that few of these places had asked to be taken under British rule and given protection was not considered a valid point. Nevertheless, the lament of colonial nationalists during times of world war — that they had never asked to be part of an imperial system of which Britain was the chief beneficiary, and that they bore no responsibility for defending it against threats stemming from the fact of being British — was essentially unanswerable.

As this chapter has shown, colonies were at the heart of imperial defence across the centuries. The next chapter considers the role played by one particular colony in imperial defence, from the eighteenth-century battles of the Napoleonic War through wars of internal conquest to participation in the world wars of the twentieth century. Ceylon, like many British colonies, had a history steeped in the military and naval affairs of the British Empire.

3

The Evolution of Ceylon as Martial Colony, 1760 to 1960

Many British colonies were intimately bound up with the military fortunes of the British Empire during periods of colonial warfare and seismic struggles among the world's most powerful nations. Ceylon was one such colony, for over 200 years its history tethered to the strategic needs of the British Empire and the regional and international wars in which it fought. In this chapter the military history of the island is examined in order to explain why a colony acquired military value in the eyes of the British, how it was conquered, and how subsequently it was used to support the system of imperial defence. Many Ceylonese people were directly affected by their island's status as a martial colony, their lives touched by the depredations of savage fighting as repeated attempts were made to conquer the island in the nineteenth century and, briefly, by Japanese bombing in the twentieth; by the demands and opportunities that were associated with the growth of a military colony hungry for military labourers and soldiers for service locally and overseas; and by the social and economic effects of war, from food shortages and propaganda to dock work, prostitution, and the influx of thousands of foreign servicemen and women during times of world war.

A land of mountains and jungle, coconut and rice, rubies and pearls, lotus flowers and flamboyant trees, elephants and sloth bears: Ceylon was the real jewel of the British Empire, notwithstanding the power and wealth of its giant northern neighbour. Britain's association with Ceylon, known to literature as the 'Island of Serendip' (Sirandim, the Isle of Rubies) and the setting of Bizet's opera *The Pearl Fishers*, began in the seventeenth century at around the time when Europeans first beheld its shores. Through Portuguese and then Dutch endeavour the island gained fame for its spices as well as its warlike inhabitants, and became significant for European powers seeking to dominate the Indian Ocean and its trade routes and sea lines of communication.

Britain's presence in the Indian Ocean grew dramatically in the eighteenth century, as new fields of imperial enterprise opened in India and the Far East and Britain strove to supplant Dutch dominance before engaging in a global struggle with France involving European and indigenous allies and commercial and military rivalry the world over. Britain's presence was by no means exclusively 'official'; traders of the East India Company drove British expansion and were often the servants of government policy. Robert Knox, an East India Company trader and the inspiration for Daniel Defoe's *Robinson Crusoe*, spent twenty years marooned on Ceylon from 1659, and British pirates entered the Indian Ocean in large numbers from the 1630s. They arrived in the East with a licence from the King to plunder 'from the Cape to China and Japan, including the Red Sea, the Persian Gulf, and the Coromandel coast'. Many pirates, including Captain Kidd, left the Caribbean for the Indian Ocean attracted by the prospect of greater riches. In 1695 Captain Every took the Mughal ship *Ganj-i-sawai* off the mouth of the Red Sea. 'The ship carried a huge and valuable cargo, including jewels and a saddle and bridle meant for the Mughal emperor Aurangzeb . . . The women were raped, the ship plundered, and some four hundred pirates got the huge sum of £1,000 each.'[6]

Piratical activities and the expansionist policies of the East India Company were sometimes endorsed by the British government, if their interests aligned, and often the forces of the British state marched or sailed alongside those of a private company, or pirates were given official sanction to go about their usually unlawful occasions, should it help His Majesty's government in its latest spat with the Spaniards or the French. A formal British state presence in the region was provided by the Royal Navy. From the early eighteenth century the natural harbour of Trincomalee was coveted by the navy because it was ideally positioned for the defence of the eastern sea lanes and both coasts of India at a time when the global struggle with France was at its height. It was one of the finest natural harbours in the world, 'its huge expanse almost entirely enclosed by palm-fringed beaches and well sheltered from the turbulent waters of the Bay of Bengal'. It was the only decent harbour on the west side of the Bay of Bengal, ideally positioned to meet intruders on either side of India and boasting ample supplies of water and fuel. It was well-placed to avoid the seasonal winds, giving it invaluable all-year-round utility. Nelson considered it 'the finest harbour on earth', and for this and other reasons it became an object of British desire as the Empire grew through war and trade.

Thus began an association between the Royal Navy and Ceylon which was to last for over 200 years. Commodore Curtis Bennett led the first East Indies Squadron into the Indian Ocean in 1744. Bombay and Madras became the principal bases for the Royal Navy in the region, but the acquisition of the excellent harbour at Trincomalee in 1795 led to its increasing use when the Fleet began more extensive operations against the Dutch East Indies during the Napoleonic Wars. Even before Ceylon became British, the Royal Navy's East Indies Fleet regularly used the island's ports, spending fifteen winters at Trincomalee between 1746 and 1795 as opposed to fourteen at its official base in Bombay. The British seized the port in 1782, though subsequently lost it to the French. But they continued to covet it, and their power in the Indian Ocean continued to grow.

The British eclipse the Dutch

In the lands of the Indian Ocean rim, as well as on the ocean waves, British power grew inexorably during the eighteenth century, supplanting the Dutch as they themselves had supplanted the Portuguese. As their power grew, it was only a matter of time before the British sought to make more permanent their claim to the harbours of Ceylon for reasons of grand strategy. As was so often the way with imperial and colonial warfare of the age, deception, diplomacy, intrigue, spies, and pretenders to the throne all played their part in Britain's campaign to acquire Ceylon. As in the famous Battle of Plassey in 1757, these factors were almost as important as military power itself.

Both the Portuguese and the Dutch had been unable to establish absolute sovereignty in Ceylon, their power confined to the coastal regions. Portuguese armies had been destroyed in 1594, 1630, and 1638 as they attempted to subjugate the inland kingdom of Kandy. In 1765 the Dutch had managed to capture Kandy, capital of the ancient Sinhalese civilization located high in the central mountains, only to be forced to retreat by the ravages of disease and guerrilla resistance. A compromise peace was arranged. The Dutch were acknowledged as sovereigns in the north, while the king of Kandy ceded the entire seaboard, to a depth of four miles, to the Dutch East Indies Company, along with the right to pick cinnamon in his domains.

Yet disputes with the Dutch over trade encouraged the King of Kandy to look to the British, growing more and more powerful in south India and the waters of the Indian Ocean, for political and military support. This was forthcoming; the 1780s and 1790s were long years of global-ized European conflict, and the British were prepared to commit precious resources to support any local ruler who could help further their inter-ests against the French and their allies. The British were on the march in Asia as the epic struggle of the Seven Years War and then the Revolutionary and Napoleonic Wars fuelled rivalry and proxy fighting throughout the world. Extensive operations were mounted by the British against the colonial estates of their rivals throughout the Indian Ocean region. The British took Penang in 1786, drove the French out of Pondicherry, annexed Malabar, and subjugated Hyderabad. It was not long before the British had taken Ceylon, the Cape, and Malacca from the Dutch, fearful that these strategic plums might fall into the hands of France and determined to purge the Orient of all European rivals. Thus strategic logic dictated colonial acquisition. The British even took Java and Sumatra, though returned them to the Dutch at the end of the war. Mauritius and Réunion were swiped from the French in classic govern-ment-private company campaigns, the soldiers of the East India Company's Madras presidency, and warships of the Honourable Company's marine, working shoulder to shoulder with the British Army and the Royal Navy.

Like the Cape and Java, Ceylon was a Dutch possession taken for fear that the French might oblige the Dutch to allow them to use it once the French satellite Batavian Republic had been established.

> The only part of the world in which British naval and combined oper-ations were entirely successful in 1795 was the East Indies. On the news of the French conquest of the Netherlands, the East Indies Squadron and troops of the East India Company were able to seize Trincomalee and Malacca in August 1795, followed by Colombo and most of the Spice Islands in early 1796. In all these cases it was the strategic value of the ports as naval bases which was uppermost in ministers' minds.[7]

Soldiers of the British Army and the East India Company, commanded by Colonel James Stuart of the 72nd Foot, arrived off Trincomalee on 1 August 1795. A thousand British infantrymen were joined by four battal-ions of Indian troops, who were directed against Trincomalee. The fortress was besieged, and surrendered on 26 August. The forts at Batticaloa and Jaffna also capitulated. British forces spread across the island encountering only limited Dutch resistance, until on 15 February 1796 Colombo was taken. The Swiss mercenary regiment of Count Charles-Daniel De Meuron, upon whom the Dutch had depended, was persuaded to transfer its allegiance to the British Crown after being released from its oath in October, its 1,000-plus men thereafter serving with distinction alongside British troops. British operations in Ceylon demonstrated the telling benefits of seapower and the penalties to be paid by those who could not wield it; whilst the Dutch were unable to reinforce, they were unable to prevent the British from doing so at will.

Thereafter, British rule clamped itself upon Ceylon, though it took half a century before a vice-like grip was established. To bolster Britain's position the 19th Regiment of Foot (later to become the Green Howards) was dispatched to Ceylon in 1796, departing Britain in April and arriving Colombo in December. The Regiment was to remain in Ceylon for the next twenty-four years. Its task was to secure the British position from internal and external threats, and to take part in imperial campaigns in the region. Thus it took part in fighting in India (for example against Tippoo Sahib in 1799), and in the Kandyan wars that were soon to come. Ceylon thus became a garrison colony, and during the nineteenth century at least twenty British line regiments spent time on the island. Supporting them were locally-recruited units, such as the Malay Regiment of Foot inherited from the Dutch, the 7th Native Infantry from India, and four battalions of the Ceylon Regiment. The Ceylon example illustrates the huge importance of indigenous military forces in gaining the Empire and subsequently providing for imperial defence.

The maritime provinces and the first Kandyan war

Initially Ceylon was ruled by the East India Company and administered from Madras. In 1798, however, it became a Crown Colony, and its acquisition from the Dutch was formally confirmed by the Treaty of Amiens in 1802. But having gained the colony because of its military and naval value, the British now found that establishing their rule *internally* required a significant and lengthy expenditure of military capital. As in so many parts of the colonial empire, British rule was not firmly established until a series of internal wars and uprisings had been attended to.

Like their Portuguese and Dutch predecessors in Ceylon, British power was at first confined to the coast, with the interior controlled by the last Kandyan king, Sri Wickrama Raja Sinha, a man with a reputation for cruelty and tyranny that invited conspiracies against his rule. His kingdom was allowed access to the ports for supplies of salt and fish and a limited trade, though the relations between the newly-established European power and the ancient indigenous power were always likely to be strained. As in other parts of the Empire where British interests were essentially maritime — such as the Cape, West Africa, and China — the British sound found themselves sucked into the interior, through the actions of the people of the interior and the over-zealous frontier engagement of the British 'men on the spot'.

In time-honoured fashion the British attempted to gain influence over the hardy, independent kingdom of Kandy by indulging in palace intrigue. The adigar, or chief minister, Pilame Talavve, had designs on the throne, and so offered to help the British depose the king soon after his accession in 1798. This offer was spurned, and Kandy refused to become a British client-state on the Indian model, jealously guarding its independence. A revolt in the provinces around Colombo was met by the Governor, The Honourable Frederick North, son of the British Prime Minister, by measures intended to be progressive: the reform of land ownership, an attempt to tackle corruption, the institution of a legal code, and improved health and education.

Nevertheless, Governor North concluded that the coastal provinces would never be secure whilst the Kandyan kingdom posed a threat from within, and determined to take decisive action. Keen to develop trade, the British had sent various embassies to Kandy even before they took the island, and had built a network of spies and links with aristocrats who disliked the king. Now, in possession of the coast, they were in a better position to bargain. In 1800 a military mission was sent to Kandy, designed to demonstrate British power and persuade the king of the benefits of British protection. The mission was met with much protocol but achieved little, other than providing some useful intelligence for the full-scale British invasion that was to come.

Tiring of endless negotiations, in 1803 North used the theft of goods from indigenous merchants as a pretext for invasion. His resources, however, were inadequate for the task and, true to form, the British thought that they would be facing an uncivilized foe no match for the British in the art of warfare. It was to be the British, however, who proved unfit for the task, fielding inexperienced and ill-equipped troops unable to fight the climate and the terrain let alone deal with a clever enemy that used the landscape and inferior weaponry to advantage. 'The British were more kitted out for Napoleonic warfare than Ceylon's tropical rainforests, malarial swamps, and saw-toothed mountains.'[8] The Kandyans had grown wise in the art of guerrilla warfare since the Portuguese had first landed on the island intent on plunder, and now were to offer the British some valuable lessons.

North had two British battalions (19th and 51st), and elements of a third (80th), a native infantry battalion, two companies of Bengal artillery, a company of Malays, about 1,000 men of the Ceylon Native Infantry, and thousands of coolies (nineteenth-century armies were always outnumbered by camp followers, from officers' personal servants to muleteers, mahouts, and porters carrying weapons and equipment). The invasion began in January 1803 under Major-General Hay Macdowell. Two columns reached Kandy on 21 February, only to find the city deserted. The inhabitants had moved into the mountains of Uva, taking with them treasure, arms, provisions, and religious relics. The British proceeded to enthrone Muttusamy, brother of three of the late king's wives. He struck a forlorn and ignored figure in Kandy, a king without a people in an empty capital. Meanwhile King Sri Wikrama was eighteen miles away in a palace at Hunguranketa. For the British the campaign now developed into a lacklustre and potentially very dangerous affair. The Kandyans pretended to enter into meaningful negotiations, all the time happy in the knowledge that the British were marooned in a deserted and half-burned city constantly harassed by guerrillas and ravaged by disease, as their Dutch predecessors had been when they had 'conquered' Kandy four decades earlier.

Conditions for the garrison in Kandy deteriorated. Baggage-handlers were targeted, snipers roamed the surrounding countryside, and stragglers were murdered, encouraged by a bounty placed by the king on European heads. Disease and poor sanitation took their toll. Finally, under a flag of truce, General Macdowell withdrew most of his force, leaving behind a small detachment of the 19th Foot and the Malays under Major Adam Davie of the Malay Regiment. This force was promptly surrounded. In June 1803, with his column devastated by sickness and cut off from help, Davie surrendered to Pilame Talavve and was granted safe passage to march his defeated garrison to Trincomalee. Davie led a bedraggled force of thirty-four Europeans, 250 Malays, a few Bengali gunners, and 'King' Muttusamy and his entourage. 'Safe passage' did not extend very far, however, and soon after leaving Davie's party was surrounded, disarmed, and executed by swordsmen working in relays. Muttusamy and his court were beheaded, whilst Davie and a fellow officer escaped the butchery and were taken into captivity. Indians and Malays were spared if they were prepared to switch sides, though those who remained loyal to their oath were killed. The wounded, including 150 Europeans, had been left behind in Kandy to fend for themselves, huddled in a makeshift hospital in the palace complex. A massacre ensued. Corporal Barnsley of the 19th managed, despite serious injuries, to escape. He stumbled alone from the site of the massacre and found a British column at Fort Macdowell. With this force he then journeyed to Trincomalee, supporting his head with his hands throughout the journey, for the blow of the sword upon his neck had severed the tendons. Thus news of the disaster reached the coast and the ears of Governor North.

Not satisfied with this striking victory, the King of Kandy and his lowland supporters then invaded British territory on the coast. The British community was much depleted by war and disease. At the start of 1803 there had been 5,000 able-bodied men, though six months later 2,000 of them were dead, missing, or sick. Opposed by tens of thousands of natives massed only five miles from the city, Governor North raised a militia and created a striking force under General Macdowell. This force met the Kandyans head on, causing them to retire in disarray. Such bold forward tactics proved repeatedly successful, and dismayed the Kandyans. Sri Wickrama personally led an attack on Colombo by a force that included Malabar Guards, Malays, and 12,000 Kandyans. It was defeated with considerable carnage. Nearly 200 gun lascars captured at Kandy rejoined the British, having hampered the Kandyan attack by loading their guns with grapeshot which made little impression against the solid walls of the fort. Sri Wickrama blamed his general for the disaster and had him beheaded before retreating inland. The British pursued them, catching the numerically superior but much demoralized Kandyans in a pincer movement. Stores were destroyed and a thousand huts burned as scorched earth tactics were employed to deny the enemy food and shelter. Reinforcements arrived from India, including African slave soldiers, who terrified the Sinhalese. These engagements demonstrated the value of light mobile columns, and North prepared for a campaign of fast-moving strikes across the island.

Despite general British success, confused orders led Captain Arthur Johnston to take a column of troops, unsupported, against Kandy. He was supposed to have led his troops into the kingdom in tandem with several other columns, cause as much disruption as possible, and then retire to the safety of British territory. Johnston, however, believed his orders were to advance on the capital itself. Learning from British tactics encountered thus far, the Kandyans ensured that all villages on Johnston's route were emptied, stores and animals dispersed. On reaching Kandy, Johnston shared the experience of British, Dutch, and Portuguese commanders before him, entering an empty city, the skeletons of the remnants of Davie's force hanging from the treetops. Ravaged by disease, Johnston's column returned to Trincomalee.

A stalemate ensued, Britain too weak to conquer the inland kingdom, Kandy to weak to push the British into the sea. In July 1805 Major-General Sir Thomas Maitland succeeded North as governor and military commander. Hostilities with Kandy were ended, and Maitland set about restoring the fiscal state of the colony and reducing the excessive military spending. Reorganization and consolidation were the watchwords during Maitland's tenure as governor. The Kingdom of Kandy released its British prisoners, though Major Davie remained captive until his death in 1812. Stand-offs on the imperial frontier tended not to last long, however, and soon the British mustered themselves for another assault upon Kandyan independence. The King of Kandy's position was weakening as his unpopularity grew with the oppression of his people and rivalry from within the Sinhalese elite (the royal family was more Dravidian than Sinhalese, marrying brides imported from south India. The Sinhala aristocracy was unable to unite in order to appoint a Sinhala candidate). Governor Maitland approached the Kandyan priesthood, seeking a treaty, which proved elusive. He grew tired of dealing with the royal house, and constructed a web of secret alliances with important chiefs, further undermining Sri Wikrama.

Brownrigg's tenure as governor and the second Kandyan war

In October 1811 Maitland was succeeded by Lieutenant-General Sir Robert Brownrigg. A protégé of the Duke of York, noted by the Duke of Wellington, he was a soldiering man, gazetted as an ensign in the 14th Regiment at the age of sixteen and subsequently serving in America, Jamaica, and the Netherlands. He had no previous experience as an administrator, or of working with non-Europeans, and the appointment of such a man signalled Britain's resolve to have the island subjugated once and for all. Brownrigg did not disappoint, and he soon laid plans for a new invasion of Ceylon's central highlands spearheaded by five columns approaching Kandy by different routes.

Not supported by London in his desire to march on the ancient city, Brownrigg had to await a suitable pretext for action. It was not long in coming. Kandy had a new prime minister as Talavve had been executed and succeeded by his nephew, Ehelepola. Soon he too fell out of favour with the king, ever suspicious of plots against his throne. This was Ehelepola's cue to begin scheming with the British. His intermediary was John D'Oyly, a government official who was an expert on the Sinhalese and their language and corresponded with numerous Kandyan chiefs, their missives arriving at his door written on dried palm leaves. D'Oyly's expertise meant that he was entrusted with British negotiations with the Kandyan court, serving as Chief Translator to the government. Ehelepola proposed that the British occupy Kandy and there followed an abortive rebellion. Ehelepola's family were caught and executed, his wife forced to grind the heads of her dead children with a pestle and mortar before being murdered herself. Stricken with grief, Ehelepola fled to British territory and was received by Lord and Lady Brownrigg at the Governor's Palace at Mount Lavinia.* There had been other atrocities. The King:

> Extended his atrocities beyond his own people to include the British. Always fearful of spies, he captured a group of merchants from the village of Mahara near Colombo who traded in Kandy. Accusing them of spying, he had them mutilated and sent back to Colombo with the body parts strung around their necks. Out of the ten men, nine are said to have died on the road to Colombo, each having had his nose, right ear, and right arm cut off. The Governor described this as a "wanton, arbitrary, and barbarous piece of cruelty".[9]

To top it all, Kandyan forces attacked a British garrison at Sitawaka. Brownrigg now had the 'invasion' that could trigger punitive action. In January 1815 the attack went in.

Brownrigg, who during the invasion moved about the island with his wife and a bad case of gout, mustered a mixed army of 3,744 men, divided into eight divisions, including Africans, Britons, Indians, Malays, and Sinhalese. None were lost to enemy action in this latest invasion, one that proved much more successful than its predecessors. It met with little

---

* The history of this residence, now part of the Mount Lavnia Hotel, is fascinating. Brownrigg's predecessor, General Sir Thomas Maitland, had chosen this picturesque spot, known as Galkissa, as the site of his palace. Whilst there, he fell deeply in love with a dancing girl, Lovina, of Portuguese and Sinhalese extraction. In order to keep their ensuing affair secret, he had a tunnel constructed that linked his wine cellar with the well in her father's house. The affair ended when he left to become Governor of Malta in 1811. He died a bachelor that same year. Galkissa subsequently became known as Mount Lavinia (Lovina).

resistance, secured the deposition of the king on 10 February 1815, and brought the kingdom's annexation to the British Empire in a treaty, known as the Kandyan Convention, signed by the Kandyan chiefs in March 1815. Thus more than 2,350 years of Sinhalese independence came to an end. Back in Britain, Brownrigg was hailed as 'the conqueror of the Kingdom of Kandy'. George III granted him permission to bear the crown, sceptre, and banner of the King of Kandy on his coat of arms. Britain pledged to honour Kandyan customs, protect the powers and privileges of the chiefs, and guarantee the inviolable rights of the Buddhist community. King Sri Wikrama was sent into exile aboard a British warship, his personal treasure and the historic royal regalia dispersed. The ceremonial throne and footstool were found on the day that the King was captured. The throne was covered in gold and studded with precious stones. The arms were crafted in the form of lions couchant, with eyes of amethyst larger than musket balls. Together with the King's lion standard, they were shipped to England in the custody of Major Brownrigg, the Governor's son, and presented to the Prince Regent. Housed at Windsor Castle, the throne was used throughout the nineteenth century for the ceremony of investing Knights of the Garter. Along with the footstool, crown, sword of state, and golden staff, it was returned to Ceylon in 1934. Sri Wickrama remained a prisoner of the British, living on a pension with his two wives, before dying at the Vellore Fort in Delhi in 1832.

The demise of the monarchy turned out to be a problem for the British for decades to come for, as Governor Brownrigg told the Colonial Office, the Kandyan nation 'wanted a king whom they could see, and before whom they could prostrate and obtain summary justice'. The struggle between the British and the Kandyans simmered on despite the conquest. Ehelepola and other Kandyan nobles realized quickly that the British were not going to be malleable, and potentially replaceable, overlords. There was unease concerning the British and their foreign religion. Light rule from the British permitted intrigue. Whilst people were grateful that the king had been deposed, they saw little reason for the British to remain. The impartiality of British justice was not universally popular, nor was the reduction in the status of the chiefs; before annexation, no one was above the king and the chiefs. Now, every officer in the army was, and the common soldier paid them scant regard.

This developed into a popular revolt and a brutal war, sometimes known as the third Kandyan war, or the Uva Rebellion of 1817–18, which pitched the Kandyan court and commoners against Britain. Brownrigg moved in person to Kandy to conduct operations. He arrived in a procession that included elephants decorated with bells, mounted dragoons, and palanquins. Brownrigg and his wife were conveyed in tom-johns-comfortable — armchairs with hoods born by four bearers — because they were cooler than the heavy palanquins. Brownrigg's position was clear. As he told the Secretary of State in London, he couldn't allow 'a great military nation to be ejected by a horde of semi-civilized barbarians'. The conflict that ensued led to a 'complete extirpation of the ancient Buddhist culture'. Given that the 'rebels' were not easily brought to direct battle, the British had to resort to scorched earth, burning villages and laying waste to crops. In their turn, the rebels did the same in provinces that failed adequately to support their cause. Nearly 10 percent of the population died from disease, famine, war, and executions. The British recovered 8,000 muskets, pistols, and gingals along with bows and arrows. 'The central symbols of the Kandyan kingdom, including the fabled Tooth of the Buddha, were destroyed; the old ritual link between the court and the village was wiped out, to be replaced by the pragmatic relationship of taxpayer to ruler. Buddhism, once the organization of society expressed in the form of a cult, became no more than a popular religion.'[10] On 25 November 1818 Brownrigg returned to Colombo; his short tour of inspection of the highlands had turned into an eighteen-month sojourn away from his headquarters.

With the entire island well and truly pacified and British rule firmly established, its imperial rulers could concentrate on getting Ceylon to fulfil its imperial purpose. This meant preparing it for use as a military base whilst economic development was encouraged. A new class of British settler arrived and cinnamon, coffee, and tea were developed as export crops; the central mountains began to be covered in tea estates which brought in massive waves of Tamil migrants from India. Europeans, such as a young Samuel Baker (later a noted African explorer), started farms on the island. A permanent garrison of British troops was maintained to protect the island from external aggression and to ensure that the Kandyans did not revolt again. Roads, tunnels, and hairpin bends brought the highlands into contact with the rest of the island, and railways were constructed from the 1860s. Ceylon remained important to the Empire, right down until the 1950s, for the reason that it had first been acquired: its strategic position. The island provided a base for the protection of India and the Indian Ocean trade routes to the eastern Empire.

Ceylon functioned as a strategic redoubt whenever the Empire was threatened and became an important link in the network of trade routes that connected the British world. Aside from its importance for the navy,

Ceylon remained a hugely important location for the world's mercantile traffic. During the period of the Revolutionary and Napoleonic wars the port of Galle was the island's premier port, and the main assembly point for homeward bound trade from India. It was eventually eclipsed by Colombo because it was unable to handle the large steamers that began to ply the ocean highways. As well as being able to cater for large vessels, Colombo was better positioned to service ships going from the Red Sea to South-east Asia, the Bay of Bengal, and Australia. 'By the 1880s Colombo had been provided with a basin of 203 hectares of sheltered water up to ten metres deep, which could take twenty-five of the largest steamers at the same time. In the 1890s more breakwaters, a fishery harbour, and a coaling depot with eighteen jetties was completed.'[11] In 1910 Colombo was the seventh busiest port in the world in terms of tonnage entering.

Ceylon and the army: Locally-raised military formations and the imperial garrison

Ceylon had been taken by the British because it was coveted by the East India Company and seen from London as a valuable springboard for the projection of naval power in the Indian Ocean. Given its strategic value, it was a position that had to be denied to European enemies. Though Ceylon's role as a naval base was paramount, the presence of a British garrison, and the recruitment of Ceylonese military forces, meant that it developed and retained a strong army dimension. Right from the start of Britain's rule in Ceylon, indigenous and imported non-European troops formed part of the military force along with British troops, a common phenomenon throughout the colonial world. As with many of the tropical appointments that might be the lot of the British officer and common soldier, garrison service in Ceylon was as likely to end in death through disease as it was through battle for the soldiers stationed there. During its tour in Ceylon between 1796 and 1820 the 19th Foot lost 10 percent of its strength each year through disease, accidents, and battle. The regiment left behind the graves of fifty officers and 1,500 other ranks. But what the Lord taketh with one hand He giveth with the other, and when the regiment departed in 1820 'a great crowd of Sinhalese women saw them off, some of them with three or four children by soldiers of the regiment'.

The 'British' forces maintained on Ceylon, from the time of its conquest until the final lowering of the Union Flag over a century and a half later, were thoroughly multiethnic in their composition. Malays, originally part of the Dutch garrison, were transferred to the East India Company for service in Ceylon. In 1801 they were transferred to the King's service as the Malay Regiment. In 1802 a Sinhalese battalion was formed, whereupon the Malay Corps became the 1st Battalion The Ceylon Regiment, and the new formation, known as the Sepoy Corps, became the 2nd Battalion. In 1802–3 more Malays were used to form the 3rd Battalion, recruited from among ex-Dutch Malay soldiers imprisoned on St Helena, part of the massive displacement of humanity that followed in the wake of world wars. Governor North was given permission to purchase slaves, and in 1814 the 4th Ceylon Regiment was formed, consisting entirely of Africans. In 1820 the 1st Regiment became a rifle corps, changing its name to the Ceylon Rifle Regiment in 1827. The Ceylon Engineers was also raised in this early period and in 1821 Governor Sir Edward Barnes formed the Ceylon Pioneer Corps. This unit consisted of ten companies of 200 men each used for the construction of military roads throughout the island, and was disbanded in 1833. It was vitally important in opening up the central highlands and the territory of the old kingdom of Kandy to those moving from the coast, ensuring the growth of local and export trade and bringing accessibility for troops should internal rebellion ever feature in the island's affairs again. Ceylon's impressive non-European military establishment was employed beyond the island itself; in 1847, for example, six of the regiment's twenty-two companies garrisoning Hong Kong. In 1848 it took part in suppressing the Kandy rebellion, caused by land dispossession under British rule. As land was developed for coffee estates, Sinhala peasants tried desperately to avoid plantation work, resulting in Britain's importation of Tamil workers from India. When Governor Torrington, a cousin of the Prime Minister Lord Russell, was sent to Ceylon by Queen Victoria, he imposed a system of direct taxation that further alienated the peasantry. The suppression of the rebellion transformed the nature of Sinhalese society and secured British rule of the island once and for all.

In 1874 the Ceylon Rifle Regiment was disbanded. This was because there were simply no security threats remaining. The Indian Ocean was a 'British lake' and internally, Ceylon was at peace, its last rebellious breath expended. It wasn't long, however, before a new military formation came into existence that was to form the kernel of the island's defence forces for the next seventy years and become the forerunner of today's Sri Lanka armed forces. A movement amongst the British mercantile elite for the creation of a reserve military force led to the formation of the Ceylon Volunteers in 1881. The first battalion was designated the 1st Battalion The Ceylon Light Infantry (CLI), and this was the first step in the development of the Ceylon Defence Force, the Ceylon Mounted Infantry being raised in 1892. The Prince of Wales (later King Edward VII) was Colonel-in-Chief (the unit changed its name to become the Ceylon Mounted Rifles in 1906). The CLI served as the core unit that provided the foundation for additional structural expansion and specialization in later years. These units formed the mainstay of Ceylon's strategic manpower reserve under the Ceylon Volunteer Force, renamed the Ceylon Defence Force in 1910. From its creation the CDF numbered the rough equivalent of a British Army brigade, maintaining a peacetime strength of 2,500 to 3,500 reservists.

Ceylon's military forces were involved in Britain's imperial wars. In January 1900 Ceylon's Legislative Council voted to send a contingent to support imperial forces in the Boer War. The 1st Contingent of the Ceylon Mounted Infantry duly departed in the following month, and served in South Africa for just under a year. The contingent of 125 officers and men was commanded by Major Murray Menzies. It arrived in South Africa and was sent to join Lord Roberts' advance on Bloemfontein, serving as part of the 4th Brigade of Mounted Infantry. The regiment saw action at Poplar Grove, Stinkhoutboom, Driefontein, Heideberg, Johannesburg, Diamond Hill, Nooitgedacht, and Wittebergen. During the conflict Ceylon became one of numerous imperial territories used as an internment camp for Boer prisoners of war. Over 5,000 were transported to Ceylon, and the main camp at Diyatalawa later became a naval rest camp visited by thousands of British and imperial service personnel. A second contingent of the Ceylon mounted infantry was sent to South Africa but arrived too late to see action. Participation in imperial war brought commensurate imperial honour. In February 1901, the Governor, Sir Joseph West Ridgeway, unveiled a memorial window in St Paul's Church, Kandy, dedicated to the men of Ceylon who had fallen. The Ceylon Mounted Infantry was represented in London at the coronation of King Edward VII upon Victoria's death in 1901. The Kandy Boer War memorial statue was moved from its original spot in the late 1960s, and now stands in a corner of the parade ground at Army Camp Kandy City, home of the 2nd Volunteer Sri Lanka Sinhala Regiment.

A banner marking the regiment's service in the conflict was presented by the Duke of Cornwall and York (later King George V) on his visit to Kandy in April 1901. He was visiting the island as part of an Empire Tour that had as its centrepiece the opening of the new federal parliament in Australia. His visit to Ceylon was attended by the military and naval pomp expected from one of the Empire's main martial colonies:

Under the usual salute from the war-ships and the fort we pass into the spacious harbour, and are moored ahead of the *Highflyer*, the flagship of Admiral Bosanquet, Commander-in-Chief of the East Indies Squadron. Besides the *Highflyer*, the ships in the East Indies Squadron are: the *Pomone*, the *Marathon*, and the *Racoon*. At noon their Royal Highnesses go ashore, the Duke in white naval uniform. The Royal barge threads its way quickly among the ironclads, gaily dressed and firing the customary salute, and the less imposing but equally picturesque smaller craft of various sorts and sizes with which the harbour is crowded. At the landing-stage the Duke and Duchess shake hands with the Governor, Sir West Ridgeway, the Admiral, and other chief officials, civil, naval, and military, and are conducted to a large pandal of the reception-hall type, thronged with all the leading people of the place.[12]

In the year following the visit of the Duke, Major-General Sir Hector Macdonald became Commander-in-Chief Ceylon, responsible for all locally-raised Ceylonese troops and the British line battalion and other British units stationed on the island. He came to occupy a place of notoriety as Ceylon gained something of a reputation as a place of sexual licence, and added a colourful if tragic chapter to the island's military history. 'Fighting Mac' was a classic Victorian soldier hero, who had enjoyed a meteoric rise from private soldier to general. The son of a crofter, he had enlisted as a private in the 92nd Highlanders in 1870 and rose to the rank of major-general. He had served in Afghanistan, fought heroically at Majuba Hill in 1881, was noted for his superlative leadership by Winston Churchill and General Sir Herbert Kitchener during the Battle of Omdurman, and commanded the Highland Brigade during the Boer War. Yet Ceylon led to his downfall, with allegations — possibly entirely baseless and motivated by jealousy, snobbery, rumour, and the personal animosity of the Governor — of gross sexual misconduct. According to Ronald Hyam:

> Ceylon furnished Macdonald with a lethal combination of a military command which was inactive and uninteresting and a community of boys who were interesting and very active. He soon became aware of the bonzes' catamites at the temples, the obliging waiters of the Grand Orient Hotel, the up-country rest house dancing boys, the ubiquitous nude bathing boys on the beaches, perhaps even of the Tamil boy prostitutes in the Colombo docks. He became friendly with a Burgher family called de Saran, and this led to his undoing. White planter society [which he shunned] disliked the friendship, and noted that he seemed to spend

too much time with the two de Saran boys, with whom, it was suspected, he was having a sexual relationship . . . And then came the famous denouement in a railway carriage at Kandy. Macdonald was discovered in a compartment (with the blinds down) in company with four Sinhalese boys . . . The planter, who had probably interrupted a communal masturbation session, spread the gossip in such a way that a number of schoolmasters and two clergymen were induced to lay charges before the governor. There were seven or eight cases thus alleged, but the governor was assured that more would follow if the scandal became public knowledge . . . Up to seventy witnesses could have been called. Apparently Macdonald was engaged in a systematic pattern of serious sexual activities with possibly scores of boys aged twelve and upwards. "Some, indeed most of his victims, whose cases were dealt with", wrote Governor Ridgeway, "are the sons of the best known men in the colony, English and Native".[13]

With the storm about to break, Macdonald was summoned back to England. 'Fighting Mac' had until this point been an archetypal imperial hero as a result of his exploits in the Sudan campaign and two Boer wars. Yet the British military and political establishment seems to have turned savagely on him. Field Marshal Lord Roberts told him in London that he must either clear his name or leave the army, and that in any event he should return to Ceylon to face a court-martial. Whilst in England MacDonald was also called to a meeting with King Edward VII, and although it is not known what was said, there has been speculation that the King may have told him to take his own life. The story broke in the European edition of the *New York Herald*, and Macdonald took his own life whilst staying at the Hotel Regina in Paris on his way back to Ceylon. A Government Commission sat in Colombo, and on 29 June 1903 concluded that there was 'absolutely no reason or crime whatsoever' that should have led to his suicide, and that 'we find that the late Sir Hector MacDonald has been cruelly assassinated by vile and slanderous tongues'.

Ceylon's role as a martial colony continued in the years leading up to the First World War. In March 1907 the Inspector-General of Forces, Prince Arthur, Duke of Connaught, inspected the Ceylon Mounted Rifles at Kandy and unveiled an equestrian statue of a trooper signalling 'Enemy advancing in large numbers' to commemorate the island's role in the Boer War. In 1909 the regiment was inspected by General Sir John French (later Field Marshal the Earl of Ypres), and was represented at the coronation of King George V in London in June 1911. Royal visits to

56

Ceylon, and the participation of Ceylonese units at major imperial events in Britain, signified the island's martial heritage. It was a colony that had been added to the Empire by blood and cordite because of its strategic value, and thereafter it committed forces to imperial struggles wherever they took place in the world, and performed the role of colonial military base into the second half of the twentieth century. During the First World War Ceylon sent men to Europe, Egypt, Gallipoli, and Mesopotamia, where the Ceylon Sanitary Corps was employed. The Ceylon Planters Rifle Corps sent a contingent to Egypt and the regiment suffered 80 killed and 99 wounded during the war. Showing classic public school patriotism, a platoon from Trinity College Kandy marched to Colombo in order to enlist, though was not allowed to do so. (The College still possesses a Japanese machine-gun given by Lord Mountbatten, who used the College during his time on the island as Supreme Allied Commander South East Asia.)

In October 1914 Major J. Hall Brown led 236 men of the Ceylon Planters Rifle Corps to Egypt, where they helped guard the Suez Canal before being attached to the Australia and New Zealand Army Corps. They were then sent to Anzac Cove, Gallipoli, to provide guards for the headquarters staff, including the GOC, Lieutenant-General William Birdwood. In 1918 the Ceylon Sanitary Section in Mesopotamia was attached to the Baqubah Refugee Camp commanded by Brigadier H. H. Austin. This temporary city of 3,000 tents, thirty-three miles north-east of Baghdad, was home to 50,000 Assyrian and Armenian Christians who had fled oppression from Muslims in Turkey and Persia.

As a main base for the Royal Navy's East Indies Station, Ceylon's ports were busy with war activity, and, though the Station's naval units were engaged on patrol or in support of operations in the Persian Gulf and Red Sea, its facilities remained important. Any lull in operations in the Gulf, for example, led to sloops returning to Ceylon for health reasons and for the good of the ships. Whilst refits were performed in Colombo the crews hot-footed it to the rest camp at Diyatalawa in the hills. As Wilfred Nunn, captain of the sloop HMS *Espiègle*, recounts:

> The sea voyage, the change of scene, and life in the hill-camp undoubtedly worked wonders with our health, and probably saved many lives. It made one feel proud of Admiralty methods [the Admiralty had insisted that all crews employed in the rivers of Mesopotamia be rested in Ceylon], and impressed the Army, that such care was taken of our welfare.[14]

The war also had a military dimension within Ceylon itself. Ethnic tension between Buddhists and Muslims spilled over in 1915 into major civil unrest involving angry crowds, looting, damage to property, the destruction of mosques and temples, and deaths and injuries. Governor Sir Robert Chalmers mobilized the CDF and declared Martial Law. In the House of Commons in London, the Under-Secretary of State for Colonies, Sir Arthur Steel-Maitland, speculated that German intrigue might have been the cause of the riots. The CDF worked alongside 300 regular infantrymen of the Indian Army's 28th Punjabis, there on garrison duty. At least 116 people were killed. The 28th Punjabis left for the war in Mesopotamia, and was replaced in January 1917 by the 80th Carnatics. When this battalion left — the last Regular Army unit to be stationed in Ceylon on garrison duties — a Mobilized Detachment of the Ceylon Light Infantry (CLI) was made operational.

Ceylon's participation in the war deepened the colony's martial heritage and earned British gratitude. In 1922 the island was visited by the Prince of Wales, heir to the throne, aboard the battlecruiser HMS *Renown*. This was part of a massive Empire Tour intended to thank the Empire for its support during the First World War:

> The presentation of colours to the Ceylon Light Infantry . . . brought his Royal Highness in touch with many ex-servicemen. They saluted him in the barrack square of the old Fort: nearly a thousand veterans of all colours, castes, and creeds, who had served in the Sanitary Corps and other units in Mesopotamia, and facing them, other ex-soldiers in a strange variety of uniforms — men in police kit; men in white drill; men in Highland kilts; men in worn khaki. After the presentation of the colours the Prince shook hands with every man.[15]

During the inter-war years, Ceylon kept up its proud martial and royal traditions. Units such as the Ceylon Mounted Rifles held their annual camp and annual regimental dinner, and the Ceylon Mounted Rifles Polo Club thrived. Mechanization, a trend among the Western armies during this period, even reached Ceylon, and in 1933 at Diyatalawa Camp the regiment paraded as one mounted and one mechanized squadron. The regiment was inspected in that year by Prince Henry, Duke of Gloucester, visiting the island to restore to the people of Ceylon the ancient regalia of the last King of Kandy. In 1938 the regiment was disbanded and its remnants amalgamated with the Ceylon Planters Rifle Corps.

The Second World War brought great expansion to Ceylon's military forces and thousands of imperial servicemen from Africa, Australia, Britain, Canada, and India were based on the island as it became a major strategic asset in Britain's war against Japan. By 1945, of the 26,000 Ceylonese enrolled in military formations, 14,922 officers and other ranks came under the aegis of the Ceylon Defence Force, which grew from a strength of 2,300 in 1938. The CDF was rapidly expanded after Japan entered the war and an attack seemed very likely. It included the Ceylon Light Infantry (five battalions), the Ceylon Garrison Artillery, medical detachments, an anti-aircraft regiment, coastal artillery, signallers, the Ceylon Engineers (scheduled to number 3,585), Pioneers (military labourers), and service corps personnel. A contingent of the Ceylon Garrison Artillery was the first Ceylonese unit to leave the island when it was sent to the Seychelles in April 1941 to defend possible landing places with rifles and Bren guns. Port Victoria was defended from Pointe Conan by two elderly six-inch guns recently installed after their removal from HMS *Gnat*. Another artillery contingent was sent to the Cocos-Keeling Islands to protect the Cable & Wireless station, and a detachment of the Ceylon Light Infantry escorted enemy prisoners-of-war to the Middle East.

The Ceylon Planters Rifle Corps sent several fifty-man contingents for officer training at Dera Dun in India. Early in the war it had been assigned guard duties at vulnerable civilian installations, after pressure had been put on the government to give the Corps something con-structive to do. Another locally-recruited military outfit was the Ceylon Railways Engineering Corps that operated an armoured train equipped with First World War machine guns between Colombo and Mount Lavinia. The Corps was formed by 'the militarization of pivotal railway personnel' and the arrival from India of an Anglo-Indian Railway Personnel detachment. There was also a military role for the personnel of the excise department, who organized a coast-watching system to report shipping movements.

Of Ceylon's total military mobilization of 26,000, approximately 6,800 served in the British Army as opposed to locally-raised units like the CDF and Ceylon Planters Rifle Corps. They served in the Royal Army Service Corps, the Royal Pioneer Corps, the Royal Artillery (the Ceylon Royal Artillery came to number 1,488 by 1943 and was stationed at Trincomalee), and the Royal Engineers. Some served in Ceylon itself, but 4,500 of them served overseas mainly in the Royal Pioneer Corps, providing military labour and clerical support for the Eighth Army, seeing service in the Middle East, Sicily, Greece, Italy, and France. According to standard British racial categorization, Ceylonese troops were preferred in light motor transport or clerical work 'because of their high standard of education and poor physique', just as Africans were preferred for physical work.

Ceylon and the Royal Navy: The East Indies Station and the shore establishment

The projection of British naval power around the world depended upon an extensive network of shore bases and ports. These were essential if warships were to be stationed overseas for long periods. They provided defended anchorages and all manner of facilities for dry docking, repairing, provisioning, and ammunitioning ships. They provided wharves and chandleries, bunkers, barracks, and offices. In the twentieth century, facilities were extended to keep up with technology, including anti-torpedo defences, oil tanks, wireless installations, intelligence-gathering facilities, and runways and aerodromes for the aircraft of the Fleet Air Arm, the navy's own air force.

As home to one of the Royal Navy's more important overseas stations, all manner of facilities developed in Ceylon. In 1809 the Admiralty instructed that the whole naval establishment at Madras be removed to Trincomalee as soon as it could maintain ships. In 1813 Vice-Admiral Sir Samuel Hood Bart, Commander-in-Chief East Indies, recommended to the Admiralty that Trincomalee should be developed as 'the principal Station for the British Navy in India . . . the most desirable Place in the Eastern World for fixing the Establishment in contemplation'. One of its numerous attractions was that it lay in a Crown colony, not in the territory of the East India Company.

With Ceylon's importance as a naval base established, an Admiralty House was opened in Trincomalee for the use of the Commander-in-Chief East Indies Station, a standard British practice in important overseas stations. Admiralty House was built on a beautiful twenty-acre estate on the shore of the harbour, purchased by the Admiralty in 1814 from an enterprising officer of the 19th Foot, the long-serving line regiment that provided the island's imperial garrison during the first quarter-century of British rule. Captain Robson had bought the property for £1,312 in 1811, and offered it for sale to the navy at £2,000. An Order-in-Council of 1816 approved the planned establishment of a major dockyard at Trincomalee, and the dockyard responsibilities and officers were transferred from Madras.

Ceylon thus became the Royal Navy's principal home in the Indian

Ocean region, a distinction that it was to retain for most of the next 142 years until the Royal Navy left its ports for the last time. Nevertheless, the drastic reduction of the Royal Navy after the Napoleonic Wars (the active fleet was reduced from 230 ships of the line in 1814 to forty-nine in 1820), cut the East Indies Squadron to a handful of frigates and sloops and scaled down Trincomalee's anticipated growth. But this was all that was needed given the Royal Navy's crushing pre-eminence at sea following Trafalgar, and the fact remained that Trincomalee could command both the Coromandel and Malabar coasts and that along with Colombo it was an essential port for the trade and protection of the British Empire.

As Ceylon's naval importance grew, its infrastructure was extended and developed. Between 1817 and 1822 Admiralty House was extensively redesigned by a Master Shipwright to provide a rounded verandah known as the 'Sternwalk', and a central space 'like that of a sailing ship's wardroom', used until after the Second World War as a dining room. In 1827 the then Commander-in-Chief East Indies, Rear Admiral Sir John Gage, planted coconut trees around the house, and at about the same time a banyan tree took root to become a major feature of the property that by 1955 had a canopy perimeter of 309 yards enclosing over two-thirds of an acre of the grounds.

Ceylon suffered a transient diminution of its naval importance in 1887 when the headquarters of the East Indies Fleet was transferred to Bombay. The development of a naval base at Singapore and the establishment of the China Fleet had somewhat reduced the standing of the East Indies Fleet, whose area of responsibility no longer included the islands of the East Indies, and whose main function was the suppression of piracy in the western Indian Ocean (the irony of this was that when Singapore failed to live up to its strategic role, Trincomalee had to be hastily upgraded in order to act as a surrogate centre of British naval power east of Suez). Admiralty House was closed down in 1905, reopened two years later, then closed again in 1909, and much of the furniture was removed to Bombay. Recreational amenities attached to Admiralty House remained open, however, including bungalows on Sober Island for the use of officers and a Naval Rest Camp on sixteen acres of Admiralty-owned land, used extensively by off-duty ships' companies, the colonial government permitting the landing of duty-free beer and tobacco for the sailors. The Naval Stores Depot was reopened in 1911, though closed again in 1915.

Britain's overseas naval stations between 1815 and 1914, aside from the Mediterranean Fleet, consisted of ships primarily intended to protect trade and deal with local unrest. The victory won at Trafalgar meant that there were no first-class naval rivals threatening Britain's command of the ocean. In June 1906 the East Indies Station comprised four cruisers (HMS *Fox*, *Hermes*, *Perseus*, and *Prosperine*), two gunboats (HMS *Lapwing* and *Redbreast*), and HMS *Sphinx*. This limited force was sufficient given the threats to British interests that pertained: 'The presence of even two or three sloops cruising the Malacca Straits or along the west coast of the Malayan Peninsula bolstered confidence among the trading community . . . and certainly discouraged any major operations by pirates . . . A small emergency naval force, the East India Squadron . . . was insufficient to quell the ubiquitous pirates and slavers, but as a symbol it was potent enough to keep the Indian Ocean a *mare clausum* to major hostile forces.'[16] British naval forces were committed to securing the seaborne trade upon which the Empire rested, and so the Royal Navy's main role in the Indian Ocean was as a trade protection force. Work involved the suppression of piracy around Aden and Malaya, the interdiction of slavers sailing from East Africa to the Persian Gulf, and survey work that produced the charts upon which mariners in the Indian Ocean soon came to depend.

The East Indies Fleet remained the Royal Navy's main force in the seas between Africa and China, and made extensive use of all of the bases developed by the Royal Navy in the region, from Africa and the Persian Gulf to the coasts of India and islands such as Ceylon and Mauritius. During the First World War, east of Suez naval operations in the Persian Gulf and western Indian Ocean against German and Turkish forces were better supported from bases in Aden, Bombay, and Mombasa, though Trincomalee was used as a base to hunt German raiders (see next chapter). During the inter-war years the Singapore strategy was devised in order to meet the threat of Japanese expansionism and naval power, and Ceylon's status as an important naval base revived. Singapore was ideally suited for operations in the China Sea as well as the Indian Ocean, and for the defence of the Australasian Dominions. Ceylon was well positioned to support it. In 1922 it was decided that oil fuel storage facilities should be built at Trincomalee as part of the Royal Navy's general scheme for replacing the old coaling stations that spanned the globe. Ceylon developed as a sophisticated naval base, equipped with an armament depot, wireless stations, and the largest oil reserve outside of Britain, housed in enormous cylindrical tanks in the jungle surrounding Trincomalee.

The 'Route to the East' was growing in strategic importance, and in 1923 the Admiralty announced its intention to withdraw the headquarters of the East Indies Fleet from Bombay and reinstall them at

Trincomalee, where the stores depot was to be reopened, along with an armament depot with a gun-wharf. The Matara wireless station was also to be modernized. Admiralty House was completely renovated and electrified, and the furniture moved back from Bombay. Vice-Admiral Sir Herbert Richmond was the first occupant of the reopened house, and discovered that the garden had returned to jungle on the landward side, covering the tennis court. He had the flower beds re-laid and carefully planned the plant species introduced. Another Commander-in-Chief, Rear Admiral E. J. A. Fullerton, arrived with his wife, the Honourable Mrs Dorothy Fullerton (daughter of Admiral of the Fleet Lord Fisher, who had been born in Ceylon), over Christmas 1929, and took great interest in the property. Forty-nine coconut palms were delivered from the Andaman Islands and planted along the foreshore to provide a screen. A pair of bougainvilleas were procured from the Royal Botanical Gardens at Peradineya near Kandy (later headquarters of Admiral Lord Louis Mountbatten's South East Asia Command) and planted near the tennis court. Bread fruit trees were introduced in 1937, and wild orchids introduced from the jungle in the following year.

The East Indies Station's main strength in the inter-war period was provided by a cruiser squadron and lighter forces distributed in the main Indian Ocean annexes, particularly the Red Sea and the Persian Gulf divisions. In 1932, for example, the East Indies Station, commanded by Rear Admiral M. E. Dunbar-Nasmith, consisted of the 4th Cruiser Squadron, three sloops, a special service vessel, and a survey ship. On the outbreak of war in 1939, the ships of Rear Admiral R. Leatham's East Indies Station included the 4th Cruiser Squadron, the Red Sea Division (sloops), the Persian Gulf Division (sloops), the submarine HMS *Seal*, and the submarine depot ship HMS *Lucia* (the Station soon received submarine reinforcements from the China Station, a battleship squadron, and aircraft carriers in order to hunt for enemy submarines and raiders and protect convoys). By the end of the war it numbered nearly 250 vessels.

During the war Ceylon's own fledgling naval forces expanded and offered valuable assistance to the Royal Navy in policing the island's coastal waters. Founded in 1928, the Ceylon Naval Volunteer Force (CNVF) rose from a strength of 150 officers and ratings in 1939 to over 1,200 in 1945. Its primary object in war-time was to keep Colombo harbour open, and to provide adequate protection for merchant shipping, thus reducing the tasks of the Royal Navy. During the war its activities were extended, and it acquired the armed trawler *Overdale Wyke*, collected from Port Said and used for minesweeping and escort duties. Anti-submarine and mine-sweeping patrols were extended to

Trincomalee, and the Force undertook escort duties between Colombo and Cochin, Madras and Trincomalee. Two hundred and thirty victims of Japanese air attacks were fished out of Ceylon's waters by the Force. In 1943 the Royal Navy assumed responsibility for the CNVF, and it became the Ceylon Royal Naval Volunteer Reserve. Its base was commissioned as HMS *Gamunu* (a base with 1,500 personnel by the end of the war). In early 1944 a Royal Navy Aircraft Ceylonese Training Establishment was created to train Ceylonese for work at the Navy's air stations thus releasing Fleet Air Arm (FAA) personnel for service aboard the Eastern Fleet's carriers.

Colonial ports were also vital for the repair and maintenance of vessels 'in theatre'. Refitting a ship at Singapore, Colombo, or Durban saved time and a long journey home. During the Second World War, when British shipyards were working flat out, overseas docks were crucial to the maintenance of naval formations far from home. For example, a civilian company in Colombo turned its hand to war work, and over the course of the war repaired or refitted 167 major warships, 332 minor warships and 1,932 merchant vessels (as well as producing over 39,000 articles of furniture for Mountbatten's South East Asia Command head-quarters, dummy Hurricanes, Bofors guns, and wireless transmitters designed to foil Japanese aerial reconnaissance).

During the Second World War naval shore establishments, ports, and large standing naval forces kept the sea lanes of the Indian Ocean open for international commerce and for the transit of Allied troops and war materials. Most important of all were hundreds of thousands of troops escorted through the waters of the East Indies Station, aid sent to Russia via the Persian Gulf, the flow of precious Gulf oil, and the delivery of military supplies to the fighting fronts in the Middle East, South Asia, and the Far East. Naval power was centred upon shore bases and port instal-lations in Ceylon, the west and east coasts of India, and elsewhere, and by Britain's control of key choke points such as the Suez Canal, the Malacca Straits, and the Cape. Outstations of British naval power were to be found in the Persian Gulf, the Arabian Peninsula, the Red Sea, South Africa's major ports, and on the Swahili coast, and there were repair, refuelling, and provisioning facilities on mid-ocean islands such as the Seychelles, the Chagos Archipelago, Mauritius, and the Maldives, home to the secret fleet base Port T on Addu Atoll (which remained in use as RAF Gan until 1976). The Commander-in-Chief East Indies was responsible for shore bases in Ceylon, such as HMS *Highflyer* and HMS *Lanka*, as well as HMS *Euphrates* (Persian Gulf), HMS *Ironclad* (Madagascar), HMS *Jufair* (Bahrain), HMS *Maraga* (Addu Atoll in the

Maldives), HMS *Oman* (Kuwait), HMS *Sambur* (Mauritius), HMS *Sangdragon* (Seychelles), HMS *Sheba* (Aden) and HMS *Tana* (Kilindini, Mombasa). Until the British Pacific Fleet sailed for its new home base in Australia, the main strength leaving in January 1945, Trincomalee remained home for the battleships and aircraft carriers that would take part in the final stages of the war against Japan. On VJ Day 1945, Admiral Sir Arthur Power's East Indies Fleet comprised two battleships, sixteen escort carriers; thirteen cruisers, forty-three destroyers, two monitors, three gunboats, thirteen submarines, forty-three frigates, nine sloops, sixteen corvettes, thirty-one fleet minesweepers, four trawlers, ten depot and repair ships, seven surveying vessels, two boom carriers, three minelaying trawlers, one salvage ships, twenty-one landing ships, twenty-three base and depot ships, and eight Royal Naval Air Stations. Ceylon, had played a major role in supporting Britain's global war effoert.

The post-war period

In the post-war period there was plenty of work for the ships of the East Indies Station in a region recovering from the effects of war and the instability brought by South Asian decolonization, and Ceylon still had a vital role to play in the work of the Royal Navy and the pursuit of Britain's traditional defence and security interests east of Suez. Paddy Vincent recalls the assistance rendered to the fledgling Indian Navy at Bombay as it sought to suppress mutinies, and the awareness of the crew aboard his ship, HMS *Norfolk*, of the strife attending India's bloody partition. Elsewhere in the region, a naval presence was required in Eritrea to assist the Italian authorities in dealing with insurrection. There were also ceremonial duties to be performed. In 1946 HMS *Norfolk* returned the senior member of the Clunies-Ross family (the rulers) to the Cocos-Keeling Islands, and in 1948 was involved in the visit of the Duke and Duchess of Gloucester to Ceylon, representing the King as the island gained its independence from Britain.

Despite South Asian independence (Burma, Ceylon, India, and Pakistan all became independent in 1947–48), the role of the Royal Navy east of Suez changed surprisingly little, even though the political wallpaper had been recoloured by the dawning of the superpower and the decolonization age. The business of the East Indies Station in the post-war years was diverse, and quite traditional. Britain remained the prime external power in the Indian Ocean–Persian Gulf region, and the importance of Britain's naval presence was augmented by the onset of the Cold

War. Ceylon remained the headquarters of the East Indies Station despite national independence in 1948. The job of Royal Navy vessels on the East Indies Station was to deliver fighting power in support of British foreign policy — in major warfighting (Korea) and low intensity operations such as counterinsurgency (Malaya) — and to offer a British military presence in support of national policy (showing the flag in Gulf states experiencing political turmoil, escorting shipping during times of tension, or acting as a deterrent). The navy was also expected to guarantee the security of international merchant traffic in the region from Africa to the Far East by patrolling sea lanes and seeking to deter those that would threaten them.

Maintaining a visible presence was part of the essence of the Royal Navy's relationship with the overseas world and its support of British foreign policy. Visiting foreign countries and showing the flag in colonial ports was a vital part of the navy's work. This involved showing a smart ship and a capable weapon to friend and potential foe alike, performing ceremonial duties, participating in joint exercises and socializing — cocktail parties on the quarterdeck under the sun awning, concerts by the bands of the Royal Marines, and playing the locals at polo, cricket, and football.

All of these roles were performed by the ships of the East Indies Station, and in order to accomplish them the Fleet relied upon the infrastructure of ports in British colonies or states with which a defence agreement had been concluded. These ports remained the essential providers of facilities for repairing, revictualling, and refitting ships, and, just as importantly, resting and entertaining weary crewmen. The importance of foreign ports in performing these roles cannot be overstated. Despite the experience of operating with a fleet train gained in the Pacific in the final year of the war, the Royal Navy had traditionally relied upon dry land for its replenishment, and this meant ports with stores of oil, ammunition, food, and water.

Policing the post-war Indian Ocean region was achieved by clocking up sea hours, visiting ports, hosting and contributing to public events, taking part in military exercises (particularly important in attempting to keep New Commonwealth states, such as Ceylon, India, and Pakistan, 'on side'), and conducting military operations. It is clear from the records of ships serving on the East Indies Station that touring and maintaining a visible presence was crucial to the work of the navy east of Suez. Jack Calston served aboard HMS *Mauritius* on the East Indies Station between April 1949 and March 1951. During this commission the cruiser, an old hand in the Indian Ocean, travelled 42,976 miles and spent 143 days at sea. After leaving Portsmouth and calling at Gibraltar, Malta, Port Said, and Aden on the way to Colombo, *Mauritius* visited Abadan (throughout 1950 pressure was growing within Iran that was to lead to the nationalization of BP's huge stake in the country's oil industry in March 1951, including the Abadan oil refinery), Bombay, Karachi, Calcutta, Madras, Bahrein, Basra, Kuwait, Mena-el-Ahmedi, Muscat, Singapore, the Seychelles, Mombasa, Zanzibar, Dar-es-Salaan, Tanga, Mauritius, Khor Kuwai, and Cochin. These visits were the key to the work of the East Indies Station and Britain's post-war relationship with newly independent Commonwealth countries.

Frank Fountain served as a Gunnery Rating-Able Seaman aboard the Colony class cruiser HMS *Newfoundland* during her East Indies commission between 1952 and 1955. After sea speed and gunnery trials off Plymouth Sound, the ship left Devonport on 8 January 1953. On her way out she stopped at Gibraltar and Malta, from where she spent a few days at sea working up. She then visited Port Said, Aden, Muckulla, Mogadishu, and Mombasa before arriving at Trincomalee on 24 March 1953. A highlight of this tour occurred when members of the ship's company took part in a special Coronation service held in Mombasa Cathedral to mark Elizabeth II's accession to the throne. On 19 May *Newfoundland* began the East African Cruise, lasting until the ship departed Mauritius on 13 July. Two weeks were then spent at sea around Ceylon, before the Persian Gulf Cruise began on 16 October 1953. This took *Newfoundland* to Bahrein, Kuwait, Mena-el-Ahmedi, Ras Tanura, Umm Said, Sharja, and Muscat, before she returned to Trincomalee by way of Bombay.

Newfoundland then underwent a refit at Singapore, before embarking on a Royal Cruise to the Cocos Islands, Colombo, Aden, and Berbera in British Somaliland. *Newfoundland* then transferred to the Far East Station, based at Singapore. During this period she visited Hong Kong, Penang, and Sandakan in British Borneo, as well as numerous Japanese ports and Subic Bay in the Philippines. She also exercised with the American fleet off Okinawa and spent a few days in Korea. In June 1954 *Newfoundland* was twice called upon to bombard Kedah Peak off Penang as part of British operations against Chinese insurgents during the Malayan Emergency. After four months on the Far East Station, *Newfoundland* returned to the East Indies Station on 28 September 1954. On 19 October she left for a final Persian Gulf Cruise before returning home via the Mediterranean, arriving off Spithead on 17 February 1955.

Peter Relf served aboard HMS *Superb* between February and July

1956. Whilst in the Mediterranean en route to Ceylon there was a report of trouble in the Gulf which had resulted 'in the local Sheiks asking for a Naval presence. We proceeded at a fast rate stopping only at Port Said and Aden for water . . . On arrival the Marines went ashore with the band just to show the flag and all was quiet'. 'There were no bombs but the people causing trouble were driving nails through beer bottle tops and spreading them on the roads. A march through the neighbourhood by the "Booties" with the band seemed to be effective'. After this episode, *Superb* 'toured the Gulf entertaining visitors' and conducting firepower demonstrations 'with 40mm Bofors and perhaps a blank round from a 4-inch, but definitely not the 6-inch main armament'.[17]

Superb then sailed for Trincomalee, though 'as soon as we arrived we were summoned back to the Gulf. This meant provisioning ship in twenty-four hours instead of about three days. Having returned to the Gulf we spent several weeks visiting various ports and entertaining local groups on the ship. As a member of the ship's water polo team I had several good runs ashore to play the local Brits with lavish entertainment after the matches, which we usually lost.' The speed of the ship's journey east, hastened by the reported trouble in the Gulf, had caused an 'A' bracket to crack, and this required dry-docking in Colombo. 'We did not have any air conditioning and the water coolers constantly broke down through too much use. We all slept in the altogether, the lucky ones having camp beds on the upper deck . . . While in dry dock most of us went up into the hills to Diyatalawa where we spent the week playing golf and swimming while the repairs were carried out.'

HMS *Gambia* served as East Indies Station flagship in 1955–56 and again in 1957–58. Band Corporal Michael Hutton served aboard the cruiser during her 1957–58 commission. She sailed from Chatham on 17 October 1957 to relieve HMS *Ceylon*, then the East Indies Station flagship. The two ships met at Bahrein, where, on 6 November 1957, *Gambia* received the flag of the Commander-in-Chief East Indies Station. *Gambia* spent a month visiting places such as Um Qassar, Abadan, and Basra, 'where the ship's concert party gave its first performance, then back to Aden for Christmas'.[18] On board were twenty-five Somalian ratings under Chief Tindal, Noor Sulliman, a man with thirty-two years of Royal Navy experience behind him. They had been collected from British Somaliland on the way, and remained working on board the ship throughout its commission. Whilst in the Gulf *Gambia* took part in Exercise Crescent, a NATO and Baghdad Pact exercise involving the cruiser and two frigates from Britain, along with vessels from America, Iran, Pakistan, and Turkey.

After Christmas the ship sailed for Ceylon via Berbera in British Somaliland, where the band Beat Retreat on the beach. At Trincomalee half the ship's company went on leave, after which the Indian Cruise began, bringing visits to Madras, Vizagapatan, and Calcutta. Returning to Ceylon for minor repairs in dry dock, the crew went to the rest camp at Diyatalawa. Most of the band members were billeted with tea planters families, though Hutton spent a dry week with the Reverend Tom Arnold, who 'played a mean piano' but was 'a bit short on the hard stuff'. After Ceylon, *Gambia* visited the west coast of India and called at Malé in the Maldives, where the band performed numerous concert parties and Beat Retreat. It was then on to Bombay, and, the Indian Cruise at an end, to Aden, 'where we stayed for some time due to local trouble'. A second Persian Gulf Cruise was cancelled, so the ship returned to Ceylon for the annual JET exercises, stopping off for a week in Karachi en route. 'Here there were many engagements to cope with, cocktail parties, dinners ashore at the High Commissioner's residence, and return visits on the *Gambia*.' The last week of the JET exercises were spent ashore by the band, who had acted as lookouts whilst the ship was at defence stations during the exercise. Now the task was to train with the Indian and Ceylon Navy Bands for the combined Massed Bands Retreat that would herald the end of the JET exercises. HMS *Gambia* then embarked on 'the best and busiest part of the year, the East African Cruise, lots of hard work ahead but plenty of pleasure too'.[19] Mauritius, the Seychelles, Dar-es-Salaam, Zanzibar, and Mombasa were visited before the ship returned to Aden and then sailed home to Chatham.

HMS *Ceylon* was paid off into the Reserve Fleet in late 1945, though was recommissioned in 1950 in order to relieve the cruiser HMS *Birmingham* on the East Indies Station. The Korean War broke out shortly after her arrival at Trincomalee, and on 27 July 1950 she and HMS *Belfast* left for the Pacific. She was employed for the next two years fighting and working off Korea, before being refitted at Singapore and recommissioned. She visited the Maldive Islands in January 1953, and in February 1954 arrived in Hobart to take part in the celebration of the 150th anniversary of the first Tasmanian settlement, marked by a visit by the Queen during her Australian tour. *Ceylon* escorted the Queen's ship, SS *Gothic*, from the Cocos Islands to Tasmania.

Ceylon returned to Portsmouth in October 1954 for a refit which lasted until August 1956. She was then recommissioned for the Home Fleet, but Suez supervened and she was sent to the eastern Mediterranean. In January 1957 she was sent to the South Atlantic, and was present at the independence of Ghana before taking part in the handing over of the Simonstown base in South Africa. By the end of the year *Ceylon* was back with the East Indies Station in Ceylon as flagship for the handing over of the naval base at Trincomalee to the government of Ceylon. After a return to Britain via the West Indies, Cuba, Canada, and Bermuda, *Ceylon* yet again found herself east of Suez in late 1958, taking part in the evacuation of British troops from Jordan to Mombasa (after a British intervention following the coup in Iraq). In early 1959 she flew the flag of Rear Admiral V. C. Begg, second in command of the Far East Station, during a cruise to New Zealand, and then took part in the JET exercises with Commonwealth forces off Ceylon. On 18 December 1959 she returned to Britain for the last time, and was sold to the Peruvian navy.

The East Indies Station offered plenty of shore jobs for sailors. The Royal Navy maintained a communications station on Ceylon which served the ships of the East Indies Station and merchant ships in what was known as 'Area III', and acted as a major communications relay facility east of Suez, though an alternative site was required given Ceylon's independence. David Hanson joined the navy in 1948 as a boy telegraphist, and was attracted by the opportunity to get postings abroad, including places such as Bermuda, Malta, Simonstown, Mauritius, Gibraltar, Singapore, Hong Kong, Australia, and Ceylon. He ended up in Rangalla, a small village in central Ceylon. In 1952 Hanson was on the staff of the Commander-in-Chief East Indies. Signals traffic between the commander, his ships, the Admiralty and the rest of the world had to pass though the area wireless station at Negombo, near Colombo. The link between Negombo and the naval headquarters in Trincomalee was by teleprinter and overland cables. These cables were often broken, either by wildlife or local people, so it was decided to build a VHF radio relay between the two. Trincomalee was 350 miles from Negombo, with a 5,000 feet high mountain range in between, so it was decided to put a relay station on top of the mountain. Radio sets, aerials, two diesel generators, fuel, and accommodation therefore appeared up the mountain and a path was cut through primary jungle rising from a tea plantation at the foot. The equipment was conveyed by elephants and dozens of locals. Two Royal Navy telegraphists were detailed to man the station, along with a Royal Ceylonese Naval steward/cook, and two coolies who climbed the mountain each morning and brought water from the nearby stream and emptied the Elson toilets.

The demise of the East Indies Station and Britain's Ceylonese bases

As independence came to colonies such as Ceylon, the indigenous military forces that had for so long supported Britain and the British Army in internal and external wars became the armies of new nation states. Thus the Ceylon Defence Force and its constituent parts became servants of new masters upon independence in 1948, though British methods and traditions remained strong, and British commanding officers lasted in many states until long into the first decade of national independence. In Ceylon, even after independence, Britain retained substantial naval facilities under the Anglo-Ceylonese defence agreement, which allowed Trincomalee and other bases to continue to provide a home for the East Indies Station and its extensive operations across the Indian Ocean.

In the 1950s Britain began to close its overseas naval commands. Whilst partly a result of the contraction of British power, this was not the whole story, and some of the closures had as much to do with changing ways of doing business in a new technological age and the evolution of new allied command structures that emphasized inter-state cooperation above the unilateral military structures that had been the standard way of doing business in the pre-war years. Whenever a command came to an end, British interests in a region continued, and military responsibilities were shared out among neighbouring commands. Until the late 1960s, the British intended to remain a global military power, notwithstanding the rapid loss of empire, for there still remained key British and Western interests in every part of the world that required protection.

The demise of the America and West Indies Station provides an example of these two trends — the merging of British commands within a NATO structure and the division of responsibilities when a command ended. The Commander-in-Chief America and West Indies lowered his flag 'to ensure the most efficient deployment of our naval forces in more important strategic areas, and to integrate our command arrangements with NATO allies in the vital North Atlantic zone'.[20] The erstwhile Commander-in-Chief West Indies thus became Deputy Supreme Commander, Atlantic, based at NATO headquarters in Norfolk, Virginia, and a Commodore flew his pendant in a frigate as the new Senior Naval Officer, Caribbean, with responsibility for British possessions and interests in that region. Responsibility for the southern portion of the old America and West Indies Station was transferred to the South

Atlantic, whose Commander-in-Chief assumed the new title of Commander-in-Chief South Atlantic and South America.

The East Indies Station's days were numbered when, at the Commonwealth Prime Ministers' conference of June 1956, future naval strategy and the vulnerability of Britain's worldwide chain of static bases in the event of a nuclear war were discussed. Sea-based support provided by fleet auxiliaries was coming more to the fore, providing a 'fleet train' to operate alongside a trimmed down network of bases and fleet anchorages. In the light of these deliberations and the general direction of naval policy, when the Ceylon representatives at the conference asked to take over the Trincomalee naval base in accordance with the provisions of the 1947 Defence Agreement, Britain acceded. The government of Ceylon agreed to make certain facilities available for communications, movements, and storage, with Britain in return providing training and assistance for the expanding Ceylonese armed forces. The agreement allowed Britain to use the island's naval and air facilities in future emergencies.

The arrangement with Ceylon ended, however, when in the aftermath of the Suez invasion the Ceylonese government requested Britain not to use bases on the island during the crisis. Subsequently, the Prime Minister of Ceylon stated that this ban would extend to apply in any future emergency. Ceylon thus became useless as a base for British forces, and an alternative was sought in order to bridge the gap across the Indian Ocean. Gan Island in the Maldives was developed, and fuelling stations were maintained at Mombasa and Aden. A naval wireless station on Mauritius took over the tasks formerly performed by HMS *Highflyer* in Ceylon. Mauritius had been selected as a suitable sight in 1957 and construction of a new station began in 1959, involving three separate sights for the transmitter, receivers, and the central control station. It remained open until 1975.

Vice-Admiral H. W. Biggs arrived in Ceylon as Commander-in-Chief East Indies in July 1957, aware that he would be the last holder of that office. The recent Ceylonese general election had returned the People's United Front, for whom the removal of British military bases had been an electoral pledge. The last major social event was a farewell dance given for the Biggs' daughters in August 1957 and the last formal occasion was the handing over of the Naval Yard and Admiralty House to the government of Ceylon on 15 October 1957. A Royal Marines band played 'God Save the Queen', the White Ensign was lowered over the shore establishment HMS *Highflyer*, and on the following day the East Indies Station flagship, HMS *Ceylon*, sailed from Trincomalee for the last time.

Admiral Biggs and his ships thus departed Ceylon, though the East Indies Station continued to exist, now based in Bahrain. But this was only a stay of execution. The East Indies command was to be abolished before 1959, and the Senior Naval Officer, Persian Gulf, based on Bahrain and formerly responsible for the Persian Gulf Squadron on behalf of the Commander-in-Chief East Indies, became an independent commander. Taking the title 'Commodore, Arabian Seas and Persian Gulf', he was responsible for the operation of British naval forces in the Arabian Sea, the Persian Gulf, the Gulf of Aden, and the Red Sea. The remainder of the responsibilities of the Commander-in-Chief, East Indies, were to be divided between the Commander-in-Chief, Far East, and the Commander-in-Chief, South Atlantic and South America.

In the 1958–59 Naval Estimates the Admiralty policy of increasing the ability of the Fleet to operate without the support of bases was again emphasized. To guard British and Commonwealth interests in the Indian Ocean region, a battlegroup centred on an aircraft carrier was to be continuously maintained east of Suez. It would share Singapore as a base with the Far East Fleet. Thus another chapter of the Navy's history, lit with famous names and daring deeds, came to an end when at nine o'clock on the morning of 7 September 1958, 'the flag of the one-hundredth Commander in Chief of the East Indies Station, Vice-Admiral Sir Hilary Biggs, was hauled down over HMS *Jufair*, the [British] naval base in Bahrain . . . Two months after Admiral Biggs struck his flag at Bahrain, the Queen's Colours of the station were ceremonially laid up at the church of St Martin-in-the-Fields'.

Despite this, Britain continued to be the premier power in the Indian Ocean region for a further decade, though this was to end under the Labour government of Harold Wilson with its landmark decision to close Britain's remaining major bases east of Suez (Aden and Singapore), and to hand over stewardship of the region to a reluctant America. The last Commander-in-Chief Far East took the salute as his ships left Singapore for good in 1971. Nevertheless, even this did not mark the end of Britain's naval interest in the Indian Ocean, whatever the apparent finality of government policy. With Australian and New Zealand support Britain retained a small force of surface vessels at Singapore, ANZUK Force, until 1974, and Royal Navy vessels continued to sail in the Indian Ocean region, and to deploy regularly for exercises with allied forces. British military facilities remained in the Maldives, Masirah, and Mauritius until the mid-1970s.

Even today Britain remains actively attached to the Indian Ocean region through its association with the Five Power Defence Agreement signed in 1971 to guarantee Malaysia's security. Regular exercises of military forces from the five powers take place in South-East Asian waters, and Britain remains an Indian Ocean power through its possession of British Indian Ocean Territory, part of which forms one of America's most important overseas military bases. There is also Britain's standing commitment to the Persian Gulf. The Armilla Patrol was formed in 1979 to protect shipping in this most vital, yet troubled, region, and today Britain regularly contributes vessels to allied naval formations such as Task Force 58 in the Northern Arabian Gulf, and Task Force 150 in the Horn of Africa region, and to project power at sea and on land, as in the Gulf wars. So, whilst empires have fallen and the world has changed, British sailors and their ships continue to operate in the Indian Ocean region, performing tasks that would have been familiar to their forebears in the post-war years.

4

The First World War in the Indian Ocean Region

When the British Empire was at war, colonies not only provided military bases for regional operations, they provided valuable movable resources such as military manpower and raw materials. They also continued to be vital to the Empire's trade as well, which had to continue in war as in peace if the Empire were to survive. Britain was uniquely dependent upon the unfettered movement of goods around the world; by 1913, for example, 80 percent of Britain's wheat was imported, as was 50 percent of its meat. Fifty percent of the nation's pig iron was made from imported ore, and the latest naval behemoths, the super-dreadnoughts of the Queen Elizabeth class, were motionless without imported oil.

The security of the colonies and trade routes that made up the Empire — and Britain's capacity to use them — was threatened in times of war by enemy action, and their defence was a prime call upon the Empire's armed forces. Sometimes the enemy threat developed from the land, as in the Second World War when Japanese troops moved with stunning speed across South-east Asia and Italian forces pushed the garrison out of British Somaliland. But usually, the threat to colonies came from the sea, as enemies sought either to raid or to occupy them, or to disrupt the trade routes and sea lanes that enabled the British Empire to survive and to conduct military operations all over the world. The threat from the oceans could bring economic ruin to a colony as its export crop waited to be collected by ships that could not sail, and as vital imports of food and other goods failed to materialize. The actions of enemy submarines and warships also hampered Britain's ability to move soldiers and material from theatre to theatre and from base to base. This chapter describes the war at sea as it affected the Indian Ocean region in the First World War.

75

Germany's naval challenge

After a century of peace on the high seas following the Battle of Trafalgar, the British Indian Ocean world, connecting the heartlands of empire in Africa, Asia, and Australasia, faced grave new threats as the twentieth century dawned. The first threat to the command of the oceans won at Trafalgar developed as Germany attempted to build a High Seas Fleet capable of beating the British Grand Fleet. To have done so would have wrested command of the oceans from the Royal Navy. The Kaiser's plan for defeating Britain echoed that of Napoleon Bonaparte a hundred years before. It depended on overcoming the Royal Navy in order to clear the way for an invasion of the British Isles, whilst conducting a *guerre de course* against British shipping throughout the world (approximately 34 percent of the world's shipping was British) intended to fracture the Empire's unity, its ability to feed itself and to protect itself and to wage war. This strategy, together with Germany's alliance with the Ottoman Empire in the Middle East and Germany's position as an imperial power with colonies in Africa, the Far East, and the Pacific, brought the First World War to the many territories of the British Empire that sprawled across the continents and peninsulas from the eastern Mediterranean and east coast of Africa to the ports of South-east Asia and the Central Pacific.

The Indian Ocean rim was the scene of significant fighting during the First World War, in the form of prolonged campaigns in East Africa, Mesopotamia — where British oil interests were already entrenched — and Sinai. Supplying these fighting fronts, where hundreds of thousands of imperial troops fought and laboured, required British control of the Indian Ocean and its annexes the Persian Gulf and the Red Sea. The British sought to shore up their command of the waters east of Suez by attempting to destroy the German Pacific Squadron, by hunting down German raiders, and by ceaselessly patrolling the trade routes. German raiders operated in the Indian Ocean throughout the war, though a potentially fatal threat to British command of the sea could only have come about through a major German victory in European waters — a decisive Jutland, say. But such an engagement did not take place, and British sea power, and all of the benefits that it bestowed, remained intact. The British could shunt troopships and supply ships around the world, and the thousands of British-flagged merchant vessels could go about their lawful occasions and keep the Empire's trade in motion. Vigilance was still required, however, because of Germany's use of surface raiders and its declaration of unrestricted submarine warfare. This heralded a revolutionary new threat to the command of the oceans won at Trafalgar.

British naval power in the early twentieth century was centred upon an armada of dreadnoughts based in Home Waters and a network of overseas stations from which cruisers, destroyers, and sloops operated as policemen patrolling the sea highways of the world. East of Suez these stations were known as the China Station and the East Indies Station, establishments built around cruiser squadrons and destroyer flotillas as well as river gunboats, sloops, submarines, and survey ships. The ships of the East Indies Station were responsible for policing the sea lanes of the Indian Ocean and its annexes, and providing the visible presence that was a central element in the projection of naval power. This could be variously achieved: by intercepting dhows running contraband from Oman to the Swahili coast; by naval gunfire demonstrations to cow unruly chiefs and potentates; by landing the Royal Marines to show the flag in a town affected by civil unrest; or by dressing the ship overall, putting awnings on deck, opening the cocktail cabinet, and striking up the band in order to entertain the great and the good in Mombasa, Port Louis, and Penang.

As in most imperial wars, ranging as they did over disparate lands and involving multiple layers of indigenous and imperial authority, the First World War was not just a military struggle. It entailed a worldwide battle for allies pursued through the deployment of economic, financial, and cultural power, the building of alliances and the employment of subterfuge and deception. British and German diplomats vied for the favour of the Shah in Tehran, attempting to out do each other with attractive bank loans; Germans wooed the Iraqis and threatened the overland route to India with their proposed Berlin to Baghdad railway, causing consternation in London and Calcutta; German bases and commerce grew on the shores of the gouty Chinese Empire; German diplomats and agents courted powerful Arabs tired of Britain's imperial sway, and whispered promises of a non-British future; German shipping companies attempted to break into Britain's near monopoly east of Suez; and as traders from South America to the South China Seas, the Germans presented a threat to British supremacy that was impossible to ignore.

The rise of Japan

In the period leading up to the outbreak of the First World War rapid industrialization in America, Europe, and Japan, and the intensifying arms race manifest in the form of warship building programmes, laid the foundations for the near-fatal challenge to British hegemony in the Indian Ocean that was to come in the 1940s. The threat posed by German military strength in Europe, and the meteoric rise of Japan as an advanced industrial and military power in the East, forced Britain to renounce paramountcy in the Far East. The mark of this renunciation was the Anglo-Japanese Alliance of 1902, which signalled Britain's inability singlehandedly to guarantee the security of its Far Eastern colonies and Dominions because of the need to concentrate the most powerful units of the fleet in European waters. Thereafter, Britain's Far Eastern holdings were secured by the Royal Navy *in alliance* with the Imperial Japanese Navy, as capital ships concentrated in Home Waters to face the German High Seas Fleet. To underline its arrival as a Great Power, Japan registered breathtaking victories on land and at sea during the 1904–1905 Russo-Japanese War.

In the global power struggle that broke out in Europe in 1914, Japanese naval forces operated alongside the Royal Navy in the Mediterranean, the Indian Ocean, and the Pacific, escorting troops convoys from the Pacific to the Middle East across the Indian Ocean, and hunting German vessels. This development greatly worried the Dominions, who felt uncomfortable depending for protection upon the land from which the 'yellow peril' emanated, and whose thinly-disguised territorial ambitions began to manifest themselves in China before the war had ended. Inevitably, this veiled British retreat from paramountcy in the Far East had direct and serious repercussions for the Indian Ocean. By 1914, 'with greater naval forces than she had ever before possessed [Britain] was compelled to renounce or farm out her overseas commitments . . . Atlantic supremacy was no longer identical with two-hemisphere supremacy', because the southern hemisphere now contained first-class military powers of its own.[21] This was to have important ramifications in the inter-war years, when Britain sought to compensate for this inability to maintain two-hemisphere supremacy by investing in the Singapore strategy, and abandoning its alliance with Japan at the behest of the Americans, to the great displeasure of the former.

Although the main burden of Germany's naval challenge during the First World War was in Europe, victory there would have led to sweeping German victories in the other oceans of the world where the white ensign held sway. It was exactly the same security equation that had been the cornerstone of the globalized European struggles of the eighteenth and nineteenth centuries; the naval war was vital not just in deciding the security of the Channel and of the British Isles themselves, but in enabling the Empire to be held, utilized, and even extended. The

Kaiser's Germany adopted the same strategy as Napoleon: defeat British land forces in Europe and prepare the way for invasion by removing Britain's naval shield, whilst conducting a *guerre de course* in the wider world. *Guerre de course* — a war of commerce raiding and hit and run attacks all over the world — was designed to ruin British colonies, disrupt intra-imperial trade, and dissipate Britain's military resources by obliging them to move away from Europe in order to protect merchant convoys and hunt the deadly but elusive German raiders that menaced them. Thus German commerce-raiding operations in the Indian Ocean were intended to occupy British forces more urgently required elsewhere by threatening British possessions and the security of shipping lanes, whilst the High Seas Fleet in the North Sea sought a knock out blow against the Grand Fleet venturing forth from its lonely Orkney's redoubt.

Britain's response to this German strategy also followed historical form: attempt to counter the threat in Home Waters by knocking out or immobilizing the enemy's main strength; blockade his ports in order to deny him access to seaborne resources; and sweep his merchant marine from the oceans of the world whilst hunting down his raiders as they sought to interdict British and Allied shipping. This worked well initially, though the defence of Britain's own merchant marine was made almost impossibly difficult by the advent of the submarine. In 1915 Germany began a blockade of the British Isles, and in 1917 launched a campaign of unrestricted submarine warfare throughout the world. In response, the British had to relearn the art of convoy in order to end the sinkings that by 1917 were gravely threatening the British and Allied war effort (Germany sunk over thirteen millions tons of Allied shipping during the war, six million tons going down in 1917 alone).

An island colony at war

All colonies in the Indian Ocean region supported the war effort, even the smallest specks in the ocean. Mauritius, for example, provided a Labour Battalion of 1,700 men, shipped overseas to work in Mesopotamia in the campaign against the Ottoman Empire, and over 500 white Mauritians volunteered for service with the British and French armies on the Western Front. The formation of the Mauritius Volunteer Force of over 500 men released hundreds of British garrison troops for duties elsewhere. In October 1915 the 1,000-strong British garrison was therefore reduced, the troops leaving variously for Britain, India, and Mombasa. The Mauritius Volunteer Force consisted of three infantry companies, an artillery company, an engineering company, and an ambulance corps, costing £4,460 a year to maintain.

Mauritius became a link in the wireless telegraphy chain across the Indian Ocean when a wireless facility was opened at Rose Belle during the war allowing uninterrupted communication with other countries and ships within radius, and had its electric searchlights upgraded in order to better monitor the night-time approaches to the island's main anchorages. When the war began the Governor of Mauritius was Sir John Chancellor, a former officer in the Royal Engineers who had seen action in the Sudan and on the North-West Frontier, and had served as secretary to the Colonial Defence Committee in London. When he left for the governorship of Trinidad in 1916, his place was taken by an equally experienced imperial administrator, Sir Hesketh Bell, who had long West Indian and African experience behind him.

Mauritius was dependent on British command of the seas because it was utterly dependent on the export of its annual sugar crop, and the import of over nine-tenths of its foodstuffs. Mauritius had a significant pedigree as a military redoubt, having served as the headquarters for French military operations in the Indian Ocean region before its capitulation in 1810 to Lieutenant-General Sir John Abercromby's invasion force of over 10,000 men. Mauritius had been captured largely because it possessed an excellent harbour, and once it became a British colony it developed as a fortified and garrisoned imperial coaling station and a cable station on the Cape to Australia submarine telegraphy line. This status as a link on the imperial communications and trade routes benefited the island during the First World War, as the constant coming and going of warships was a huge reassurance to the population and a deterrent to enemy raiders. There was a need to be vigilant given the activities of German raiders such as *Emden* and *Wolf*, which at one point approached the island and carried off a small sailing vessel to Germany. In 1916 the Governor, Sir Hesketh Bell, was a passenger aboard the cruiser HMS *Talbot* as she searched the Cargados Carajos group for a reported German raider. Keeping the sea lanes around Mauritius secure was a boon, for the ships that fetched the sugar brought in the food. Though rice imports from India decreased, maize was imported as a substitute. Here, the difference between ruin — that would have resulted had Germany gained command of the seas — and relative prosperity as its sugar was in great demand, was starkly illustrated.

Throughout the war the island raised contributions for the war effort by voluntary donations, a special tax on sugar exports, and gifts to the imperial treasury from government surpluses. Among other things, the island purchased thirty aircraft for the British forces. Monies were collected for charities such as the Belgian Relief Find, the Red Cross, and the Union Jack Club; a thousand tons of sugar was gifted to the British Army and the Royal Navy. In order to save Mauritius from ruin in the event of sea lanes being disrupted, the British government under-took to buy the entire sugar crop regardless of the colony's ability to deliver. Mauritius had responsibilities of its own, as the Governor of Mauritius was also responsible for the 'lesser dependencies' of the Agalega Islands, the Cargados Carajos group, the Chagos Archipelago, and Rodrigues. So that it could remain in contact with these outer islands, the Government of Mauritius requisitioned the ship *Secunder*. Mauritius also needed to keep in contact with Madagascar, the major source of imported meat. With food imports declining, the government stimulated the production of wheat, maize, and manioc in an effort to lower food prices. The difficulty in getting freight because of the steady decrease in the available tonnage due to the German submarine campaign meant that freight, and therefore food prices, were rising. A Food and Trade Controller was appointed, and there was a 66 percent increase in the land under food cultivation.

War on the Indian Ocean rim

It was not just the sea lanes of the imperial world that were affected by the global proportions of the First World War. The lands of the Indian Ocean rim were the scene of costly military campaigns. Heavy fighting occurred in East Africa, Mesopotamia, and Palestine, 'sideshows' to those fixated by the war on the Western Front but theatres of strategic moment and as likely a place to die as the battlefields of France and Belgium for the hundreds of thousands of imperial troops and colonial porters who fought there. The ability of the British Empire to sustain these fighting fronts rested upon sea power, delivered by the ships of the East Indies and Egypt Station and based upon the Grand Fleet's containment of the German High Seas Fleet in European waters.

The main threat to Britain's imperial position in the southern hemi-sphere was posed by the German navy, the German colonial empire, and German alliance with the Ottoman Empire. German naval squadrons, raiders, and submarines posed a threat in every ocean of the world, as did — by implication of its possible victory in a knock-out showdown with the Grand Fleet in European waters — the formidable High Seas Fleet. Germany's naval operations around the world were supported by its colonial holdings and the installations therein, including, in Africa, colonial land forces able to present the British with a serious challenge. Finally, German military support for the Ottoman Empire extended the war deep into Africa, the Mediterranean, and the Middle East. Conflict between the British Empire and the Ottoman Empire involved prolonged fighting in the Dardanelles, Mesopotamia, the Sinai Peninsula, and Palestine. All land operations against the Turks in Arabia and the Persian Gulf were supported throughout the conflict by the ships of the Royal Navy and the merchant marine, together with their counterparts from India, as well as by the labour resources of colonies such as Ceylon, Mauritius, and the East Africa Protectorate.

Elsewhere in the Indian Ocean region, another major battle front was to be found in Africa, extending along the Swahili coast and reaching inland towards the great lakes. The protracted campaign in East Africa came to pin down over 150,000 imperial troops from Britain, East Africa, India, South Africa, and West Africa, and hundreds of thousands of military labourers drawn from across the region. Whilst German forces practiced guerrilla warfare, living off the land as they moved, the British imperial forces adopted more conventional and ponderous tactics, necessitating a huge supply chain. This led to inspirational organization, under the leadership of an East Africa Protectorate district commissioner, Oscar Ferris Watkins. Educated at Marlborough and All Souls College, Oxford as Founders Kin, he had served in the Oxfordshire and Buckinghamshire Light Infantry during the Boer War and subsequently in the South African Police. During the First World War, as Commandant of the Carrier Corps, he built an organization that recruited over 400,000 labourers, a process which had a profound effect upon East African society.

At the outbreak of war the British were anxious to destroy or capture German wireless stations, like those in Togoland and at Dar-es-Salaam, which threatened British shipping in the Atlantic and Indian Ocean by providing intelligence to German warships. Imperial politicians such as Leo Amery, Winston Churchill, Lloyd George, and Lord Alfred Milner did not allow events in Europe to cloud their focus on the broader strategic picture and the need to buttress the Empire's defences, and were determined to take the German possessions in the southern hemisphere.

Whilst German colonies in the Pacific, West Africa, and South West Africa soon fell to British imperial forces — New Zealanders conquering German Samoa, Australians taking the Bismarck Archipelago and New Guinea, South Africans conquering South West Africa, and British forces (including West Indian troops) invading German Cameroon and Togoland — East Africa was to prove an all together greater challenge.

The fighting, across terrain dominated by jungles and plains in which motor transport was of limited use, involved the recruitment of hundreds of thousands of African porters for the Carrier Corps, many of whom were to die of disease or exhaustion in the process. German-led African troops under the command of Colonel Paul Von Lettow Vorbeck mastered guerrilla warfare and the elusiveness of the Scarlet Pimpernel, and kept imperial forces, led initially by the South African Boer War general Jan Smuts, occupied until weeks *after* the Armistice was signed on 11 November 1918.

During the campaigns in East Africa, the Middle East, and the Persian Gulf, British sea power in the Indian Ocean enabled imperial forces to be moved and sustained, whilst their German foes were cut off from external assistance. Seapower was vital in the campaigns that occurred in the Indian Ocean region, delivering troops and supplies to Basra or Mombasa and protecting the sea lanes that brought thousands of Australasians to Egypt and that kept the trade of the Empire, no less vital in war than in peace, flowing. The First World War demonstrated Britain's capacity to mobilize the resources of its Empire and carry them far across the seas.

At the outbreak of war Vice-Admiral Graf von Spee's German East Asiatic Cruiser Squadron (also referred to as the Pacific Squadron) posed the greatest threat to British and Allied shipping in the Pacific and the Indian Ocean, and it was an Admiralty priority to hunt it down and destroy it. The purpose of Von Spee's squadron in wartime was 'to disrupt communications and supply movement between the colonies of the Triple Entente and the homelands'.[22] His command embraced the Pacific and Indian oceans, stretching from the Mexican coast to the Cape of Good Hope and the waters of the Red Sea. The Squadron was a powerful force built around the modern armoured cruisers *Gneisenau* and *Scharnhost*. Based in the Yellow Sea at Tsingtao on the Shantung peninsula, the Squadron was visiting the Caroline Islands when war broke out. It managed to evade British and Japanese warships as it steamed towards South America, detaching the cruiser *Emden* for operations in the Indian Ocean. On 7 November Tsingtao had surrendered to Japanese forces. Before leaving the Pacific the German squadron began to fulfil its intended role, disrupting British shipping lanes and imperial communications. On 14 September 1914, for example, the cruiser *Nürnberg* appeared off Fanning Island, a speck of coral in the middle of the Pacific that served as a mid-ocean station on the All-Red Trans-Pacific Submarine Cable route. Armed parties were landed, and they proceeded to smash up the telegraph instruments and cut the cable.

The British were given a much more devastating taste of German naval capabilities on 1 November 1914 when von Spee's ironclads routed Rear Admiral Sir Christopher Cradock's 4th Cruiser Squadron at the Battle of Coronel in the Pacific. In this battle HMS *Monmouth* and *Good Hope* were lost with all hands and British dead exceeded 1,600, a stunning reverse that led to much recrimination in London and criticism of the fleet dispositions of the First Lord of the Admiralty, Winston Churchill. Revenge, however, came swiftly, at what came to be known as the Battle of the Falklands. The British concentrated powerful fleet units on the South Atlantic colony of the Falklands, and laid in wait for the German squadron. In the ensuing battle, von Spee's force was all but annihilated on 8 December by Vice-Admiral Sir Doveton Sturdee's battlecruiser force; 2,200 Germans perished.

Corsair: The cruise of the *Emden*

The solitary vessel to escape this holocaust in the South Atlantic was the light cruiser *Emden*, detached from the squadron by von Spee and ordered to prey on merchant shipping in the Indian Ocean. This was after the German Asiatic Squadron's commander, Admiral von Spee, and his captains decided that the British could not be allowed to think that there were no German warships at sea in the wider world, for this would allow them to concentrate all of their strength in Europe. The cruise of the *Emden* provides an excellent example of the threat that a solitary surface raider could pose, and the effectiveness of *guerre de course* against a trading nation as dependent on the movement of goods around the world as Britain. It was a strategy that the Germans, struck by *Emden*'s success, were to invest in more heavily during the Second World War. Her cruise demonstrated the effectiveness of lone raiders as opposed to battle squadrons when facing an enemy possessed of a superior navy but also a sprawling empire. *Emden* on her own was to cause far more disruption than the rest of the Pacific Squadron combined.

Emden, commanded by Fregattenkapitän Karl Von Müller, had been specially designed for this very purpose, a commerce raider from the keel up. The Germans had led the world in the development of a naval vessel designed for commerce raiding. *Emden* was launched in 1908, capable of steaming for 6,000 miles without refuelling, a major breakthrough in naval technology. 'She was built to be the twentieth century equivalent of the privateer. The French had a word for this class of cruiser: they called it *corsaire*'.[23] Crewed by thirty-four officers and 360 men, one of whom was the Kaiser's nephew, Prince Franz Joseph von Hohenzollern, *Emden* mounted ten four-inch guns. She was to have a swashbuckling career, tying down dozens of British ships and menacing Allied merchant shipping and threatening British colonies. The Indian Ocean was assigned as her area of operations and a dummy, fourth funnel was added. This was because disguise, deception, and surprise were key weapons in the armoury of the commerce raider. It worked, and early in the war numerous sightings were made of a warship taken to be the British cruiser HMS *Hampshire*, which was, in fact, desperately trying to track the German raider down.* *Hampshire* actually passed *Emden* in the opening days of the war near the Sumatran coast as she sailed towards the steamer lane between Sumatra and Colombo. *Emden* did not travel alone, as she needed to carry supplies and fuel with her. She began her cruise with *Prince Eitel Friedrich* in company as an auxiliary warship, disguised as a Peninsular and Oriental liner, and the coaler *Markomannia*.

Captain von Müller knew that his ship, by the very nature of its purpose, was unlikely to survive for long. It was imperative, therefore, that she act speedily in order to cause as much havoc as possible. Whilst doing so, *Emden* would live as a cannibal, feeding off the ships she captured, using their fuel, food, ammunition, and spare parts before sending them to the bottom. As long as she could evade the many warships that the British could bring to bear against her she would survive. Von Müller knew that when he took the *Emden* through the Strait of Lombok he was steaming into a trap; huge as it might be, the Indian Ocean was still a cage to him and his points of exit were few and easily guarded. In charge of the hunt for *Emden* was Vice-Admiral Sir Thomas Jerram, Commander-in-Chief of the Royal Navy's China Station. He transferred his headquarters to Singapore in order to better coordinate the hunt.

Though ultimately she was to be caught in the trap, and never left the Indian Ocean again, during her time she captured a large number of Allied merchant vessels, spread panic in Indian Ocean shipping circles, and held up the departure of Australian troops bound for Britain — a good value-for-money return for a lone vessel. Not content with harassing ships on the high seas, *Emden* also attacked British targets ashore and terrorized coastal populations across the Indian Ocean region. Back in London, meanwhile, the Admiralty tried desperately to marshal

---

* *Hampshire* struck a mine in June 1916. Field Marshal Lord Kitchener, Secretary of State for War, was among those who drowned.

resources and plot the course of reported sightings in order to track her down and destroy her.

Emden's first action of the war was to capture as a prize the Russian ship *Rjasan*, the first hostile act in the war between Germany and the Russian Empire. Captured southeast of Korea, *Rjasan* was sent with a prize crew to the Asiatic Squadron's headquarters at Tsingtao, and there converted into an armed merchant raider, recommissioned on 10 August as *Cormoran II*. This was an excellent example of the utility of merchant raiders. *Emden* soon began her Indian Ocean campaign, capturing the Greek ship *Pontoporos* and then the British ship *Indus*, packed with food and supplies and destined to be converted into a troopship. From 11 September 1914 the prizes began to come rapidly. She sank the *Lovat*, another British ship equipped to carry troops and on her way to Bombay to collect Indian soldiers destined for the war in France. Lurking on the Calcutta–Colombo steamer route more prizes soon came the way of the German raider, including the *Kabinga* bound for New York with a cargo of jute. She was spared destruction, however, and joined *Markommania* and *Pontoporos* in the *Emden*'s convoy. Then the *Killin*, taking coal from Calcutta to Bombay, was sent to the bottom followed by the *Diplomat* carrying a thousand tons of tea from Calcutta to London. *Emden* then moved north onto the steamer route from Madras to Calcutta. Here the *Trabbock* was taken, then the *Clan Matheson* from Southampton to Calcutta, carrying Rolls-Royce automobiles, locomotives, typewriters, and other precision equipment. Also on board were a number of race-horses, one of which was destined for the stables of the Calcutta Racing Club, a favourite to win the forthcoming Calcutta Sweepstakes. The animals were shot before the ship was sunk.

The 17th of September 1914 found the *Emden* cruising in the upper Bay of Bengal, crossing the Madras—Rangoon steamer route and the Calcutta—Singapore route. Intent upon frightening the people of the region, von Müller decided to attack British territory, and chose the Indian city of Madras. Here, on 22 September 1914, at a range of 3,000 yards, *Emden* mounted an audacious attack against the Burmah Oil Company's storage tanks. The port city, stretching along the coastline and ablaze with lights illuminating the shore, was taken completely by surprise. Nearly 130 rounds were fired and the oil tanks set ablaze, some shells being fired into the city itself. The defending artillery did no damage to the *Emden*. Most of the harbour guns were in fact unmanned, perhaps because a large dinner was in progress at the Madras club that night, celebrating the joyful news of yesterday: the supposed sinking of Germany's solitary ship in Indian waters, the *Emden*. Müller succeeded in frightening people; thousands of Indians fled inland and, on the other side of the Bay of Bengal, for two weeks not a single ship entered or left Rangoon harbour, so great was the fear that the *Emden* would return. By this time sixteen Allied warships were engaged in the hunt.

On 25 September *Emden* passed around the southern tip of Ceylon and moved inshore to a point about twenty miles from the beach. On the Colombo–Penang–Singapore route she sunk the *King Lud*. As night fell, four searchlights from Colombo 'stabbed out to sea from the naval base . . . All night long they ranged back and forth. Colombo was not going to be surprised as Madras had been'.[24] They later saw a ship coming out of Colombo, silhouetted time and again against the searchlights inside. She was the British steamer *Tymeric*, carrying sugar to Britain. The following day *Gryfevale* was captured and rather than being sunk was added to *Emden*'s train, used to accommodate the prisoners captured so far. On 27 September a much-needed coal ship, the *Buresk*, was captured. The coal intended for Vice-Admiral Jerram's ships was used instead to fuel the solitary raider that they were hunting. *Emden*'s thirteenth capture in three weeks, the *Ribera*, gave the Germans fresh provisions, a valuable British signals book, and a record of a wireless message to the captain reporting a port embargo in the Bay of Bengal region due to the *Emden*'s activities. Captain Müller knew, therefore, that he should hunt in other areas, and headed for the Maldives.

Looking for a place to rest, *Emden* then headed for the British colonial territory of the Chagos Archipelago. On 10 October 1914 *Emden* docked at Diego Garcia. Diego Garcia was connected to the outside world only by a twice-yearly steamer from Mauritius. Not yet aware of the fact that there was a war on, the islanders welcomed *Emden* with excitement and offered hospitality to her crew. Entertaining local leaders on board, the wardroom was hastily cleared of all German newspapers. The raider was even beached so that her keep could be scraped. The locals showered the *Emden*'s crew with chickens, pigs, fish, and fresh fruit. Having availed herself of an unknowing enemy's hospitality, *Emden* resumed her commissioned business, hunting in the shipping lanes of Cape Comorin off India's southern tip, sinking more merchant vessels and causing chaos ashore. Two days after her departure, HMS *Hampshire* and the auxiliary cruiser *Empress of Russia* arrived at Diego Garcia, and learned of the recent departure of their prey. On 15 October *Emden* captured the *Clan Grant*, packed with cigarettes and beer, then later the same day the *Ben Mohr*. On 19 October Müller decided to try his luck on the Colombo—Bombay shipping route, and captured the Blue Funnel liner *Troilus*, carrying a valuable cargo of metals and rubber destined for Britain. That same day she also captured *St Egbert* and *Exford*.

Müller next conceived a bold strike on the British harbour of Georgetown in Penang. The *Emden* and her two colliers steamed ahead, blacked out, and were unobserved. Later the men of the *Emden* discovered that they had been criss-crossing the path of the *Hampshire* and the *Empress of Russia*. The Germans passed through the Maldives and rounded the southern tip of Ceylon, and on 22 October the men had a party to mark the birthday of the Kaiserin. On 26 October *Emden* pulled into Nancowrie harbour in the Nicobar Islands — making use of more British territory — to coal before the Penang enterprise. At Penang she found the Russian cruiser *Yemtschuk* (*Jemstchoung*). 'The battle flags were run up the masts . . . and she turned hard aport to bring the port torpedo tube to bear on the beam of the Russian cruiser. At 500 yards, as the dawn broke from the bridge, the captain and the torpedo officer could see a steam pinnace pulling away from the Russian, towards the town of Georgetown.'[25] The torpedo was released, and then *Emden* shifted position to unleash the starboard torpedo. Some of the unsuspecting Russians managed to get guns to bear, and shells began to be fired at the *Emden*. But the Russian cruiser was ill-prepared to resist. Amazingly she had fewer rounds of ready ammunition (thirteen) aboard than prostitutes below decks (sixty). The *Emden*'s second torpedo broke the Russian cruiser in two, and there was a rush to abandon ship. 'There was a sizzling and a hissing in the water and a cloud spread around and above the Russian cruiser.'[26] The Germans rushed to leave the harbour, not tarrying to deal with the French destroyer *D'Iberville* that had engaged her. Upon leaving the harbour, however, the French destroyer *Mousquet* was encountered returning from sea, and was promptly sunk.

On 30 October *Emden* captured the *Newburn*. In less than three months she had accounted for twenty-three merchantmen and two warships. Now, no fewer than seventy-eight Allied ships were searching for her. Müller next set course for the British Cocos-Keeling Islands, where the cables of the British All-Red cable route crossed, one going from Australia to India, another from Australia to Zanzibar and Africa. The mission was to destroy the wireless station and cut the cable. On 9 November 1914 *Emden* appeared off Direction Island in the Cocos-Keeling group. A fully armed raiding party of fifty men was put ashore led by First Officer Helmuth von Mücke. There they encountered D. A. G. de H. Farrant, head of the Eastern Extension Telegraph Company's station on the island. He obligingly told the Germans where all the equipment was, though had secretly secured other lines, and was able to send out repeated distress signals — 'SOS, *Emden* here' — and exchange information with the British warship HMS *Minotaur*. It happened that a large convoy of Australian and New Zealand troops heading for the Middle East was sailing fifty-five miles to the north, escorted by *Minotaur*, HMAS *Melbourne*, HMAS *Sydney*, and the Japanese warship *Ibuki*, fulfilling the terms of the Anglo-Japanese Alliance and helping the British war effort. The task force commander ordered *Sydney* to leave the convoy and go and investigate. From on board the German ship a smoke cloud was seen on the horizon and *Sydney*, a heavy armoured cruiser, hove into view. 'After three months of solid good fortune, the fates of war had turned on the *Emden*.'[27] Detecting an enemy raider, *Sydney* opened fire with her six eight-inch guns. At 5,600 yards, *Emden* knocked out her opponent's automatic fire-control with a direct hit. The *Sydney* drew away in order to use her longer-range guns to advantage, past 7,000 yards and out of range. 'Then she began to cut the German cruiser to pieces.'[28] When *Emden* had been beaten to a wreck, her funnels shot away, it was discovered that her torpedo room was completely useless, and so Müller decided to run her aground on the reefs of North Keeling Island. Over 150 men had been killed on board the *Emden* during the engagement and many more wounded. Those remaining were taken prisoner, 230 being sent to Colombo aboard SS *Empress of Russia* before onward movement to Aden, Suez, and finally to a prisoner of war camp in Malta.

Von Mücke's raiding party, meanwhile, escaped the carnage and subsequent capture, and began an epic voyage aboard a barely seaworthy schooner, the *Ayesha*. First they made landfall at Padang in the Dutch East Indies. Then, at sea, the men transferred to the German ship *Choising*, which von Mücke took over. Initially, he planned to head across the Indian Ocean for East Africa, and there link up with the warship *Königsberg*. He learned from *Choising*'s captain, however, that she was lost or sunk. In the end, he decided to head for Arabia and the Red Sea and Germany's ally, Turkey. The crossing of the Indian Ocean was made in twenty-two days.

Königsberg and *Pegasus* and the naval war in East Africa

The *Königsberg*, contrary to von Mücke's information, had not yet been sunk. As *Emden* had been holding down dozens of British and Allied vessels in the eastern Indian Ocean, *Königsberg* was obliging the British to commit significant resources in the western Indian Ocean. A modern cruiser of 3,000 tons, she had arrived in East African waters in June 1914 under the command of Kapitän Max Looff. Britain had a squadron of elderly cruisers based in the region (one of which, HMS *Astraea*, had attacked the German wireless station at Dar-es-Salaam on 8 August 1914) and that had the destruction of *Königsberg* as a pressing task. Two days before the attack on Dar-es-Salaam the *Königsberg* had claimed the first British merchant victim of the war, scuttling the *City of Winchester* in the Gulf of Aden.

On the 19th of September 1914 Looff learned that HMS *Pegasus*, an elderly vessel of 2,000 tons and part of the cruiser squadron commanded by Rear Admiral Sir George King-Hall as Commander-in-Chief Cape and East Africa Station, had put into Zanzibar for boiler maintenance after spending weeks burning poor quality Natal coal. 'At 0510 the following morning the crew awoke to the scream and crash of five shells exploding alongside. *Königsberg* had arrived and opened fire at 9,000 yards. Seconds later the ship received a savage blow as the second salvo struck home . . . Eight minutes into the action and [*Pegasus'*] gun crews ceased firing, most had either been killed or severely wounded. Commander Ingles took the unprecedented action of striking the colours. A white sheet was raised and *Königsberg* departed into the early morning haze leaving *Pegasus* on fire and sinking.'[29]

This prompted the Admiralty to send a powerful force of modern cruisers to gain revenge. HMS *Chatham*, *Dartmouth*, and *Weymouth*, however, were unable to reach the German cruiser, which was hiding out of range of their guns in the Rufiji Delta. The British force proceeded to block the entry to the delta, and to experiment with various ways of winkling the German ship out. At first air power was tried, though several aircraft were lost. The Admiralty then sent an Expeditionary Squadron flying Sopwith seaplanes. It failed. Next, in March 1915, a pre-dreadnought battleship, HMS *Goliath*, was dispatched, to see if her 12-inch guns could reach the German vessel. They could not. The solution was finally arrived at with the appearance of two shallow draft monitors, HMS *Mersey* and *Severn*, from Malta. They were able to get close enough to engage in a gun duel which on 11 July 1915 crippled the German ship. But German troops salvaged the guns from the *Königsberg*'s smouldering wreck.

The guns of *Königsberg* and *Pegasus* were to encounter each other again, this time on land in the East Africa campaign, stripped from their stricken vessels to live again as artillery pieces hauled overland by teams of African porters. All ten of the German cruiser's 4.5-inch guns were removed and mounted on wheels. Two of *Pegasus*'s six four-inch guns were mounted at Zanzibar and one at Mombasa, and another was railed to Lake Victoria and mounted on a steamer. The remaining two formed No. 10 Heavy Battery during the advance into German East Africa in 1916. In June 1916 the ex-*Pegasus* guns opened fire on the German garrison at Kondoa Irangi. Salvoes from the *Königsberg*'s main armament replied, as a duel involving naval pieces developed deep in the Africa interior.

There was more naval action in this region demonstrating the benefits bestowed by sea power. In November the British attacked in the foothills of Mount Kilmanjaro, and made an amphibious assault on Tanga, attempting to land two Indian brigades and knock German East Africa out of the war in one fell swoop. Over 8,000 British and Indian troops under Major-General A. E. Aitken led the invasion, landing unopposed and advancing towards Tanga, Aitken 'observing from the bridge of a converted liner'.[30] Though outnumbered eight to one, Lettow-Vorbeck's troops opened fire and caused some of the Indian troops to panic and run. Others fought on in to Tanga, where both sides endured attacks from angry bees. Steady German fire obliged the imperial force to remain on the beaches and then re-embark, leaving behind their arms, ammunition, and supplies that lasted the German defenders for much of the next two years. The invading force suffered 10 percent casualties, and Aitken lost his command.

Following the disastrous British attempt to invade German East Africa in November 1914, the next main Allied thrust came from British East Africa, supported by troops from other European colonial powers. Symbolizing both the British alliance with moderate Afrikaners and the territorial ambitions of South Africa, it was Jan Smuts who led subsequent operations in East Africa. His force included 13,000 South African and 7,000 Indian and African troops. Four Allied columns totalling 40,000 men were launched into German East Africa, two from Kenya and Nyasaland, a Portuguese one from Mozambique, and a Belgian one from the Congo. The Germans were assailed from Lake Victoria, the Rift Valley, and Lake Nyasa. Despite British sea power, the Germans were still able to make use of blockade runners, and in April and May 1915 some 50,000 African porters delivered supplies landed by the *Maria von Stettin*, and the German High Command even tried to resupply its forces by dirigible flown from Germany. In January 1917 Smuts handed over command to Major-General Arthur Reginald Hoskins of the King's African Rifles. There were to be further German victories, and in May 1917 Hoskins was replaced by General Jacob van Deventer.

The naval war in East Africa reached even further into the interior of the Dark Continent. Two wooden motor boats were dispatched to

Central Africa by the Admiralty in June 1915 to destroy German gunboats on Lake Tanganyika which had been brought in sections from Dar-es-Salaam on the coast. Given the British and Allied offensive in the region, the strategic significance of Lake Tanganyika came to rest on the Germans' ability to ship troops across it and insert them behind Allied lines. The Germans ability to do this was augmented by the presence on the lake of a number of gunboats. The big game hunter John Lee took his plan to sink the German vessels to the Admiralty, where he had an interview with the First Sea Lord, who gave his backing, as did the Foreign Office and the Colonial Office. Lee procured two forty-foot motor boats, named HMS *Mimi* and *Toutou*, which were fitted with three pounders on the foredeck and Maxim machine guns in the stern. Lieutenant-Commander Geoffrey Spicer-Simson was given command of the expedition, totalling twenty-three officers and men. The party arrived at Cape Town and then travelled overland across Africa for two months, by rail, road, and river. The boats finally arrived on the shores of the Central African lake on 22 December 1914. They did not have long to wait before tasting action. On Boxing Day the two vessels gave chase to the German ship *Kingani*, which happened to sail by, and forced her to surrender after landing a direct hit on her foredeck, killing the captain. She was taken under service and commissioned as HMS *Fifi*. On the strength of this action the satisfied Admiralty promoted Spicer-Simson to commander, and on 9 February 1915 the force added to its conquests when *Mimi* and *Fifi* sank the *Wissman*. The episode, a footnote to history, nevertheless illustrates the reach of naval power and the unusual manifestations of an empire at war.

Protecting the shipping lanes of the Indian Ocean

Despite these various victories over the German navy in the Indian Ocean region, the shipping lanes still required protection. In the month that the *Emden* was destroyed in the eastern reaches of the Indian Ocean, Admiral Rosslyn Wemyss, who had begun the war by escorting a convoy of 40,000 Canadian troops across the Atlantic, transferred his flag to HMS *Euryalus*. Early in 1915 he arrived at the Suez Canal, where *Euryalus* became the flagship of Admiral Peirse, Commander-in-Chief East Indies and Egypt Station. In January 1916 Wemyss assumed command of the East Indies and Egypt Station himself. He established his headquarters ashore at Ismailia, his flagship anchored half a mile away on Lake Timsah. John Godfrey accompanied Wemyss from the Atlantic to the

Mediterranean, and thus began his association with the Indian Ocean region, which was eventually to see him command the Royal Indian Navy in the Second World War.

The East Indies and Egypt Station during the First World War was a vast command, extending from Crete to Colombo. The Station's responsibilities included:

> The defence of the Suez Canal; the seaborne aspects of the defence of Egypt's western frontier; anti-submarine activities throughout the whole of the Levant south of Crete and as far west as Corfu; cooperation against the Turkish outposts in the Levant and Arabia; naval support of the Mesopotamia campaign; and convoy and shipping protection in the Red Sea, Indian Ocean, and Persian Gulf. In addition, as Commander-in-Chief Wemyss was also Naval Adviser to the High Commissioner in Cairo, and to the Viceroy and Government of India.[31]

With the eastern Mediterranean and Middle East being such active theatres of conflict during the war, it was inevitable that much of Admiral Wemyss's time would be taken up with Britain's struggle against the Ottoman Empire and its German ally. This required extensive action in two of the Indian Ocean's annexes, the Persian Gulf and the Red Sea. The power of the Royal Navy in these waters meant that all manner of operations could be contemplated on either side of the Arabian peninsula. In Godfrey's words, Wemyss was 'deeply interested in Arabia and the possibility of aiding the Arab leaders not only to detach themselves from their Turkish overlords but to give us their active support, [and] in applying himself to the problem of Arabia:

> Admiral Wemyss was destined to become a political force transcending his purely naval role as Commander-in-Chief East Indies and Egypt . . . In September 1916 we found ourselves at Jidda, the port of Mecca, attending the ceremonial landing of the Holy Carpet from Egypt. Although Jidda was technically in enemy territory HMS *Euryalus* anchored inside the reefs, dressed ship, and fired a salute. Wemyss was bound for Port Sudan in order to visit Sir Reginald Wingate at Khartoum, a journey by warship and train that T. E. Lawrence took with the Admiral after asking for a lift.[32]

Thus East Indies and Egypt Station warships were active in the Red Sea and the Persian Gulf as Ottoman power in the Arabian peninsula was attacked from the narrow waters either side. On Arabia's western flank, 'the Red Sea Patrol consisted of the aircraft carrier HMS *Ben-my-Chree*, HMS *Clio*, *Espiègle*, *Odin*, *Topaze*, *Fox*, *Lama*, *Lunka*, *Slieve Foy*, the monitor *M. 31* and from time to time the cruiser *Euryalus*.[33] HMS *Ben-my-Chree*, launched in 1908 as the Isle of Man Steam Packet, had been transformed into a seaplane carrier and commissioned into the Royal Navy in 1915. She became flagship of the East Indies and Egypt Station when it was initially formed in January 1916. Ordered to Aden later in 1916 to join the Red Sea Patrol as flagship, she took part in the bombing of Jeddah and attacks on Arab camps, and her seaplanes 'routinely bombarded the Turkish railway infrastructure.' One of *Ben-my-Chree*'s crew was Captain William Wedgewood Benn, DSO, DFC, later Lord Stansgate (father of Tony Benn), who served as an observer in one of the ship's aircraft until she was sunk by a Turkish shore battery off Castellorizo in the Mediterranean. Another aerial observer serving aboard *Ben-my-Chree* during her time in the Red Sea was Lieutenant Robert Erskine Childers, author of *Riddle of the Sands*.

The East Indies and Egypt Station's Red Sea Patrol, commanded by Captain W. A. D. Boyle (later Admiral of the Fleet the Earl of Cork and Orrery), was reinforced by HMAS *Perth* and the Royal Indian Marine ships *Dufferin*, *Hardinge*, *Northbrook*, and *Minto*. The Royal Indian Marine was, in peacetime, a non-combatant trooping and surveying service. In war its ships were commissioned and armed. 'Manned by their Muslim Indian crews and a mixture of Royal Indian Marine and Royal Navy officers, they did admirable service in the Red Sea, Persian Gulf, and Indian and Burmese coasts.'[34] As well as its activities at sea, the Red Sea Patrol was required to conduct 'a lot of semi-political work collaborating with the Arab chieftains and in general terms conciliating and helping the Arabs while keeping up hostilities with the Turks on a coast that was still part of the Ottoman Empire and garrisoned by troops under Turkish command'.

The East Indies Station maintained its home in the Ceylonese ports of Colombo and Trincomalee. It was responsible for providing essential naval support for the British imperial army that floundered through the Tigris marshlands and towards the conquest of Baghdad during the sapping Mesopotamian campaign, which involved the deployment of over 400,000 imperial troops, mostly labourers, and caused over 90,000 imperial casualties. In particular, the navy provided artillery support for the land forces. At the outbreak of war Wilfred Nunn and his ship, HMS *Espiègle*, was on the East Indies Station. 'After rounding up as prizes some German merchantmen off Ceylon, and patrolling the trade routes in the vicinity, we were ordered to the Shatt al Arab, where the Turks were already creating a difficult situation'. Thus began Nunn's lengthy association with the East Indies Station's Persian Gulf Division. Though 'to be in the East at that time was a great disappointment to all in the Force' — the world over, Britons desired only to rush to Europe — this was to prove to be vital, and costly, war work. Though, as Nunn wrote, all soldiers wanted to be in France, and all sailors in the North Sea 'at the delivery — long prepared for and expected — of a rapid *coup de grâce* to the German Fleet' — this was not, of course, how the war was to be won.[35] The stalemate on the Western Front lasted until the end of the war, the German High Seas Fleet survived it intact. The work on the fringes of the European conflict was vital to eventual victory and to securing the manifold strategic objectives of the British Empire beyond those focused upon the balance of power in continental Europe. But this was not apparent to men such as Wilfred Nunn on the outbreak of a keenly-anticipated war in the late summer of 1914. Feeling remote from the fulcrum of events in European, Nunn, commander of the Cadmus class sloop HMS *Espiègle* (the last Royal Navy ship built with a figure-head), was at anchor in Colombo when on 12 September orders were received to proceed to the Persian Gulf. The ship departed on the following day, coaling at Maskat en route, arriving at the entrance of Shatt al Arab on 29 September.

After spending the first two months of his tenure as commander of the East Indies and Egypt Station at Ismailia, aiding the war efforts of Allenby, Lawrence, and Wingate, Wemyss decided to visit the eastern part of his command, having concluded that the situation in Egypt and Arabia was stable and that a Turkish attack on the Suez Canal was no longer imminent. A pressing reason for the visit was Wemyss's need to confer with his next door neighbour, the Commander-in-Chief China Station. Thus, wrote Godfrey, 'on 27 March 1916 we left Suez for Aden, the Persian Gulf, Bombay, Colombo, Trincomalee, and Penang, where [Wemyss] met Admiral Grant, Commander-in-Chief China'. The two admirals met in late June at a conference in Penang, where plans were put in place to meet the raider threat which still hung over the Indian Ocean. 'These plans involved the dispersal of merchant vessels, the patrol of focal points by the Royal Navy (the Malacca Strait, the Sunda Strait, and the waters around Aden and Colombo), and the convoy of troop transports. The principle in devising this new routing system was to scatter shipping as much as possible and to do away with the continuous and congested traffic streams round the coasts of India and Ceylon by providing ships with several alternative tracks'.

After four months in the Indian Ocean, Godfrey returned to Egypt to set in motion the measures needed to survey in detail certain dangerous areas through which ships were constantly passing and groundings frequently occurring. This was because dozens of ships were operating on a hostile coast encumbered with uncharted, or roughly charted, coral reefs. The Royal Indian Marine tug *Enterprise* and the special service vessel *Imogene* (in peacetime the British Ambassador to Constantinople's yacht) were dispatched as survey vessels. Godfrey set about plotting all the new routes on a chart of the Indian Ocean. He had been charged with the task of plotting new trade routes and organizing the control of shipping so as to secure a united policy throughout the Indian Ocean and South China Sea. 'As in the Atlantic the general purpose of the scheme was to see that all ships kept away from the ordinary routes and to make sure that naval protection was provided at points where traffic was bound to congregate, such as the waters to the south of Colombo, those off Bombay, and the mouth of the Hugli, and in the Gulf of Aden. This was done by plotting a number of new tracks on either side of the normal routes between any two places, and by giving vessels special sailing orders at their ports of departure.'[36] From three to seven routes emanated from the Cape and from Mombasa, the Gulf of Aden, the Persian Gulf, Bombay, Colombo, Calcutta, the Malacca Strait, the Sunda Strait, and Western Australia, with a different set for troop transports. Upon completion of this work the Surveyor-General of Egypt, Ernest Dawson, drafted new charts, which within three months were being issued to ships.

This was necessary work, for the raider threat existed as long as the German navy remained a potent force and the British Empire continued to depend on seaborne trade and the movement of troops all over the world. At the end of November 1916 Kapitän Nerger commissioned the ex-Hansa Line vessel *Wachtfels*, a 3,600-ton ship armed with two six-inch and four four-inch guns and 500 mines, and equipped with a small scouting seaplane. The vessel was thus reborn as the auxiliary cruiser *Wolf*, the most successful German raider of the war, and Nerger's orders upon departing Kiel were to operate against Allied shipping in the Indian Ocean and the Far East. Early in 1917 news of a German commerce raider that had laid a minefield off Cape Agulhas and passed into the Indian Ocean was received by British naval stations throughout the region. The light cruiser HMAS *Brisbane* had sailed to the Mediterranean early in the war at Admiralty request, spending two months based at Malta before the disappearance of vessels in the Indian Ocean led to her transfer to the East Indies Station at Colombo. There she was joined by the French cruiser *Pothuau* and the British seaplane carrier *Raven II*, a converted ex-German prize carrying four Short 184s (two-seat reconnaissance, bomber, and torpedo-carrying aircraft), and a Sopwith Baby. The latter was transferred to *Brisbane*, the Royal Australian Navy's first experiment with aircraft at sea. The force scoured the seas around Colombo and the Maldives for two months hunting the *Wolf*, with no success.

After entering the Indian Ocean and laying her mines off the Cape on the way, *Wolf* proceeded to lay mines off Aden, Bombay, and Colombo. Her success in avoiding destruction was largely due to her carrying a seaplane, named the Wolf Cub. She lived by capturing coal as she went about the business of capturing Allied and neutral merchant vessels, taking their cargoes for the German war effort and their crews as prisoners of war. During her record-breaking cruise, she destroyed thirty-five merchant vessels and two warships. Despite Allied efforts to hunt her down, she returned to Kiel after 451 days, the longest voyage of any First World War warship. The cargo that she returned to Germany betrayed the importance of colonial goods which, having lost its own small empire, the Germans were now having to plunder where and when they could. Along with 450 prisoners, *Wolf*'s hold contained rubber, copper, zinc, brass, silk, copra, and cocoa.

Allied victory in 1918 removed the German threat to the Indian Ocean, and Britain gained vast new imperial holdings in the region. British power in the Indian Ocean remained unshaken, and it is little surprise that in the inter-war years traditional formulations of imperial military geography and imperial defence prevailed. Indian Ocean security continued to be predicated on the assumption of British command of the sea, ultimately based on capital ships deterring Great Power rivals, and overseas bases, cruiser squadrons, RAF bases, and army garrisons going about the day-to-day tasks of showing the flag, policing the Empire, and guarding the sea lanes. The war had only served to reinforce the importance of sea power and control of the world's sea lanes if the Empire were to survive. The war had been fought and the final decision reached on land; but the land campaign was rendered possible only by reinforcements and supply from overseas. As the Admiralty summarized the situation in a secret memorandum:

The armies of the Western Front, where the main offensive lay, have to a great extent been transported thither across the seas. The passage of the allied troops to the Dardanelles, Salonika, Egypt, Palestine, and Mesopotamia depended entirely on the security of our sea communications. The campaigns of East Africa, Samoa, New Guinea, South West Africa, and the Cameroons, and of Archangel in the far north rested on the same foundation. All these depended mainly on the supremacy of the allies at sea — guaranteed by the Grand Fleet — and on the carrying power of the British Mercantile marine. The Navy and the Mercantile Marine of Great Britain have, in fact, been the spearshaft of which the Allied armies have been the point.[37]

5

The First World War in a Colonial Backwater

The Bechuanaland Protectorate and the Caprivi Strip

Throughout the [First World War] the inhabitants of the [Bechuanaland] Protectorate, both white and black, gave marked proof of their unswerving loyalty to His Majesty the King; *inter alia*, they subscribed liberally to the War Funds, and although the natives were at first somewhat timid when approached on the subject of their supplying a company for service with the SANLC [South African Native labour Contingent], yet, in the end, they answered the call so readily in the Southern Protectorate, that the number required was soon reached . . . As those who had been accepted . . . were by no means all Christians, and witchcraft still plays an important part in the lives of many, the cause of sea-sickness was duly explained to them before they left the Territory [for France], and it was with great relief that their dusky wives and other friends hear that they had safely reached 'the ford on the opposite side of the Great River', where we must leave them for the present, fulfilling their duty to King and Country.[38]

So reported the Government Secretary of the Bechuanaland Protectorate to his superiors at the Colonial Office in London in 1918. Colonial annual reports, for which this summary was composed, were ever a picture of African contentment and tranquillity, laced with a dash of local colour intended for the delectation of deskbound officials back in Whitehall. During the First World War colonial annual reports created an image of uneventful and overwhelmingly loyal wartime participation on the part of distant colonial populations. The Government Secretary's prose, written in the condescending tones with which 'civilized' Europeans commonly wrote of 'uncivilized' Africans, might have been further embellished. He might have mentioned that these dusky simpletons, when they reached the other side of the 'Great River', would find their European paragons slaughtering each other with an industrial efficiency that surpassed anything previously contrived by man. But that would have been considered far from amusing.

The percolation of information upwards from colonial officials on the ground to pen-pushers and policy-makers in Whitehall offered scope for such neat bureaucratic airbrushing, invention, and judicious omission, and it certainly did the trick; this anodyne summary of the Bechuanaland Protectorate's wartime experience was subsequently repeated in the official histories of the territory and of the British Empire's participation in the 1914–18 war. The official history of the war, Sir Charles Lucas's five-volume *The Empire at War*, concluded that for Bechuanaland the war was 'a story of contentment with the *status quo*, readiness to uphold it, and confidence in the ultimate result of the war'. Thus the ramifications of a distant war did nothing to shake 'timeless', 'unchanging' Africa from its torpor, or threaten the munificence of British rule, at least, not if this meaningless drivel is to be believed. Yet this official version of the Protectorate's war history was symptomatic of a historiography of two-dimensional simplicity that was far from the truth. It is a historiography, however, that has remained largely unchallenged because the war experience of Bechuanaland — and many other British colonies apparently too peripheral to bother with — has received scant scholarly attention. But despite this, even here, in the middle of Africa, there was a surprising degree of war-related activity that deserves to be acknowledged. The participation of its people should be saluted in modern-day Botswana, in Britain, and beyond, if we are to do full justice to the extent of that war and remember those colonial subjects who participated and were affected by war because of the politics of their leaders and their association with the world's premier imperial power.

The foundations of British rule

On the outbreak of war in August 1914 Bechuanaland had been a British protectorate for thirty years. Its topography was dominated by the sands and camel thorn scrub of the Kalahari desert, though it was possessed of a vast region of swamp and lagoon in the Okavango and a narrow fertile strip on the eastern border with Southern Rhodesia, running along the banks of Kipling's 'great grey green greasy' Limpopo. According to the 1911 census, the huge territory (224,607 square miles) supported an estimated population of 123,658 Africans, 1,692 Europeans, 355 coloureds, 323,911 cattle, and 350,335 small stock. Most Africans relied for their livelihood on subsistence agriculture and stock rearing, though with the penetration of Western economic forces, and the demand for hut tax payments from 1899, the need for waged employment was growing. But there were few employment opportunities in a Protectorate that possessed no industry and only a handful of government appointments. A little gold was mined for export in the northeast, and some timber was exported to Kimberley for use as mine props. Cattle sales to the Union of South Africa were restricted by that Dominion's protectionist policies, manifest in the form of weight restrictions that debarred the Protectorate's under-weight stock from the markets of Johannesburg. There was growing employment in the South African mineral mines, and in 1910 an estimated 2,255 Bechuanaland Africans were in the industrial regions of South Africa, a figure that was soon to rise dramatically.

Bizarrely, Bechuanaland's annexation had had more to do with affairs *outside* of what became the Protectorate than affairs within it. It was not gained for economic reasons, nor as a potential destination for settlers. Rather, the extension of British authority was viewed as a necessary burden on the imperial exchequer if settler interests in the region were to be kept at bay — particularly German ambitions to link their territories in southwest Africa with those in East Africa, thereby potentially cutting off Britain's dreamed-of Cape to Cairo highway. There was also the continual threat of Boer expansion from the Transvaal, and the possibility of Boers allying with Germans now formally established in East and South West Africa. Missionaries had been active in lobbying the British government to 'save' the friendly tribes of Bechuanaland from the predations of Boer expansion, and the chiefs of Basutoland, Bechuanaland, and Swaziland had all at some point asked for British protection against the Boers.

These strategic reasons, foisted upon London by vigorous imperial agents 'on the spot', most notably Britain's High Commissioner to South Africa and the London Missionary Society, led to a significant military expedition to claim the territory for the Crown. The British government's resolve was steeled when the British agent Christopher Bethell was murdered by Boers in Mafeking. Major-General Sir Charles Warren, a classic Victorian general (and later the Commissioner of Police in London at the time of the Jack the Ripper murders), was appointed Her Majesty's Special Commissioner and Military Commander and dispatched to Bechuanaland at the head of a potent force. The Warren Expedition, sent to break up the fledgling Boer states of Goschen and Stellaland and to eject Boers from Bechuanaland, to 'restore the natives to their land', was made up of over 4,000 men. Warren's force included two field batteries, Royal Engineers, the 6th Dragoons, the 1st Royal Scots Regiment, a Cape artillery battery, Bantu Guides, and three mounted rifles regiments recruited from Britain, the Cape, and Kimberley and each consisting of 600 men. They marched inland from the Cape, laying a 225-mile telegraph line as they progressed, communicating via heliographs, and employing an Army Balloon Section in order to reconnoitre the terrain ahead of the column.

Thus Bechuanaland was born of a military expedition and began life formally under military rule. The territory south of the Molopo River became British Bechuanaland (transferred to the Cape colony ten years later), and to the north of that river the Bechuanaland Protectorate came into existence (today's Botswana). To serve the two new territories, two regiments of mounted rifles were established. One of them, known as Carrington's Horse, became the Bechuanaland Border Police, a force of 500 men supported by artillery. They took part in the Matabele War in neighbouring Southern Rhodesia and were the first British colonial troops to use the Maxim gun in action in 1893 (at one point four Maxims and fifty men fighting off over 5,000 Ndebele warriors). When British Bechuanaland was transferred from British to Cape administration in 1895, the Bechuanaland Border Police was disbanded. The British South Africa Police had a role in policing the Protectorate, and in 1897 the Bechuanaland Native Police was established. In the same year the Bechuanaland Rifles, a Cape unit, was formed at Mafeking. During the Boer War a Protectorate Regiment was formed by Baden-Powell and based at Ramatlabama. Thus military formations were deeply involved in protecting and policing the Protectorate in the early years of its life.

Because the British government had sanctioned the declaration of a protectorate in order to neutralize threats from outside, it was keen to keep the financial costs of the commitment to a bare minimum. The very nature of a protectorate, in terms of international law, was that the protecting power offered protection to the indigenous people whilst leaving them to continue to manage their own internal affairs. This meant that the indigenous chiefs were left with a significant amount of real power. The Protectorate's thinly-staffed British administration relied on alliance with the chiefs, and was supported in its work by African hut tax revenue and an annual grant in aid from the British Treasury to balance its budget. In 1913–14 government revenue stood at £65,139, expenditure at £66,749. Other than a railway running along the Protectorate's eastern fringe, linking Mafeking to Bulawayo and paid for by Cecil Rhodes and his British South Africa Company (BSAC) — intended to connect Southern Rhodesia to the South African coast rather than to serve Bechuanaland — modern transport infrastructure was non-existent. Bechuanaland, therefore, was a genuine Cinderella colony, gained to stop others from having it, overshadowed and threatened by its dynamic settler-led neighbours Southern Rhodesia and South Africa, and run on a shoestring. But it still had a part to play in the war that from August 1914 reverberated around the world.

Given its peripheral status within the British Empire, and its remoteness from the major scenes of conflict during the First World War, it would have come as little surprise if the war had entirely bypassed Bechuanaland. But, of course, that was the thing about the world wars of the twentieth century; they were genuinely global, and the power of empire meant that even such remote places as this could be mobilized, and affected by the economic, political, and social ramifications of industrial conflict, be they measured in terms of econometrics, the demand for manpower, or the spread of disease. It was 'their' war as much as a meteor striking the earth would be 'our' problem. In physical terms Bechuanaland was affected by the war because it was, ultimately, a war for imperial re-division of colonial spoils. Defeat would have led to either Boer or German rule for Bechuanaland. German forces made incursions into Bechuanaland as British Africa fought German Africa. With the British winning the day, Bechuanaland became an unlikely territorial beneficiary of conflict, actually growing in size through conquest when it assumed control of the neighbouring German territory called the Caprivi Strip, one of the first territorial blows struck against Germany's short-lived empire.

As well as engaging in local military activities, the Protectorate made financial contributions to the wider war effort and recruited a battalion of soldiers for the South African Native Labour Contingent that served in France. Hundreds more Batswana served with the 67,000 South African troops that invaded German South West Africa in January 1915. This surprising level of mobilization was achieved because Bechuanaland's African elite was overwhelmingly — though for its own political reasons — loyal to British rule. In Basutoland, Bechuanaland, and Swaziland the imperial monarch was commonly viewed as a protector, having saved the territory from the fate of Boer rule. The chiefs of the eight main tribal kingdoms that formed the Protectorate were anxious for British protection to continue, and used their loyal participation in the war effort to further fend off the prospect of the territory being absorbed within South Africa or the territories of the BSAC, both ambitious for expansion and with predatory intentions towards Bechuanaland. The territorial competition between Britain, South Africa, and Southern Rhodesia was a feature of the war years and lasted until the 1950s. Though Bechuanaland, Southern Rhodesia, and South Africa were all 'red on the map' and therefore 'British', they were ruled by elites with different visions of Africa's future. During the war, Whitehall used Bechuanaland in order to thwart the ambitions of Southern Rhodesia and the BSAC for westward expansion. The war also had an impact on the colonial home front, bringing inflation, a widening market for cattle exports, the spread of fear and rumours, and the Spanish influenza epidemic that devastated communities around the world in 1918.

In 1914 British rule in the vast Protectorate was light, characterized by rudimentary transport and communications and a lack of local knowledge on the part of the skeletal British administration, which numbered no more than thirty-five Europeans at any time during the war. Nine of them left to join the forces, depleting the administrative ranks, a common problem throughout the colonial empire during times of world war. The ranks of the European administration were supported by the Bechuanaland Protectorate Police (BPP), a force that comprised thirteen white officers and three white warrant officers, forty-seven white troopers (sixteen of whom left for the forces), seventy-two Basotho policemen, and forty Batswana employed as police messengers. This police force expanded to 226 in 1916 as more Batswana messengers were taken on in order to engage in intelligence-gathering activities against the Germans in neighbouring South West Africa.

Reasons for African chiefly support: South African and Rhodesian territorial ambitions

The huge lump of land that became the Bechuanaland Protectorate had been traversed by all manner of Europeans for decades prior to the establishment of formal colonial rule in 1885. Explorers, artists, traders, concessionaries and missionaries (including Thomas Baines and David Livingstone) had established contact with most of the main tribal groups by the time of the 'Scramble for Africa' in the 1880s and 1890s. The territory's African rulers, therefore, were experienced in both the problems and the opportunities associated with European encroachment. They feared the hostility of warlike neighbouring tribes, such as the Ndebele of Southern Rhodesia, as well as the territorial ambitions of the Transvaal Afrikaners and the commercial ambitions of Cecil Rhodes' BSAC after its creation by Royal Charter in 1889. British rule — imperial protection — was seen as a means of *maintaining* independence in the face of their adversaries. On numerous occasions before the declaration of the British protectorate the chiefs had asked for British protection, supported by powerful missionary interests marshalled by the London Missionary Society, in the face of Boer and Ndebele encroachment. Deaf ears in Whitehall had finally been unblocked when a number of factors threatened to bar Britain's route to Central Africa and tilt the balance of power in the region, most visibly expressed in Germany's shock eruption onto the African colonial stage in 1884–85. The triggers of British action were mineral discoveries and other economic developments in the region, together with continued Boer expansion and the appearance of massive German colonial holdings in the region when Bismarck annexed South-West Africa (1884) and German East Africa (1885).

Under the terms of the new protectorate, African chiefs would be left alone to rule their people as before (though with certain powers circumscribed and invested in the British administrators), whilst the British would guarantee the territorial integrity of the chiefdoms under the Protectorate umbrella. Though the British administration became the supreme power in the land, therefore a large measure of autonomy remained invested in the 'independent' chiefs of the Protectorate's eight tribes (the Bangwato, Bakwena, Batawana, Bangwaketse, Bakgatla, Balete, Batlokwa, and Barolong). The chiefs remained convinced that the British presence was essential given the undiminished threat of South African expansion, though this did not mean that they readily accepted some of the restrictive impositions that trailed in the wake of British rule, nor the concomitant diminution of their own power. As will be seen, their position had not changed by the time of the Second World War.

This foundation meant that British rule was based upon *shared* rule, not upon the right of conquest as was the case in many other British colonies. Embedded in the creation of the Bechuanaland Protectorate, and present in its very name, was the notion of *protection*. It was implicit in the relationship subsequently forged by the Queen's representatives on the ground, headed by the Resident Commissioner, and the African chiefs, that the extension of British protection required *reciprocation*. The idea and rhetoric of imperial protection was central to the Protectorate's mobilization during the First World War, and the same applied in Basutoland and Swaziland.

Thus the idea that the Batswana should be grateful for British protection from Boer land hunger was firmly established in the Protectorate's 'official mind', a powerful foundation myth that defined the relationship between the British and the African chiefs. On the outbreak of war in August 1914 the administration speedily gathered the executive powers necessary to control the dissemination of news and to prevent 'the spread of false intelligence'. Twenty-four war-related Proclamations were passed, including one allowing for the internment of the Protectorate's small Austrian and German populations. The chiefs were asked to attend a special conference at the Protectorate's capital. This was the only capital in the world located beyond the territory's borders (and remained so until Gaborone was constructed as a new capital city as national independence approached in the 1960s), known as the Imperial Reserve in the South African town of Mafeking. Here the Resident Commissioner, Colonel Frederick Panzera, reassured himself of the loyalty of the eight chiefs and explained the war situation. As Panzera told them, Britain 'had done so much for them, by spending money for years without return, and by finding men for their protection, and to preserve intact for them and their children the land held by their fathers'. At this Mafeking '*indaba*' Panzera told them that they and their people must now help Britain defeat Germany. The war had started because the Germans 'violated the territory of a small country under British Protection' (Belgium), drawing the obvious, if tenuous, connection between Britain's protective role in Bechuanaland.

The chiefs, for their part, were generally keen to display loyalty and further distance the possibility of Bechuanaland's absorption into the Union of South Africa, an option provided for in the terms of the 1909 Union of South Africa Act. Clause 151 anticipated that one day Bechuanaland would become part of the Union. With the BSAC and its homeland, Southern Rhodesia, presenting another overbearing suitor for the Bechuanaland Protectorate, it was the imperial trusteeship of the British government, and their minimalist local administration, that held the ring between settler and commercial interests.

The chiefs were dead set against any form of absorption, having seen at first hand the fate that befell other African kingdoms absorbed into the settler states of South Africa and Southern Rhodesia. In 1895, three Bechuanaland chiefs had actually toured Britain under the auspices of the London Missionary Society, and met Queen Victoria, in a well-choreographed and media-conscious attempt to drum up support for their cause (Victoria presented Khama III with a Bible bearing the inscription 'The Secret of Khama's Greatness'). Vigilance was essential, because even within the imperial structure there were powerful advocates for transferring the territory to South African or BSAC rule; the ultimate future of all three High Commission Territories remained up in the air throughout the period of British rule. As recently as 1911 the BSAC had formally pressed its claim on the British government, and in 1913 Leander Starr Jameson, who had launched the notorious Jameson Raid on the Transvaal from Bechuanaland in 1895, renewed the BSAC claim, to the anger of the South African government.

The wartime High Commissioner, Lord Gladstone, preferred the South African claim, and officially argued for transfer. He was contemptuous of the 'unprogressive' Batswana people, arguing that the northwest of the country was 'occupied by 18,000 natives who are doing nothing. It is a country which could perhaps be made to support millions of men'. The implicit assumption was that white rule was just what was needed to chivvy these lazy Africans into action (probably by taking their land and making them work for whites), and this would allow another patch of God's earth to reach its full agricultural and industrial potential. In 1916 Gladstone's successor as High Commissioner, Lord Buxton, suggested a partition of Bechuanaland between South Africa and Southern Rhodesia (which would also get the Caprivi Strip).

South Africa continued to formally ask for the High Commission Territories throughout the twentieth century. In 1913 the South African Prime Minister, Louis Botha, had asked for the transfer of Swaziland, one of Bechuanaland's High Commission Territory peers. But the Colonial Secretary, Lewis Harcourt, was determined to delay decision on this matter and dampen the High Commissioner Lord Gladstone's ardour. Nevertheless, the Colonial Office assured South Africa that the BSAC claim to Bechuanaland would not be upheld. This claim was based upon the fact that the territory had been included in the original sphere of the BSAC Charter. Even some of the missionaries, for long champions of Bechuanaland's 'independence' from the settler states, were by 1914 advocating absorption, worn down by years of poor returns in terms of converts. Perhaps 'backward' and 'oppressive' chiefs would prove less resistant to the gospel if Europeans took over the land.

The chiefs, therefore, had every reason to cling to the imperial coat tails in order to retain their land and their autonomy, and this ensured a loyal response to the imperial call to arms in 1914. Supporting the war effort, they reasoned, morally bound the British *not* to hand them over to South Africa. Chief Seepapitso of the Bangwaketse enthusiastically backed recruitment and fund-raising. The future Bakwena chief, Sebele, served in the army and met members of the British royal family in Paris in 1917 (Sebele's age-regiment was named *MaThubantwa* in recognition of the many ex-servicemen who underwent initiation rites with him). Chief Khama of the Bangwato, meanwhile, leader of the Protectorate's largest tribe, supported fund-raising but refused to send men, while Chief Linchwe of the Bakgatla supported both.

The British administration and the coming of war

Before the war imperial defence evaluations had cast an eye upon even relatively unimportant territories such as Bechuanaland as the system of imperial defence came to have real meaning at the local and international level. Statistics of the defensive capabilities and strategic position of every colony in the British Empire were compiled and reported to London. In 1911 Major-General F. T. Clayton of British Army Headquarters in Pretoria asked for an appraisal of the Protectorate's defensive capabilities. Resident Commissioner Panzera reported that the Batswana 'could not be considered a warlike people'. His assessment demonstrated that at this period — thirty years into the life of a British protectorate that ran for eighty years — it was felt that security risks were more often within one's own borders than without: 'They are not of good physique as a rule and although normally organized in 'regiments' may be regarded more or less as an armed rabble, who would be easily cowed by European mounted troops, especially if supported by Field Artillery and Pom-Poms' (an onomatopoeic name for a model of the Maxim machine-gun that fired a one-pound explosive shell).

Clearly suffering from the 'siege mentality' of the early colonial state, Panzera concluded that there was 'no probability of mutual support' among the eight main tribes: 'this has been our salvation on many occasions and it is this which has enabled us to hold the country with so small a force'. Largely in order to counter the threat of African uprising, the war was seen as an opportunity to strengthen the Protectorate's European military forces. The administrative officer of 1914 was already rather paramilitary, armed and used to life in the saddle, whereas his inter-war successor was unarmed, increasingly deskbound, and usually travelled in a truck. British administrators and their paramilitary partners in the First World War era were outdoorsmen, men such as Captain E. Salmon, who in October 1914 was patrolling in the Caprivi Strip with a party of fifty NCOs and soldiers, a Maxim gun, nineteen African porters, two boats, a wagon, and 20,000 rounds of .303 Lee Enfield ammunition. Many administrators in Britain's scattered colonies shared with their countrymen back home an impatience to taste action in the war against Germany, and felt marginalized in apparent backwaters that, in the case of a colony like Bechuanaland, was always likely to be peripheral even to the 'peripheral' war theatres of Africa. But they could not all simply be released to make the journey home, by steamer from the Cape, in order to enlist. Even though colonial administrations were depleted, colonies did not run themselves, and even seemingly remote colonies had a war role to perform. Those destined to remain, therefore, were likely to respond enthusiastically should a military role for their colony become apparent. Such was the case in Bechuanaland, not only concerned by rumours of 'native uprising', but bordered by German territory for many hundreds of miles.

Almost as soon as war had been declared the Resident Commissioner asked the High Commissioner in Pretoria, Lord Buxton, for permission to form a European volunteer force. It was to be drawn from men with previous military experience, of whom there tended to be a large number among settler populations. Panzera himself had a military background, having been in the British South Africa Police and having commanded Colonel Robert Baden-Powell's artillery during the famous siege of Mafeking in the Boer War. Panzera argued that the force would be 'invaluable in case of native trouble' or should a Boer uprising take place. The men would provide their own horses and uniforms (a dashing colour scheme had already been conceived) and the only official outlay would be the provision of rifles and Maxim guns.

The force would also revamp the Protectorate's paramilitary police force, whose 'keen spirit of esprit de corps' had been 'practically destroyed' since the Boer War. Panzera was clearly excited by the prospect of forming a new military force. The Bechuanaland Protectorate Police, as he claimed, was demoralized, and with imperial troops leaving South Africa for service in Europe, more police were needed to fill a void in which Africans or Boers with rebellious intentions might choose to act. Such a force would constitute a 'loyal reserve' in times of trouble. Another reason for increasing the military force at the disposal of the Bechuanaland administration was the inadvisability of using South African troops to deal with any African rising. Revealing a surprising degree of African animosity, Panzera wrote that:

> The Natives are so intensely distrustful of the Colonial Government that the employment of a contingent of Union forces would have the opposite effect of stamping out any simmering rebellion, by, if possible, uniting the wavering tribes against them as a common enemy.[39]

Among Bechuanaland's settler community there was 'alarm at the withdrawal of imperial forces from inland South Africa' and the prospect of Boer rebellion that this invited. British troops had remained in South Africa after the Boer War, a source of continuing tension. Though ostensibly the garrison remained in case of 'native uprising' and to protect the High Commission Territories, the Boers knew their more important calling — to suppress any attempt on their part to reverse the decision of the 1902 Treaty of Vereeniging that had ended the Boer War. Boers thought it showed a continuing distrust of the erstwhile enemy. The issue was resolved upon the outbreak of war when Prime Minister Louis Botha offered to undertake full defensive responsibility for the region (the Union Defence Force had been formed in 1912), an offer that the hard-pressed British government was happy to accept. Despite thoughts of local uprisings, either from Africans or Boers, more worthwhile opportunities for martial excitement were soon to present themselves because of Bechuanaland's shared border with German South West Africa, and the labour demands of the war in distant Europe, particularly those associated with the massive Somme offensive of 1916.

The occupation of the Caprivi Strip

The Caprivi Strip — named after Bismarck's successor as Chancellor, Georg Graf von Caprivi — was a geographical quirk that owed its existence to Germany's desire for access to the Zambezi River. The British had duly obliged, ceding a narrow corridor of territory that linked Germany's new colony of South West Africa with the Zambezi, just above the Victoria Falls. Bechuanaland, therefore, shared with the enemy a border that ran for hundreds of miles along the entirety of its northern and western perimeters. Given this contiguity, the Bechuanaland administration needed to take precautions against German invasion, and was required to support offensive action intended to amputate the geographical tentacle of the Caprivi Strip. The strategic reason for this action was to stymie any German threat to the Rhodesias or attempts to use the Strip as a bridge between Germans forces in East Africa and those fighting in South West Africa. This threat was taken seriously, and Jan Smuts even offered to release the Rhodesia Regiment from his army operating in German South West Africa in order to help defend its homeland.

A number of factors accounted for the British campaign to annex the Caprivi Strip. First, there was the not inconsiderable matter of prestige. The capture of the German base at Schuckmannsburg, it was thought, would 'inspire native confidence' in the British. There was mounting evidence that British prestige was being damaged: the BSAC Administrator of Northern Rhodesia reported that Chief Letia of the Barotse, whose kingdom bordered the Caprivi Strip, had asked why the British allowed the Germans to stay now that they were enemies, remarking dismissively that his people could easily take the position. Barotse territorial ambitions came into play here, for they had long claimed the Caprivi region as their own. They had been angered when their 'special winter grazing grounds' had been lost to the German colony in the first place, and now saw an opportunity, if the Germans were defeated, of getting them back.

Apart from the continued German presence being 'bad for prestige' among the Africans, the BSAC Resident Commissioner of Southern Rhodesia, Colonel Burns-Begg, reported that it kept British troops occupied in guarding the Victoria Falls Bridge, troops that could ill be spared. Conquest would remove this threat to the strategically important railway line and release the troops for other duties. Burns-Begg told the High Commissioner in Pretoria that the occupation of Schuckmannsburg was all that would be required to capture the entire Caprivi Strip. He reported that there was 'growing annoyance' expressed in the Rhodesian press about the 'policy of inactivity' on the part of the British. A further reason for annexing the Strip was the fear that it would act as a focus for Germans trying to cross Africa from one side to the other, leaving South West Africa, where German forces were in retreat, for East Africa, where they were holding their own.

A proposal to capture the Caprivi Strip was put to the Secretary of State for the Colonies on 22 August 1914. From the Colonial Office in Downing Street, London, Lewis Harcourt responded without enthusiasm, ordering no occupation unless it was necessary to secure British interests. He also made it clear that in mind of the 'eventual settlement of colonial claims [that was to come at Versailles in 1919] occupation, if deemed necessary, should not be undertaken by BSAC forces alone', for fear of the company claiming territorial rights. Thus in granting the 'man on the spot' the power to annexe if he considered it necessary, Harcourt requested that the High Commissioner consult the Resident Commissioner of Bechuanaland about the possibility of the Bechuanaland Protectorate Police (BPP) participating in any operations to secure the Strip. This would give an important *imperial* stake in what would otherwise be an exclusively BSAC operation. The Bechuanaland Protectorate and its scant administrative and police establishment was being used as a pawn in a regional game, required to establish British imperial control rather than allowing settler or African expansion to claim the prize of the Caprivi Strip.

On 7 September 1914 the BSAC repeated its earlier claim that the Caprivi Strip should be taken in order to remove the German threat to the Victoria Falls Bridge. Five days later Lord Buxton authorized the 'occupation of Schuckmannsburg and as much of the eastern end of the Caprivi Strip as felt essential to protect trade routes and prevent German aggression'. Justifying his actions to the Colonial Secretary back in London, Buxton wrote that he had permitted the attack on the 'urgent recommendation of the local officers'. Reports of German reinforcements making their way to Schuckmannsburg had been received from the BSAC fort at Sesheke. Harcourt replied to his fellow peer with the assumption — a *sotto voce* order — that unless the fort at Schuckmannsburg could be occupied by the BPP, it must be destroyed. This again indicated Whitehall's unwillingness to allow the BSAC to be in a position to make a territorial claim. Following this prompt, the High Commissioner made it clear that when he had given permission to move against the Caprivi Strip, any territory taken 'would have to be at the disposal of the Imperial Government at the conclusion of hostilities'; there was to be no automatic gain for the settler state of Southern Rhodesia and its ruling chartered company.

The annexation of the Caprivi Strip was thus entrusted to Rhodesian forces with support from the BPP, who provided intelligence and, most importantly, represented an imperial stake in a venture that would otherwise have been entirely in the hands of the armed forces of a private company. The bloodless conquest was completed by 21 September 1914. The German commander at Schuckmannsburg surrendered to Major Capell who had led the Victoria Falls detachment to Sesheke in order to launch the attack. As Whitehall had feared, the BSAC immediately sought to extend its control over the new territory, the BSAC Administrator of Northern Rhodesia, L. A. Wallace, suggesting that he should take over its administration. The High Commisioner, given the injunction against BSAC claims from his superior in Whitehall, could not accept this. 'As long as I am responsible for military measures in the Strip I must also have direct control of any civil authority', he wrote to Wallace and to the Resident Commissioner in Salisbury on 15 October 1914. Instead, the High Commissioner ensured that the Bechuanaland administration was able to take over responsibility for the Strip. He proposed a withdrawal of all BSAC forces and the positioning of 120 Africans at Sesheke armed with Maxim guns. He asked if Bechuanaland could provide an officer for civil administration, as, in the High Commissioner's words to the Resident Commissioner of Bechuanaland, if left to the BSAC they 'might make this the basis of a territorial claim'. Colonel Panzera replied in the affirmative on the following day, 7 October 1914, and said he had sent a 'very good NCO' for the purpose. Soon afterwards Captain H. V. Eason was appointed Special Commissioner for the Caprivi Strip.

Bechuanaland, therefore, became part of the asset-stripping of the German Empire in Africa, responsible from October 1914 for administering the Caprivi Strip. In the first two years of the war the Germans lost all of their colonies — save for long-contested Tanganyika — to forces from the Belgian, British, French, and Japanese empires. In August 1914 New Zealand troops occupied Samoa, and Togo fell to British and French troops; in September 1914 Australian troops occupied New Guinea, and in Southern Africa, the Caprivi Strip was surrendered to the British on 21 September 1914, ten months before the completion of the conquest of German South West Africa. Unlike these other colonial gains in Africa and the Pacific — motivated largely by the 'sub imperial' ambitions of insecure and territorially-greedy Dominions — the Caprivi Strip was destined to remain under direct British rule for some time. This was partly because of the need to forestall Southern Rhodesian ambitions to acquire new real estate, though the Rhodesians kept up a sustained campaign for the Strip's absorption. The BSAC Administrator of Northern Rhodesia continued to insist that the Strip was better off under his control. He repeated the grievance of Chief Letia of the Barotse concerning the loss of his tribe's grazing grounds, and argued that handing the land over to Bechuanaland would cause unrest. The Barotse claim was pushed hard by the BSAC in forwarding its own claim, and a potted history of the tribe's claim was sent to the Colonial Secretary in London. As the Colonial Office noted, 'the history is designed to show that Lewanika's people have the strongest claim to the Strip, having owned the country for several generations before the [German] occupation'.

The British South Africa Company would not relinquish its claim, and another ruse employed was to emphasize the prospect of a German recrudescence that only BSAC forces — as opposed to Bechuanaland's one-man band — could deter or suppress. The Administrator of Northern Rhodesia wrote directly to the Colonial Secretary, Lewis Harcourt, urging greater defensive measures for the Strip, for fear of a German attempt to cross Africa or raid Barotseland. Harcourt asked the High Commissioner for his opinion on this, and Lord Buxton in turn consulted the Resident Commissioner of Bechuanaland, a neat illustration of the passage of enquiries and information up and down the imperial chain of authority. The Resident Commissioner thought the Rhodesian fears greatly exaggerated and regarded a German move through the Strip as 'exceedingly improbable'.

At the local level, the BSAC attempted to disrupt Bechuanaland administration of the Strip in order to further its campaign for a takeover. Lieutenant Hornsby, officer commanding the BSAC post at Sesheke, wrote to the Strip's Special Commissioner, W. B. Surmon (who had replaced Captain Eason) complaining about ex-German African policeman being allowed to settle in the Strip as it would damage his intelligence operations should they be used as German spies. The High Commissioner brushed off this concern. The Administrator of Northern Rhodesia emphasized the threat of German reinforcements making their way into the area. He reported that *Induna* Nsiku had been sent to the Mashi River and found that thirty Africans and 'a great many more whites' had arrived at Andara at the western end of the Strip.

Concerns that a large German party might seek to cross Africa in order to link up with forces in 'German East' as the South African invasion squeezed them out of German South West, required continued vigilance. There were acrimonious differences on this subject between the authorities in Bechuanaland and Southern Rhodesia, illustrating the potential for friction even between contiguous 'British' territories. A conference was called by the High Commissioner to clear the air, the prospects of defending the Caprivi–Barotseland region from a German trek were discussed, and agreement was reached that the Bechuanaland administration would enlist African scouts to form an 'Intelligence Department' reporting German movements to the Strip's Special Commissioner. Colonel Panzera, the Bechuanaland Resident Commissioner, remained sceptical about the efficacy of some Africans as scouts, however, because of the Damara 'dread of the Germans and their consequent fear of entering German territory' (the ferocious German suppression of the Nama and Herero uprisings of 1904–5 had led many people to flee from South West Africa and settle as refugees in Bechuanaland).

What of the people who actually lived in this watery sliver of Central Africa? For a period, they were frightened by the prospect of violence. J. H. Venning, Assistant Magistrate at Sesheke, reported in February 1915 that the people of eight villages had fled, fearing military action. The shift in the Strip's proprietorship brought about by the British occupation also roused concern. The Assistant Magistrate at Sesheke reported to the BSAC Administrator at Livingstone that sixty *indunas* and headmen from the Strip had come to see him. He told them of the change of government and took them to see the Barotse chief Letia, to assure them that they had nothing to fear from the Barotse, formerly their overlords. The Barotse coveted the Caprivi Strip not only for its grazing, but for its reeds, the main material used in the construction of huts, its rich fish stocks, and its suitability for winter crops (winter was the dry season; the Strip's was very wet, hence ideal for growing crops when they struggled to grow elsewhere). The Africans who inhabited the Caprivi Strip had been relieved from Barotse overrule when the Germans took it over in 1893. They feared the return of the Barotse now that the Germans had been ousted. They were right to do so for as of 28 January 1916, the Barotse were allowed access to the Strip.

Proclamation No. 22 of 1922 brought the Strip formally under Bechuanaland administration and therefore British, as opposed to Southern Rhodesian or South African rule. This followed the establishment of the Mandate system at Versailles. Tax collection began in that year. The Strip remained a lightly-administered drain on the Protectorate's scant resources until 1930, when it was transferred to South Africa as part of its League of Nations mandate over South West Africa (although until the 1950s Bechuanaland police helped maintain law and order there).

Reliance upon Africans and African indifference

A clear theme to emerge from the Bechuanaland Protectorate's war record is the administration's absolute reliance on Africans for information and intelligence-gathering. It also reveals the indifference and fear evinced by Africans often unwilling to be co-opted to support the administration and afraid, in equal measure, of both the British and the Germans. A paucity of manpower meant that the administration relied heavily on Africans to govern themselves — hence the residual power of the chiefly structures — and for intelligence. This was especially true in the Protectorate's more remote regions, which corresponded precisely with those closest to the German borders along its western and northern boundaries. It also meant that the inhabitants of these regions were less familiar with Europeans; there were still people who had never seen a white man. The sheer size of the country informed the British presence, as did its inhospitable climate and transport difficulties in areas such as the Kalahari Desert and the Okavango Delta. Here the climate could defeat the European intruder. In late 1914, for example, the greatest fear of Captain Salmon and his column patrolling the Caprivi Strip were floods caused by early rains and the menace of horse sickness. In September 1917 the missionary G. Cullen Reed died of blackwater fever at Kavimba on the Chobe River in the Caprivi Strip. The Resident Commissioner wrote in frustration of the 'swamps, [tsetse] fly belt, and fever' that made the northern reaches of Bechuanaland so difficult to administer and to develop. The administration of such a colonial territory was conducted by men in the saddle trekking great distances across desert, swamp, and scrub, operating hundreds of miles away from the Protectorate's head-quarters in Mafeking.

Despite the difficulties of terrain and climate, it was still necessary for the Bechuanaland administration to acquire intelligence about German movements. In administrative reports Africans often appear as part of an observed landscape, rather like game. Occasionally they are encountered, interviewed, and then left to go about their business. Roaming in the Okavango and Caprivi regions in February 1915, for example, we encounter two BSAC intelligence agents, European pinpricks in a vast African landscape. They had mounted a forty-two day patrol in search of Germans, though despite many rumours, had failed to track any down. Forty wagons and 400 men had been reported leaving Grootfontein in the north of South West Africa, heading towards the Caprivi Strip. A Damara 'native' told them of a German who 'puts a hat on his head and talks back to Windhoek', referring, so Agent Johnson thought, to a wire-less set. The Africans in the area were unwilling to talk because the retreating German Resident for the Caprivi Strip had said that the Germans would 'make it hot for them on their return if anyone helped the Company — the name by which the Rhodesian government is known'. Thinking defensively, Johnson believed that 100 men could make it a 'difficult and dangerous enterprise' for a force of 1,000 Germans to get within 200 miles of the Zambezi.

On the outbreak of war Africans were told to report German activi-ties in the Caprivi Strip to Lieutenant Charles Keat Brown, Officer Commanding the Bechuanaland Protectorate Police post at Kazungula on the banks of the Chobe River that separated Bechuanaland from the Strip. Headmen along the Linyanti were employed to report strangers, and the Resident Magistrate at Kazungula sent African scouts to Andara at the westernmost end of the Strip. On 18 September 1914 he reported that 'David, the young chief of the Ba-Sekgoma, has offered to provide 300 men for any service required', on the condition that the administra-tion provided arms and ammunition. African territorial aggrandizement was again at work here, for Sekgoma's tribe as well as the Barotse in Northern Rhodesia claimed the Caprivi Strip as its own.

It is clear that many Africans feared backing the wrong European horse in the conflict, and would really have preferred it if the Europeans weren't there in the first place. In December 1914 the Resident Magistrate at Tsau in the Okavango Delta reported that, after warnings, Chief Mathiba of the Batawana had offered to assist Britain in the war, arriving with headman Mogalakwe and a couple of regiments:

> It appears that Mathiba at Maun [the Batawana capital] in discussing the war situation with the gang of degenerate young Batawana of his own age . . . is supposed to have agreed with them that since it was 'impossible to see the outcome of the war', they had better 'sit on the fence' . . . The majority of young Batawana being both lazy, feeble, and pusillanimous, this idea would commend itself to them.[40]

In the *kgotla* (tribal council), headman Mogolakwe rebuked Mathiba and the young men, and was supported by the elders in his contention that the Batawana should aid the British administration in prosecuting the war. Fearing loss of land, he complained that Mathiba was 'doing his best to alienate the Government from the tribe and cause them to lose their Reserve'. The Resident Magistrate considered Mathiba to be 'pitiably weak and unable to command respect'. Mathiba was 'spoken to very severely' by the Protectorate's Resident Commissioner later in the war, allegedly for torturing people. Despite these clear differences with Mathiba, the official history of the war poured healing balm upon these disputes, and contented itself with noting that 'the Resident Magistrate and the few police under him were also loyally assisted by Chief Mathiba and his people in putting their headquarters in a state of defence in anticipation of an attack, and in patrolling the northern and western borders'.

The 'loyal' Mogalakwe led a party of 'well mounted Batawana' to the northern border at Muhembo, whence spies were sent forward to Andara. The South African government asked the Bechuanaland administration to send spies to patrol between Grootfontein and the Okavango, supported by a network of runners for the transmission of information. This was done, partly through an agreement with Chief Mathiba for the employment of mounted Batawana. On the western border, the Batawana sent out patrols 'mounted on oxen, which for work in heavy sand and long stretches of thirst, do better than horses'. The Damara people living in the extreme northwest of the Protectorate were refugees from the 'thorough doing' meted out by the Germans in their suppression of the Nama and Herero uprisings a decade earlier. Despite this horrific experience having, in the words of A. G. Stigand, the Resident Magistrate at Tsau, 'put the terror of Germans into them for a couple of generations', they were anxious in this latest conflict to hedge their bets, and therefore not loyally committed to the British cause. The trepidation with which the Damara approached and crossed the border between British and German territory was noted by Stigand.

The region's inhabitants quite understandably feared for their safety. Lieutenant Hornsby of the BSAC reported in December 1914 that Siombosso's village at Lebebe (next to Andara) was 'found deserted when called upon by the Assistant Magistrate and the chief Letia, and cannot be relied upon to bring us information should a party of Germans appear there'. Rumour was rife in this area, where Africans clearly had no special love of either the British or the Germans. Special Commissioner for the Caprivi Strip Captain Eason reported the 'wild and unauthenticated native rumours which are in frequent circulation'. The situation was deliberately worsened by German propaganda, intended to spread disaffection among the Damara and Batawana of Ngamiland and the Okavango region. The Germans distributed letters explaining that they were at war with the British, not the African people. Fear remained a standard African response to the appearance of white strangers throughout the war. In 1918 G. E. Nettelton, Sub-Inspector of the BPP, was sent to intercept Germans spotted in Ngamiland. Upon sighting his party, the whole village of Mompakush took to the swamps, 'fearing that they wanted to make war'.

On the Protectorate's western border the administration prepared for German incursions through the Kalahari as well as the Okavango. Both routes would require the invasion of the Batawana Reserve (Ngamiland) and the capture of the region's administrative headquarters at Tsau. It was estimated that this would require a raiding force of at least a hundred men. On 9 November 1914 a German force around twenty strong attacked the BPP station at Kwakhanai in the Ghanzi District, killing a Damara police messenger, Jonas (who is commemorated on the war memorial outside of the parliament buildings in Gaborone). The Resident Commissioner requested that the High Commissioner dispatch arms, ammunition, and hospital supplies. He sent twenty Lee Enfield rifles to his Magistrate at Tsau. Chief Khama III of the Bangwato offered to provide scouts in the western Kalahari to report German movements. In February 1915 British military intelligence reported a force of Germans marching towards Lake Ngami.

The Resident Commissioner in distant Mafeking kept a close eye on the situation. There were known to be German forces at Sandfontein near the Bechuanaland–South West Africa border. As well as feeling unable to trust some of its own African population, the Bechuanaland administration also had to watch elements of its white population. In and around Ghanzi near the western border lived Boer settlers, likely to sympathize with the German cause. The administration was so concerned that it wanted to concentrate them and their livestock for surveillance purposes. But the Ghanzi Boers were probably more interested in what was in the war for them. The Resident Magistrate at Tsau, who had entrenched and sandbagged his camp, reported that they were 'talking about their hopes of looting German horses and rifles'. The Lewis brother and a man named Drotzky arrived at his headquarters offering their services against the Germans. They came equipped with horses, rifles and, in their saddle packs, fourteen days-worth of biltong and rusk rations. Drotzky had been one of the original Boer settlers sent to establish the town of Ghanzi in the 1890s, itself a measure aimed at establishing a 'British' presence on the fringe of the vast Protectorate in order to fore-stall any possible German claim for extension into 'unoccupied' land.

Financial and military assistance to the imperial war effort

Even though a thousand miles from Europe and in a land only recently colonized, Batswana people contributed money for the war effort, and endured the inflation that trailed in its wake. 'Gradual all-round price increases' were reported, but no countermeasures were taken because it was believed that the 'natives' could subsist quite easily. In 1916 the Protectorate balanced its budget for the first time, even recording a surplus of £1,600. This, the Resident Commissioner wrote, was due to 'increased customs and licensing revenue, to savings in salaries under various heads, and, in view of the European war and of the consequent high cost of certain materials, to the abandonment of some proposed public works'. Batswana provided gifts and comforts for servicemen overseas, such as the 'hundreds of pairs of socks knitted for troops over-seas by native girls and boys of the Bangwaketse Industrial School, Kanye'.

One sector of the economy that profited because of the war was the cattle industry. The war was a time of heightened world demand and the Protectorate duly benefited from an increase in the market for its cattle given the insatiable global appetite for food. The weight restrictions were dropped so that the cattle could be sold on the South African meat market, the Dominion's white breeders not needing protection in a time of boom. The Bechuanaland administration took its cut when in 1916 it imposed a Cattle Export Tax. Quarantine camps were established at Ramatlabana and Sikwane on the southern border with South Africa, Exports then escalated rapidly, from 12,000 head in 1913–14 to 19,000 in 1916–17, and 31,000 in 1920–21. After that the market slumped, and the weight restrictions were re-imposed. But the main and growing source of cash remuneration was migration to the diamond and gold mines of South Africa.

The administration placed a certain amount of pressure on the chiefs to ensure that their people donated money. In November 1915 Jules Ellenberger, Assistant Magistrate at Gaberones, wrote to Chief Linchwe of the Bakgatla to remind him of his peoples' 'duty' to support the war effort in line with the King's subjects around the world. Linchwe replied that he had reminded them, resulting in the 'gift' of £356 that accompanied the letter. The Resident Commissioner had circulated a letter aimed at preventing undue chiefly pressure to contribute, in which he reminded magistrates that hut tax collection — the bedrock of administration finances — remained the revenue priority. It is difficult to believe, however, that all contributions were genuinely voluntary, and the High Commissioner thought that the memorandum worsened the situation, as it 'was bound to be regarded by a native Chief as being in the nature of a solicitation which it would be difficult for him to refuse'. The Resident Commissioner would have winced at this censure from his superior in Pretoria.

The Financial Secretary of the Bechuanaland administration put the Protectorate's total war contribution at £10,205. European communities, including 'the ladies of Serowe', gave money to war-related charities such as the Red Cross. The Bangwato tribe made by far the largest collective contribution, amounting to £1,642. But despite the tribe's largesse, the administration was highly irritated by the decision of its chief, the famous Khama III, not to send men to join the army. The administration saw this as an embarrassment, and, given this, tried to make Khama feel embarrassed as a way of putting pressure on him to change his mind. The new Resident Commissioner, Edward Charles Garraway (Panzera had taken over as Commandant of the 26,000 prisoners of war at the Isle of Man Alien Detention Camp in 1916) wrote thus:

All the other Chiefs in the Protectorate have sent men and are sending more, but they are asking me: 'Why does Khama not send some of his men?' . . . Your name is well-known in England and I should be very sorry to be asked from England why it is that Khama alone, of all the Bechuanaland Chiefs, has not sent any men to help England in her hour of need . . . This letter, my friend Khama, is only written to you in friendship, and is not meant as a reproof.[41]

But Khama stood his ground. Fortunately for the administration, other chiefs were prepared to send troops. They joined a unit called the South African Native Labour Contingent (SANLC), formed in September 1916. It comprised over 21,000 men and was sent for service in France as military labour, created 'in response to urgent requests from Imperial authorities for manpower to expand the British military infrastructure for the gigantic Somme offensive'. In total, Bechuanaland send 1,058 men to war. Of this number, 106 Europeans served in Imperial, Rhodesian, and South African units, 555 Africans joined the SANLC, 405 worked on the railways in the South West Africa campaign, and twenty-one served with South Africa's Transport Corps in East Africa. To qualify for service in the SANLC men had to be 'capable of carrying a distance of a hundred yards a sack containing one hundred pounds of earth or sand'. Overall casualties are not available, but of the Bakgatla who served in the SANLC, 10 percent died. The men who joined the army or supporting services were usually called out by their chiefs in age-regiments. When asked to send men to help in the South West Africa campaign, for example, 'volunteers from the *Majanko*, *Mantwane*, and *Makuka* regiments' of the Bakgatla tribe were sent to the Cape and thence by sea to South West Africa where they worked for South African Railways on the military extension of the Prieska line into the colony's interior. Of the men sent to South West Africa, 312 were Bakgatla, the rest Balete. The Bakgatla regiments were sent under the leadership of Ramorotong and Motshwane, both relatives of Chief Linchwe and therefore royals able to exercise authority over the men. Chief Linchwe was insistent that a Dutch Reformed Church chaplain accompany his men. The SANLC contingent in which the Bechuanaland men were included arrived at Le Havre in February 1917 after thirty-five days at sea. In France they were housed in a compound surrounded by ten-foot high barbed wire fence, 'right out in the country and in no way in contact with the French people'.

Jules Ellenberger, a Bechuanaland official, recalls meeting three Bakgatla men who had been returned from Rosebank Camp in South Africa as unfit:

'I was from a regiment sent forward by the Chief Linchwe'. He told me that the regiment has been sent by ship to South West Africa and must now have 'got across the broad river'. He has been returned because he had six toes on each foot. He wanted the extra toes removed so that he could 'do his bit'. I forget what the other two were returned for but when I asked them what had struck them most at the Cape the one replied, 'The size of the fish! I had never before seen a fish as long as a man is tall'; the other was amazed at the quantity of cases, bales, and other articles that could be stowed away in a ship.[42]

Uprising

Though there was no chance of the British being 'kicked out' of Bechuanaland, official documents reveal a fear of potential African uprising at the time of the war. Perhaps this reflected the paramilitary nature of the early colonial administration, which was very different in character to the public school and Oxbridge colonial administration common by the 1930s. There were dark murmurings about the possibility of 'native uprisings'. Settlers and administrators remained vigilantly on the lookout for signs of 'restiveness'. This 'rising psychosis' was symptomatic of the fear amongst European settlers in the midst of recently subjugated Africans, as well as their lack of intimate local knowledge, and their awareness of the numerous occasions on which colonized people had risen against their overlords.

But there was a much more realistic and threatening source of potential rebellion in 1914; continued Boer hostility towards British rule. This came to a head in the form of a serious Boer uprising in the early winter of 1914 that involved over 12,000 Boers. The Bechuanaland administration had an early warning of the rebellion. In November 1914 Colonel Panzera informed the High Commissioner that Chief Linchwe of the Bakgatla was increasingly uneasy after receiving messages from the Bakgatla living in the Transvaal, reporting that Boers in the area, not wanting to fight on the side of the British, planned to cross into the Protectorate with their cattle. Panzera reminded Lord Buxton that a threat to the Protectorate's cattle originating in the Transvaal was anthrax. He mentioned the loyalty that the Bakgatla tribe had shown to the British during the Boer War, and how greatly it had suffered in the past from anthrax introduced from over the border. As a result of this, African guards were enlisted to patrol the Bakgatla Reserve–Transvaal border, and Chief Baitlotle of the Balete tribe was told to be watchful along his Reserve's stretch of border with the Transvaal.

Soon afterwards the Bechuanaland administration was warned that the Boer War general Jacques Pienaar and a party of rebels were on their way into the Protectorate, seeking to cross the Kalahari and link up with German forces in South West Africa to fight the British. As the official history of the Empire at war records:

> On receipt in the dead of night of a warning message from the Assistant Commissioner at Gaberones, Baitlotle immediately summoned up his men and ordered detachments to proceed with all speed to guard railway bridges and culverts in his Reserve . . . Meanwhile a detachment of the Kimberley Regiment was being rushed up by rail from the south and reinforced the Protectorate Police at Lobatsi, Ramoutswa, and Gaberones, also relieving Baitlotle's men at Metsimaewaane railway bridge.[43]

On 26 October 1914, hearing that a rebel movement was likely, two additional South African units, the 13th Dismounted Rifles (Lichtenberg Ruiters) and 9th Mounted Rifles (Bechuanaland Rifles) were mobilized at Potchefstroom and Kimberley. Detachments of the Bechuanaland Rifles were sent to Mafeking and Ramoutswa. Elsewhere in the Protectorate, rifles were dispatched to the European community in Lobatsi, whence a patrol of motor-cars set out in pursuit of the Boers, soon running out of petrol in the desert. Telegrams were sent to Chief Baitlotle and Chief Gaseitsiwe Seepapitso of the Bangwaketse, saying that they would be rewarded if the Boers were intercepted. Again, as in Bechuanaland's other 'war theatres', the administration relied upon its African subjects. The Bangwaketse chief dispatched age-regiments. Whilst offering rewards for the capture of the Boers, it was made clear by the administration that 'any native assisting them in any way, or failing to obstruct them, would be punishable by death', a rather severe injunction.

Colonel Cowan and twenty-five Britons — mostly 'old Matabele hands' who had been with Cecil Rhodes' Pioneer Column when it advanced into Southern Rhodesia in 1890 — were sent to Ramoutswa, the Balete capital. The Resident Commissioner left the Imperial Reserve in Mafeking, the Protectorate's headquarters, and moved to Lobatsi so as to be nearer the action. The Boer rebels crossed the border into Bechuanaland six miles south of Ramoutswa. The Bangwaketse chief sent fifty armed and mounted men out to scour the country. They were joined in the hunt by local traders. Near Segwagwa the rebels, swerving to avoid the Bangwaketse force, ran into Commandant du Plessis of the Union Defence Force. But some of the Boer rebels escaped from this encounter and soon afterwards Chief Seepapitso 'received a report that they had been seen in the eastern part of his territory, and that they were probably making for the Segwagwa Hills, about twenty miles south-west of Kanye. He ordered all available men to join him on horseback at Segwagwa . . . The rebels were caught up, and surrendered without firing a shot. Seepapitso then handed them over to the government troops who were pursuing them'. This action took place on New Year's Day 1915. The Resident Commissioner reported that 'as a result of the surrounding movements the enemy were captured', and praised 'the loyal, hearty, and ready assistance rendered by the natives'.

Rumours of African uprising were heard throughout the territory. In November 1917 a trader reported to the South African authorities that weapons were being sold to Africans in Lobatsi and that unrest was likely. In March 1917 a settler, H. G. Robins, made allegations of 'unrest' — one of the great catch-all words in the colonial lexicon — among the population. He reported that within six week's the Bangwato chief Khama III's son would lead an uprising. This would be a signal for an uprising in neighbouring Northern Rhodesia among the Barotse, 'then a universal conflagration right down to Zululand'. Even Ethiopian religious movements were apparently to be involved. According to Robins' source, a BSAC corporal, this was part of a continent-wide 'plot to kill all the white people'. The Bechuanaland administration had the good sense to realize that this was at least 90 percent nonsense, the product of the late-night verandah and the empty whisky bottle. But it did suggest how vulnerable Europeans felt in Africa, and one only has to recall the deep scars left by the Indian Mutiny — still feared on the eve of independence ninety years later — to comprehend how wary many Europeans felt.

Africa had had plenty of its own uprisings in the years since colonization. The 1890s and 1900s had witnessed serious rebellions in Southern Rhodesia and South Africa, 1915 brought John Chilembwe's rising in Nyasaland, and throughout the region the Watch Tower movement frightened settlers and administrators alike. German and Boer malcontents were suspected of fomenting African unrest aimed at undermining British rule, and Africans across South Africa were still smarting from the dispossession visited upon them by the 1913 Land Act, which reserved 87 percent of South Africa's land for white settlers (strengthening the resolve of Africans in Bechuanaland to resist South African takeover). The sinking of the *Lusitania* in May 1915 triggered riots in Cape Town, Durban, and Johannesburg. The lessons of *Prester John* were still being taken to heart by the white man in Africa. Even at the summit of imperial authority, military commanders took note of the matter. In 1917 the

Intelligence Department of the General Staff sent a secret memorandum to African governors warning of the dangers of pan-Africanism. As at least a partial antidote, they underlined the importance of fostering local tribal awareness.

Spanish influenza and the end of the war

Spanish influenza reached Africa in the autumn of 1918, possibly arriving at Cape Town via a contingent of SANLC troops returning from Europe in September. The rail network facilitated its passage throughout South-central Africa, a grim example of technology and man's inventiveness speeding his demise. The flu reached Bechuanaland in October. Even the blithe tones of the colonial annual report could not disguise the fact that the resulting discomfort was widespread. The disease had engulfed most of the country by 1919, obscuring 'malaria in its usual form'. As the Annual Report for 1918–19 put it:

> In October 1918 the disease known as 'Spanish Influenza' broke out in the Southern Protectorate, and, spreading rapidly, eventually affected the whole of the Territory except the Western Kalahari and the Ngami littoral, as they were concentrated in large communities or scattered. The mortality, all round, amongst them, from the disease and its complications, has been estimated at between four and five percentum.[44]

Based on 1911 census figures, this represents a death toll of approximately 6,500, and is in all probability on the cautious side. The London Missionary Society minister in Serowe estimated that 7.5 percent of the people of the Bangwato Reserve had died and the flu also caused a recrudescence of lung sickness in cattle.

In November 1918 news of the Armistice that brought the war to a close was conveyed to the chiefs and their people. To mark the occasion, 18 November was proclaimed a public holiday, 'but owing to the epidemic of influenza which was then raging in the Territory, it was not possible for the natives to take advantage of this holiday', according to the Annual Report. At a meeting in Serowe two weeks later, however, the chiefs 'took this opportunity to renew to His Majesty the King their promise of loyalty and obedience'. As this chapter has shown, the idiom of loyalty and reportage of happy African participation did little to represent the true experiences and problems faced by the Protectorate's population during the war, though a war record which emphasized loyal participation did at least serve the political ends of the chiefs, anxious to escape the tender embraces of South Africa or Southern Rhodesia. Though Bechuanaland had been peripheral to the main theatres of First World War conflict, the significant fact is that this under-populated, vast, and inhospitable land should have been involved at all. It not only played a part in operations against the enemy within the region itself, it had grown in size and furnished men and money for a remote cause barely perceived by the majority of its people. This was the power, and the price, of empire. The demands made upon the Empire, and the extent to which the war involved distant colonies and oceans, has been the theme of the last two chapters. We now turn to some studies of the role of colonies in the Second World War.

6

Recruiting Colonial Soldiers
The Case of the High Commission Territories

As the previous chapter showed, Southern African colonies played a part in the Empire's war effort between 1914 and 1918. During the Second World War Bechuanaland and the other two High Commission Territories (HCT), Basutoland and Swaziland, were much more deeply affected by conflict. All together, these three distant colonies contributed 36,000 men to the estimated 470,000 Africans who by 1945 were in British uniform, either in fighting regiments like the King's African Rifles (KAR) and Royal West African Frontier Force (RWAFF), or in labour and support units such as the Royal Army Service Corps and the Royal Pioneer Corps (where they formed the African Pioneer Corps), and the East African Military Labour Service. Until 1943 Africa was a central battlefield in the war between the British Empire and the Germans and Italians. From late 1942 American forces were also engaged in the African conflict in large numbers. Because of the fighting on the continent and the danger to normal supply routes through the Mediterranean and the Suez Canal, Africa also became a vital overland supply route for armies fighting in the Middle East. In addition, Africa was a source of strategic raw materials without which the Allied war effort would have faltered. African colonies also contributed hundreds of thousands of pounds to the imperial war effort, funding, for example, a Basutoland Spitfire Squadron that served in the Battle of Britain and the defence of Malta. African infantrymen played an important role in the British Army, serving with distinction in the Burma campaign and throughout the East African theatre, and bearing the major responsibility for the defence of British

West Africa in the face of a significant Vichy threat early in the war. Africa was the source of a vast labour army that made a crucial logistical contribution to Allied victory as part of the British Army's service branches and its Royal Pioneer Corps forming, for example, the essential labour component for the Eighth Army as it marched across Africa and invaded Italy.

What was particularly impressive about the war effort of colonies such as Basutoland, Bechuanaland, and Swaziland — and many other British territories around the world — was that they had no peacetime military tradition to draw upon, no extant military structures, and yet managed to produce large and effective contingents of troops and labourers in a short space of time. Imperial improvisation was much in evidence. The question that this chapter addresses is *how* this was achieved — how colonies that were not expected at the start of the war to have any military role were mobilized to play a significant role. This was achieved not at the point of the bayonet, but through collaboration with indigenous leaders, inducement, cajolery, and sometimes coercion.

Once in the past outbreak of war rumour was heard,
The rumour of war which spread all over the world,
It spread and roared to reach awareness of Great King George VI, 'Hee!
Hee!', he said, 'Come to help, ye British Protectorates'.
Prompt acceptance was the response of the Bakwena of Mmamagana,
Mobilization and recruitment immediately took place,
A call from Chief Kgari Sechele-a-Motswasele covered all Bakwena,
Thus each sitting man double marched to the call,
Every man danced war cry and rushed to meet the Chief's call.
                                    — Selebatso Gofetakgosi Masimega

Thus wrote Selebatso Masimega, a Tribal Clerk in the office of the Chief of the Bakwena, Bechuanaland's senior tribe. The year was 1944, and Masimega was soon to volunteer for military service with the High Commission Territories Corps which served with the British Army in the Middle East from 1946 to 1949. This chapter reveals how Basutoland, Bechuanaland, and Swaziland were mobilized for the recruitment of over 40,000 imperial soldiers to serve thousands of miles away as part of the British Army. It examines the reasons why the British administration of Bechuanaland and the territory's African chiefs supported military recruitment so strongly, and how ordinary people viewed and reacted to the call to arms — whether with the willing alacrity suggested in this wartime praise poem, or with the sullen acquiescence of 'conscripted volunteers'.

The importance of the imperial monarchy

As was seen in the last chapter, in Bechuanaland and the other High Commission Territories it was widely believed that Britain was a protector, an idea that had its roots in historical fact as well as in imperial rhetoric and repetition. Britain had protected them from the Ndebele, the Boers, and from the British South Africa Company, and the meeting of the three principal chiefs of Bechuanaland with Queen Victoria in 1895 had become a part of common folklore. Fifty years later, the monarchy was still conceptualized by many in the High Commission Territories as a schizophrenic institution in which King George reigned whilst Queen Victoria hovered spectrally in the background. Selogwe Pilane of Mochudi lucidly explained this enduring memory of the longdead Queen:

> Yes, she had passed away. But we here in Botswana always refer to her and she was well liked and known. Like among us Bakgatla. There was a Chief who governed a long time ago, Chief Pedi, the father of Pilane, father of Kgamanyane, father of Lentswe. We still refer to Bakgatla as people of that Chief, for example when we greet, *ban a ba ga Pedi* (Pedi's children) — but of course we all know that he is long dead. It is him who fathered Pilane, who fathered Kgamanyane, who fathered Lentswe I. Lentswe II is our Chief today, but we still call ourselves' *bana ba ga Pedi*.[45]

According to this popular lore, in 1941 the protectress called to friends and loyal subjects for help against Germany, not to subjugated people. There was the clear understanding that a contract existed. The belief in this transaction between two independent parties bound together by common interest was important even though historically somewhat inaccurate. Ex-serviceman Ephraim Molatlhwe offered a standard recapitulation of this widespread historical view:

> In the year of 1940 we heard that abroad in European lands a war had started between the Germans and the English. This meant that the Queen asked for help from her colonies in Southern Africa. This was done through the office of the High Commissioner of the Protectorates.

It took some time for this message to arrive and to be discussed and be heard by the people. This meant that the chiefs were able to take the message and explain that a message had arrived and you know that we are under protection of the Queen. For this reason we have to go and help.

Interviewed in the 1980s, Miriam Pilane recalled:

We were so frightened to hear that our husbands were going to war . . . had no slight idea what. the war was about, the thing is, we only heard that Queen Elizabeth [here confused with Victoria] has asked for help. They are going to fight for the Queen. We then know that this involves us, if they [the Germans] are fighting the Queen, as we were her people. We were under her, and she helped us against our enemies and with other things, so we had to help her. We didn't know how long they were going to take there. Even if we were afraid we just encouraged them to go in the name of God, we will also pray for them whilst gone, so that they can help the Queen as she helped us.

The reputation of the British as protectors and benevolent helpers was strengthened by the continued existence across the border of the 'bad whites', the Boers. In the opinion of ex-serviceman Odirile Mogwe, 'the old Chiefs went overseas to go and ask *Mmamosadinyana* to protect them [the 1895 visit of three chiefs to Britain which featured a meeting with the Queen]. We regarded them as our protectors, not as our enemies, no, no, no. If Germany or the Boers had ruled, there would have been devastation in Botswana!' This view of the British presence in Bechuanaland, shared equally in Basutoland and Swaziland, meant that Batswana were more easily able to rationalize their participation in the war, unlike the Africans of the Union whose failure to identify with the Empire's plight so 'astonished' Tshekedi Khama upon his visit to South Africa in 1940. This flattering view of the British formed part of the meaning that Batswana invested in the world around them, and was called in to play when they were asked to go to war; for many people now had to build a picture of the wide world beyond their own locality and the migratory thoroughfares of southern Africa, a picture that encompassed places such as Cairo, Jerusalem, and Rome.

The outlook of the British and the chiefs

The African political elite in the High Commission Territories had further reasons for wishing to support the imperial war effort to the utmost, a central political consideration as important in 1939–45 as it had been during the 1914–18 war (see chapter 5). The African leaders concerned were the Paramount Chief and his Basutoland National Council; the Paramount Chief, Queen Mother, and Council in Swaziland; and the eight 'independent' chiefs of the Bechuanaland Protectorate. By demonstrating their outstanding loyalty to the imperial connection, the chiefs were determined to fend off the prospect of a political transfer of their territories from British colonial rule to South African rule. This threat to the territories had been enshrined in the Union of South Africa's founding Act in 1909, which looked forward to the day when their incorporation would fulfil South Africa's geographical destiny. It was still very much alive in the 1940s. The prospect of transfer was viewed by the leaders of all three High Commission Territories with unmitigated alarm, causing them to cling to the imperial connection. The South African government hoped that the distractions of a world war, and the service rendered by Prime Minister Jan Smuts in bringing the wavering Union to war on Britain's side in September 1939, would enable the final realization of the dream of incorporation. Indeed, soon after going to war, the South African government made a formal request for the transfer of Swaziland. Some chiefs had personal reasons for throwing their weight behind army recruitment. Molefi Pilane, for example, had recently been reinstalled as chief of the Bakgatla following his deposition in 1937, and was keen to impress the British.

In Basutoland the Paramount Chief Seeiso declared his nation's loyalty to Britain and willingness to send men to war in 1940, though the Basutoland National Council at its October 1940 meeting expressed concern about sending men to join the South African Native Labour Corps. After Paramount Chief Seeiso's unexpected death in December 1940 his Queen, Mansebo, became the nation's first ever female regent. At a *pitso* attended by the High Commissioner in 1941 she reaffirmed the loyalty of the Basotho people and their willingness to assume any burden required 'to help His Majesty's Government to achieve victory'. After this, in June 1941, came the *mokhosi oa ntoa*, the call to arms, a message spread throughout the land through local *pitso* meetings ahead of the official start of recruiting for the British Army on 29 July 1941. As in Bechuanaland, chiefs were the main force in recruitment.

As in other parts of Africa, the HCT political elite recognized the evil of Nazism. Though some African leaders considered the conflict a white man's war and thought the stories of Hitler exaggerated, men like King Sobhuza of Swaziland came to realize the threat posed by Hitler's racial ideas. The Nazi threat could be understood by observant Southern Africans, given their existence amidst a similarly 'advanced' racist society which boasted neo-Nazi groups like the Afrikaner Ossewabrandwag. Elsewhere in Africa, traditional and educated elites favoured the defeat of Nazism, even if some of them — like the educated elite in Nigeria — expected political concessions from the British as a reward for African participation in the war.

For the first two years of the war the military mobilization of the Protectorate was minimal, as its territorial integrity was not threatened and a military role for the African population was not envisaged despite the rapid contraction of the white male population. Until the call for African soldiers came the administration's policy was to encourage Africans wanting to join up to cross the border and enlist in the Union Defence Force's Native Military Corps (NMC). But this suggestion was anathema to the chiefs of Bechuanaland who did not want the Protectorate's war effort subsumed by that of its overbearing neighbour. Their war aim, and that of the rulers of Basutoland and Swaziland, was to secure long-term independence from South Africa, both political and economic, and they wanted their war contributions would be entirely distinct from those of the giant Dominion on their doorstep. In Basutoland and Swaziland, recruitment took place for the Native Military Corps. In 1940 a company of Basotho and a company of Swazi soldiers joined the 4th Battalion of the NMC to guard strategically vital points in the Union, Basutoland's first NMC company of 145 men leaving for the Union in September 1940. Batswana troops were earmarked for the Southern Rhodesian Labour Corps, though hostility to the NMC remained strong. After visiting Batswana troops in the Middle East in 1942, the Resident Commissioner reported that 'one of the effects of the trip was to prejudice the chiefs even more strongly against the Native Military Corps and the Union'. The men of the three protectorates tended to support this view, and many of those who had joined the Native Military Corps in 1939–40 expressed a desire to join 'my own country's kraal', meaning the distinct Basutoland, Bechuanaland, and Swaziland units, upon the creation of the African Pioneer Corps in the summer of 1941. Both Basutoland NMC companies transferred to the African Pioneer Corps upon its formation. In February 1941 Tshekedi Khama insisted that the Bangwato serve under the British, not the South

Africans. The local British authorities supported this, though they had to tread carefully given the delicacy of British–South African relations.

The outlook of the British administrations to African participation in the war was disarmingly straightforward. Bechuanaland, as in the days of Resident Commissioner Frederick Panzera earlier in the century, was participating in the war as a loyal part of the British Empire according to the colonial administrators. Britain had since the Warren Expedition of 1885 afforded protection to the Batswana, and because of this protection, it was reasoned, they enjoyed freedom. In the minds of the administrators of Bechuanaland, the torch of imperial trusteeship still burned brightly. Rewards for participation in the war effort would be the 'maintenance of freedom' and, as an added post-war boon, an increase in development expenditure under the Colonial Development and Welfare Act. The fight for 'freedom' rallying cry used by the British to try and engender support for the war against Nazism was more potent among Basotho, Batswana, and Swazi than it was among Africans in the Union, for they were aware of the benefits of not living under the racially oppressive South African regime.

Though the desire to prevent the territory's transfer to South Africa lay at the heart of chiefly support for the war effort, overt political bargaining was not tolerated by the administration. In 1943 the administration asked for messages from the chiefs to be conveyed to their soldiers. The response from Chief Montshiwa of the Baralong, and its rejection by the Resident Commissioner, illustrates the difference of outlook between the administration and the chiefs. Montshiwa wrote to his men that 'war service is the means by which we are requesting through the Head of our Administration, to the members of the forthcoming peace conference, that we may be considered and declared as citizens of the British Nation, and as such entitled to receive all rights of citizenship, politically, industrially and socially'. Though the administration was keenly aware of how the chiefs were hoping to bind Britain closer by demonstrating unfailing loyalty during the war, the nature of Montshiwa's message was unacceptable. Resident Commissioner Aubrey Forsyth Thompson minuted 'this bargaining message won't do', and altered it to conform to the administration's position on African participation in the war: 'War service is the means by which we are showing our gratitude for the Protection which the sovereign has extended to us for so many years.'

Though aware of South African racial sensitivities, and the need to maintain the flow of High Commission Territories labour to the South African mines (one of the main war roles identified for the HCT to perform), the British administrations were generally ambivalent towards South Africa and its influence upon 'their' territories. They insisted therefore that HCT troops bear arms, despite Union alarm at the prospect of 'black armies' on its borders and the common settler fear that training a man for war meant training him for violence. Rita Headrick writes that HCT troops were 'not trained for combat probably out of respect for South African feeling'. Although it is true that HCT troops were never considered for infantry duties, this was not because of their proximity to the Union, but because African infantrymen were more sensibly drawn from long-established infantry regiments like the King's African Rifles. With scant regard for Union racial sensitivities, HCT troops were mixed with white units and employed in Palestine, although Union authorities considered the Arab–Jew conflict unfit for African eyes. Most importantly, particularly for their own self-image, they were armed, trained to fight, and proud. Charles Arden Clarke, Resident Commissioner of Bechuanaland at the start of the war and Basutoland at the end of it, was anxious that the HCT be seen as 'shop windows' of enlightened British rule juxtaposed against the more illiberal rule of a white minority in South Africa. Given this, the HCT administrations were keen for their men to be treated as imperial soldiers, in marked contrast to the unarmed men of the NMC who were treated as little more than labourers and menial servants.

In considering the actions of the kings and chiefs of the High Commission Territories during the Second World War, the pejorative word 'collaboration' must be eschewed. The calculated moves of the chiefs were aimed at political gain, 'insurance premiums' against the possibility of transfer to South Africa. In Bechuanaland the war was in no conceivable way the prelude to decolonization, and the chiefs, ineluctably led by Tshekedi Khama and Bathoen II, sent their men to war in the hope of preventing a British withdrawal from their land. Had the chiefs acted in concert and refused to send men to the army, then they could not have been compelled to do so. The Bechuanaland administration lacked the means to coerce effectively, and could never have allowed the Union government the pleasure of seeing open compulsion used against Bechuanaland's 'natives', especially after Colonel Rey and Rear Admiral Evans' risible escapade with the Royal Marines in 1933, when a naval detachment towed artillery pieces all the way from Cape Town to preside over a deposition ceremony after Chief Tshekedi Khama had allegedly flogged a white man. The guns became stuck in the Kalahari sands, and members of the tribe they were supposed to intimidate had had to help drag them out.

Desperate to send men to war in pursuit of their own political ends, Tshekedi and Bathoen came up with a proposal to pay for the raising and training of over 1,000 men for the war effort. In a letter to the Resident Commissioner they made their feelings known:

> The Chiefs of the Bechuanaland Protectorate together with their people have desired from the outbreak of hostilities to take their full share in Britain's War Effort and immediately tendered their services . . . We are unhappy to note that whilst other territories are making all efforts for the successful prosecution of the war, by placing men and munitions at the disposal of the British Government and British Crown, we have not taken our full share in this fight for World domination by Germany.[46]

But according to the imperial government, there was still no military role for the High Commission Territories at this stage, and the Bechuanaland administration could not allow the tail to wag the dog. Bechuanaland had to fit into the orchestrated war plans of the Empire as defined by London. In 1941 Chief Moremi, also keen to send men to war, pleaded that the people of Ngamiland be allowed to join the newly-established African Pioneer Corps. Considered to be 'tropical' Africans and therefore unfit for service in cold climates, Moremi offered his men despite the increased risk of disease: 'We ask that we should be permitted to join the Corps, even if we are going to face death. We know that we will be a diseased Corps, and that there will be a lot of death amongst us.' The administration fully understood why the chiefs were almost falling over themselves to get men into British army uniforms. Forsyth Thompson wrote in 1943 that 'there is little doubt that the political implications of their contribution to the war in men and money looms large in the minds of the Chiefs and Councillors, led by Tshekedi . . . Their attitude, as I understand it, is this: the more we can place the Imperial Government under an obligation to us the harder will it be for them to hand us over to the Union'.

A further key to understanding the chiefs enthusiasm for the war effort is the fact that the territory's two most powerful chiefdoms — the Bangwato and the Bangwaketse — were 'at peace' with the local British administration. In the 1930s, there had been constant feuding between the administration and these powerful African polities, fuelled by the then Resident Commissioner Charles Rey's desire to assert his authority over the chiefs, and, in turn, the desire of these still-powerful chiefs to thwart his designs. Their disputes with Charles Rey in no way signalled a weakening of their devotion to the imperial link, but rather their willingness to challenge the policies of the colonial administration when they impinged upon their power. The relationship established between Rey's successor as Resident Commissioner in 1937, Charles Arden-Clarke, and Tshekedi Khama was pivotal in closing the breach that had marred relations between the chiefs and the British. Arden-Clarke realized that Rey's problem, and the reason for the political impasse of the 1930s, lay in his relationship with Tshekedi, and promptly took remedial action. At peace with the Bangwato and the Bangwaketse, the administration had little to fear from the chiefs during the war years.

Another motive behind the chiefs support was that they saw recruitment for the army in particular, and the war effort in general, as a means of re-establishing control over the labour of their people. Before the war their lack of control over men migrating to work in South Africa had greatly concerned the chiefs and the administration. Even though the British exhorted the chiefs to encourage people to go to the mines to help the war effort, they were reluctant to comply, and British officials evinced a good deal of ambivalence on the subject. Their difficulty in maintaining tribal restraints among migrating labourers worried the chiefs; along with the administration, they were caught on the horns of one of Bechuanaland's greatest historical dilemmas. Whilst deploring the social effects of migration and the threat to chiefly power entailed by men drifting beyond tribal control, the money earned by mine workers formed the greatest part of central (i.e. British administration) revenue and Native Administration (i.e. the tribal headquarters of the eight chiefs) revenue.

Repeatedly throughout the war chiefs asked the administration to obtain permission for them to travel to the mines to address their men, ostensibly to get them, especially those who had fled from military recruitment, to join the army. Recruitment was being used in an attempt to reassert chiefly control, to get men home where their disobedience could be dealt with, or to get them into the army where control strategies were easier to devise and maintain. Further, military service was politically more useful to the chiefs than mine work. But repeated requests to the Chamber of Mines for permission for the chiefs to visit the compounds were rejected, as the mine owners jealously guarded their ability to attract Batswana workers. Even during army recruitment drives when mine recruitment was officially suspended, men could simply walk across the border and attest at a 'bolt hole', and this 'largely nullified' the effectiveness of suspending mine recruitment in order to engender African Pioneer Corps enlistment during 1942. The mine owners were quick to point out that given the importance of South African gold and minerals to the Allied war effort, their call upon the men of Bechuanaland was at least as pressing as that of the army.

For Tshekedi Khama, thinking of the Protectorate's long-term future, recruitment was an officially-sanctioned means of exerting control over his people. His desire to demonstrate that the whole country was loyal to the Crown meant that he pushed recruitment hard upon his people, and they were expected to obey. In June 1941 Tshekedi said to the Resident Commissioner: 'I see that some of the Chiefs have some doubts about their followers — if there is any difficulty, I can send more men. My people are eager to go'. Whilst enthusiasm was not uncommon, particularly in 1941, Tshekedi overstated the desire of his people to go to war. He appreciated more keenly than other African leaders the importance of sending signals that would percolate upwards, from a lowly district commissioner on the ground in Africa to the seat of power in distant London. According to three eminent Botswana historians, military recruitment played a part in Tshekedi's political downfall in 1949: 'Tshekedi pushed his people hard and rode roughshod over objections to army recruitment . . . Tshekedi used military recruitment and regimentation to remove rivals and to exert social control over dissident groups.'[47]

The methods of recruitment

Tradition, even if it be invented tradition, was a cornerstone of British rule in Africa and naturally came into play when continent-wide mobilization for a world war was required. District administrations throughout Africa used chiefs and headmen to the greatest extent possible. In South Africa's reserves, chiefs and headmen were considered to have more influence than white Native Commissioners. Senior traditional figures, like the Asantehene in the Gold Coast, publicly supported the call to arms. In Bechuanaland, for example, the chiefs called out communal labour to cultivate the 'warlands', a collective growing and storage programme aimed at food self-sufficiency in order to help the war effort and overcome war-induced shortages. Many African societies, including those of the High Commission Territories, maintained an age-regiment system that could be used to mobilize men and women for military service and communal war-related tasks. Young people were initiated into age-regiments, a rite of passage conferring valuable social knowledge and providing an organized group that could be called upon by a chief to perform tribal services. Rooted in the pre-colonial past, the British felt partially absolved from moral contumely if traditional African practice sanctioned conscription as opposed to volunteerism. Throughout British Africa, methods of recruitment had many similarities, though the HCT stand out as territories in which the traditional chiefly structures were more effective than elsewhere. A number of factors explain this. The Colonial Office was reluctant to approve official conscription and expected very good reasons from any governor who advocated it. Formal conscription (usually resting on an official Labour Ordinance) was used in British Africa where either (a) settlers were able to put sufficient pressure upon the colonial government for the supply of agricultural labour, or (b) vital raw materials or war infrastructure works urgently required local labour. The tin mines in Nigeria (worked by over 100,000 conscripts), 'civil labour' in Kenya (where the settlers had 20,000 Africans conscripted under this heading in 1945), sisal production in Tanganyika (involving over 80,000 people), the naval defence works at Freetown in Sierra Leone, and the air base at Takoradi in the Gold Coast, all required the use of official conscription. But the HCT had neither a powerful settler lobby nor vital indigenous industries or defence installations that warranted official conscription.

Despite the eventual scale of their military participation, in 1939 no military role for the High Commission Territories was envisaged. The HCT war effort was to concentrate upon home front and regional front tasks that would indirectly support the imperial war effort, such as increasing agricultural production, continuing to furnish mine labour for South Africa, and cutting financial dependence upon annual imperial exchequer grants-in-aid. Despite the fact that early in the war a military role for the High Commission Territories was not envisaged, from 1939 people in the HCT wanted more active war participation — so at least said the chiefs, who were held by the British to be representative of the people. The British welcomed the ardent desire of these authorities to get their people involved in the war against Adolf Hitler's Germany. In late 1940 Sir Eric Machtig, Permanent Under-Secretary of State at the Dominions Office, told the High Commissioner in Pretoria about 'much evidence from correspondence from Basutoland that the Basuto were anxious to take a more active part in the war' and were distressed at not being allowed to do so. In Britain, a headline in *The Times* read 'Basuto Offer Army to Britain'.

When a military role for the HCT finally materialized in 1941, the edifice of traditional authority — the chiefs and their subordinates — was called into action. In Basutoland and Swaziland recruitment was carried out by the order of the Paramount Chief. In Bechuanaland, the basis of traditional mobilization was the call of the chiefs for the turning out of age-regiments for service to the tribe. Paramount Chief Sobhuza II sent war messengers to all Swazi chiefs and charged them with the responsibility of furnishing men, as well as accounting for absentees. Subordinate chiefs were anxious to court the favour of their superiors. Though officially the British did not countenance compulsion, they turned a blind eye as African leaders obtained men in traditional ways; thus, the weight of recruitment was borne by the traditional structure, not the colonial authorities. With minimal support and encouragement from district commissioners and a handful of army recruitment officers, the African leaders produced recruits. In late 1943 the three resident commissioners and the High Commissioner considered the practicability of replacing soldiers coming home on leave with new recruits. The Basutoland National Council was adamant that conscription was the only fair way. According to Resident Commissioner Charles Arden Clarke, 'voluntary recruitment' did not exist, only, as he unequivocally described it, 'compulsion, naked and unashamed'.

The effectiveness of traditional recruitment methods in the HCT can be attributed to a number of factors. First, the three territories were *protectorates*, not colonies, in which the British presence had developed through the request of indigenous powers for protection from neighbouring African and European states, rather than through British conquest of arms. Because of this, power-sharing was a foundation of colonial rule and shaped the British–African political relationship until independence in the 1960s. Inevitably this power dynamic informed the way in which the protectorates were mobilized for war. British rule in the protectorates bolstered the power of the chiefs in relation to their subjects, and depended upon them to provide settled government. Not until the 1930s was any serious attempt made to rein in the autocratic powers of the High Commission Territories' chiefs through legislation in order to bring them more into line with chiefs elsewhere in Africa. The requisite legislation, however, was successfully challenged by the chiefs, who hoped that support for the war effort would remove the prospect of further attempts to limit their powers. So, come the Second World War, chiefly power remained effective, more so than in colonies where the power of chiefs had been consistently undermined by colonial rule. Men like Sobhuza II in Swaziland and Tshekedi Khama in Bechuanaland remained, as far as their people were concerned, as powerful as 'little gods'.

Beyond the small coterie of councillors, royals and educated people, few Batswana had any idea about how their services had been provisionally committed before news of military recruitment burst into village homes and *dikgotla* in 1941. Because of the consultation that had already taken place between the chiefs and the administration, Bechuanaland was speedily able to assent to the request of General Sir Claude Auchinleck, Commander-in-Chief Middle East from July 1941, for soldiers to help bolster Britain's parlous position in the Middle East. Within six months 5,500 men had been recruited, trained and dispatched, a remarkable feat for a territory with no experience of large-scale recruitment and no existing military formation to draw upon. So the situation changed; at the start of the war, the War Cabinet envisaged no military role for the Southern African colonies, though in 1941 it became apparent that a significant military contribution was desirable. What had changed everything was the arrival of Rommel in Africa, and the expansion of the responsibilities of Middle East Command to meet an increasingly challenging war situation in Africa, the Mediterranean, and the Middle East.

The administrations' attitude to the method of recruitment was ambiguous. Sensitive to taunts of coercion or conscription in a war of 'freedom' versus 'tyranny', the Dominions Secretary insisted that all men be volunteers. This fiction was dutifully maintained in Bechuanaland and in many other parts of British Africa. In effect, it meant turning a blind eye while chiefs exercised their customary power over the labour of their people. The chiefs were the only medium through which recruitment could be attempted as they possessed real and effective powers little fettered at the local level by British rule. It is too simplistic, however, to see the chiefs' order for men to join the army as a sign of 'exploitation' for, as many Africans in the High Commission Territories believed, and as the chiefs maintained, it was their traditional right to call their people, especially when their interests were threatened, as they were by German aggression during the war. British defeat would have entailed either German or Boer rule. Asking for volunteers rather than conscripts created a dilemma, for traditionally a chief did not ask for volunteers; he told people to perform a duty and they were expected to obey. As the old men still say, this was Setswana custom. In 1941 the District Commissioner at Molepolole wrote to the Government Secretary about the progress of recruitment in the Bakwena Reserve, sympathetically reporting Chief Kgari's disapproval of voluntary recruitment: 'Every one of the headmen dislikes the idea of calling for volunteers, even the young men have grumbled about it to me. They say that the Chief should call the men who are to go and that Voluntary Service is absolutely unknown to the Bakwena.' Selebatso Masimega of the Bakwena still speaks with the voice of traditional authority on the subject: 'Regimental service is compulsory. When a regiment is called by the chief to perform a duty it is a matter of no one has to resist, if that man resists he must be punished. It is a law. When a regiment is called the Batswana believe it is by the orders of the law. The chief has the right to issue such an order.'

The anxiety of the Dominions Secretary in London concerning 'camouflage conscription' could not be squared with the facts of life on the ground in Africa. As the Resident Commissioner of Bechuanaland told his staff before the 1942 recruiting drive, 'it has how been agreed that Native Authorities may continue to utilize their customary powers for obtaining recruits. . . but care must be taken to ensure that these powers are not abused'. But with a tiny administrative establishment already severely reduced by the war and with a constantly overstretched police force, the chances of abuses being detected were slim. During the recruitment drive of 1941 the role of British officials was very much that of back up for the chiefs; a few rousing speeches, a little pomp and circumstance, and in the weaker chiefdoms a lot of cajolery in the *dikgotla*. When the call came, the Resident Commissioner embarked upon a tour of all the main villages, to explain in open *kgotla* the need for men. At these dramatic *kgotla* and *letsholo* meetings, the assembled men would be addressed by their chief, the local district commissioner and sometimes by a military recruitment officer. The object was to impress upon the men the fact that their protector King George was calling for help, and that it was their duty to respond favourably in order to reciprocate for the protection afforded them since the reign of Queen Victoria. Hitler was portrayed as an evil oppressor, and the Axis presence in East and North Africa was highlighted. A threat to the territorial integrity of Bechuanaland itself was also suggested. The Batswana had a historical memory of previous hostilities against Germans and Boers. In 1940, for example, an accidental though massive railway explosion at Foley Bridge in the Bangwato Reserve was widely believed to have been due to enemy bombing.

During the recruitment drive of 1942 the Resident Commissioner again toured the Protectorate accompanied by the chiefs. The entourage included the Bechuana Drum and Bugle Band, army-trained musicians who marched in formation wearing leopard skins, and an epidiascope so that pictures of the war and of the Batswana then participating in it could be widely seen. As elsewhere in Africa, propaganda value was derived from films, marching men and military bands. Such techniques certainly stimulated great interest in the villages, and encouraged social pressure to be put upon men to join. In 1942, the bottom of Bechuanaland's manpower barrel was scraped in order to raise another 5,000 men for the Army. As the Resident Commissioner wrote in August 1942, 'the spirit of loyalty and the desire to help is stronger than ever, but all say that there are no more men . . . Tshekedi said that he was doing his best against his better judgement, since he was denuding his country of men'. Revealing figures from the Bangwato reserve for the recruitment campaign between August and October 1942 show how the extra men were found. Of 1,869 recruits, 841 were returning mine workers, 556 were previous medical rejects, 216 were previously unreleased by Tshekedi, and 256 were fresh recruits.

A number of discernible factors accounted for the success or failure of recruitment. It depended upon people's proximity to a chief or headman, and whether that chief or headman was weak or strong, enthusiastic about recruitment or not. It also depended upon their proximity to the South African border across which they could move unhindered to avoid recruitment, and to geographical features like the Okavango swamps or remote Kalahari bush, where they could hide. Strong and enthusiastic chiefs and headmen such as Tshekedi Khama and Rasebolai Kgamane (his representative in the Bokalaka district), recruited successfully. N. Khama of Serowe remembered that 'men went to please Tshekedi, whose word was law'. Bangwato 'passivity and obedience might have been due to Tshekedi's firm hold over his people'. In some notable cases recruitment was used by the chiefs to assert their authority over 'recalcitrant' subject communities, like the Mswazwi people of the Bangwato Reserve, the Balete of Gabane in the Bakwena Reserve and the Herero of the Batawana Reserve.

Resistance or indifference towards recruitment was more likely to be encountered among such subject communities, or where disobedient headmen held sway as in Lentsweletau, where Headman Kgosidintsi sent only four men to Molepolole to be attested, arguing that the needs of domestic agriculture took precedence over the call to arms. Unenthusiastic headmen sometimes needed a visitation from their chief. In September 1942 Chief Bathoen toured the Bakwena Reserve, and according to the District Commissioner Kanye, 'at Ranaka, Kika and Manyana he trounced the Headmen and men and women present for the response to the call for men. The duty of women to knit was also stressed'. After speaking, Bathoen read out a list of names of those who were to present themselves in Kanye for medical inspection, 'these being men the Headmen admitted were hiding close to the village'. Supervising the call up, village and ward headmen were supposed to see that enough men remained to continue essential tasks like ploughing and cattle rearing, and to avoid taking more men than a family could spare. Though evidence on this point is negligible, the pivotal role of headmen must have presented ample opportunity for patronage to be extended or withheld.

Recruitment, in theory at least, was done in age-regiments. A chief would name a regiment and order it to present itself at the *kgotla*. Men would then be expected to have a medical inspection, and if fit, to attest for the army. In more populous reserves this system worked properly, especially where the regimental system was commonly used in peace time and the chief was strong, but in the smaller reserves men often failed to present themselves. In line with traditional concepts of seniority and maturity the older regiment were called up first, like the Bangwato regiment Masokolo. This regiment had been 'built' in 1911, so the men would have been around fifty years of age in 1941. The District Surgeon at Kanye wrote that 'some of the older men (even fifty and on up towards sixty) were very anxious to go'. As Molatlhwe remembers, 'if you were under forty it was thought that you were not mature'. The rate of medical rejection was high.

Methods other than verbal reasoning and the appeal to tradition could be used to stimulate recruitment, from social pressure to physical compulsion. Those who did not want to go to war and who had no mitigating reason such as ill health, were liable to encounter social pressure from people who believed in the duty of a man to obey his chief and his King, especially those who had relatives already serving. District commissioners even encouraged this in areas where recruiting was unsuccessful. The District Commissioner at Gaberones reported in March 1942 that 'the matter has been kept before the Chief and I have spoken in *kgotla* and to the dependants of the men who have joined the Pioneer Corps urging them to act like women in the last war who had nothing to do with slackers'.

Chief Matlala of the Batlokwa denounced his son publicly in the *kgotla* at Tlokweng for refusing to join the army and threatened to deprive him of his inheritance. Another man was fined for refusing to go. The District Commissioner at Gaberones reported in July 1941 that 'the Batlokwa have thought better of their refusal to join the Bechuanaland Protectorate African Auxiliary Pioneer Corps'. A tradition of free migration between Bechuanaland and South Africa largely accounts for the failure of the chiefs in the tiny south eastern reserves such as the Batlokwa Reserve to get their men to join the army. An even greater degree of coercion was met by a few men, though evidence of punitive action taken by chiefs or headmen is difficult to find. This does not mean, however, that it did not occur; the District Commissioner at Maun reported that some men recruited from Ngamiland had been 'grossly abused' in the process. In October 1941 the District Commissioner at Gaberones received a complaint after two of L. S. Glover's employees had been snatched for the army by the men of Chief Kgari Sechele. Such coercion, however, appears to have been rare and oral testimonies reveal no tradition of widespread resistance or rancour arising from the recruitment process.

Reasons other than the use of Labour Ordinances or the traditional demands of chiefs account for the large numbers of Africans joining the army. The proscription of other forms of employment could be used to increase military recruitment. A second army recruitment drive in the HCT in 1942 saw the suspension of recruitment for the South African mines, the main destination for HCT labour migrants and, through their wages, the main source of HCT revenue. This manipulation of the labour supply had to be used with caution; in the HCT, it was simple enough for men to cross the border and attest. Likewise, when the authorities in Nyasaland banned labour migration to increase King's African Rifles recruitment, South Africa and Southern Rhodesia protested and threatened to ignore the ban.

In the High Commission Territories, unlike the colonies of East and Central Africa, there were no painful memories of the Carrier Corps to prevent Africans from volunteering. The African Pioneer Corps and the East African Military Labour Service did not recruit in Nyasaland because, Timothy Parsons claims, the bitter experiences of the Carrier Corps would have led to significant resistance. Following economic instinct, however, some Nyasaland men joined the High Commission Territories African Pioneer Corps and the South African Native Military Corps, where good rates of pay obtained. Though not subject to peacetime military recruitment, the HCT were experienced labour migration societies, used to funnelling men from rural homes to the urban heartlands of South Africa. Subsequently, the territories had adapted to coping with the absence of a huge proportion of their male population. The HCT administrations were not as politically constrained as some colonial governments in making manpower decisions. The lack of urban and industrial areas in the High Commission Territories lessened fears of rural–urban drain and meant that potentially awkward factors in industrial relations, such as the views of settlers or trades unions, were not in play. The HCT did not experience the level of state intervention in the economy witnessed elsewhere in British Africa, resulting in less disruption of people's lives. Unlike colonies such as Nigeria and Kenya, no critical educated elite maintained links with sympathetic British Members of Parliament, and no indigenous press hounded the British administrations and debated war policy. The HCT contained no vital military bases, strategic raw material deposits, or essential industries, the existence of which would have made the manpower tightrope that much more difficult to navigate. Perhaps most significantly, the HCT had no powerful settler communities, unlike Kenya, where the war greatly augmented the settlers' political power as the colonial administration conceded ground in its pursuit of total mobilization.

Throughout Africa the press, radio, posters, and films were used in recruitment propaganda. South Africa's media and communications network was more sophisticated than that in most parts of Africa, though the war gave a boost to modern media techniques across the continent. Recruitment was supported by the official tours of governors, chiefs, army recruitment officers, military bands, and uniformed troops on leave. In a contemporary newsletter, Sergeant E. Mohapeloa of 1902 Basuto Company Brass Band recalled the music that had drawn him to the army, using language that, if the editor had considered its implications, he might have hesitated to print: 'Many of our young men were spirited away by the deadly rhythm of that band, and before they knew it they found themselves in the Army.'

Some Africans were attracted to military life by ideas and sentiments common all over the world: the quest for adventure, the appeal of soldierly paraphernalia, curiosity, boredom, unemployment, and peer pressure. The army offered prestige, care, and the healthy effects of military life. Some men, such as in Kenya, were motivated by the fear of enemy invasion. Others were influenced at least partially by notions of loyalty to King and Empire, perhaps hoping for improvements in colonial political and economic conditions after the war. In East Africa many desired to defend Emperor Haile Selassie of Ethiopia, victim of Italy's aggressive conquest in 1935–36. Recruitment propaganda in the HCT used the semi-mythical notion that, long after her death, Queen Victoria protected the people of the HCT from South African land grabs and political oppression, and that therefore reciprocation could be legitimately called for in the form of war service. A colonial official wrote that in Basutoland Queen Victoria was 'almost a Goddess'.

Throughout Africa, personal economic reasons were a major factor in recruitment. In exploding the colonial myth of the 'martial race' — the military aptitude of certain African tribes — Parsons writes convincingly of the 'political economy of recruitment'. He links the army's popularity in Kenyan reserves to its remunerative rewards and the lack of competitive alternative employment: 'The extent to which Africans found military service lucrative and appealing largely determined the level of

145

coercion needed to secure recruits'. He claims that because of a surplus of recruits in Kenya, the 'government rarely had to conscript Africans for combat or specialist units', even for the least prestigious military services like the African Pioneer Corps and the East African Military Labour Service. The push–pull factor was the same for both military recruitment and labour migration; for example, many of South Africa's 80,000 NMC recruits came from the Northern Transvaal, where agricultural conditions were particularly poor.

Most High Commission Territories' troops, especially those from the 1941 recruitment drive, were enthusiastic or at least acquiescent recruits. This usually meant that although they had not actually volunteered, they had not resisted the order of a chief or headman to present themselves. Some chiefs were simply not to be disobeyed, and men did exactly as they were told; for example, 'in Serowe [Tshekedi Khama's capital] they were put inside the big kraal at the *kgotla* [chief's court] and told they were to go to war'. In the Matsekheng Ward in Basutoland's Berea District some chiefs actually threatened to confiscate livestock and land if men did not join up. Elsewhere in this ward, a *pitso* meeting for recruitment held at the District Commissioner's office in Teyateyaneng involved free beer and the singing of war songs, including the simulated trampling of Hitler, as a crude but effective recruitment technique.

Families might try to stop men from heeding the call to arms, as other agencies tried to dissuade them. In Swaziland, Afrikaner farmers spread rumours about the horrors of army life to try to stop potential farm hands joining up. In Basutoland, French Canadian Roman Catholic missionaries discouraged recruitment and attacked the territory's colonial administration. Every soldier had a tale to tell about how he came to join the army. Sixteen-year-old Julius Segano lied about his age in order to join up, whilst others hid when recruiters were in the area, sustained at night by relatives who pretended to be calling livestock to feed. Some men were simply grabbed, as subordinate chiefs sought to fill their quotas. This practice was thoroughly unacceptable to the British authorities, but such was the substance and vigour of African–African power relations *beneath* the British line of vision, that such practices rarely came to their attention. Chiefs insisted that they had the right to enlist their men for the defence of their land and people, and that asking for volunteers was alien to customary practice. Hamilton Simelane labels the 1941 recruitment drive the 'triumph of tradition', but identifies 1942 as the 'time of coercion', as finding men became more difficult. Many potential recruits believed that the soldiers of the earlier draft had all died, and that they were being asked to face a similar fate.

Responses of the people

Most men summoned to war heeded the call, willing volunteers or reluctant obedients. Though compulsion was a factor in recruitment, the image of tens of thousands of hapless men being dragged off to military camps by chiefly minions is inaccurate. Over 10,000 men from the Bechuanaland Protectorate joined the African Pioneer Corps, a further 700 joined the South African Native Military Corps, the latter all being volunteers, and 3,500 joined the post-war High Commission Territories Corps. Basutoland recruited 21,463 for the African Pioneer Corps, 2,000 for the Native Military Corps, and 4,000 for the High Commission Territories Corps. Swaziland recruited over 3,500 Pioneers. Fear of the unknown was a common reason for not wanting to go to war, as well as the possibility of death. How could the Batswana, rural people unused to modern warfare, be expected to fight the dreaded Hitler and *Majermane*? As Robert Kgasa recalls, when war was discussed by the people of Kanye, 'some people were saying, "No we can't go to war. What are we going to fight for? How can we fight? Do you know how to handle a gun?"' Not aware of the distinctions between front line and base areas, combat duties and labour duties, these were fair questions to pose. People's knowledge of the war, its methods, causes and geography, was extremely vague, if it existed at all. For nearly two years the war had been distant, and local manifestations like tax increases and the introduction of the communal food growing scheme known as the warlands did little to bring the prospect of fighting closer.

Reasons for attestation were numerous. Some went for the money, perhaps intent upon raising sufficient capital to afford bridewealth and get married. Excitement and enthusiasm, especially when buoyed along by one's friends and relatives, was common, as was curiosity, adventurism and a desire for the accoutrements of soldiering, including firearms. Despite the sensitivity of the Union government and its military establishment on the subject of 'black armies', it was indicative of the power of the kings and chiefs in Basutoland, Bechuanaland, and Swaziland that the men of the High Commission Territories were to carry rifles. Many viewed the whole thing with indifference and resignation. People in the territory's remote areas often failed to understand what all the fuss was about. The Resident Commissioner noted on a visit to Ngamiland in 1940 that 'some people in the Reserve do not understand. They don't know what Government is and why anybody is fighting at all'.

Interviews provide an insight into the recruitment of soldiers as

147

remembered by elderly Batswana and allow some penetration of the realm of individual motivation — 'the private reasons why' — as Colley entitles an illuminating section on recruitment for the Napoleonic Wars in her book *Britons*. Robert Kgasa recalled a discussion about recruitment at the *kgotla* in Kanye:

> At a recruiting meeting Chief Bathoen said: 'Hey, look. I'm doing this because His Majesty is at war with Germany and they're going to beat the whole world. And what are we doing about it? We should have our young men join the Army'. It wasn't forced on people. But some were scared of this and ran away. They said, 'We are going to die'. Those who understood, like me, we are volunteering. Some were forced to go: 'Your own regiment has left. Why are you here? You must go!'

Selogwe Pilane recalls the call to arms among the Bakgatla:

> We heard in 1939 that the Germans were starting a war. The chiefs were told by the district commissioners. The Chiefs told us this in a *kgotla* meeting . . . This was just to inform us. They said the Government had not yet made a decision as to whether we would be involved, but that we should be ready to go at short notice, and that each person should do what they can to help the war effort . . . There was then another meeting at the *kgotla* — last one. The Chief stood up and asked the people, 'Where are we? Are we still under Britain?'. The people responded, 'Yes!'. 'But the war has started', the Chief declared, 'and as you said, we are under the English. Men, you are going to war. Hitler is indignant, and the war is at its height'. That time we were under the English. They governed this land and they needed help. We were like their child that goes if its parent sends it. Also, the English had been helping us against the Boers, so it would be unfair for us to deny them our assistance.

Julius Segano, a Morolong from Lobatsi and one of the youngest men from Bechuanaland to go to war, offered a personal account of why he enlisted:

> Well, as a young man, you know young people are always enthusiastic, so now we just saw soldiers around, marching, and we were very much impressed and we said to ourselves we would like to join. That time I was sixteen years old so I was not qualified to join. However I insisted

148

and then my parents said, 'Well, at least try to finish your Standard 6 at school'. So it was December, I remember well 1st December 1942 that I joined the army here at Lobatsi. I was not in any way forced like some of our tribes when the chiefs got them to join — we are in a detribalized place [Lobatsi was a town and was not subject to the rule of a powerful tribal chief] so I was just attracted to join because we found it to be thrilling. No one who joined from here was forced.

A boy would like to show he's a man. I didn't think that to be a soldier was a risky life. I didn't think about fighting and that I might be killed. I didn't entertain those thoughts in my mind. My father didn't in any way try to discourage me from service. My first Sunday after having joined the army, I put on my boots and everything, and found it to be a very good Sunday for me because I heard the church ringing the first bells, and thought I'd only go when the congregation was in, and then I'll *march*, with my boots you know, on the floor. So then each and every person in there can look at me!

After completing their training at the Lobatsi military camp, the first companies of soldiers returned to their villages to bid farewell to their friends and families and to be officially dispatched by their chief, but also to show the remaining males what army life did for a man. In September 1941 the first Bangwato company returned to Serowe, where they attended a church service in their honour. The Witwatersrand Native Labour Association's band added to the occasion, as did a 'torchlight procession' and a 'European dance'. Such spectacles stimulated voluntary enlistment, or mollified resistance to the idea of military service. Kgasa recalls returning briefly to Kanye with his company and the sense of pride that went with being a soldier: 'We were so excited, and we were not afraid. We were allowed to return for a day to say goodbye to our people. We didn't have one single man who absconded'.

Selogwe Pilane remembers:

There was a lot of rejoicing as we left, the whole village came to see us go, and they sang for us and praised us . . . When we were leaving an old man called Moloi stood up and told those who were going to war — and his words were true — 'This, the *kgotla* of Kgamanyane, Lentswe I's father, has laid the foundation. This too is the *kgotla* of Lentswe I who was built on that foundation. Their hearts are with you as you go'. From there we left, and were not afraid at all.

Alongside government officials, chiefs, councillors and military personnel, the clergymen of the London Missionary Society helped encourage and sanction military service. Traditional doctors and Setswana medicines were also very important in providing comfort and reassurance to men going off into the unknown. Masimega recalls:

> The administration of traditional medicine is usually done. The ritual was performed for every group going away. It is done on the basis of a ritual done when the regiment is built. It is ritual doctoring. There is one *pheko* [a charm or potion] that first goes to the most senior man. It may be sprinkled on the person, or taken. Here I remember old man Jacobus Kgari, renowned for such rituals, administered charms. The Batswana believe that under such pheko one will be lucky and safe from being hurt.

Men who did not want to join the army hid in various places, some displaying greater ingenuity than others, using the natural advantages for concealment afforded by geographical features like the Okavango Delta. Some men stayed deep in the bush at their cattle posts, and just waited; if they were to go to war, someone would have to come and find them. Others hid in their homes, or dug holes when recruiters were about. Kwatle Makati of Metsimotlhabe hid inside the hut of a woman and her newly-born child. The door was barred with sticks, for it was considered taboo for men to enter during a woman's confinement. His wife, recalling the experience with him, teased him about being a coward and running away. Sometimes a man's reluctance to join the army was due to quite obscure reasoning; Molatlhwe recalls that some men in Gabane 'heard that when they were there [in the army] they would not pay tax. They thus concluded that a person who did not pay tax was a dead person'. Discord between those who had supported recruitment and those who had not is still evident today. Miriam Pilane said: 'If I was a man, I would have been the first to go, unlike those who behaved like pigs and frightened horses running around hiding — cowards! We knew that the war was ours.' Selogwe Pilane also recalls the behaviour of men in Mochudi who did not want to go to war:

> If men were needed to look after cows, their parents would appeal to the chief, and the chief would say, 'Okay they can stay'. Those that didn't want to go for their own reasons would go and hide in the bush, and be fed under the cover of darkness by their parents . . . At first a lot of people were willing, and many even came from the cattle posts and volunteered themselves, saying, 'Here we are, we want to go and fight'.

It was only later on that people started trying to avoid being enlisted. They would go into the bush, in the hills, with an animal skin over them. When a man heard his wife walking through the bush saying, 'Oo-keyo, keyo', he would know that she was looking for him and he would make some bird sound in reply. He would then climb down to get the food she had brought him.

In Basutoland there was evidence of self-inflicted wounds in order to prevent enlistment (perhaps the pulling of teeth) or the faking of lunacy, as was also the case among members of The Mauritius Regiment intent on avoiding overseas service (see chapter 9).

Robert Kgasa recalls that 'some who ran were recaptured and sent. We used to call them meerkats, because when it sees you it stands up like that, and then runs into a hole! Some men went to South Africa to work and stayed there to avoid being recruited. In July 1942 the District Commissioner at Maun, reporting on a tour of Ngamiland, noted that 'most of the young men have already left to the swamps'.

Even men already in the army could contest their recruitment. In November 1941 the anticolonial Lekhotla-la-Bafo movement in Basutoland provoked an embarrassing desertion of 1,300 APC recruits from Walker's Camp, leading to the banning of the organization's meetings and the incarceration of its leaders. A red-faced High Commissioner told the Secretary of State for the Dominions that the men had 'gone AWOL . . . and intended to return', as opposed to having 'deserted'. He asserted that the Basotho were 'particularly anxious for military service'. The desertion had been:

Confined to the men newly recruited from the Leribe district and Butha Buthe sub-district (both in the extreme north) where, owing to personal factors, political situation is normally not so satisfactory as remainder of Basutoland and in consequence subversive activities of Lekhotla-la-Bafo had been more active. The trouble was essentially local in character.

The incident reflects the gulf that could exist between the High Commission Territories' chiefs desire to support the war effort through military recruitment, and that of the men whom they sought to offer in this role.

After having been attested in his village and dispatched to the Pioneer Corps Base Depot training establishment at Lobatsi, a man's knowledge of his conditions or location of service was still negligible. So the prospect of a certain wage or certain conditions could not act as a motivating factor for any of the men. This omission was later to engender much confusion about what the army offered in the way of pensions and gratuities upon demobilization. At the time of recruitment some chiefs and headmen held out the prospect of large rewards, while others, like Tshekedi, said that service was to be voluntary. The scope for speculation was unlimited because of this maladroit approach and still engages the attention and debate of ex-servicemen all over Botswana. However, even arrival at the military training camp did not necessarily end a man's chances of avoiding service if he wanted to. Molatlhwe recalled that 'when a doctor was checking us for the last time at Lobatsi he would ask if you really wanted to go. If you said no, he would write "reject"'. From the Lobatsi military camp the Batswana recruits left by train for Durban, there to meet the ships that were to take them to war.

The British administration of Bechuanaland regarded the war service of the Batswana as a duty, because of the prevalent belief that the British were in Bechuanaland as protectors and the knowledge that the territory was a net drain on the imperial exchequer. The same applied to the other two High Commission Territories. The African elite had one overriding political objective in offering their wholehearted support for the war effort, though other factors, like the cordial relations with the British ushered in by Arden-Clarke's accession, were also important in setting the climate. Though the issue of the transfer of the High Commission Territories to South Africa was not properly interred until the 1960s, the chief's war strategy was effective; at the end of the war even High Commissioner Evelyn Baring believed that Britain was 'morally bound' not to transfer the High Commission Territories to the Union. Unlike other parts of Africa, the elite in Bechuanaland did not attempt to use their war-time efforts as bargaining counters to be exchanged for political concessions towards national independence; they aimed to prolong British rule and reinforce the edifice of traditional authority. The nature of British rule meant that chiefs like Tshekedi and Bathoen were not the expendable bureaucratic appendages of a colonial state, but that their co-operation was essential to the successful outcome of policies like the Protectorate's mobilization for war.

The evidence concerning the other chiefs of the Protectorate is less abundant, though a few observations can be made. Molefi Pilane regained his chieftainship as a direct result of active service and his successful efforts to get the Bakgatla to support the war effort at home and abroad. Kgari Sechele's army service improved his sometimes unenviable reputation with the administration, and earned him respect among the Bakwena people with whom he was anxious to establish his legitimacy. Bathoen reaffirmed his status as the Protectorate's second most important and indispensable chief, and his authority among the Bangwaketse remained undiminished. The unfortunate Moremi never managed to lose his 'bad chief' image and killed himself in an alcohol-related driving accident in 1946.

As for the effects of the war upon the chiefs in relation to their people, it did nothing to weaken their grip on the reins of power or diminish the prestige and authority of office. The fact that no discontent is recorded in the archives or in the memories of people interviewed suggests that whatever hardships the war imposed, they were not sufficient to provoke discontent that escaped the framework of traditional authority and came to the attention of the British. The war's impact upon the home front (price rises, profiteering, a failed communal agriculture scheme, family disruption) was not detrimental enough to create active protest. The ex-servicemen were quickly reabsorbed into their communities and became a conservative rather than a radical force, maintaining no group homogeneity. The mythology surrounding the imperial monarchy, the prestige and authority of the chiefs, together with a host of individual motives, meant that many men went to war without direct compulsion being necessary, just as many women readily supported their chiefs and their husbands and backed the war effort. Yet many others decided to run, hide or ignore, unimpressed by the King's call or the chief's command.

7

The Military Contribution of the High Commission Territories Soldiers during the Second World War

Having seen how soldiers were recruited from the High Commission Territories, this chapter examines the nature of their war service and the range of military tasks they performed. It considers the war situation in the Middle East into which the African soldiers were deployed, the provenance of Pioneer labour in the history of the British Army, and the role of the African Pioneer Corps in the North Africa campaign and the Allied invasion of Southern Europe. The chapter also examines why, reversing the trend in East Africa, High Commission Territories' civil authorities were prepared to allow their troops to be employed in Europe, but not in the Far East (where 120,000 East and West African colonial troops served in Ceylon, India, and Burma). Attention is drawn to the fact that the HCT troops were not 'just' Pioneers soldiers devoted to rear echelon labour tasks, but were also successfully used to 'dilute' British Heavy Anti-Aircraft (HAA) gun batteries and specialist service and fighting branches (like mountain regiments) in order to release white troops for the Allied invasion of France in 1944. The recruitment, utilization, and demobilization of African soldiers represented an outstanding success on the part of military authorities in the war zones and civil authorities back in the colonies. The military contribution of the Empire was part of a quite remarkable imperial war effort that provided a never-to-be-repeated lesson in the art of metropolitan mobilization of an empire's resources.

War in the Middle East and Europe and the provenance of the Pioneer Corps

Perhaps the most valuable military contribution of the colonial empire to the war effort was its provision of the military labour force upon which imperial troops fighting in the Middle East and southern Europe depended. By early 1941 the British had won spectacular victories in Abyssinia, Libya, and Somaliland, destroying Italy's military forces and imperial ambitions in North Africa. Yet these bold early successes were overshadowed in February 1941 by the arrival in Africa of General Erwin Rommel and the Afrika Korps. The British proved unable to hold onto the spoils of their early victories largely because of the distractions of the Greece and Crete operations in April and May 1941 that led to the diminution of the hitherto victorious Eighth Army (previously the Western Desert Force, or in Churchill's more romantic and evocative language, the Army of the Nile). The stage was set for the titanic desert struggle that seesawed across Egypt, Libya, and Tunisia and that eventually — after many thrusts, counter thrusts, and false dawns — went decisively the British way after the second battle of El Alamein in October 1942. The massive Anglo-American 'Torch' landings in Morocco and Algeria in November 1942 opened an Allied front squeezing Rommel from the west as the Eighth Army pressed in from the east, and in May 1943 Axis forces were finally ejected from Africa. Thereafter, the Allied focus shifted to the invasion of southern Europe via Sicily. With the arrival of American forces in the Mediterranean theatre in late 1942, British African Pioneer Corps labour began to support the new ally, and thus American forces benefited directly from the recruitment of over 100,000 troops from Britain's African and Indian Ocean colonies. Colonial soldiers of the Pioneer Corps were an integral part of all of this action, Mauritians, for example, forming part of the Eighth Army's order of battle from the day of its creation.

The British army that fought these battles was a truly imperial army, comprising Indian, New Zealand, Australian, British, and South African infantry and armoured divisions (as well as Poles, Greeks, and Free French). What is seldom realized, and omitted from all major histories of the Desert War, is that a host of lesser-known imperial territories provided the soldiers that made up the military labour force supporting them. The fact that this force of over 100,000 men has become a ghost army is a ringing indictment of the unbalanced memory of the war that has developed, and confirms the need to stress the role played by colonies in British imperial warfare. Egypt, particularly the Suez Canal Zone, was the British Empire's main military base and the 'largest military complex of its kind'. Middle East Command (MEC) covered a vast area bristling with threats to British territories and strategic interests. Within the ambit of MEC there were enemy threats to British East Africa, to Egypt and the vital Suez Canal, to the oil of Arabia, to the eastern Mediterranean, and to the Balkans. Middle East Command had to contend with the Vichy French position in Syria, German influence in Turkey and Iraq, and Axis operations against Greece and Crete. The Middle East region was also vital for the transportation of Lend-Lease supplies to the Soviet Union via the Persian Gulf.

The crucial function of 'supplying war' was that to which the HCT troops contributed through service in the African Pioneer Corps (APC), created as part of the Royal Pioneer Corps (RPC) specifically to recruit Africans. The fact that 'supplying war' — the vital role of logistics — is such an unfashionable branch of military history has compounded the reasons for the colonial soldiers being forgotten in the popular, and even the scholarly, memory of the war. Colonial Pioneers, supplemented by civilian and prisoner-of-war labour units, kept armies like the British Eighth and American Fifth in the fight. HCT troops recruited into the APC were often farmed out to other service branches of the British Army like the Royal Army Service Corps, the Royal Army Medical Corps, and even — through a policy known as dilution — to military branches like the Royal Artillery. Without the army service branches and the labour muscle provided by Pioneers, fighting could not have been sustained; in the British– Canadian 21st Army Group in France in August 1944 only 56 percent of the troops were fighting men; the other 44 percent belonged to the service branches. Of the 660,000 personnel involved, only 14 percent were infantry soldiers. Ten percent alone were from the RPC.

In the Desert War the issue of supply hampered all commanders. In making dashes across the desert, their effectiveness depended on the ability of service branches of the army to keep them supplied with food, fuel, water, and ammunition. As the distance between fighting units and supply bases increased, supply lines tautened, and supply dumps in the open desert had to be established. Egypt had no railway beyond Mersa Matruh, and the only road ran along the coast. Therefore Mediterranean ports like Tobruk, Benghazi, and Tripoli were great prizes, for they enabled the occupying army to receive supplies by sea. HCT troops worked these ports on many occasions, and along with other imperial Pioneers were the carriers of the supplies that kept the infantry and the armour fighting, and salvaged the planes of the Western Desert Air Force and removed them to the cavernous repair factories supporting the imperial war effort and located in Cairo.

Pioneers were the essential labour force of the British Army, mentioned as early as 1346 in the Muster of Pay Rolls of the British Garrison at Calais. A Labour Corps was formally raised during the First World War, when a Labour Directorate was formed 'to co-ordinate the demand for labour and apportioning the available labour as the tactical situation demanded'. Infantry battalions were converted to form the British element of the Corps, and foreign and imperial manpower was mobilized. By 1918, there were 80,000 British Pioneers and 1,500,000 foreign nationals and imperial subjects. The Corps badge was 'a rifle, a shovel and a pick "piled" on them a laurel wreath, all ensigned with a crown. Beneath, the motto *Labor Omnia Vincit* [Work Conquers All]'. The Corps was disbanded in 1919, as 'no nation could afford in peacetime the luxury of a regular Corps of unskilled labour in its Order of Battle'.

The huge demands on imperial manpower made by the Second World War led to the most elaborate logistical arrangements in British military history, including, not surprisingly, the revival of the labour corps and the use of civilian labour on a truly epic scale. In October 1939 Army Order 200 established the Auxiliary Military Pioneer Corps (AMPC), initially formed as a combatant corps. In August 1940 a Directorate of Labour was created under the Quartermaster General's Department with the task of allocating civilian and military labour for the army, and the AMPC became the Royal Pioneer Corps. The 'Auxiliary' in the title was dropped as it was disliked for being non-martial and inappropriate, especially after Pioneers had fought alongside the infantry at Dunkirk in May and June 1940. Furthermore, the task of the Pioneers in aiding British fighting formations was about to become crucial, and the colonial empire was to take the leading role:

> After Dunkirk, the Middle East became the most important overseas base outside of the UK. A Directorate of Labour was formed at GHQ [General Headquarters] Middle East in May 1940. At that time three Pioneer Companies had been formed — two Palestinian and one Cypriot [a Pioneer unit raised in the Sudan could not be used much beyond the Condominium itself], and the Army was employing about 10,000 civilians. . . . The Greece and Crete campaigns of April and May 1941 proved extremely costly to the Corps, some 80 percent (about 50 officers and 4,500 men) fell into enemy hands or were listed as missing.

. . . The greater part of the Pioneer Corps in the Middle East had been lost, and we had to begin all over again.[48]

This was where Africa entered the manpower equation. At the time war broke out, the Colonial Office had not envisaged the large-scale recruitment of colonial soldiers. On 25 March 1940 the War Cabinet decided to orient colonial manpower towards agricultural and mineral production at home, with the provision, where necessary, of *local* defence formations to release British garrison troops for service elsewhere. One constraint on raising colonial units was the shortage of military equipment. The existing African fighting formations, the King's African Rifles, Northern Rhodesian Regiment, Royal West African Frontier Force, Somaliland Camel Corps, and Sudan Defence Force, were to be maintained as an African Division for possible service in the Middle East and North Africa. Other units included the Sudan Defence Force, the Somali Camel Corps, the Northern Rhodesia Regiment, the Rhodesia Rifles, and the South African Union Defence Force. At a future date colonial manpower might be directed towards Pioneer labour, though this possibility was to remain in abeyance.

But events were to hijack the War Cabinet's timetable. Even before the heavy Pioneer losses sustained in Greece and Crete, the Cabinet recognized that new sources of Pioneer labour would have to be identified. In the dark days of 1941, the Commander-in-Chief MEC, General Sir Claude Auchinleck, turned to the HCT and then in the spring of 1942 urgently appealed to the colonies for a further 130,000 military labourers. By October 1942 MEC was supported by 36,000 men from the HCT, 18,400 from West Africa, 30,000 from East Africa, 5,600 from Cyprus, 4,500 from Palestine, and 5,000 from the Indian Ocean colonies. Forty Indian companies (15,000 men) were raised for service in the Middle East. The Arab Native Labour Corps (including many Libyans) reached a total strength of 30,000 civilians, and seventy-five companies of Italian POWs were also employed.

Training, organization, and discipline

When in 1941 the call for men finally came from the beleaguered Commander-in-Chief Middle East, Basutoland and Bechuanaland were prepared to respond, with chiefs in the latter territory having already drawn up lists of able-bodied men. Swaziland remained to be convinced, and the role of Colonel Herbert Johnson, sent out to recruit and train the Swazi, was crucial in securing their participation. As has been seen in the last chapter, mobilization of the men of the HCT for war service would have been impossible without the sanction and support of traditional authorities. Unlike Kenya and Nigeria, the HCT had no existing military institutions. So, once the traditional call had brought forth recruits, the HCT needed a structure to begin turning the recruits into soldiers prior to their shipment overseas. This structure was imported from Britain in the form of three Pioneer Corps Headquarters based at camps hastily built by the public works departments. In Basutoland, Walker's Camp was constructed near Maseru. 54 Group, commanded by Colonel Johnson, was sent to the former Agricultural Show Ground at Bremersdorp in Swaziland. In Bechuanaland, 64 Group went to the converted Imperial Cold Storage Warehouse site that became the Lobatsi Camp.

Men who arrived at these new military camps had been inspected in their villages by medical officers and, if passed fit, attested. Medical standards for joining the APC were lower than for the regular army, but even after standards were dropped in 1942 when recruits became scarce, the rate of rejection could be high. Still, more of Bechuanaland's adult male population (about 20 percent) went to war than in any other African colonial territory.

The High Commission Territories' Pioneer companies were variously attached to the British Eighth, Ninth, and Tenth Armies (created to defend Iran and Iraq from German invasion), and the American Fifth Army. They served in North Africa (with the Eighth Army all the way from Alamein to Tunisia), the Middle East (Suez, Syria, Lebanon, and Palestine), and Europe (Malta, Sicily, Italy, even as far as Yugoslavia and Austria). Basotho and Batswana troops served extensively in Palestine until protests from the Dominions Office led the Cabinet Defence Committee to end the practice (see next chapter). One detachment of Basotho troops even ended up in India by mistake. More would have travelled in that direction had the War Office been able to obtain permission to use the men in the Far East campaign after victory in Europe, though a significant battle in Whitehall eventually prevented this. The HCT administrations enlisted the support of the High Commissioner in Pretoria and the Dominions Office in order to oppose the Commander-in-Chief in Cairo and the War Office, as HCT Africans understood — correctly — that they had joined the Army before the Japanese war had begun, in order to help the King defeat Hitler and Mussolini, and that repatriation would follow immediately thereafter. It was a point of honour on which Middle East Command and the War Office had to concede. The HCT administrations would allow their men to go to the Far East only if a new recruitment drive was mounted specifically for that purpose (see next chapter).

Thus the West and East African situations were reversed in the case of the High Commission Territories: HCT troops served in Europe, but not in the Far East. They served in Europe because the HCT had no powerful settler population able to demand that they be kept away from Europeans. Such was the case in Kenya, where 'to allay fears that A[uxiliary] APC askaris might pick up unsuitable ideas whilst they were abroad, the Middle East Command promised never to send East Africans to Europe or to mix African Pioneer Corps companies with other imperial units'. One of the reasons that British officers came to view HCT troops so favourably was because neither of these restrictions, born of the racial situation in the home colony, applied to them.

The speedy recruitment, training, and deployment of over 36,000 soldiers from the High Commission Territories was a significant achievement, because unlike other British African territories, the HCT had no peacetime Western military tradition to draw upon, no King's African Rifles or Royal West African Frontier Force, no veteran soldiers leavening the lump of society. As Simelane remarks, however, they did have a 'long tradition of militarism' and were 'still organized in a regimental formation'. The thousands of men who passed through the army training camps at Lobatsi, Maseru, and Bremersdorp were raw recruits from the villages, where many, before leaving, had been 'doctored' in accordance with traditional methods of preparing men for war. In Swaziland this involved the slaughter and consumption of a fierce black bull. Prince Dabede, sent to war by Paramount Chief Sobhuza in the traditional post of royal representative, was given a ritual baton containing the Paramount Chief's magical power. Despite the lack of a western military tradition, past experiences could prove useful in adapting to the demands of army life. Initiation into age-regiments had taught many a sense of regimental pride and discipline, and mine work in South Africa had introduced many to compound life, strict discipline, white supervision, and the Western fixation with industrial time. It had also given many men a familiarity with technology such as drills and dynamite, and this was to prove useful when Southern African soldiers were employed to blast cuttings through rock during the construction of military railways. The Pathfinders — an adapted form of the British Boy Scout movement popular in Southern Africa — had taught others quasi-military skills and notions of loyalty, discipline, rank, and group organization. At the training camps, the men were made into soldiers — drilling and more drilling is the dominant memory of ex-servicemen, who are all still able to present arms and mimic the sonorous commands of their drill instructors. In Bechuanaland some — not knowing the difference between left and right — carried grass in one hand and paper in the other, and would shout, 'grass (the 'g' pronounced as the guttural Setswana 'h'), *pamperi, grass, pamperi!*' as they marched, instead of 'left right, left right'.

A Pioneer company consisted of 365 men divided into sections of twenty-five, each under a sergeant. African authorities in all three territories insisted that their men serve in tribal units, so that, for example, the effort of the Bangwato was not watered down through service with other Bechuanaland tribes, so that Swazi troops served together rather than be mixed with those from Basutoland or Bechuanaland, and so that tribal discipline could be more easily maintained. It was also, of course, a time-honoured technique of British colonial containment. A further proviso in Swaziland was that all of the Swazi companies had to be kept strictly segregated and together under Colonel Johnson, to whom Paramount Chief Sobhuza II officially handed them. Upon his arrival from Britain in August 1941, Johnson 'soon established a remarkable rapport with the Paramount Chief, the Queen Mother and the Swazi people'. On first meeting the local African and British authorities, Colonel Johnson:

> Pointed out that if they could get enough recruits for their own Army Group they would not be mixed up with other tribes. . . . He attended at the Lombaba Krall on 25 August 1941 to learn the result of the deliberations of the Paramount Chief and the National Council of the Swazi nation. The Paramount Chief announced that the Council had decided to issue a '*hlaba mkosi*' calling their men up for war.[49]

Johnson then addressed the assembly, promising to look after the troops and to be worthy of the friendship invested in him by the nation. The nine Swazi companies were handed over:

> In accordance with Swazi custom; Colonel Johnson was given the delegated authority of the Paramount Chief and provided with the Chiefs personal warrior bodyguard. . . . He has commented that the Group idea [i.e. the plan to keep all Swazi together and segregated] was the only way to arouse any enthusiasm and produce recruits . . . Later, the Paramount Chief informed Brigadier Mills DPL [Director of Pioneers and Labour]: . . . 'It is the desire of the Swazi Nation that our troops should not be divided and that their care should always be under Colonel

.Johnson who has faithfully promised that he will return our young men at the cessation of hostilities. . . . Colonel Johnson has learnt as much of us as we have learnt of him and therefore regard him as part of ourselves.

The Batswana, Basotho, and Swazi came from societies in which age and social status were important variables in political control, and civilian power realities were carried into the army. The highest ranks attainable by Africans — Company Sergeant Major (CSM) and Regimental Sergeant Major (RSM) — almost always went to chiefs or other royals who were able to ensure that, even though thousands of miles from home and in an alien military establishment, traditional discipline was maintained. RSMs included Basotho chiefs Theko Makhaola (cousin of the Paramount Chief) and Mahlomola Masupha, Prince Dabede Dhlamini of Swaziland, Chief Kgari Sechele (head of Bechuanaland's most senior tribe), Chief Molefi Pilane of the Bakgatla, and Molwa Sekgoma, a Chief's Representative from Bechuanaland's Bangwato Reserve.

CSMs and sergeants were essential cogs in the military wheel, working to connect Africans with no knowledge of English or military procedure to the British officers and men whom they were to serve under and work alongside. Their role was crucial to the success of High Commission Territories troops. Also important was the projection into the military structure of the eyes and ears of the home colonial governments, in the form of welfare officers appointed to the Adjutant General's staff, and district commissioners seconded to the army as junior officers in HCT companies.

War Service

The tasks allotted to the Royal Pioneer Corps were legion: transporting and unloading supplies for forward fighting formations; dock work at crucial ports such as Benghazi, Tripoli, and Tobruk; building and repairing military infrastructure on a fluid battle front (bridges, docks, aerodromes, tank traps, railways, roads); camouflaging vehicles and supply dumps, building dummy tanks and partaking in movement deception measures; building vast supply dumps; guarding supply dumps from an acquisitive local population; providing smoke-screen cover for amphibious infantry landings; guarding prisoners; forming fire-fighting and military salvage units; providing garrison troops in base areas; manning anti-aircraft batteries; and providing a range of craftsmen, from mechanics and drivers to carpenters and metal workers. Though not trained as infantry soldiers, the men of the HCT were armed and often within range of enemy gunfire, or were employed in potentially hostile environments as a deterrent (like the stationing of 1949 Basuto Company in Beirut when the local population began attacking the French).

After basic training in Basutoland, Bechuanaland, and Swaziland, most of the men got their first-ever glimpse of the sea as they arrived in Durban for embarkation to the Middle East. Stories are told of diviners being obliged to throw their divining bones into the sea for fear of the ships sinking, although they later fashioned replacements from driftwood (the boneless meat that formed part of their rations proving unfit for the task). Upon disembarking at Suez they travelled by train and lorry to a remarkable military camp that had sprung from the desert wastes near the site of the famous battle of Tel-el-Kebir. This was the Pioneer Corps Base Depot (PCBD) at Qassassin, a huge, isolated camp where Pioneers from all over the world completed their training and acclimatized. It accommodated up to 26,000 men on a site spread over four and a half square miles. Established in 1941 'to deal with the rapidly expanding Pioneer organization in the Middle East', it served as the Reinforcement and Training Depot and Equipping Centre for all Pioneer units coming to the Middle East, and also the dispersal camp during demobilization. Here the men were properly armed, many at first with Mannlicher rifles captured from the Italians and later with Lee Enfields. The provision of weapons was in line with British Army policy, which had been revised after unarmed Pioneers had to be formed into fighting units at Dunkirk and after many defenceless Pioneers had been lost in Greece and Crete.

High Commission Territories' troops were deployed in three distinct phases. Under the original plan, they were to serve with the Ninth Army in the Delta, Palestine, and Syria. The Ninth Army had been formed from British Troops Palestine and Trans-Jordan under General Sir Henry Maitland Wilson in November 1941. The task of defending the Middle East from a potential German attack through the Caucasus meant that the Lebanon and Anti-Lebanon mountains in Syria had to be turned into a gigantic fortified position. From Qassassin many HCT soldiers left for Syria, where they built tank traps, fortifications, and the strategic railway from Haifa to Tripoli. The second phase of HCT troop deployment began in 1942 and involved supporting the Eighth Army in the Western Desert. During the third phase they were sent to Europe to participate in the long Allied push through Sicily and Italy, supporting, as they had towards the end of the war in Africa, both British and

American armies. This meant that HCT companies invariably ended the war with a service history of diverse tasks and locations. For example, 1989 Bechuana Company served in Syria at the docks and airport, in Palestine with the Royal Army Ordnance Corps, in Egypt and Sicily with heavy anti-aircraft (HAA) batteries, in Palestine (again) as a garrison company, on an Army Forage Farm, and finally as guards for German prisoners-of-war alongside Gurkha troops. Pioneer companies were organized into groups providing labour pools dotted around the war theatre. The Eighth Army in the Western Desert, for example, was supported by 62 Group at Tobruk, 59 Group at Fort Capuzzo, 44 Group at Bardira, 55 Group at Sollum, 58 Group at Mischiefa, and 73 Group at Mersa Matruh. One group comprised six or more Pioneer companies.

The build up to Montgomery's Alamein offensive required massive preparation. In the autumn of 1942 Basotho companies were sent to the Western Desert to prepare for the imperial advance that was to come. They 'built up supply dumps at rail heads, or loaded the endless streams of lorries that took the ammunition, petrol and food, to the forward troops'. HCT Pioneers became particularly important to Eighth Army operations in these months prior to the battles of Alamein; they replaced East African Pioneers who were removed from frontline duties and switched to base area garrison duties and construction work after a 'breakdown' during the retreat from Tobruk in spring 1942. After the defeat of Axis forces in Africa in 1943, the Allies turned their attention to the invasions of Sicily and Italy. For this task the British formed Central Mediterranean Forces (CMF) under MEC from an amalgamation of the British First and Eighth armies. Pioneer Corps labour was important in opening up this new theatre as a great supply stockpile had to be built up, and aerodromes constructed. The initial invasion of Italy involved the movement of 160,000 fighting troops, 14,000 vehicles, 600 tanks, and 1,800 guns. Throughout 1944 the CMF labour establishment consisted of five Mauritian, one Rodriguan, one Seychellois, twelve Basutoland, eleven Bechuanaland, and nine Swaziland RPC companies — an impressive labour force of over 14,000 men.

When the Eighth Army invaded Italy on 3 September 1943, 1501 and 1502 Mauritian Companies and 1918 Basuto and 1977 Bechuana Companies 'hit the beach alongside the infantry' and 'began stockpiling supplies'. On 9 September a further 400 Mauritians, along with 400 Seychellois, landed right behind the American Fifth Army infantry at Salerno, in the face of fierce opposition. They spent the following three weeks unloading landing ships under German shellfire. Nine British

Pioneer Corps companies, 1508 Mauritian Company, 1941 Basuto Company, and 1991 Swazi Company supported a simultaneous British commando landing north of Salerno.

Dilution

Military policy regarding the High Commission Territories troops shifted dramatically in 1943. Given the excellent reputation that had been won by the 36,000 men from Britain's Southern African protectorates, they were considered the best Pioneer troops to use in an innovative development in the use of colonial manpower. The idea was to release British troops for duties in the re-invasion of Europe by replacing them with African soldiers. Thus Heavy Anti-Aircraft (HAA)regiments of the Royal Artillery retained a core of British troops but were 'diluted' by Africans. This was because British soldiers were being recalled to Britain to join the 21st Army Group ahead of the Normandy landings. As they were withdrawn from units in the Middle East and Italy, HCT soldiers filled their places. Successfully performing this role enhanced the reputation of HCT troops among senior officers. Other Pioneers, like those from East Africa, were banned from dilution for political reasons. The first experiments, conducted with 2,000 Basotho troops, took place in March 1942. Dilution necessitated careful negotiation and meticulous planning as HCT companies were broken up and mixed with British units similarly disrupted. This required a high degree of civil–military cooperation, involving authorities at the highest level in London, in the Middle East, and the colonial administrations and African chiefs back in the protectorates. The Army was not in a position simply to dictate terms and do what it pleased with the manpower it had drawn from the Empire. In the case of HCT troops, permission had to be sought from the colonial authorities of the territories. The chiefs had to be consulted, and their opposition would have stymied the proposal — as was to be the case with the Swazi.

On dilution High Commission Territories' troops performed a multitude of tasks with all service branches of the army. Their most notable role was with Royal Artillery HAA Regiments, in which thousands of Basotho and Batswana trained as 3.7-inch mobile gunners. They operated in ground-to-ground and ground-to-air roles, like 1944 Basuto Company, attached to 55th HAA Regiment, which gave American infantry ground support prior to the taking of Leghorn. 'At one point' according to B. Gray, 'there were thirty-two of these heavy 3.7-inch guns manned by Basuto, massed together within a quarter of a mile of each other and hammering the German line before Leghorn.'

Service with HAA regiments allowed HCT troops to engage the enemy directly for the first time, and notably shifted the men's perceptions of their role, making them feel like 'real' soldiers. As one wrote to his chief in a letter accompanying a photo of a 3.7-inch anti-aircraft gun:

> With the aid of this gun the enemy can hardly succeed in shooting or capturing us . . . If the enemy gets lost and comes near us in his plane then it is his last day. . . As Pioneers [i.e. labourers] we were mere women and children, but today we arc calm and collected under all circumstances, burning only with the desire to get to grips with the enemy and so great is our ardour that we feel like tearing him with our teeth.[50]

Companies, or sections of companies, were attached to British units from most service branches, though kept under the supervision of the Pioneer Corps, to which they still technically belonged. The officers of the host British formations were responsible for training and administration, whilst the officers of the HCT companies maintained control of discipline, promotion, and welfare (see next chapter). It is quite clear that dilution was a highly successful military utilization of imperial manpower resources. Aside from their artillery role, HCT troops were diluted to join imperial units performing an astonishing range of essential tasks. Some trained to provide smoke-screen cover, notably performing this duty as the Allied invasion of Europe began with the landings in Sicily and Italy. Some trained at the Army Fire-Fighting Centre in Abbassia:

> For three years Basuto fire-brigades of sixteen men each and two or three UK NCOs gave protection to vital points throughout the Middle East. Virtually every military fire-brigade in the Middle East was diluted with Basuto and it may fairly be said that they were the firemen of the Middle East.[51]

Others became lorry drivers, mechanics, and hospital orderlies. Two companies were trained as salvage units to recover reusable wreckage from land and air battles. Basotho and Batswana troops joined the Corps of Military Police, passing out with the Corps's red sash, white puttees and brass shoulder titles. Basotho soldiers were drafted into the Royal Artillery's mountain regiments, where 'their knowledge of horses has been given full scope and has proved of inestimable value to units dependent on pack transport'. Also useful was their familiarity with mountainous conditions, especially when they served in the Apennine region (the final German defensive line in Italy):

> The 85th Mountain Regiment was to give infantry artillery support in mountains . . . in Italy, where in many places there are no roads or tracks good enough for the normal tractors or lorry-drawn field guns. The 85th was therefore equipped with special light guns. . . that could easily be taken to pieces and packed on mules and so carried off along difficult narrow tracks and set up again in places quite inaccessible to any other artillery. To look after the mules they needed men of confidence, naturally good with animals.[52]

This led to 560 Basotho of 1921 and 1929 Companies being trained as muleteers in autumn 1943. 1941, 1943, and 1944 Basuto Companies worked as porters for infantry brigades in the Italian mountains. Mule trains carried the supplies as far as they could go, but the latter stages of the journey had to be made by the men, each carrying sixty pounds of ammunition and supplies. Some Basotho served for three years in the 19 Field Survey Company Royal Engineers producing military maps, and were 'all fit to be Printers Assistants in civilian life', according to their commanding officer. In Beirut, 1931 Basuto Company formed part of the Royal Army Veterinary Corps' 3 Remount Depot, learning Animal Management with mules and training as farriers, saddlers, and smiths. From the same company, 180 Basotho joined a Royal Engineers Camouflage Unit in Cyrenaica, constructing dummy planes, tanks, and installations, and camouflaging real ones. This was all part of military deception measures. 1951 Basuto Company, working with an Airfield Construction Group, moved into newly captured territory and constructed airfields for the landing of supplies and reinforcements. 1947 Basuto Company served with the Royal Electrical and Mechanical Engineers and for some time operated a tank servicing bay. 1928 Basuto Company formed a Bridge and Road Construction Company. 1907 and 1930 Basuto Companies were temporarily employed at Suez unpacking and assembling American and Canadian lorries, delivered in kit form due to the severe shortage of Allied shipping.

Meanwhile, 1914, 1915, and 1916 Companies guarded military installations in Alexandria, and 1901 and 1913 Companies were sent from Syria to join 1917 Company at Port Said docks. 1912 and 1928 Companies built roads at Aqaba in the British Mandate of Trans-Jordan, enlarging the harbour in case Egypt was lost. Basotho and Batswana served with the Royal Army Ordinance Corps and the Royal Corps of

Signals. As part of the latter, three to four hundred Basotho were trained in the construction of telephone lines. One of their assignments was to put up an important connection between Brindisi and Bari on the south-east coast of Italy:

> Where were situated the Headquarters which were directing our 'behind the lines' operations against Germans in Yugoslavia and Greece. The job involved the erection of 2,300 poles. . . . Alone of Basuto units, a Basuto Line Section, No. 521, crossed the northern border of Italy into Austria.[53]

As medical orderlies with the Royal Army Medical Corps, Basotho received patients from ambulances at Casualty Clearing Stations and transferred them to hospital for treatment. As stretcher-bearers Basotho brought wounded troops down from the perilous Italian mountains. For example, 1941 Company worked simultaneously for 140 Field Regiment carrying ammunition, and for 140 Medical Dressing Station carrying stretchers — the means and the ends, as it were.

1926 Basuto Company provided essential support during the advance across the Sangro River, bridge building (cutting down seven hundred trees for the purpose) and laying tracks for tanks. They bridged the river under heavy fire, and during the operation were the farthest unit north, all of the fighting units waiting on the southern side until the bridge had been built. According to Gray, 'prior to the successful bridging of the Sangro, 1943 [Company] had the job of conveying ammunition over five miles of sea at the estuary'. As the Allies moved north, the same company was called on to fill gaps in a canal bank dynamited by the retreating Germans. The British advance resumed after the company used 44-gallon oil drums and sandbags filled with earth to plug the holes.

A few men had a more exotic calling: each territory had a military band and dancers, performing at parades and troop entertainment shows. The Bechuana Drum and Bugle Band, for example, attired in leopard skins, beat retreat in front of 18,000 servicemen and the British Resident in Egypt, Lord Killearn, at the Alamein Club, Cairo, after a South African Springboks versus New Zealand rugby match. In the victory procession through Tripoli in May 1942 the Swazi military band bore the Swazi flag and the Swazi royal colours, made especially by the Queen Mother and her ladies (the origin of today's Swazi national flag), on the 'first [and only] day in the history of Swaziland to have its flag march through a conquered city'.

The Swazi 'Enclave'

The case of the Swazi illustrates the triumph of tradition in the recruitment and use of HCT troops. The Swazi remained undiluted for the simple reason that the Paramount Chief would not allow it. The strict racial segregation in the Swazi case represents a striking contrast with the Basutoland–Bechuanaland dilution and integration with European units. One condition upon which the Swazi were recruited was that they would be kept together under the officer to whom they had been ceremonially entrusted, Colonel Johnson. The first six companies to leave Swaziland as part of 54 Group were sent from Qassassin to join the Ninth Army in Palestine in February 1942. Johnson's second in command, Major D. P. Desborough, took them up. In July 1942 four of the six companies were sent to Syria, thus splitting the group. When Johnson arrived from Swaziland with the remaining companies to take command, he immediately set about getting the Swazi regrouped. He wrote to the military authorities that this was necessary:

> To keep faith with the Paramount Chief. . . The political relationship between the Swazi Nation and the Administration is such that not a single company could have been raised by the Administration. The Paramount Chief, his Council, and his people are to this day full of suspicion and distrust of the British.

Colonel Johnson appended a letter from Paramount Chief Sobhuza, stressing the need for the Army authorities to follow his own advice when dealing with the Swazi:

> It is the desire and wishes of the Swazi Nation that our Swazi troops should not be divided, and that their care should always be under Colonel Johnson who has faithfully promised that he personally will return our young men at the cessation of hostilities. . . . [He] will know how essential it is that these wishes should always be given first consideration wherever possible and that it is one of the chief conditions that influence our WAR CALL.

The Swaziland Resident Commissioner strongly supported Johnson's appeal for the Swazi to be reunited. This wish was implemented when 54 Group joined the Eighth Army in the Western Desert, the military authorities demonstrating the flexibility of a colonial–military system responsive to the local political demands of the colonies from which manpower was drawn. Thenceforth, Colonel Johnson had the great majority of the four thousand Swazis under his command and formed a self-contained unit known as the Swazi 'enclave', with its own news-paper, provosts, Field Punishment Centre, hospital, and leave camps.

The Swazis served in the Western Desert for long periods, starting at Mersa Matruh just after the Battle of Alamein. Then from December 1942 to February 1943 they worked at Tobruk alongside 5,500 Civil Labour prisoners-of-war and two Indian and two Basotho Pioneer companies. From February 1943 to June 1944 they were stationed in Tripoli, where during one stage the port was almost entirely worked by Swazis in order to keep the Eighth Army supplied (particularly with petrol for the tanks) as it pursued Rommel's forces. The Swazis had an extended stay (June to November 1944) at the port of Bône in Algeria, where they 'acquired a special skill in unloading war stores and supplies in docks. By their work as stevedores they affected a valuable saving in European manpower'. One company went to Algiers, while 'a large number . . . were also trained as machine gunners and were used to deal with organized groups of Italians engaged in raiding petrol and oil dumps'. The Swazis provide an example of how HCT troops were used to free British troops for frontline tasks; their move to Tunisia released Italian companies for Pioneer labour in Britain, thereby freeing British troops for service in France.

The one Swazi company that was not kept under Johnson's direct eye as part of the 54 Group Swazi 'enclave' was 1991 Company, detached under Major D. W. Pasea to participate in the landings at Salerno in September 1943. The company had been trained as a smokescreen unit to conceal the Allied landings from the enemy. The company's war diary for 13 September recorded 'nuisance raids and machine-gunning during night. Two African Other Ranks wounded on Sugar Beach. By night-fall [smoke] screen extended to cover 46 Division front'. By 16 September, the Swazi smoke screen was fourteen thousand feet long. Part of the company was transferred to 201 Guards Brigade:

> For portering arms and ammo to the front line. Lieutenant Scullion with similar party to 169 Infantry Brigade for similar duty. Two sergeants and 40 men to Grenadier Guards. . . . All men have shown admirable powers of endurance, climbing mountains with heavy, uncomfortable loads of rations and water. Rain has fallen heavily, sleep out of the question. The men have been without food and sleep for 36 hours. In many cases carrying wounded down on their backs on the return journey.[54]

The company landed at Anzio at 8.30 a.m. on 23 January 1944, again coming under heavy fire. During the landing the company operated as a machine-gun unit.

Men of 1991 Company had the distinction of being the first soldiers into Rome behind the infantry in June 1944, but a damning report concerning its unfitness to serve in Europe gave the company an undeserved reputation in official circles. The war diary noted a company inspection by Colonel Pearman, who reported that the company was 'not fit to carry on with smoke duties. Should not remain in European country — women and drink'. Colonial officials, ever sensitive to matters of race and concerned about the soldiers' eventual repatriation to Southern Africa, blew this out of proportion and duly damaged the company's reputation, even though it continued to do outstanding work and to suffer casualties in the Allied cause. The other eight Swazi companies left Bône and arrived at Taranto in November 1944, proceeding to the port of Ancona on the Adriatic coast, where 1991 Company joined them.

Welfare, Discipline, Communications, and Recreation

The British Army successfully provided for the welfare of the thousands of colonial soldiers in the Pioneer Corps. The military authorities were kept up to the mark by colonial governments anxious to look after the interests of their men and ensure that ex-servicemen did not become a political threat upon their demobilization. For these reasons demobilization plans were made at the highest level years before the end of the war, and pressure was kept on the military authorities to handle the colonial troops in the way most conducive to a smooth demobilization process. The use of troops from different parts of the Empire made the task of military commanders even more difficult, because their fighting formations were made up largely of Dominions troops commanded by generals who were subject to political pressure from their home governments. Likewise the colonial troops of the Pioneer Corps were represented at GHQ Middle East by representatives of the colonial governments, always quick to protest when they considered that their troops were not getting a square deal or that they were being encouraged to harbour post-war expectations that could not be met.

The Adjutant General's branch established a welfare organization known as 'A' branch. Official attention to the welfare of HCT troops was impressive; these men bore no resemblance to the wretched African Carrier Corps of the First World War. The world of 1940 was in some ways a more sophisticated place. On the one hand, the British Army realized that to gain maximum efficiency from the thousands of colonial soldiers, the best possible 'deal' was needed for the troops. On the other hand, colonial civil servants were determined to look after the welfare of their men whilst in the army. On a number of occasions colonial authorities did battle with military authorities in Whitehall and MEC. To their credit, the colonial officials almost always won the day, sticking up doggedly for the rights of HCT Africans.

A crucial variable in the 'kid glove' treatment received by colonial soldiers was the fact that there *would have been no military participation* had the African rulers of the territories not wholeheartedly backed the plan. The authorities never forgot the fact that they were answerable to these rulers. The paternalistic British administrators in the HCT broadly conceived themselves to be trustees, knowing what was 'best' for the African. They were concerned to keep their men away from 'harmful' influences that might make them an unruly element in colonial society upon demobilization, hence the grave concerns later in the war about the effects of service in Europe, the lengthy absences from home without leave, and the resultant breakups of families. Maintaining contact was considered essential for the well-being of the men, for family and social cohesion, and for colonial and traditional authority. It is notable that amidst a vast military bureaucracy worthy of a far-flung empire at war, the authorities pursued individual welfare cases. Soldiers were easily worried by bad news from home (and always concerned about land allocations and the fidelity of wives). Again, the way in which such matters were handled reveals the skill of British civil and military authorities, for colonial troops like those from the HCT lacked the historic advantage of a family welfare network like that of the Indian Army, the Gurkhas, or the King's African Rifles.

An efficient structure for welfare and liaison operated on a number of levels. Of great everyday importance was the work of the CSMs and sergeants, looking after the men, dealing with problems, liaising with the company officers and NCOs, especially on disciplinary matters where they had to deal on the spot with differences of language and culture. The roving RSMs, acting as trouble-shooters and direct conduits between leaders at home and the men in the field, were channels for welfare, problem-resolution, and the projection of traditional authority. Throughout the war, missionaries from the HCT worked tirelessly, touring among the companies, bringing gifts and comforts from home,

Get in the Scrap Knock Out the Jap

'Every sixteen ounces of Salvage are another pound behind the Allied punch – the punch that is going to knock the Nazis and the Japs right out of business.' A war poster from the Government of Ceylon's Department of Information, c. 1942.

(Courtesy of Sri Lanka National Archives in Colombo)

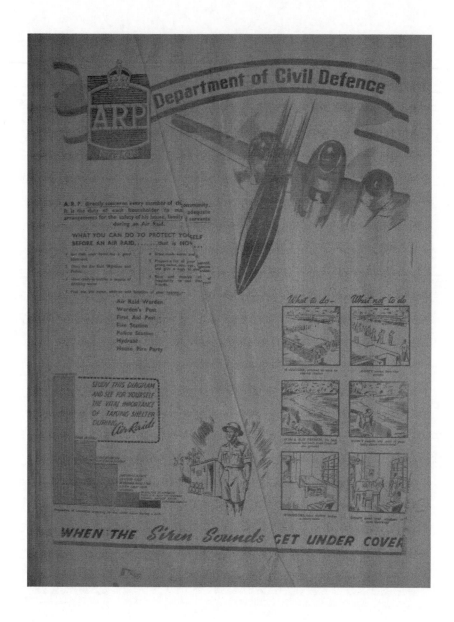

ARP Department of Civil Defence

It wasn't only in Britain that ARP and civil defence measures were familiar to the population of cities and coastal regions. Fire gaps cleared in slum areas, ARP posts, underground shelters, ARP wardens, and fire-watching measures were familiar in wartime Ceylon.

(Courtesy of Sri Lanka National Archives in Colombo)

Careless words

A variation on the famous 'Careless Words Cost Lives' poster familiar in Britain, this poster shows the Japanese high command perusing a map of Ceylon after the interception of an indiscreet letter from the island.

(Courtesy of Sri Lanka National Archives in Colombo)

In the grip of Japanese Co-prosperity

With the Japanese having conquered neighbouring Burma and Malaya, an attack on Ceylon was entirely possible. It was necessary, therefore, to try and steel the resolve of the Ceylonese people. October 1943.

Lanka calling

A recruitment poster that appeals to Lankan national sentiment as well as martial spirit, dating from April 1942, the month of the Japanese raids on Colombo and Trincomalee. By the end of the war, over 26,000 Ceylonese men were in uniform, and many women too.

(Courtesy of Sri Lanka National Archives in Colombo)

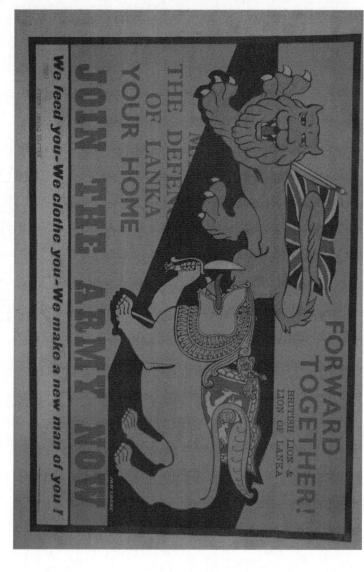

Forward Together!

A striking recruitment poster that uses Ceylonese national sentiment – an appeal to the Lion of Lanka and the need to defend the homeland. The Lion of Lanka (now at the centre of the Sri Lankan national flag) walks along side the British lion.

(Courtesy of Sri Lanka National Archives in Colombo)

Victory is in sight

A slightly premature poster aimed at the morale of the people of Ceylon, dating from January 1943.

(Courtesy of Sri Lanka National Archives in Colombo)

Askari wetu washinda wajapani

A recruitment poster aimed at the people of Britain's East African colonies.

Our allies the colonies

A soldier of the Royal West African Frontier Force, and the names of all of Britain's colonies.

(Both images courtesy of the Imperial War Museum)

The Western Front, 24 June 1917: South African Native Labour Contingent War Dance and Sports at Dannes: Zulus ready for the war dance.

(Courtesy of the Imperial War Museum)

17 July 1944: Admiral Sir James Somerville, Commander-in-Chief Eastern Fleet and formerly Commander of Force H based at Gibraltar, inspecting Wrens serving with the Eastern Fleet in Colombo, Ceylon. To celebrate his sixty-second birthday he held an inspection of Wrens, with nearly 250 of them on parade. After the inspection they marched past the saluting base to music from a Royal Marines band. As the Admiral was leaving the Wrens sang 'Happy Birthday to You'. There is no record as to whether or not Admiral Somerville invited any male sailors to attend the ceremony.

(Courtesy of the Imperial War Museum)

September 1944: Sinhalese women labourers line up for bucket loads of gravel, dug by the men, to repair the hard standing areas of the flying boat station at Red Hills Lake, Ceylon. Parked behind them are Consolidated Catalina Mark IVs of No. 240 Squadron RAF.

(Courtesy of the Imperial War Museum)

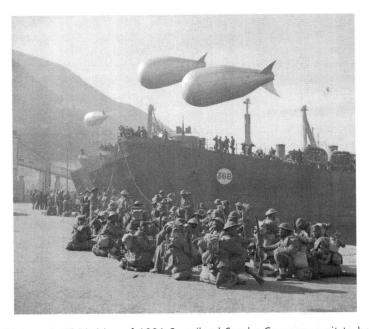

17–22 January 1944: Men of 1991 Swaziland Smoke Company wait to board landing craft at Castellammare before sailing for Anzio. The unit was responsible for creating smokescreens over the invasion area.

(Courtesy of the Imperial War Museum)

2 February 1945: A 75mm howitzer of 461 Battery, 85th Mountain Regiment, Royal Artillery, on the Monte Di Rontana. The guns were firing at German positions in Isola. A mule train with Basuto muleteers bringing up ammunition can be seen in the background.

(Courtesy of the Imperial War Museum)

February 1941: Women from Palapye in the Bechuanaland Protectorate knit woollen comforts for the Navy League.

The value of colonies and colonial manpower: Air Vice Marshal Sir Keith Park climbs away from Malta in his personal Supermarine Spitfire Mark V on 15 May 1943, after his ceremonial take off to mark the opening of Malta's new airfield at Safi. He is watched by RAF personnel, Basuto and Mauritian Troops and Maltese civilian workers.

January 1943: Basuto 'hangar boys' clean and polish Miles Master 2036 at No. 23 Air School at Waterkloof near Pretoria, part of the British Empire Air Training Scheme.

(Courtesy of the Imperial War Museum)

August 1942: Gun crews of the Colony class cruiser HMS *Mauritius*, part of the Eastern Fleet based on Ceylon, sit on the barrels of the 6-inch guns so they can clean them on returning to harbour.

(Courtesy of the Imperial War Museum)

September 1943: Marines at drill with three 40 mm Bofors guns at the Royal Marine Group Mobile Naval Base Defence Organisation Instructional Wing, Chatham Camp, Colombo, Ceylon.

(Courtesy of the Imperial War Museum)

Imperial soldiers remained vital to the Empire's internal and external security for decades after the end of the Second World War. This piece of mess silver, presented to the British Army's Staff College in 1960 by the Army of Rhodesia and Nyasaland (serving the Central African Federation, 1953–1963), depicts an African soldier. Upon independence colonial armed forces formed the core of new national armies.

(Courtesy of the Commandant, Joint Services Command and Staff College) offering encouragement and prayers, and passing news both ways. From Bechuanaland came missionaries of the London Missionary Society, Reverend Arthur Sandilands being attached as a Deputy Chaplain General to MEC. Roman Catholic, Church of England, and Paris Evangelical ministers travelled from Basutoland. After requests from Colonel Johnson, the Swazi 'enclave' received its own minister in early 1943.

Communications were important both for the purposes of colonial control and in order to keep families in touch. A prime concern was to avoid splitting families, who were encouraged to correspond in order to maintain psychological contact. Also of help were the woollen comforts knitted by African and European women to send to the men. Servicemen often sent photos, and films of the troops were shown back at home. Both the home administrations and their men 'up north' exchanged newsletters. Early on in the war the Native Military Corps newspaper, *Indlovu/Tlou*, added a Bechuanaland supplement. The Swazi published the *Swazi Gazette*. The war was an important stimulus for modern media techniques, and the widespread use of the wireless for information and propaganda began in this period. The Bechuanaland administration, seeing news flowing in both directions, established a ground-breaking tabloid, *Naledi ya Batswana* (Star of the Batswana), to serve both the men at war and the people at home. Unlike King's African Rifles recruits, no effort was made to separate HCT soldiers from their home life in order to induce regime loyalty and an elite sense of self-identity. Quite the reverse was true: HCT troops were short-term recruits in uniform only until Hitler had been defeated, and efforts centred upon extending tribal control into the army and maintaining psychological contact between a soldier, his family, and his tribal community.

Missionaries and officers repeatedly asked the HCT administrations to get families to write more often to their men, requests that met with only limited success in largely preliterate societies. More often, the men wrote to their families. Letters were a way of passing on news, having a say in domestic affairs, and of maintaining some kind of control — a soldier over his wife, or a father over his soldier son. In one series of letters, dozens of soldiers wrote to their chief asking for help in looking after money and recovering or caring for property, or complaining about errant wives and relatives. Letters also enabled chiefs to keep control over their men through their appointees serving in the Army.

Recreation for HCT troops was the same as that for all British soldiers, including ubiquitous football matches (as the diarist of 1991 Swazi Company ruefully noted, 'lost to 188 Company in semi-final of Anzio

Football Cup') and sporting competitions, African Clubs in cities like Cairo, leave camps, NAAFI's (Navy, Army, Air Force Institute, providing canteens and shops), music, singing, games (especially the ever-popular African board game *marabaraba),* magazines, tobacco, and sleeping. Other traditional soldierly attractions — such as women and alcohol — were available only with difficulty, and HCT troops had a record better than that of most British units when it came to the avoidance of venereal diseases and drink-related charges. Thousands took up smoking for the first time. It was hard not to with a free ration of fifty cigarettes a week. Towards the end of the war, education sergeants were appointed to each company. Many hoped that Army education would be a way of training a new class of responsible post-war citizens. But the issue was a sensitive one. New ideas and a broader world picture were inevitable results of the war, but colonial authorities did not want men who would become 'trouble-makers' upon repatriation. The HCT administrations insisted that army education suit the colonial setting that the men were to return to. Suitable educational topics were to be rural and uncontroversial. Also, with the 'New Jerusalem' dawning in Britain and casting a pale light on the colonial empire through the Colonial Development and Welfare Acts, the authorities considered it important that HCT soldiers not be led to expect massive transformations in their own societies. They were not to return to lands where well-paid jobs were 'as plentiful as apples on trees'.

Constantly touring among the troops were the welfare officers of AG10 (fully, DAAG10 — Deputy Assistant Adjutant General 10). The head of this unit was the Basutoland Government Secretary, Lieutenant Colonel D. W. How, who as the High Commissioner's 'eyes and ears' in the Middle East, was responsible for the welfare of the HCT men and for all communications between the military authorities and the home administrations. Throughout the war the unit consisted primarily of officers who in civilian life were HCT district commissioners. When large numbers of HCT troops began to be deployed in Europe from 1943, A7 was established to perform the same role as AG10 among Colonial and Local Troops (CLT) in Central Mediterranean Forces. Finally, the troops received visits from Resident Commissioners such as Arden Clarke in 1943 and Featherstone in 1944. Tshekedi Khama and Bathoen II of Bechuanaland called on the troops in 1942, though Sobhuza was prevented from going by his Swazi Council, who took the view that a king's place was at home with his people, not amidst the fighting.

The war situation in the Middle East called for the identification of new sources of military labour, primarily to augment the service branches and the labour wing of the British Army. As this chapter has shown, HCT soldiers performed a wide range of essential military tasks, demonstrating the vital role of colonial soldiers in fighting imperial wars. They were enlisted from territories whose leaders had a keen interest in maintaining the imperial link with Britain, and were therefore willing to put the full weight of traditional authority behind military recruitment. Without this support, recruitment would hardly have been possible. The men performed vital military tasks as part of a support army that numbered over one hundred thousand. Many men died for an imperial cause and for the cause of their political leaders, the chiefs. Though the 36,000 HCT soldiers had an overall 'sick rate lower than that of British troops', disease, accidents, and military action took their toll. Basutoland lost 1,216 men, 633 perishing when the troopship SS *Erinpura*, en route to Malta in company with twenty-two other merchant vessels, was sunk thirty miles north of Benghazi by a torpedo-carrying plane on 1 May 1943. Of over 10,000 Batswana serving in the African Pioneer Corps about 400 died, the majority from disease (particularly respiratory disease), and 61 also died on the *Erinpura*. Swaziland lost 122 men.

The men of the HCT won high praise from contemporary army officers who worked with them and from the official RPC historian. Colonel Collins, head of welfare and liaison, wrote that 'the men from the HCT showed more promise as soldiers in various arms of the Services than any other Africans and it is important that the value of these men should not be forgotten'. This view was endorsed by the officer in charge of Pioneer labour himself. Another senior Royal Pioneer Corps officer called the HCT troops the 'find' of the war, and the official RPC historian described them as 'the best of our African Pioneers'.

The military role of the HCT did not end with the war, and the RPC — unlike after the First World War — was not disbanded when hostilities ceased. Between 1946 and 1949 a further 3,500 HCT men served in the High Commission Territories Corps (HCTC), a unit formed in 1946. They were stationed mainly in the Suez Canal Zone and in Palestine before Britain returned the Mandate to the United Nations in 1948. They also served in Libya, where the desert campaigns had led to the creation of a 'veiled protectorate' upheld by a significant British military presence and which lasted until 1969, when Colonel Gaddafi came to power. The RPC survived until 1993, when it was merged with the Royal Army Service Corps, Royal Army Catering Corps, and Royal Army Ordnance Corps, to form the Royal Logistics Corps.

One is often moved, when contemplating the Second World War in all its complexity and global magnitude, to wonder how such a war effort was ever orchestrated. Though luck and chance played their part, though many things went wrong, though some consider it unacceptable to identify anything positive with Britain's imperial past, we should not be so mean as to deny credit where credit is due. The mobilization of an empire for war was a remarkable achievement. Engaged upon the monumental task of bringing an empire to war, and mindful of the calamities that would ensue should defeat occur, the transformation of hundreds of thousands of Africans from farmers to soldiers and back into farmers again was just one more sweep of the magic wand that imperial military and civilian officials planned with minimal fuss, and executed with aplomb.

8

African Soldiers and Imperial Authorities

Unrest among High Commission Territories Soldiers in the British Army

The last two chapters have shown how colonial manpower was recruited and utilized in pursuit of imperial victory in the Second World War. The use of colonial manpower was not without its problems, however, and the next two chapters examine factors that could contribute to unrest and even mutiny. As we have seen, thousands of men from the High Commission Territories joined the British Army during the war. Although their service was a success from a military perspective, numerous problems arose that threatened their usefulness and led to serious unrest. The problems stemmed from the use of seconded colonial administrative officers in the Army, and the differences that they had with Regular Army officers; the former group wanted to control the manner in which 'their' Africans were employed, with at least half an eye on ensuring that they did not become 'troublemakers' upon their return to Africa. The latter group, meanwhile, more concerned with exclusively military matters, was not interested in issues relating to colonial authority and the position of ex-soldiers in post-war colonial society.

Because of these diverging priorities between army officers and colonial civil servants in army officers' uniform 'for the duration', British Regular Army officers often complained about colonial service officers drafted into the Army as 'experts'. Interestingly, so too did the Africans themselves. As in the case of the mutiny of The Mauritius Regiment (see next chapter), colonial authorities who claimed to 'know the African'

177

proved unpopular and contributed to indiscipline and unrest. Africans also complained about not being allowed commissions, and problems arose over seniority between British Non Commissioned Officers (NCOs) and their African counterparts. African service among 'demoralized' whites in newly recaptured Sicily and Italy also caused racial tensions, as did the service of Africans in close quarters with British soldiers who received more pay. A slow demobilization process, that saw the military authorities renege on a promise to repatriate Africans as soon as Hitler was defeated, led to a great deal of resentment, which manifested itself in depression, disobedience, strikes, and even riots. This led to questions in the House of Commons and to battles between British colonial administrators and British military authorities, both backed up by their Whitehall departments, as the colonial authorities in the African territories and in the Army sought to care for the welfare of their men as well as to prepare them for a return to an unchanged rural life.

'I have never met a good Englishman yet', said a private soldier of 1931 Basuto Company in late 1945 as he waited in the Middle East to be repatriated to his homeland after four years at war. Another soldier accused Basotho Regimental Sergeant Majors (RSM) of 'siding with the British and making our life difficult'. Though the war against Germany, Italy, and Japan had ended three months before, like thousands of their fellow African soldiers these men were still in the British Army and still in the danger zone. Their mounting dejection disturbed the imperial authorities, because it was adversely affecting their military performance and potentially storing up troubles for their return to African society. Despite promises that they would be repatriated as soon as Hitler had been defeated, for up to a year after this had been achieved in May 1945 HCT troops found themselves working on supply lines for the war that continued to rage in the Far East until the atomic bombs were dropped in August 1945, and also involved in the escalating Jewish–Arab conflict in the British Mandate of Palestine.

Though the 36,000 High Commission Territories troops earned an enviable record during their service as part of the British Army, rounded off by a smooth reabsorption into home society, a number of problems arose that worried officials during the war, and that, especially in its later stages, affected their military efficacy. These episodes represent an important aspect of the military experience of the HCT troops during the war and reveal differences in the attitudes of colonial authorities and military authorities. The successful mobilization of African troops from the HCT required consultation at every level, and study of the Empire at war presents a cross-section view of the mechanics of British world power at work. The case of HCT military participation shows British imperial and colonial authority working in 'metropolitan' and 'peripheral' power centres: the British Cabinet, the House of Commons, the War Office, and the Dominions Office and its staff in London; the High Commissioner and the three resident commissioners in Southern Africa, along with the African chiefs in their tribal headquarters; the Commander-in-Chief Middle East and his staff in Cairo; and officers commanding the HCT companies and numerous HCT district commissioners serving with the Army as company officers and as roving welfare officers. All of these tiers of imperial and military authority were involved in the mobilization, participation, and demobilization of HCT troops in the Second World War. This chapter shows how imperial authority was exercised at all of these levels.

Differences between Regular Army officers and Colonial Service Officers in the Army, and between Africans and Colonial Service Officers

Throughout the war both African servicemen and regular British Army officers complained about district commissioners serving in the Army, and the divisions between army officers and colonial service officers during the war is very instructive. Regular Army officers often presented a more progressive, liberal face of British rule over colonial peoples than their counterparts serving as colonial administrators. In order to keep African soldiers content and 'unchanged' — and therefore manageable upon repatriation — colonial authorities had to ensure that their welfare was cared for as effectively as possible, and to shield them from influences considered detrimental to post-war colonial rule. Fear of 'detribalized' Africans and the effects of urban living on supposedly 'rural' people was common. British colonial policy was founded upon the twin pillars of altruism and control. Set against the colonial administrators, Regular Army officers could appear more liberal and progressive, encouraging an African interest in the post-war development of their countries that colonial officials would rather had not been fostered. In particular, these Regular Army officers were concerned purely with military matters, and did not care, and often frowned upon, the colonial officers' attempts to control what Africans thought or experienced, particularly when this conflicted with military imperatives.

Colonial officials serving in the Army irritated Regular Army officers. On the one hand, Army officers, used to unhindered command, were annoyed because they could not do as they pleased with the HCT troops under them. This was because colonial officials on secondment to the Army formed an additional tier in the hierarchy of Army authority, and were successful in establishing the right to look after the welfare of their men and interposing their opinions and methods. As the historian of the Royal Pioneer Corps ruefully commented, 'advisers and welfare officers were frequently more concerned with post-war problems in the territory for which they spoke than with the immediate military requirements'. On the other hand, the intervention of colonial authority in the Army was a reflection of what could be the stifling hand of colonialism, holding people back in the name of control, 'good government', and settled colonial administration. Africans were supposed to belong to a 'changeless' society, and so needed to be shielded from new ideas and experiences to the greatest extent possible so that they did not rock the boat of 'unchanging' colonial society upon demobilization.

The common practice was for district commissioners to join the Army as seconds-in-command of Pioneer Corps companies, or as staff attached to the Adjutant-General's Department, known variously as DAAG (Deputy Assistant Adjutant General) 10, AG 10, or 'A' branch. The Adjutant-General and his staff were responsible for all matters relating to military administration, personnel, and discipline, and therefore played a very important role as entirely new military units comprising tens of thousands of Africans became a part of the British Army during a time of war. The Adjutant-General's Department was responsible for all communications between the colonial authorities in Basutoland, Bechuanaland, and Swaziland and the Pioneer companies in which their men were serving. Its head was the High Commissioner's representative to General Army Headquarters; it was primarily concerned with the welfare of the troops, and acted as the High Commissioner's 'eyes and ears' in the Middle East, where all of the troops served at some point under Middle East Command (MEC). When HCT troops moved into Europe and came under a different command — Central Mediterranean Forces (CMF) — a new branch, A7, was established in order to share the burden of keeping the home fronts in touch with their men as they became dispersed. This dispersal presented a problem for the administrations, chiefs, and families trying to keep in touch with the servicemen. By 1944, HCT troops were serving under four separate commands: MEC, CMF, Allied Armies Italy, and British North African Forces.

It was expected that colonial service officers seconded to the Army, with their first-hand knowledge of African culture and language, would help Africans adjust to Army life, thus making them more efficient soldiers. They were also to take a keen interest in the welfare of the men; the British as colonial rulers were naturally paternal, and were also answerable for the welfare of the African soldiers to the chiefs, without whose sanction HCT military participation would not have been possible. It is also clear that the colonial administrations back in the three territories — like the chiefs — wanted to extend their control into the Army. This was in order to ensure that the men returned home without any 'dangerous' ideas, attitudes, or habits, and still subject to the tribal structures under which they lived.

Colonel H.G.L. Prynne was Director of Pioneers and Labour at Middle East Command, and he wrote a damning report on the role of colonial authorities serving with the Army. He wrote of the 'futility of most of the so called "expert advisers"'. They arrived with the highest credentials from their local Government authorities and were backed by 'A' branch at GHQ. They usually had no idea of the military problem and were far more interested in domestic native problems at home than in the military problems presented by these natives joining the British Army. It will thus be realized that their activities were very often subversive to discipline and their advice was based on post-war problems at home rather than military requirements'. Prynne wrote that most of the senior Pioneer officers in the Middle East were of the 'robust' no-nonsense type, so the colonial administration officers (the 'expert advisers') were given short shrift, except by the Adjutant-General's Department. Prynne reserved special scorn for the 'experts' serving with the East African Pioneers:

> The East African 'advisers', for instance, were backed by their own Government who exerted pressure on General Headquarters Middle East to have East African Pioneers run as their 'advisers' directed. The result was that these East African troops, badly officered, badly led, and badly administered, all in accordance with the expert advice, failed us completely on the withdrawal to El Alamein and were never again trusted with operational work.[55]

The East Africans were considered 'the [Royal Pioneer]Corps' problem child'. Fortunately for the HCT troops (who took over tasks in the Western Desert that East African Pioneers were now considered unfit to perform), 'it also happened that the two senior advisers from the HCT were outstanding exceptions (lieutenant colonels Charnock and Collins, and, before his death, the Basutoland Government Secretary, D.W. How), which is why HCT units progressed so much further and were so much more useful to us than any others'.

After this praise, Prynne returned to the attack on the colonial officers sent to the Army as 'experts'. They could only offer advice based on customs in the specific African territories that they came from. 'Thus though these individuals could advise on what had worked satisfactorily [in the past], they could not really advise on the practicability of any new ideas, because they had very rarely seen any new ideas tried out', a telling criticism of the static nature of colonial rule. The advisers wanted all 'tribal' customs observed in the Army, even down to meal-time habits. 'But we decided that now they were soldiers there was only one standard — that of the British Army'. So all marched to get meals, 'regardless of race, caste, nationality, or custom'. Prynne concluded that this treatment of the men as soldiers rather than Africans had worked well. In this, the chaplains proved helpful (themselves often egregious critics of the conservative tendencies of colonial rule), as they 'had for long believed that the natives would respond to opportunities to improve their status'.

The Swazi case shows how Africans resented the conservatism of colonial administration, and of how Army officers could fall foul of it. In November 1941, Colonel Herbert Johnson, leader of the Swazi Pioneers, requested that J.F.B. Purcell, an Assistant District Commissioner, be released to join the Army to help in preparing the men for their eventual return to civilian life. This, however, was not a particularly popular move with the Africans:

Company Sergeant Major (CSM) Sukati tells Sergeants of 1992 Company that Mr Purcell of the Swaziland Administration may be coming to the Middle East as an officer to go round the Companies in a welfare and educational capacity, discussing reconstruction after the war, etc. No enthusiasm is shown. One man says they have known Mr Purcell for years, and he hasn't done anything for them. Why should they think he is interested now? Sukati spoke of the natives getting together and running their own stores on a co-operative basis. This aroused considerable interest, with the feeling that though something might be done with the Colonel's help, afterwards the Administration and Europeans generally would sabotage anything of the kind, just as various natives have in the past been stopped from running shops by the real or imagined threat of the law etc.[56]

Johnson, like many Regular Army officers ignorant of the intricacies of life and rule in the colonies that so preoccupied colonial officials, was very keen to help the Swazis to a better life. This included taking an interest in post-war development in Swaziland, and in stimulating African discussion of it. He wrote to the Administration: 'I am most anxious to get news of what Administration is planning for these men on their return. You have no idea how keen they are to know what life has in store for them.' This is what the Administration did not really want to hear, because it did not have a lot to offer, and did not want the men filled with unrealistic expectations. Despite the Colonial Development and Welfare Act of 1945, there was to be no money for a Welfare State in the colonies.

In May 1944, CSM Mkwanazi wrote to Johnson to say that the motor drivers of 54 Group (the 3,500 Swazi soldiers under Johnson) had had a meeting to discuss ways of making a livelihood upon their return home. 'They intended to open a Motor Drivers Association that would fit in with schemes being made to develop the country.' Johnson sent a copy to the Paramount Chief via the Swaziland Administration (he was not allowed to write direct, an example of exasperating colonial formality):

It is evidence of the thought which is being given by the Swazis to their future. I am doing my utmost to prepare them to accept any scheme which is put before them as a result of the united thought of all those who have their future welfare at heart. It has been my ambition to get the Swazis 'work-minded' . . . I have trained them to do highly skilled work, so that they might gain confidence in their own ability to do things. That they desire to form a Motor Drivers Association shows that they have confidence in themselves.

But the Swaziland Administration did not share Johnson's enthusiasm: 'We are interested to hear of this but the Resident Commissioner hopes that the men will not get the idea that all those trained as drivers during the war will be able to follow that calling when they return to civil life'. The Colonel wrote in the margin: 'This was typical of the Administration — Cold water to damp down enthusiasm.' Colonial administrators, however, were not just killjoys, and would have rigorously defended their position. Charles Arden Clarke, Resident Commissioner of Basutoland, when visiting the Middle East in 1944 had spoken to some soldiers 'who were drivers, and they all had the same idea, that they should on their return home secure employment as lorry drivers and the result may be that along our 400 miles of main road we shall have one long line of derelict lorries. We are running a grave risk. Everything possible had been done to stop the men from thinking that they were returning to "heaven on earth"'.

There were numerous complaints about Bechuanaland district commissioners serving in the Army. Tshekedi Khama found after a tour of Batswana companies in the Middle East in 1942 that some soldiers expressed a preference for regular British Army officers rather than those 'supposed to have knowledge of the Bechuana people'. Gerald Nettelton, the Government Secretary of Bechuanaland who was accompanying the chiefs on their tour, reported that in Tshekedi's eyes Bechuanaland administration officers 'became more peremptory and less friendly' in the Army, and that the men wanted British officers 'who do not claim to know the African'.

There were numerous reasons for these problems between Africans and the district commissioners serving in the Army. Before joining the Army, British district commissioners and Africans had only seen each other at a distance, and encounters had been formal, ritualized, and rare. In the High Commission Territories, African traditional authority remained very much a reality, with district commissioners indirectly ruling in the background. But the Army meant years of close contact, with district commissioners now appearing as direct military superiors. They might present their 'expert' knowledge of African law and custom as a codified, finite, and rigid code enshrining what Africans could *not* do, rather than as an enabling and fluid corpus. Complaints extended beyond the war. In 1946, Monametsi Chiepe told the Bechuanaland Administration that 'the European officers who came from Britain were well disposed towards them but when their own officers, who came from the Territory, got to their Companies, relations immediately changed for the worse'.

The Resident Commissioner of Bechuanaland, Aubrey Forsyth Thompson, wrote that 'petty Army jealousies have all along operated against the full utilization of officers with knowledge of the Bechuanaland Protectorate'. But it is possible that the racial attitudes of district commissioners, seen by Africans at close quarters in the Army, tended to reflect those prevalent among white South Africans. This was in contrast to the more liberal and idealistic attitudes of men coming out fresh from Britain to serve in the forces. Peter Fawcus, a district commissioner in Basutoland immediately after the war and later Resident Commissioner of Bechuanaland, said that Africans were used to district commissioners *as* district commissioners, conducting relations through negotiation and persuasion, and not to district commissioners as Army officers, passing on orders that were to be obeyed without question.

As has been seen, Colonel Johnson, leader of the nine companies of Swazi Pioneers, experienced such 'petty jealousies'. He had had the care of the Swazis entrusted to him by the Swazi King, Sobhuza II, and the Swazi National Council. Johnson's prestige and influence over the Swazi soldiers was unrivalled. It was a condition of their service that they were to stay together under his command. But as was seen in the last chapter, 1991 Company was separated and sent to Italy, whilst Johnson kept the other eight Swazi companies under his command in North Africa in what became known as the Swazi 'enclave'. 'After receiving reports of internal problems', Johnson asked to be allowed to visit 1991 Company stationed at Anzio. 'He was told that AAG 10 would not recognize him as anything but a Group Commander and would not agree to his visiting 1991 Company'. The message was that Johnson was commander of the Swazis that comprised 54 Group in North Africa, but had no officially recognized right to trouble-shoot for a Swazi Company in a different command, despite the fact that there existed no one better able to assume the role and that the trust placed in him by the Swazi nation gave him such authority. As he later wrote, 'I am afraid there was jealousy caused by my influence over the Swazis . . . and the outstanding success of the Swazi Group. It did make work doubly hard and I was always conscious that, so far as AG 10 was concerned, I was "non persona grata"'.

Commissions for Africans and Relations between British and African NCOs

Colonial officials in the HCT would rather not have discussed the issue of commissions for Africans, but events forced their hands. Along with the question of jurisdiction between British and African Other Ranks, it became an issue that the authorities were anxious to shelve, hoping that a 'wait and see' stance would substitute for a clear policy. The highest rank an HCT African could hold was Regimental Sergeant Major, and the rank almost always went to royal appointees, usually chiefs or their relatives. This was an important way of maintaining tribal control of the men even at a great distance, and of keeping them in touch with their homes. The roving RSMs also acted as trouble-shooters liaising between African soldiers and the British military authorities.

The subject of commissions was discussed at a meeting of the High Commissioner, the resident commissioners of Basutoland, Bechuanaland,

and Swaziland, and the British military representatives in South Africa (this was 203 Military Mission, Pretoria, known as 'Milmis'). The biggest problem was the attitude of the South African government, and it was agreed that commissions should not even be considered for HCT troops unless they became open to other Africans. When the issue had previously been raised it had quickly been dropped, 'chiefly through opposition to such a step on the part of the Union authorities'. It had reared its head again in April 1945 when RSM Theko Makhaola (the leading Basotho soldier in the forces and a senior chief in his own right) asked for a commission based on the 'vast responsibilities I have ... shouldered'. In early 1944, two Basotho CSM Warrant Officers had applied for commissions.

Though it was acknowledged that the granting of commissions to Africans would anger the South Africans, 'assurances had been given to the effect that His Majesty's Commission is open to all British subjects irrespective of colour'. This was the dilemma, as so often, facing the colonial authorities in the HCT; whilst anxious to conform to the letter of official British policy, it was difficult to ignore the sensitivities of the South Africans. The British government had to walk a diplomatic tightrope in its relations with the pivotal but wayward Dominion of South Africa, and the issue of the High Commission Territories was a fly in the ointment between London and Pretoria. The issue of commissions for Africans annoyed African leaders too. Tshekedi Khama, touring Batswana companies in the Middle East in 1942, wrote:

> I am unhappy as to the obvious colour distinction in the AAPC. I held great hopes of an opportunity having occurred where the Bechuana would prove their worth in taking their position alongside other nations and they have exhibited their devotion to duty, obedience to their senior officers and high abilities, but they can only go as far as Sergeant Major.[57]

An attendant problem was who should receive commissions should they ever be opened to Africans. It was acknowledged that promotion should in theory at least be based on merit alone, but in the appointment of HCT RSMs, the colonial authorities had had to see that they went to chiefs or their appointees — to do otherwise would have outraged the chiefs and jeopardized HCT military participation. As the Resident Commissioner of Bechuanaland, Aubrey Forsyth Thompson, said, 'a chief is always a chief in war or peace and this fact must, I think, be recognized'. His Basutoland opposite number, Arden Clarke, agreed, stating that 'the first Basuto to have a commission will have to be the Paramount Chief's representative . . . RSM Theko Makhaola'. Fortunately for the authorities, the subject of commissions for Africans did not arise often enough to cause serious problems.

A more pressing problem was the relationship between African and British soldiers of the same rank, particularly jurisdiction between them. Was, for instance, a British private soldier to take orders from an African sergeant? It was hoped that this problem could also do without official resolution. It was a matter seldom raised before 1943, as HCT troops were serving in units where only the officers were white. With dilution, however, thousands of them served alongside British Other Ranks and NCOs. It was noted that African NCOs were vigilant in ensuring that they were not given orders by their British inferiors. Though the colonial and military authorities were not overtly racist, and upheld the King's Regulation, they naturally did not want too many non-Europeans ordering Europeans around; it simply did not fit into the world as they knew it and believed it should continue. The problem was that the rules as they stood were colour-blind, and to change them would have required an embarrassing parliamentary emendation of the Army Act. Again, the British authorities in the HCT were anxious not to upset the South Africans, a crucial though troublesome member of the Commonwealth family, depended upon by Britain for major strategic reasons. Despite this, however, they were unable (and unwilling) to adopt South Africa's characteristically blunt solution to the problem; the South African government had simply legislated against any non-European giving orders to a European.

The issue was raised by the military authorities in 1943 after an incident involving a Mosotho sergeant who had refused to obey an order from a British sergeant. The African had been put on a disciplinary charge, only for it later to be discovered that he was in the right. His appointment to the rank preceded that of his British counterpart, so technically he was senior. This type of incident, the High Commissioner noted, 'raises issues of high political significance'. He considered that it was 'much better to allow the difficulties to be solved as they arise, by . . . "tact and judicious posting"', and that action of any type would 'prove highly contentious'. At the same meeting Arden Clarke said that it was wrong to have any distinction based on colour. But if the King's Regulations were followed, 'a European corporal would have to carry out the orders of an African sergeant'. He continued: 'I think it is undesirable at present that we should have Africans ordering Europeans about', especially as the African societies of the HCT were allegedly going through a period of 'transition'. The British were caught between the logic of the rules as they stood and their own reading of what was best for long-term colonial control and the maintenance of the best possible relations with the South African government.

The War Office noted that the issue had political as well as military significance, as 'an African may now with impunity decline to obey an order given him by a European unless that European is senior to him'. A later notice from the Commander-in-Chief's office recorded that the situation was becoming increasingly difficult 'as African NCOs become more efficient and in consequence more self-confident'. An incident had occurred where a Mosotho CSM had refused to hand over a parade to a junior British NCO, and the CSM had had to be moved to another unit because, 'having won his point, [he] is tending to become difficult'. As tensions mounted among African soldiers waiting to be sent home after the defeat of Germany, such issues, exacerbated by other racial factors (discussed below), led to frequent low level incidents that worried colonial officers serving in the Army and the colonial authorities back in the three High Commission Territories to whom they reported. As Major Germond, a Bechuanaland district commissioner serving in the Army, reported:

> Fracas between British Other Ranks and African Other Ranks are becoming more frequent and there is an increasing tendency to refuse to obey any orders given by British Warrant Officers and NCOs. The development of such an attitude of mind must have most serious repercussions in the Territories and in the Union of South Africa . . . It is considered that a situation has arisen which is directly opposed to the desires of His Majesty's High Commissioner in South Africa and it is requested that application be made to the War Office for the immediate withdrawal of HCT troops as soon as hostilities cease with Germany.[58]

Service in Europe, relations with British troops, and the role of Army education

The two specific issues discussed so far formed part of wider tensions that affected all High Commission Territories soldiers. There were numerous reasons for the discontent, unrest, and even violence that sporadically affected companies after the defeat of Germany. Discontent was visible long before the end of the war. The primary cause was undoubtedly the sheer length of unbroken service overseas. As early as November 1942

Colonel Edye reported that some of the men were 'browned off, thinking they had only enlisted for a year and in fear of a second Syrian winter'. A year later the High Commissioner — along with the three administrations just as keen on planning for after the war as the military was on winning it — wrote of the 'deplorable effect on natives of unduly long separation from their homes'. He was 'very concerned at the probable adverse effect upon the AAPC [African Auxiliary Pioneers Corps] who have been away for two years or more on active service'. In summer 1943, it was reported that 1933 Basuto Company was suffering from 'disciplinary trouble' because it had been kept unduly long in the desert without relief. In August 1944, the High Commissioner reported to his superior, the Secretary of State for the Dominions in London, that the men were 'obsessed with the idea of returning to their homes'.

The High Commissioner believed that whilst the war in Europe was still on, with advances against the Germans keeping the HCT troops occupied and in good spirits, things would be all right. But he emphasized the need to get the men home as soon as possible after the German surrender, rather than keeping them loitering in the Middle East, for this situation would only encourage discontent. But this is just what happened; though the defeat of Germany in May 1945 ended the HCT troops' contract with the King, instead of returning home they were returned to the Middle East, reformed into Pioneer *labour* companies (often unpopular among men who had been serving on 'dilution' as part of the *fighting* artillery units), and put to work or kept in reserve by an Army Command that had its own priorities. This led to discontent and unrest that increased as the months went by. Unlike the colonial authorities anxiously looking to demobilization and the impact of ex-servicemen on post-war societies, the Army had one goal: finishing the military job. This entailed winning the war against Japan, quelling the rising tide of discontent in the British Mandate of Palestine, working the imperial military supply lines of which Egypt and the Canal Zone were vital parts, and clearing up in the Middle East after years of intense military activity.

With the advent of the dilution policy (that saw HCT troops split up to join British units from all branches of the Army) and the Allies' final defeat of Axis forces in Africa, all eyes turned to Europe. But colonial authorities viewed the movement of HCT troops into Europe with concern, just as they were alarmed by their close contact with white troops during their service in diluted units. Concerns were never based on military, but rather on racial, grounds. Contact might show Europeans in a bad light and corrode the racial 'balance' of Southern Africa. Sexual opportunities and the sight of impoverished whites threatened white prestige, and had implications for the return of Africans to their colonies. The problem was not really what they might *do*, but what they might *see* (and how this might change their attitudes towards whites), though this could not be openly acknowledged. Before dilution, whilst in the Middle East and North Africa, HCT troops had been stationed in the desert away from settlements and, serving in companies where the only whites were the officers, away from close contact with British Other Ranks. Moving into Sicily and Italy, they were near to local population centres, often billeted in the 'most undesirable quarters of towns and harbours . . . swarming with a poor and demoralized people'. Out of this came official worries for white prestige that, in retrospect, were largely unfounded. Alongside them grew real concerns as Africans noticed differences in the conditions of service between themselves and the British soldiers they worked with.

Lieutenant-Colonel Collins wrote that 'the temptations to which these men are subjected in Sicily and Italy are serious . . . The people are large producers of potent wine . . . [and] women of Sicily and Italy display a deplorable lack of any sense of moral decency'. This touched deep-seated fears for white prestige, particularly on the subject of sex. Charnock's concern about 'the possible effects if these troops are sent further into the continent of Europe' were twofold; 'both as regards immediate relations with the local population and in connection with the problems of eventual repatriation'. They were now dealing 'with Europeans whom they have always looked on as their masters and superiors. In Italy they have met a very different European who is ready to treat them as equals and has little colour consciousnesses'. This was because of the more relaxed racial attitudes common among southern Europeans, and because of the 'extreme poverty and want of the local population' recently liberated from Axis rule. In these circumstances, the soldier is 'necessarily in a far superior position... and is able to offer many things which they are in dire need of'. HCT soldiers were black conquerors in a white land, a novel situation for all concerned. But the problem seemed to lie more in the imaginations and prejudices of white officers; liaisons with Italian girlfriends and the sight of impoverished whites did not lessen the military effectiveness of HCT troops, or lead to lasting racial tension upon their return to Southern Africa.

Colonial fears were augmented by the fine gradations existing within the British racial 'league table'. Because 'uncivilized', HCT troops were considered more vulnerable to European temptations than 'civilized' Pioneers, like those from Mauritius and the Seychelles, who 'have experience of the impact of European living'. Racial categorization could be narrowed down even further. The peoples of the three HCTs were characterized in different ways. The Basotho had a reputation for being 'truculent', and they were by far the most troublesome of the three nations during service in the Army. The Batswana were more 'docile', largely, it was believed, because they were more subject to tribal discipline. The Swazi were considered unusually 'backward', even for Africans. This was not a view held by British soldiers with no previous experience of Africans; it was the view of the High Commissioner himself, who wrote that 'the account of the Swazi smoke company (1991 Company) in Italy is as bad as I could have anticipated. It is a mistake to send such backward people as the Swazis into such temptations'. Swazis were considered 'more backward than the other Africans of the HCT . . . It would be dangerous to send them to Europe where segregation mightn't be possible'. They were to be 'kept away from the influences of the demoralized Europeans of countries which have been occupied by the enemy'. 1991 Company's war diary reveals that on 16 December 1943 Colonel Pearman inspected the Company and reported: 'Company not fit to carry on with smoke duties. Should not remain in European country — women and drink.' This was unfair on the Swazis — and 1991 Company in particular — and blighted an excellent war record. It is a view flatly contradicted by the dozens of letters sent to the Commander of the Swazi Group on their leaving North Africa for service in Europe. As the Deputy Provost Marshal North Africa District wrote, 'from a Provost's point of view it is felt that the discipline of the Swazi Pioneer Companies in Bône has been exceptionally good'. Added to this, the Swazis were not affected by the troubles that beset Batswana and Basotho companies in the last stages of the war. It was considered that the Swazis should not go to Europe 'if this would involve a weakening of their present segregation from demoralizing influences':

> The Swazi is not suited to employment in Italy, his mental makeup is different to that of the Mosuto and Mochuana. He is much more primitive and in drink loses all restraint and becomes subject to mass hysteria. It was obvious for me that the officers in this particular Company have lost control; the men are drinking hard and womanising in general, and the officers appear powerless to do anything.[59]

Racial problems in the Army were not of the kind sometimes posited by historians — there is little evidence of a nascent brotherhood of the

191

colonized or plans to rid the homelands of the nefarious British oppressors once the war was over. In the case of HCT troops, there was little contact with other Africans, even beyond one's own tribe in one's own territory, and contact with other non-European peoples did little to stimulate mutual knowledge or friendship. E.K. Featherstone, Resident Commissioner of Swaziland, reported after visiting the troops and witnessing their behaviour on leave, that they 'had, from choice, very little contact with East and West Africans'. Lieutenant-Colonel Charnock wrote of the Arabs, 'who they generally despised'. Batswana soldiers deprecated Arab haughtiness in dealing with Africans, and identified them as the beggars and thieves against whom they were often deployed. But there were some racial problems between British and African soldiers, and though they had no discernible long-term effect, they certainly worried colonial officials conscious of the racial status quo as it existed in Southern Africa. The mutual curiosity engendered by the dilution of British squaddies (who had just lost friends withdrawn for service elsewhere) by Africans speaking very little English, can be imagined, and what is more notable than the tensions that arose is the fact that dilution worked and worked well.

Lieutenant-Colonel Collins reported that 'a matter of difficulty is the growing claim to equality irrespective of race on the part of Africans serving in dilution roles', where they saw their British counterparts at close quarters. Miss Lawrence, an official at the Dominions Office, minuted:

> [There are] various unsolved problems, the chief of these being the growth of colour prejudice. The policy of dilution can't stand the strain of a long war, and there is no remedy except victory in the next few months. Allied to this problem is that of equal pay: the men share the life of British soldiers and do the same work for less money.

This was the root of many problems — the men had been kept in the Army and prevented from returning home for too long. Resident Commissioner Featherstone wrote that 'the most serious and disturbing aspect is the increasing resentment by Africans to any form of differentiation between black and white troops, or to restrictions which have necessarily been imposed on social relations between them and the civilian population'. A feeling of colour prejudice was developing among some troops in the Middle East, though oral testimonies reveal no feelings of racial discrimination among Batswana ex-servicemen. For the sake of military efficiency, rather than for predetermined racial reasons, HCT troops serving with British units were usually given separate living and eating quarters. When in action, however, 'mucking in' together was the norm. It was the return to more rigid segregation when resting that could cause offence. But it was pay differentials that were the real problem. In August 1945, Lieutenant-Colonel Acutt wrote that 'the close contact dilutees have had with British personnel has led to a certain amount of contempt and in fact anti-white feeling'.

The problems souring the Army experience of HCT troops worried the administrators of the territories to which they were to return after the war. Demobilization was a topic regularly discussed and planned for by military and civilian authorities from 1943 onwards. The HCT governments were naturally concerned about the timing and method of the repatriation of their men, wanting as little disruption as possible upon their return. They were constantly fed information by welfare 'A' branch officers and Pioneer company officers. An interesting example was provided by Captain Muirhead, a Basutoland district commissioner serving for the duration with HCT units. He prepared a memorandum on the likely effects of war service upon the Basotho, and 'the problems to which their changed outlook will give rise'.

It was noted that the soldiers would inevitably have 'imbibed progressive ideas', and that this was acceptable, but could cause difficulty if 'the local [African] authorities . . . by active repression or by their own stagnation, drive the spirit into undesirable channels, i.e. subversive activities for which there is opportunity in the existence of native organizations such as the Lekhotla la Batho'. War experiences might lead to 'an altered regard for their Chiefs . . . a much more critical attitude towards the minor Native Authorities, and may have crystallized a dormant sense of exasperation at the delay and obstruction which in far too many cases impedes the ordinary Mosutu's progress towards settlement of his judicial and administrative problems'. The men were losing respect for the minor sub-chiefs, especially where these were 'self-seeking and ignorant'. Respect was further diminished when chiefs failed to look after a soldier's interests back at home — his stock, his land, and his wife. He noted that 25 percent of the men's complaints were to do with land allocation, mainly that 'their land was being filched away during their absence'.

The number of successful sit-down strikes, conducted by Basotho even as early as 1943, had given the men 'the knowledge of force of mass action'. Also to be taken into account when planning for the return of the men, there had been a great 'acquisition of new tastes'. For example, thousands of Basotho, given a ration of fifty free cigarettes a week, had taken up smoking. Higher standards of clothing, food, drink, and recreational pursuits had been attained by the soldiers. The return of over 21,000 Basuto would also, in the opinion of Muirhead, lead to 'political changes', partly stimulated by the dissemination of 'progressive views' and the provision of Army education. Returned soldiers 'will expect opportunities at home equalling those available in Army'. Though this could be a cause for concern, ex-servicemen would also be a valuable resource, and Muirhead recommended the creation of employment boards and the development of small handicraft industries. As an example, he suggested the development of transport services — 500 men had served as drivers 'up north'. To usefully employ Basotho he also suggested the formation of a Basotho Force available for service overseas. Muirhead's report ended up on the desk of Clement Attlee, Secretary of State for Dominion Affairs.

It was hoped that Army education would be a useful safety valve, beneficial for soldiers and for colonial society, encouraging them to become model rural citizens. It was hoped that Army education would correct 'wrong' impressions about what men could reasonably expect upon demobilization, and distract them whilst demobilization was awaited. Education and repatriation had been in the minds of colonial officials and Army officers almost from recruitment. As the leader of the Swazi Pioneers, Colonel Johnson, wrote:

> The problem of resettlement of the troops is constantly in my mind. So are the many problems facing post-war Swaziland. It will be tragic if something is not done while we have 3,500 Swazis in the Army to prepare them for their return and to educate them how to make a better land for their own habitation. These troops will learn a great deal on their travels, and they will be very different men when they return . . . With the returning troops should come many men, who as NCOs have been trained to accept responsibility and act as leaders. These men can be prepared to take over responsibility in civil life.

Colonial officials recognized that the troops would be changed by the war, and saw in this both an opportunity and a threat. At war, the men expressed a keen interest in the post-war world, unavoidable given all the talk of the Beveridge Report and fundamental changes in post-war British society, and with news of international landmarks like the Atlantic Charter in the air. The colonial administrations knew what was going on, and, up to a point, welcomed an interest in post-war society. Arden Clarke noted that 'many have heard of the Atlantic Charter and the Beveridge Report and want to know to what extent the principles underlying these statements . . . are to be applied in their own countries'. But they also wanted this interest to be 'correct', appropriate for men who had to return to a rural life and possible labour migration. Though colonial officials would have loved to have had the resources to build a New Jerusalem in Southern Africa, it was not to be, and the HCT share of the 1945 Colonial Development and Welfare Act grant of £120,000,000, was small; in the case of Bechuanaland, lower than the administration's lowest estimate. As one official memorandum stated:

> It is understood that our troops in the Middle East are asking with increasing frequency what benefits they are to derive from the war, meaning material benefits. Propaganda to deal with this matter requires the most careful thought. With all the talk about post-war reconstruction in the UK, which inevitably our men hear, the underdeveloped African may easily form the opinion of a Utopia to which he will return. Our post-war development programme should convince anyone that we do not want to perpetuate the old order, but improvement must inevitably be slow and gradual.[60]

Administrators also knew that there was little scope for employing returning servicemen in new ventures or Government posts. The Bechuanaland Administration could only find 214 jobs in the whole of the Protectorate. It was hoped that controlled Army education could help prepare men for the harsh realities of the post-war world, whilst inculcating useful knowledge that would help them to become better tribesmen and better farmers. It was also hoped that education would relieve boredom and divert attention as they waited to be demobilized. The colonial administrations wanted the 'right' type of education, and sought to control it. 'Information talks, especially about the post-war period, should be in consultation with the Protectorate Governments, as some information given by British officers might not be suitable.'

In the eyes of the colonial authorities in the High Commission Territories, the purpose of Army education was twofold: 'Education schemes may be able to correct wrong impressions and direct newly acquired ideas, experiences, and skills to the benefit of the communities in which, by virtue of their status as returned soldiers, these men will be regarded as outstanding personalities.' It is 'from them that many leaders of their generation will be found and they will be important agents for implementing development plans now being prepared in their colonies'.

The rather modest plans for development in the HCT were circulated in upbeat reports, and educational articles appeared in Army newspapers with titles like 'the African and his cow'. The HCT supplement to the South African forces newspaper, *Indlovu/Tlou*, was full of news from home (crops, schools news, weather reports, court cases), and 'safe', moralizing, and informative articles. A 'correct' syllabus consisted of lessons in geography and literacy, with a concentration on moral and practical advice. Africans were to be prepared to return to the rural way of life that, it was thought, was their ideal, natural state: 'At all costs we must avoid raising their hopes that they are coming back to a completely new world where jobs are as plentiful as apples on trees.' Army education, however, was provided solely for the benefit of the Army and not for the benefit of post-war colonial administration. Despite the hopes placed upon it by colonial authorities, it had little lasting impact, and was not enough to prevent problems of indiscipline mounting after the defeat of Germany.

Problems after the Defeat of Germany

All serious disciplinary problems among High Commission Territories companies stemmed from the sheer length of service overseas and the broken promise concerning demobilization. The 'infamous promises' of 1944 declared that HCT troops would be repatriated on the defeat of Hitler; they 'would be able to go home and the *speed* of the repatriation would be limited by availability of shipping *only*'. The Army argued that the Commander-in-Chief Middle East's statement of July 1945 cancelled this arrangement. HCT troops did not qualify for home leave until late 1944, and then it was too little too late. Things were not so bad during the war of movement before the capitulation of Hitler. Men acknowledged that they had signed on to defeat Hitler and Mussolini, but fully expected to be repatriated as soon as this was done. But on the defeat of Germany the men were regrouped in the Middle East, those that had been diluted into Royal Artillery regiments were re-formed into Pioneer companies, and they were all expected to perform further labour tasks. This was a major bone of contention. The Army wanted to keep as much labour available until the war was won, and even wanted HCT troops to serve in Palestine and the Far East. Even if this was not possible, there was plenty of work to be done in the Middle East, clearing up and working on the supply lines to the Far East. Though shortage of shipping was the ubiquitous reason given for the lengthy delays in demobilization, MEC adamantly maintained that *it* was to decide when the men were to be released, and resented all interference. MEC was 'user command', and was to decide the timing and rate of repatriation. This slow demobilization, however, amounted in the minds of the soldiers to a breach of faith and breach of their terms of service (to serve until Hitler's defeat) and of the promise made in 1944 that they would be demobilized as soon as the war in Europe had ended.

Major Germond, a Bechuanaland district commissioner serving in the Army, wrote directly to the Dominions Office, emphasizing the social cost of such long service: 'many wives, unused to being separated from their men for such a long time, have deserted their homes and children and attached themselves to other men'. He complained that the men were now being told that they must remain in the Middle East handling munitions bound for the Far East: 'Their period of service ended with the defeat of Germany . . . I speak without fear of contradiction that these troops are disillusioned and "browned off". They feel that the promises made to them have been broken.'

HCT troops had been recruited before Pearl Harbor. It was widely understood that they were joining up 'to help the King fight the Germans'. As Charles Arden Clarke wrote in 1942, 'our men have no idea of this Japanese war' and he added in 1944 that they were 'unaware of events in the Far East and the implications of a global war'. The War Office requested permission to use HCT troops in the Far East. The High Commissioner consulted the three resident commissioners, and the answer came back that this would not be possible unless, with the support of the chiefs, new recruits were found on a purely voluntary basis. Even despite this, a number of Basotho troops were mistakenly sent to India!

Equally, the men had not signed up for service in Palestine, a growing 'internal security' conflict that was not part of the world war. This was a conflict that cost HCT lives; four Basotho soldiers, for example, killed in the bombing of a Jerusalem police station in December 1945. Service in Palestine had a bad effect on the morale and behaviour of Basotho soldiers. Lieutenant-Colonel Acutt reported that 'at any moment now any of the Basuto Companies in Palestine may go on strike . . . Therefore these troops are now a liability not an asset'. Of eight Basotho companies in Palestine (known as 15 Area), none were considered reliable, and no less than five had been on strike. A problem for the military authorities facing this indiscipline was that there were not enough other troops in the area to coerce them into obedience. In the Haifa area of Palestine 1928, 1942, and 1943 Basuto companies were refusing to work. Soldiers of 1935 Basuto Company stationed at Qatana near Damascus claimed that the 'British are a lot of crooks', and that they were 'being treated worse now than during the war'. On visiting the company in December 1945

Major G.B. Gray (author of *Basuto Soldiers in Hitler's War*) noted the 'general air of slackness in the unit' and concluded that 'the mood of the men is unsatisfactory'. Though it was almost always the Basotho who went on strike, Batswana were also affected by the same grievances, causing low morale: 1988 Bechuana Company 'has been affected by the sight of many idle Basuto in the vicinity and its performance and morale are now indifferent'.

But the Army, at full stretch, was unconcerned about political ramifications in the protectorates after the war, and despite the grievances of the soldiers was determined not to disgorge manpower, even if it was of declining efficiency. The Dominions Office, however, was concerned, and only too well aware of the reason at the root of all of the trouble. An official in London minuted that 'these reports on Basuto and Bechuana Companies in Palestine make rather dismal reading. The reason for their attitude is only too clear and it is most unfortunate that they should have got the idea that they are being exploited because they are Africans . . . The root cause of all the trouble is the long waiting for repatriation'. The Dominions Office believed that 'it is very possible that serious mutiny will break out among the troops', and had to take the subject of HCT service in Palestine all the way to the Cabinet before getting satisfaction and overruling War Office policy. At a meeting of the Cabinet Defence Committee on 19 July 1946 the Prime Minister, General Montgomery, and the Colonial Secretary agreed that HCT troops should not be further used in Palestine, as this 'caused great resentment'.

On 31 December 1945 a 'notorious mutiny' of Basotho troops from 1943 Company occurred at 57 Military Prison and Detention Barracks in Egypt. Its suppression caused a furore that reached the House of Commons. The incident was symptomatic of the malaise affecting all HCT troops in the long months after the defeat of Hitler. Soldiers of the Parachute Regiment used gas and opened fire on unarmed Basotho, killing four, after the detainees had taken up sticks and stones against the European and African staff running the detention centre. Similarly, near Haifa on 22 November 1945 1934 Basuto Company was surrounded by troops from the North Staffordshire Regiment, armed with machine guns and tanks, in order to forestall a riot. The Batswana were less trouble because 'their Chiefs have much greater power over them, but on all points they agree with the Basuto'. Many of the troops were considered 'useless as a defence against any but casual thieves'. The Swazi soldiers, kept together and undiluted, were to a large extent insulated from the troubles affecting their counterparts from the other two HCTs.

It was the shooting of Basotho soldiers that brought the plight of the

HCT troops to the attention of Parliament. Henderson Stuart MP asked the Secretary of State for War 'why his department consistently refuses to announce a definite scheme of demobilization for HCT troops when a definite scheme was offered to British troops. He asked for a report on the Palestine 'mutiny' of November 1945, in an attempt to discover 'why airborne troops fired over 100 rounds at the sentenced men'. Ronald Chamberlain MP widened the debate by asking: 'Is my right honourable friend aware some are arriving home in a deplorable state?' due to inadequate medical examinations. In April 1946, the Prime Minister, Clement Attlee, was asked which Ministry should be addressed for further information on the mutiny. H. Hynd's parliamentary question, however, gives a sense of how peripheral HCT troops were to the view of the vast majority of Britons: 'Could my right honourable friend explain for the more ignorant section of the House what HCT troops are?'

In the month in which Hitler's Germany was finally defeated, Batswana and Basotho troops were involved in an explosive incident that saw the High Commissioner and his resident commissioners at odds with the Commander-in-Chief Middle East and the South African government. Since September 1944, a few hundred HCT troops had been receiving thirty days home leave. In May 1945, a draft of 109 Batswana and 303 Basotho, hearing of Victory in Europe, refused to re-board a troopship at Durban that was to return them to the Middle East. It was widely known that South African Native Military Corps troops were not being asked to return. The British Army representatives in South Africa (203 Military Mission, Pretoria) insisted that the men return, and were backed all the way by Middle East Command and the authorities in Whitehall. The High Commissioner intervened forcefully, backed up in turn by his Whitehall department. He feared a bloodbath if the men were forced to re-embark because of 'the past record of the Union Defence Force in South African racial riots'. The High Commissioner insisted that force could not be used, and said that to get the men back would require the dispatch to Durban of the African chiefs and resident commissioners from the two territories. Thwarted by the resistance of the colonial authorities on the spot and in Whitehall, the C-in-C Middle East was furious, and protested 'most vigorously . . . [It] has been constantly stressed that African troops could not expect immediate demobilization on end of war in Europe'. He wanted no interference with his unilateral authority to decide, as head of 'user command', when release would take place, and was greatly annoyed to learn of the 1944 agreement between the Dominions Office and War Office concerning demobilization.

HCT troops had little time for the excuses offered as to why they were not being sent home. They knew what had been promised them, and could see what was happening to troops from elsewhere:

Shipping is soon arranged to the Middle East [from Italy] which they regard as the first step on the way home. There is, however, in most units deep underlying uneasiness about being re-employed in the Middle East and the rumour they have heard to the effect that some CMF [Central Mediterranean Forces] units previously returned to MEF [Middle East Forces] have been sent to Syria or Palestine to work. This will be seen as directly contradictory to the clear promise formally given to them last year that they could go home when the war with Germany ended.

'Problems of lack of shipping and shortage of transport mean little to the simple and undeveloped black man', wrote one officer, but this was unconvincing as well as unfair as the authorities knew full well that the men had signed on only until the defeat of Hitler, and many officers did not believe the Army's excuses themselves. Furthermore, it did not take a particularly well-developed mind to notice when white officers and NCOs who had served in the same units as HCT troops suddenly disappeared home on the leave scheme for British troops known as 'Python'. As Deputy Chaplain-General Reverend Arthur Sandilands noted, this inevitably brought a sense of discrimination. The reason why demobilization took so long did not elude colonial officials: 'The need for Africans is still great, hence their slow rate of repatriation'. As the Resident Commissioner of Swaziland wrote, 'my fear is that user command may be driven through compulsion of losing white troops in release categories to retain HCT troops'.

On leave in England, his counterpart from Basutoland, Charles Arden Clarke, wrote directly to the Permanent Under-Secretary of State at the Dominions Office, Sir Charles Dixon. All three resident commissioners, and the High Commissioner, feared that unfair treatment would do lasting damage to relations between Africans and the colonial authorities if allowed to continue for much longer. He stated bluntly that 'in my opinion the HCT troops are not being given a square deal'. He feared that in the scramble for demobilization they were 'losing all along the line'. West and East Africans troops had won better demobilization deals, and it was seen as a weakness that the HCTs — unlike East and West Africa with their lieutenant-generals — did not have a senior officer attached to MEC. The troops were well aware of the demobilization of

British troops taking place all around them, and had 'a strong sense of what is due to them'. Officers and NCOs of HCT companies had already been sent home. He stressed the fact that they were not conscript soldiers, and that it would be a great pity if their loyalty to Britain was lost: 'They feel they are not getting honourable treatment from the Protecting Power to whose help they came.' Lieutenant-Colonel Acutt, one of the welfare officers serving with HCT troops, wanted to leave, as he 'couldn't face the Companies with such a poor prospect before him and them'.

Administration officers 'on the ground' among the troops awaiting demobilization backed up the claims of their seniors. Captain Atkinson, a young Bechuanaland district commissioner, wrote an exasperated letter to his Government Secretary from the 'burning waste' that was the Pioneer Corps Base Depot in the desert at Qassassin. He was suffering from acute depression. In his letter he wondered how long it would be before the 'truculent Basuto', armed with sticks, 'took matters into their own hands'. He said it was 'useless to talk to the men about shortage of shipping; they do not believe the story and neither do many of us'. Upon hearing of the stand taken by the leave draft refusing to return to the Middle East from South Africa, the soldiers said that 'now the *makgoa* (whites) will realize we mean what we say that we want the promise to send us home kept'. Atkinson believed that 'successful African mass disobedience is a product of this war'. He complained of the refrain that was constantly ringing in his ears from the Batswana — '*boshula ba makgoa*' — the lies of the white man. He ended by stating that 'the Bechuana will not forget, if we are unfaithful or unfair, and we shall meet with hate for our pretences, contempt for our inefficiency (order, counterorder, and disorder), and non-cooperation as an inevitable result'.

The service of HCT Africans in the British Army was a success; they served effectively and were regarded as the finest African Pioneer soldiers of the war. 'The men from the HCT showed more promise as soldiers in various arms of the Services than any other Africans and it is important that the value of these men should not be forgotten.' This opinion was echoed by the historian of the Royal Pioneer Corps. He thought that the HCT troops were 'the best of our African Pioneers'. Their service, performing the vital 'rear echelon' tasks that keep fighting men in the field, enabled thousands of white troops to be released for front-line duties. They were then successfully demobilized, and post-war society was not riven with discontent caused by dissatisfied ex-servicemen, although some did participate in the Lesotho political movement *Lekhotla la Bafo*.

The troubles encountered among the 36,000 HCT soldiers should not detract from their exceptionally creditable war record. But to contemporaries, the service of these Africans raised fears for white prestige and colonial rule in the post-war world. Racial tensions never reached breaking-point, and HCT soldiers had fewer encounters with women and drink — both major sources of minor infringements of military law — than most British units. Africans were confronted with differential treatment based on colour that many of them would have recognized from their experiences as labour migrants in South Africa. It might be concluded that the documented examples of unrest relate almost exclusively to Batswana and Basotho troops because the Swazi Companies were never 'diluted' to serve alongside British Other Ranks. Unlike their peripatetic Batswana and Basotho brothers, who served in many different theatres with white artillery units before being regrouped into labour units, the Swazi were kept sedentary and united. Continuity in location, employment, and leadership clearly related to the exemplary Swazi disciplinary record. Differences between colonial and military authorities are instructive, and it is to the credit of the HCT soldiers that, despite the unacceptable delays in their demobilization after an exhausting war, indiscipline was so limited in scale, even if the talk of it was not.

9

The 1st Battalion
The Mauritius Regiment,
Madagascar, 1943

The Archaeology of a
Colonial Mutiny

On 17 December 1943 the 1,003 officers and men of the 1st Battalion
The Mauritius Regiment (MR) boarded the troopship *Burma* at Port
Louis, capital of Mauritius, and embarked for the grand harbour of Diego
Suarez in the recently-captured French colony of Madagascar. The MR
was a new regiment of the British Army, granted its colours in principal
by King George VI in October 1943. During the crossing conditions on
board ship were poor. Arriving in Madagascar the Battalion was made to
parade in full kit in the afternoon sun before beginning a route march to
Orangea, about twelve miles inland. This was in spite of the provision of
motorized transport, and was indicative of the attitude of the Battalion's
commanding officer, Lieutenant-Colonel J. Yates, who was determined
to seize the moment and show off his troops and his own leadership. In
the course of the march order disintegrated, men began to fall out, and
the Battalion arrived at Orangea in straggling batches. Used to the high-
quality Abercromby Barracks in Mauritius, the men were unhappy with
the accommodation assigned them in Madagascar. At the camp, by accident or design, a grass hut was set alight. Others followed through
deliberate ignition. Men left the camp against orders. The following day
hundreds disobeyed an order to parade for physical training; 501 of the
soldiers mutinied, and all together over three-quarters of the Battalion
was disciplined. African soldiers of the King's African Rifles (KAR) were
ordered to round up the mutinous Mauritians, wielding machetes and

rifles with fixed bayonets. Some ringleaders were sentenced to death. The Regiment survived for a further eight months before being disbanded. This chapter presents a reconstruction of the rise and fall of one of the British Empire's least-celebrated regiments. In doing so it casts light on the considerable military preparations made in the most unlikely places on behalf of the Empire at war. As had been the case during the Indian Mutiny of 1857, the Madagascar mutiny was the result of numerous 'time bomb' factors that had been present for months or years before the touch-paper was finally lit.[61]

The word mutiny is commonly used with a degree of elasticity; for example, the 'Indian Mutiny' of 1857–8 covers what was, after the initial acts of military mutiny, a military conflict coupled with a civil uprising. Mutiny is defined as an 'open revolt against authority', and the Madagascar mutiny of the Mauritius Regiment in December1943 was certainly that. Military mutinies were not new and by no means confined to colonial troops — one historian has filled an entire book with exam-ples of mutinies affecting British and Empire armed forces. The Madagascar mutiny, from inception to suppression, witnessed no violence. As Mauritian ex-servicemen insist, it was purely passive. Maxime Labour, President of the Mauritius Branch of the British Commonwealth Ex-Services League, describes it pithily: 'it was an absence of discipline'. Another 'mutineer' writes that the men 'had never been initiated into the King's Regulations', and had no understanding of the sense of the word mutiny. They believed they could behave like strikers. But mutiny of course was the most serious offence under the Army Act.

The Mauritius Territorial Force (MTF) and Mauritius Rifles

As an earlier chapter has shown, locally-recruited military formations were raised to supplement imperial garrisons and in anticipation of the shrinkage likely in a time of war when imperial troops would leave. At the outbreak of war the Mauritius Garrison numbered 200 imperial troops. It was supported by the 200-strong MTF as well as a company of white Franco-Mauritians supporting Royal Artillery coastal defence batteries and a non-white infantry company trained to defend the island's many points of strategic importance. In their tasks they were supported in the Second World War by numerous other formations, including the Coastal Defence Squadron, the Home Guard, and the Mauritian Royal

Air Force raised to work on flying boats in the island's territorial waters. Naval raids or Japanese invasion were the perceived threats to the island's security. Mauritius also supplied 4,000 men to the Royal Pioneer Corps serving in North Africa and Southern Europe, and 8,000 others served in a Civil Labour Corps recruited for military construction tasks. Mauritius provides an excellent example of a colony utilizing numerous long-standing and ad hoc locally-recruited formations in support of an imperial garrison and the wider interests of imperial warfare.

The MTF officially became the Mauritius Regiment on 24 April 1943 when control passed to the Army Council. It thereby ceased to be a *locally-recruited* force for service only on Mauritian soil (which included Diego Garcia, Rodrigues, and the other Mauritian dependencies in the Indian Ocean), and became an *imperial* unit that could be sent anywhere in the world. This transformation of status was to be of fundamental importance. As in the case of the Indian Army's General Service Ordinance of 1856 — which provided one of the grievances leading to the sepoy mutiny because it made them liable for overseas service — the Mauritian soldiers were to come to resent this shift in their Regiment's status. Through conscription and voluntary recruitment the MTF had grown rapidly with the coming of war, performing garrison and artillery duties on Mauritius, Rodrigues, and Diego Garcia. The 1943 transformation of the MTF into the MR led to further expansion and the division of the new Regiment into two battalions, its strength rising towards 2,000 officers and other ranks.

The 1st Battalion The Mauritius Regiment (1MR) was posted to Madagascar in late 1943, swapped for a King's African Rifles battalion. The armed forces of Mauritius had a regional role to play as part of Islands Area Command, a newly-created subsidiary of General Sir William Platt's East Africa Command. Islands Area Command was responsible for supervising military affairs in Madagascar, the Seychelles, Mauritius, and its dependencies. After the departure of 1MR, the 2nd Battalion (2MR) acted as a training and reinforcement unit and maintained the Regiment's original infantry role within Mauritius. The dispatch of 1MR to Madagascar was partly motivated by the need to give the Regiment more experience. By moving from a peaceful garrison island that was home to the men and their families to a recently-conquered enemy territory, they would encounter a tougher environment. Then, if the war so dictated, the Regiment could be employed elsewhere — for example, in the Burma theatre. East Africa Command 'ordered that they should be sent to north Madagascar for battle training and toughening up' before being sent to Burma. This was where the men, few of whom had ever been overseas, thought that they were going. They were 'smartly turned out but had little field experience', and it was this that they were to gain in Madagascar. Whilst the fledgling Regiment was gaining valuable experience overseas, Mauritius — an important strategic outpost that was home to Royal Navy, RAF, Special Operations Executive, and intelligence-gathering installations — would be defended by a more experienced imperial unit provided by the King's African Rifles.

Ex-servicemen are at pains to emphasize the point that the Mauritius Regiment was a *fighting* unit, tired of the accusation that they were 'only parade-ground soldiers'. Roger Requin, a sniper sergeant, recounts an intensive training: 'grenades, route march with full marching order, bayonet fighting, free-for-all manoeuvres, mock battles, disarming techniques, compass-marching, sniper shooting, and camouflage'. 1MR's War Diary records frequent route marches, tactical exercises (for example, Operation Nippy in May 1943 involved repelling an 'attack' by the Royal Navy), and weapons training, including rifle and light machine-guns, and the 'tactical handling of 3-inch mortars'. The troops were lectured on jungle warfare and the application of camouflage. Titles of talks included 'Why Should I Fight?', 'War Aims of the United Nations', 'Japan and the Japanese', 'Japanese Tactics and Methods', 'The British Army: Its History and Traditions', 'Esprit de Corps', 'Hygiene', and 'Discipline'. Given such training, and the subject of propaganda and information lectures, it is easy to understand why Mauritius Regiment troops believed they were destined for the Far East as, indeed, they were.

The swap of 1st Battalion The Mauritius Regiment for a King's African Rifles (KAR) battalion was engineered by the Commander-in-Chief East Africa, Lieutenant-General Sir William Platt, and the Governor of Mauritius, Sir Donald Mackenzie Kennedy, for several reasons. As the latter wrote, 'I feel that the experience gained will be of immense value to the Colony after the war'. Both men also doubted the ability of the inexperienced Mauritius Regiment to defend the island in the event of a Japanese attack, and questioned the loyalty of some of the soldiers suspected, given their French heritage, of harbouring Vichy sympathies. So the Commander-in-Chief decided that imperial troops were needed 'to strengthen the defence of this part of East Africa Command'. (KAR troops remained until the Mauritius Garrison was closed in 1960 after 150 years on the island.)

Political opposition to overseas military service

Governor Sir Bede Clifford (replaced by Mackenzie Kennedy in April 1942 when Clifford was transferred to Trinidad) foresaw no political or military difficulties arising from the overseas service of the Mauritius Regiment. Provision for overseas service was introduced when the Mauritius Regiment Ordinance removed the unit's home service-only liability. Whilst some men volunteered for the MR, and some could be described as willing conscripts, others resented conscription, providing a layer in the geological bedrock of the mutiny. Suchita Ramdin remembers her brothers rubbing petrol in their eyes so that recruiters would think that the family was diseased. Maxime Labour was conscripted from college to join the Mauritius Signals unit. Ramsing Kusrutsing wanted to join the Auxiliary Police. 'I applied and on the selection day about 125 men were selected and were at once transferred to the military.' The Colonial Office was naturally concerned by such practices and the political and media attention they could attract, sensitive as it was to the issue of unfree labour (especially in a former slave colony) during a war of 'freedom' versus 'tyranny'. The issue of military service was politicized in 1941 and flared up again in 1943, when it became known that MR troops were to be sent overseas. Non-white members of the Council of Government, the island's parliament, claimed that troops being sent overseas were 'exclusively' non-white (the white company remained a coastal artillery unit). They told the Governor 'of the psychological reaction the decision of the Military [to send 1MR overseas] has had on the public mind'. Recruitment for the Pioneer Corps had not required conscription, but MR enlistment was unpopular, and the authorities blamed this on the fact that the MR was more likely to see combat, and on the ambivalent Franco-Mauritian attitude to the Allied cause. The Governor tried to assuage fears that only non-white troops were being sent overseas, and denied that the troops themselves felt disgruntled. He explained that the aim of sending MR troops overseas was to provide them with further training, so that the MR 'if called on, [can] play a full part in the military operations of the Empire . . . Personnel of these units, with very few exceptions, are most anxious to exchange the humdrum garrison life for more active participation in the war . . . It would be a thousand pities if [their morale] were undermined by the local influence which I fear is being brought to bear upon some of the men'. The Governor, however, could do little to stymie the feeling that non-whites were getting a raw deal, and overseas service remained deeply unpopular.

When Japan entered the war in December 1941 the Government was accused of importing racial discrimination into the military. Race and communalism were major factors in Mauritian politics. Dr Maurice Curé, founder of the Mauritius Labour Party, claimed that segregated recruitment harmed race relations and hindered the island's war effort. In a telegram to the Labour MP Arthur Creech Jones, he requested intervention. On 23 December 1941 the Council of Government was told that 'in regard to military service a colour bar has been *officially* established in Mauritius'. The issue was taken up by the press. Governor Sir Bede Clifford countered by reporting that there was 'a long waiting list of coloured volunteers for service and 400 Creole intellectuals had sent in their names since the [Council of Government] debate took place'.

The Secretary of State for the Colonies, Lord Moyne, and the Under Secretary, Harold Macmillan, needed information, for they were being hounded in the House of Commons by Creech Jones, who, through the Fabian Colonial Bureau, was intimate with Mauritian affairs. From Government House Clifford penned a lengthy refutation of the charges. The 'attempt to pin the blame on the Government is only an average example of the blind unreasoning prejudice against the Government and the Military Authorities in Mauritius'. He pointed to 'the intrusion once more of the colour question. . . Both [Laurent and Rivet, the politicians who raised the issue] are being prodded by a bunch of mothers, wives, aunts, and sisters who do not object to their offspring and relations drawing good pay so long as they remain at home'. The Governor assured the Colonial Office, however, that there was nothing to worry about; 'this sort of thing is a feature of one's daily life'. But this was a miscalculation, as the undercurrent of racial tension contributed to the unhealthy state of unit morale that was to see Mauritian troops mutiny on Madagascar.

Racial tension, morale, and leadership

The Government of Mauritius was acutely aware of the unofficial colour bar permeating Mauritian society and segregating the white elite, the Creoles, and the Indian majority. Racial discrimination was an issue from the foundation of the MTF, exacerbated by wartime conditions. 'The NCOs were a higher class of Creoles who resented the attitudes of the English officers towards them and their men'. Given the numerical dominance of Creoles over Indians in the MTF/MR, the latter community experienced difficulties. One ex-serviceman recalled that 'all my best friends were Creoles and avoided Indian companionship. I tried to conceal my Indian identity, feeling ashamed of my origin. . . . This stupid attitude took greater hold of me when I joined the Army where anti-Indian feeling was particularly violent and Creoles enjoyed some power'.

The considerable achievement of the British in forming military units using non-European peoples has rested on the closeness of British officers and their men. In the MR there was neither the time nor the desire to forge such bonds, and it showed. Carried into the Army was a resentment of the status of white Mauritians, whose social and economic dominance was translated wholesale into the structure of Army rank. This, according to Ramgoolam, 'ran counter to the Allied cause'. Roger Requin says that there were 'just a few officers — you can name them — who to me were very bright people. We were at school at the same time, we know their calibre. Now when you join the Army, they came and gave you orders — that's the problem. Such treatment was a proof of blatant injustice and was deeply resented throughout the Other Ranks'.

In his study of the King's African Rifles Timothy Parsons writes that 'military organizations are by nature hierarchical and authoritarian, but in colonial armies these divisions were defined almost exclusively by race.'[62] This was the way of the British Army at the time. Inequality was reflected in conditions of service that all could see. 'Officers had British pay, and we had Mauritian pay — African pay — [we were] treated as Africans.' This point is often emphasized by Mauritian ex-servicemen; they strongly resented being classified alongside Africans, who they considered inferior. Hence their great resentment at watching an African battalion march onto their island from the ship that was to take them overseas.

The racial gulf imported into the Army was also reflected in the widespread feeling among the white community that, first, it was dangerous to give non-whites military instruction, and that secondly, they would never make good fighting soldiers anyway. Likewise, British officers did not see Mauritians as particularly martial. These were standard cries of settlers throughout the colonial world. Captain Alfred North-Coombes wrote of:

> The danger it is to have these [non-white] fellows taught the use of weapons and the menace to the white community. . . To my mind our men would be more useful to the war effort if they were Pioneers or members of a Labour Corps rather than soldiers which they can never become. They have reached that state of civilization when the native

209

mind is distorted and dangerous. Higher [British] officers do not discuss these matters with Mauritian officers who, like myself, although very junior in rank, at least understand the local native mind and mentality.[63]

The Mauritius Regiment suffered from dangerously low morale. Regular entries in North-Coombes' diary refer to this problem and to a lack of respect among the officers of the Regiment's second battalion for its commanding officer, Major B. J. Landrock (seconded from the East Lancashire Regiment). Morale was acknowledged as a problem by the Officer Commanding Troops (OCT) Mauritius, Colonel Ronald Yeldham of the Sherwood Foresters:

> Training [is] difficult when you know you're not going off to do some fighting. Difficult job for officers to keep up morale. . . When you're remote from the battlefield one of the problems is maintaining morale . . . if you know you're going to the front line, it's okay.[64]

Indiscipline was a sign of low morale and did not augur well for overseas service. There were numerous cases of soldiers refusing to obey orders, for example refusing to empty latrine buckets, complaining that they had 'not enlisted for this type of work'. 'Breaking out of barracks was very common as was malingering', recalls a former soldier. The fact is that men who joined the MTF before it became the MR did so with no expectation of overseas service, and — war or no war — they did not want to leave home. Others were simply not fit enough for the exacting standards demanded when the exigencies of war turned the amateurish MTF into a Regiment under the authority of the War Office that could expect combat service overseas. As Sir (then Major) Guy Sauzier claims, the MTF 'at its formation was designed only for service on Mauritius itself, and the medical examination was relatively superficial'.

North-Coombes thought that morale had 'sunk to zero', and self-mutilation was an index of this. There were disturbing rumours 'now circulating of several men of 1MR maiming themselves so as not to leave the colony on Active Service. One man smashed his right thumb to pulp by hitting it with a heavy hammer, another broke his leg (tibia) on purpose, many are inducing 'alésées de fixation' by injecting themselves with turpentine, mostly in the chest. And so more men with barely any training are being taken from 2MR to replace them'.

Inexperienced troops were being drafted to replace men in a unit destined for front-line duties. Similarly, in October 1943 fifty other ranks from the Pioneer Corps were drafted into 1 MR. Self-mutilation did not stop when the soldiers reached Madagascar. Medical Officer (MO) Rex Salisbury Woods recalls that there were:

A few undisciplined men of low morale who. . . would run any risk to avoid being sent to Burma and battle. Some paid Chinese to lash-whip their knees to produce 'water-on-the-knee'. Others risked blindness by inducing acute gonococcal ophthalmea with pus from a friend; or amputation by pushing nails, purposely fouled with faeces, into the knee joint to provoke an infective arthritis. This sort of thing, when not spotted, notoriously inspired others, as it did when a veritable epidemic of 'low backache' followed the success of a few men in being excused duties, and the resulting sick wastage began to assume such proportions that all fresh cases had to be referred by the RMOs [Regimental Medical Officers] to me as Surgeon Specialist. Practically, none, I found, were genuine.[65]

Men of the Mauritius Regiment viewed their impending departure with gloom. A fellow officer told North-Coombes 'that the feeling of the men in 1MR was such that if they knew the time of departure of their transport it would be necessary to look for them "avec des bougies"'. When news of the Madagascar mutiny filtered back to Mauritius there were clear signs that 2MR troops did not want to follow their comrades overseas. Sergeant Felix believed 'the men's morale is such that they have been heard to say "if the [authorities] want to make us cross the sea we'll set fire to this Camp before we go"'. North-Coombes wrote that 'a strong undercurrent of passive resistance, if not blatantly apparent, is nevertheless clearly perceptible'.

The MR was poorly officered, at company and platoon level and at the higher level, where British officers had little appreciation of Mauritian problems. At the lower level, some Franco-Mauritian officers were ineffective, and the fact that communalism was a part of Mauritian life made for natural resentment and a coldness in inter-rank and inter-racial relations. Lieutenant-Colonel Fisher, who took command of 1MR after the mutiny, claimed that many officers lacked 'knowledge of man-management', too many bringing from civilian life the methods of the sugar estate or the dockside. 'Very few of these men took any interest in their men's welfare, and as most of them were drawn from the ranks of the French aristocracy of the Colony, they were *ipso facto* divorced from the confidence of their coloured troops'. There were signs of strained relations between British and Franco-Mauritian officers, and disquiet on the part of British other ranks who resented having 'part-timers' placed above them. Former members of the Mauritius Regiment insist that the 1st Battalion's ambitious commanding officer, Lieutenant-Colonel Yates, must shoulder much of the blame for the state of the Battalion that led to its mutiny. One described him as 'a tyrant in colonel's uniform'. A Government official's wife wrote that Colonel Ronald Yeldham, the Officer Commanding Troops, felt ashamed of 'the lack of hardship in his war service. . . (He) regrets the name he would like to have made'. Likewise, Yates perhaps felt that the war was passing him by. So when his opportunity came, he was determined to grasp it. Yates was 'a Regular Army officer who was, I suspect, anxious to fashion his battalion into a first-class fighting force'. With his arrival in 1942 'the troops began to lose their amateurism and be better trained'.

After the event, Yates had his own opinion as to where the blame for a mutiny that had blighted his career lay: 'The only six good officers were white non-Mauritians. A high percentage of Other Ranks were conscripts and only among Creoles was there any genuine enthusiasm to serve. . . [the] rest thought the most they should be asked to do was a little quiet training in Mauritius'. The fact that no white troops were ordered overseas led to resentment, particularly among families back at home, Yates added. NCOs were considered 'all right on parade, but had no influence when off it'.

So before 1MR even left Mauritius it was beset by problems that could lead to indiscipline and inefficiency. Lieutenant-Colonel Fisher recognized this with hindsight when attempting to reform the Battalion after the mutiny. In addition to the inferior quality of MR officers, he divined other reasons for the malaise. Because of geography, Mauritius was an insular island. The population was divided along racial and class lines, and recent disputes between employers and employed 'have become increasingly serious as the influence of militant Indian nationalism spreads [serious rioting had occurred in October 1943]. One consequence of a population divided against itself in this manner is a total absence of patriotic feelings, of any spirit of unity, or of any appreciation of civic responsibilities'. Fisher wrote that 50 percent of the troops came from the 'extremely poor' class of society, which suffered from undernourishment and a range of diseases. The war had spawned little contact between the people and the Armed Forces, 'there is no military caste', and so 'there is a complete absence of military background, and only a superficial, if any, interest is taken in the progress of the war — the majority feeling that it is NOT their war'.

Before leaving Mauritius, 'nothing had been done in regard to the education of the troops to give the necessary patriotic or military bias to their mental make-up'. The physical condition of many of the men passed A1 in Mauritius fell far short of that required for infantry troops. Fisher's analysis continued:

Many of the old peace-time territorial soldiers [members of the MTF], who constitute the backbone of the Battalion, felt aggrieved by the sudden conversion of their terms of service from voluntary service in MAURITIUS to compulsory service anywhere . . . Considerable subversive propaganda had been circulated within the Battalion by both outside and internal sources. . . on such subjects as (a) This was NOT the Mauritians' war, so why should they be used as cannon fodder? . . . (b) There might be an acceptable reason for Mauritians training as soldiers to die for their country in MAURITIUS, but there could be no reason for them to go and rot in MADAGASCAR or die in BURMA while East African soldiers used their comfortable barracks in MAURI-TIUS, and raped their sweethearts and wives. (c) The coloured population was being exploited again, witness the disproportionately few white people in 1MR and the fact that such white people hold all the best appointments.[66]

Fear of the Japanese and dislike of Africans

Rumour was endemic in Mauritius, and played a part in 'putting the wind up' soldiers who did not particularly want to serve overseas anyway. One problem was the reputation of the Japanese as ferocious soldiers — a psychological obstacle encountered by British and Indian soldiers of Burma Corps — and the currency of the belief that Mauritians were destined for the Far East as cannon fodder. George André Decotter, an MR and later a Pioneer Corps officer, recalls:

> I think that the men were reluctant — absolutely reluctant — to go to Burma. That was one of the reasons why they threw everything over the wall. Because they simply did not want to go to Burma. The offi-cial reason for our going to Madagascar given by Yates himself — I have seen it by his own hand in a minute in a file to the OCT — was they are going to Madagascar to be trained in 'ideal circumstances'.

A general unwillingness to leave the island was compounded by anger when it was learned that African soldiers were to replace them. The 17th Battalion KAR, commanded by Colonel E. F. Whitehead, was ordered to Mauritius in November 1943 to replace 1MR. Major Guy Sauzier recalls that the Mauritius Regiment 'took this badly — unhappy that African troops would be charged with the protection of their families'. Lieutenant J. F. C. Harrison recalls his KAR Battalion's arrival in Mauritius and the departure of 1MR:

Our reception was something less than enthusiastic. The big, fierce-looking askaris struck terror into the hearts of the islanders, who feared for their goods and women. . . When the KAR arrived there was a great fear that the askaris, who looked like savages to them, would molest the Mauritian womenfolk and rumours soon spread.[67]

'Most [Mauritius Regiment soldiers] were Creoles, small men, and they clearly did not want to go', and Harrison recalls the 'KAR lining the streets, seeing them off almost at bayonet point'. He continued:

Our first surprise was the emotional nature of their embarkation. As the Mauritius Regiment marched down the quay . . . amidst much waving and shouting I could not make out whether the crowds were protesting or encouraging their embarkation. There were tearful scenes as women, children, parents, and friends tried to kiss, embrace and hold on to the marching soldiers, some of whom seem to me to be reluctant to let go.

The Government of Mauritius had not learned the lesson of the hostile reception given to African troops in 1899, when, with the British garrison depleted by the Boer War, the 2nd Battalion The Central African Rifles was sent to make up the difference. The Battalion was not popular on the island, and was quickly moved offshore. Similarly, in the First World War: 'A large draft of Zulu recruits were sent to Mauritius for training. They got out of hand and sacked a village, looting shops — especially taverns — raping women etc. The Mauritians' conception of the African was based on this picture which had become distorted through time to the Africans detriment'.

Mutiny: the official version and eyewitness accounts

So the 'time bomb' factors leading to the mutiny were racial tension, poor officer–men relations, low morale caused by conscription and an unwillingness to serve overseas, and the unpopular decision to replace 1MR with African troops. It only needed a spark for the mutiny to occur, and this was provided upon arrival in Madagascar by an arduous route march and accommodation considered inadequate by the men. It is probably no coincidence that the War Diary entry for December 1943, the month in which the mutiny occurred, is missing, hindering an exact reconstruction of the course of the mutiny. The Commander-in-Chief East Africa, Lieutenant-General Platt, wrote to the War Office '[I] regret to report that 1st Mauritius Regiment on arrival at Diego Suarez from Mauritius burnt some of their huts in protest against the standards of accommodation and next day carried out a sit down strike'. The 'mass refusal to do PT' was the central act that turned insubordination and indiscipline into mutiny. 'Officially the men were said to be "browned off" . . . and angered about their removal from Mauritius'. The entire Battalion was disarmed, and 343 were arrested for being out of bounds of camp. Speculating about causes, the Governor referred to the 'over-long delay' in announcing the Battalion's departure, the politicized colour question, and the fact that there were 'more than likely subversive elements within the Battalion'. The Governor recommended a firm hand, and 'in no, repeat no, circumstances should the Battalion or any portion of it return to Mauritius until this disgrace has been lived down'.

Lieutenant-General Platt forwarded to Mauritius and Whitehall the report of his subordinate, the General Officer Commanding (GOC) Islands Area, Major-General Gerald Smallwood. The Mauritian battalion had had a twelve-mile march to their camp after landing. Upon arrival, 'discipline had virtually collapsed'. The accommodation provided was partly of old French brick barracks and partly good-standard *bandas* (grass huts) and the Mauritians 'took exception' to the latter. The following day the men refused to stay in limits, and 'were addressed by agitators'. Of nineteen interviewed, fourteen said they did not want to leave Mauritius. Many of the men had signed up not knowing that they would be required to go overseas. The GOC reported that all identified ringleaders had been court-martialled, and over 500 offenders put on minor charges.

Back in Mauritius, the 2nd Battalion of the Mauritius Regiment was not told of the mutiny for a month. Officers received 'the Official Version' from the commander:

The boat was crowded and accommodation poor but there was no sign of any trouble brewing. . . They were marched to this camp twelve miles away. Half way up the route men began to fall out. By the time they reached the camp a large number had fallen out and discipline had fallen to zero. The men were quartered in old French barracks and in *bandas*, in which even British NCOs live. That night the men set fire to some of the *bandas*. The CO tried to stop them and to obtain a hearing by the men, but they would not listen to him. Bounds were set, but the men broke bounds. More huts were set on fire, and as the position became uncontrollable two Battalions of KAR and one armoured Battalion were ordered to disarm them. The next morning a PT parade was ordered. There were 400 absentees. They are still disarmed and are now building roads [and when doing so were treated with derision by passing askari, the African soldiers]. Of 1,000 men, 300 are awaiting trial by the new commanding officer. Colonel Yates is on his way to England, but he has been found not responsible. There has been a reshuffling of the officers. Ten to fifteen men have been court martialled and sentences of three to fifteen years imprisonment passed.[68]

Resentment had mounted even during the sea voyage between Mauritius and Madagascar. It was noted that cabin accommodation had been afforded a handful of white NCOs, but coloured NCOs were billeted on the troop deck. This was 'seized upon as a case of differential treatment . . . and caused grave and general dissatisfaction'. Major Guy Sauzier had been sent ahead to Madagascar on 12 October 1943 with an Advance Party in order to prepare for the Battalion's arrival. On arrival, the men were demoralized and made to march in 'overpowering' heat. During the march:

> Some men began to leave the ranks and lie down at the roadside, without even having obtained permission of the officer in charge, already a grave indiscipline. [At the camp] Sauzier was warning the men to take care not to set fire to the huts, one went up in flames, and he exhorted the men to put it out. One of the men said, 'Let it burn'. This was the first act of insubordination. Several huts then went up in flames, and it became obvious that they were criminal acts of arson. As they struggled, largely in vain, to put out the flames, snakes emerged from the huts and added to the general fear. A few men left the camp and took refuge in a small village on a beach close by. Those left at the camp struggled to regain order . . . The next day Sauzier and other officers went to round up the men, with little success. One soldier, elbow propped against the counter of a little shop, told Sauzier, 'Sir, everything you are telling me is going in one ear and out the other'. The next evening further fires were lit and more men left the camp.[69]

Several King's African Rifles officers who took part in the round-up of the mutinous Mauritians have left written accounts. The composite battalion of African troops were armed with *pangas* and rifles with fixed bayonets. Most were in KAR units being withdrawn from Madagascar to make way for the Mauritians, who were to take over their duties garrisoning Fortress Diego — responsible for the giant island's key naval base — as they prepared to move to the Far East. They confirm the reasons for the mutiny — unwillingness to leave Mauritius, anger at their replacement by African troops, the march to Orangea, dissatisfaction with the accommodation, and insects. They point out that their treatment was quite normal by the standards of the British Army, and the accommodation was considered to be good by those standards. However, the MR was simply not experienced enough to cope, and was already in a 'mutinous mood'.

Roger Requin recalls that:

Each night for consecutive nights there had been tents on fire, with flames illuminating the sky and creating a fairy-like atmosphere, described as 'feux de joie'. That Monday night was really a nightmare. All during the night, we heard the footstep of soldiers arriving at Orangea. Exhausted, they just threw their heavy body wherever they could, using their pack as a pillow. Discipline was a dead word; they were tired and hungry, it was no use reasoning with them. On Tuesday afternoon, orders were received that every soldier must fall in for physical training on Wednesday morning, but practically on that day no one turned up. They stayed in their tents, doing nothing but playing cards or dominoes. Some strolled to the sea side and spent the day there. For about three days running, they enjoyed such sweet idleness, doing no military work, refusing orders from anyone. These do-nothing days, baptized 'Vacances Payees', were not to last forever. On Friday, they noticed from the stone buildings that African troops were lurking around their encampment. They took it that these soldiers were being deployed as part of their training and thus they did not pay any heed to their movement and continued relaxing. All of a sudden, these African soldiers, fully armed, encircled all the premises, seized all the rifles, and drove all the troops to a plain nearby.

King's African Rifles officer Tom Higginson, one of those seconded to help the Mauritius Regiment reform and retrain, offers a succinct summary of the causes of the mutiny:

Although the mutiny could not and cannot be condoned, there were reasons for it. These were raw, half-trained polyglot troops with little regimental tradition, homesick for their 'Jolie petite ile' which they had never previously left. They had been translated, for purely political reasons, over a rough sea and decanted onto a large, strange, hot and apparently hostile land, there to be forced into a long, mid-day march under a scorching tropical sun to accommodation which by their standards was primitive. An example of bad man management.[70]

After the mutiny

The MR was disbanded in August 1944 and its men parcelled off to other Army units. The Regiment, however, was *not* disbanded immediately after the mutiny, and was not disbanded *because* of the mutiny. A combination of factors caused the disbandment — the period of 'reformation' after the mutiny failed to produce sufficiently encouraging results; MR personnel could be better employed by the Army in other areas; and low standards of physical fitness and ill-health beset the Regiment. Until August 1944, however, it was still destined to be a front-line infantry unit, and a new commander and new officers were doing their best to bring it up to scratch.

The Mauritius Regiment was given a chance to re-train for its original purpose as an infantry regiment, rather than immediately being disbanded or downgraded, because senior officers did not think that the training it had received before leaving Mauritius had been adequate. That it still might be sent to the Far East is evidenced by the continual post-mutiny training, and the frequency of lectures with titles like 'Burma Front and Japanese Tactics', and 'Advance to Contact and Encounter Battle in Jungle'. Certainly the troops, always unhappy about the prospect of facing the Japanese, continued to believe that the Far East was their ultimate destination. In April 1944 CSM Fright from I (Intelligence) Branch arrived to investigate rumours in the Battalion that it was about to move East.

Immediately after the mutiny the Commander-in-Chief East Africa consulted the Governor Sir Donald Mackenzie Kennedy, and his subordinate, Islands Area Commander-in-Chief Major-General Smallwood. Platt decided that 1MR was to 'be reformed (in more senses than one, I hope!), and [the] Commanding Officer replaced'. A number of the Battalion's officers were temporarily transferred to the KAR to 'broaden their outlook', experienced KAR officers were drafted in, and some MR personnel were transferred to the Pioneer Corps. 2MR was to be converted into a training centre and depot for all Mauritian units. At this point, the purpose of the Regiment was not to be altered; it was acknowledged that problems had prevented it from becoming a 'first line unit', but these were to be overcome. On 26

January 1944 the free men of the Battalion were finally rearmed. A few days later, at a conference of officers presided over by Major-General Smallwood, it was declared that the Battalion was to be 'trained up to and become a first line unit'. The aim was for the 'physical and mental re-education of the Battalion. This is to be achieved by PT, route marches of gradually increasing length, education classes, and propaganda'. On 15 February a batch of 179 soldiers was returned to the Battalion from the Orangea Detention Camp.

The much-maligned commanding officer, Lieutenant-Colonel Yates, was replaced by Lieutenant-Colonel Jackie R. Fisher of the Royal Inniskilling Fusiliers, who was to attempt the reformation of the Battalion. All ex-servicemen remember Fisher with warm regard, in contrast to their universal condemnation of Yates. The 'ringleaders' condemned to death had their sentences commuted to seven to fifteen years imprisonment by the Commander-in-Chief. Many ex-servicemen resent their punishment to this day, feeling that it was totally unwarranted: 'My nights are still haunted by my "discharge with ignominy from the Army" and the twenty-four months spent in hell [prison]. The whole is made worse by my total innocence and the fact that I had naively wanted to serve my country.'

Guy Sauzier writes that after the mutiny, 'the General [Smallwood] instructed me to draw up a declaration, urging the men against further insubordination but exhorting them to forget the past and reform into the effective unit he had seen in Mauritius [when he visited in the autumn of 1943]'. Upon assuming command after Yates' dismissal, Lieutenant-Colonel Fisher addressed the Battalion: 'I know quite well your past behaviour, but for me it's a challenge, thus I am trusting upon your good will and discipline. Without any doubt, I am confident that you will not let me down'. As the months passed, Fisher felt that he was making progress in reforming the Battalion. In March 1944 he wrote that 'confidence in their cause, their leaders, and the progress of the war is in the initial stages of up-building; it is likely to be a lengthy process', but it was hoped that the exchange of 1MR officers for more experienced officers would help, along with 'the inauguration of a process of complete mental and physical re-education'. He kept an eye on conditions, including accommodation, messing, NAAFI (Navy, Army, and Air Force Institutes) supplies, recreation and amusements, and the mail service. In terms of efficiency, physical fitness was considered to be of a low standard, and discipline 'extremely low'. Relations between officers, NCOs, and the men were slowly improving, though Fisher noted that 'no little jealousy and ill-feeling arose over the selection of both officers and NCOs who were required in large numbers in the formation of the new Battalion in the second half of 1942'.

The second Quarterly Morale Report revealed factors hindering the Battalion's attempts to reform. Major F. R. G. Rountree, standing in for Fisher, noted that the Battalion 'would now appear to consist of a minority of approximately 150 to 200 men, excluding sixty-five Other Ranks who were recently evacuated to Mauritius on medical grounds, who are either physically unfit to serve or who have decided that, come what may, they will not serve. These men do the barest minimum amount of work to keep themselves out of trouble and report sick on every possible occasion. They thus constitute a bad moral influence on the remainder. It is felt that if these men could be replaced by better material and some prospects of a more active role held out, more satisfactory results would be obtained'.

In terms of 'confidence in their cause', the troops were optimistic, indeed rather casual, believing that it was only a matter of time before the Allies won the war. 'They seem to take these things for granted, and as a result, events like the fall of Rome and the invasion of Western Europe produce only mild enthusiasm'. The troops had confidence in their officers, though 'an underlying colour prejudice against being led by White Mauritian Officers' was still evident. 'British Officers and CSMs get markedly better results from the troops'. In terms of contentment, Rountree reported that a 'genuine antipathy' for Madagascar had developed. The men felt that the future held nothing but 'training and more training', and were anxious 'to move to a more active sphere'. It was reported that the troops were pleased to move from Sakaramy back to Orangea — even though this had been the site of the mutiny — as 'the jiggers [flesh-burrowing fleas] menace had assumed considerable psychological proportions in the minds of many of the troops'. Once at Orangea, 'all jigger infection has now disappeared'. Jiggers caused long queues at the medical centre each day, and daily sick parades were huge. On 6 March 1944, 144 men reported sick. Those adjudged to have been shamming were sent on a twelve-mile route march, and twenty men who fell out of this exercise were ordered to repeat it. On 20 March 1944, 103 men reported sick, on 17 April, 252. Ninety-six of these men were found not to be sick, and sent on a fifteen-mile march. A week later 150 reported sick, and thirty-seven of these were sent on a twelve-mile march.

Rountree noted that as a result of the 'abnormally large sick parades, I ordered my MO to examine the whole Battalion, and he found that approximately 200/250 men were below A1 category'. Discipline was 'fair', 'but the troops do NOT, probably owing to their complete lack of military background, appear to understand the necessity for military discipline. NCOs do NOT, generally speaking, enforce strict discipline unless an officer is present'.

Major-General Rowley Mans remembers that the Mauritians 'used to march past our camp en route to the hills but on the return many fell out exhausted. They were obviously not up to the physical efforts demanded. Eventually Fisher reported to GOC that they could not reach the required standard'. The Commander-in-Chief wrote that he 'consider[ed the] quality of Mauritius personnel in unit does not justify retention as first line unit'. He proposed to convert the Battalion into an Artisan Works Company and two Independent Garrison Companies, 'with consequent saving of British manpower'. The former went to the Middle East, the latter to Kenya. Some men became clerks at the Military Records Office and Pay Branch in Nairobi, and Guy Sauzier took a contingent to Gilgil (EAC's Ammunition Depot in Kenya). Those wanting to transfer to the Mauritian Pioneer Corps were told to submit their names to their Company Commander.

The Governor of Mauritius agreed with Lieutenant-General Platt's prognosis. 'Despite efforts, General Platt and I reluctantly conclude that they are not up to scratch'. He wrote of the 'shocking' military efficiency of the unit, and that the mental attitude and mediocre medical condition of many was 'most disquietening'. Lieutenant-Colonel Fisher paraded the Battalion on 8 August 1944, and after it had presented arms, announced its disbandment. 'I am afraid I have some very bad news for you', he began, before outlining the position regarding sickness and poor physical standards within the unit. With so many Pioneers in the Middle East, there were 'no longer sufficient reinforcements in Mauritius to maintain this Battalion at its correct strength and fitness'. General Platt had reluctantly decided to disband the Regiment, and 'reform it into other smaller units which can give the maximum help to the general war effort'.

The maladroit handling of Mauritian troops by their officers did not end with the mutiny, as illustrated by the treatment of 2MR after 1MR had mutinied. If ever there was a time to tread carefully, this was it. However, on 1 February 1944, 2MR was 'paraded to be told about the 1st MR by Landrock'. In North-Coombes' opinion, the commanding officer 'committed the stupid error of telling the men that "they should be ashamed for what had happened to the 1st MR". [This] particularly upset the more enlightened among the men'. He continued to record that 'Landrock also told the parade that "a General [Smallwood] would visit on Monday or Tuesday to see if they could be made into soldiers or if they should be disbanded" — another psychological mistake. I would not be surprised if many of them are absent without leave on Monday'.

On 7 February 1944 Major-General Smallwood inspected the Battalion, and the following day the Battalion's CO held a conference to tell his Company Commanders what the future had in store for the Battalion in light of the mutiny:

> The Battalion will cease to exist in a few days when it will become a Training Company of four Platoons with a fairly large HQ. Some will be transferred to the Artillery. The General says he has dealt with the 1st MR very gently this time but that he won't stand any more nonsense either there or here and men who do not comply with orders will be shot.

10

Ceylon, Mauritius, and the Indian Ocean during the Second World War

'The Queen of the Nicobar Islands is a determined looking woman of about fifty-five with four husbands and lots of grandchildren who scuffle about among the pigs, poultry, and offal. She is the sort of Queen who likes to get hold of a bottle of gin and no nonsense about mixing it with water or sharing it with anyone else'. Thus wrote John Godfrey. Who were these people, and what was this place? The Queen in question reigned over the nineteen coconut and rice-producing islands of the Nicobar group, formed by the peaks of a submerged mountain range in the Bay of Bengal. The islands were invaded by the Japanese in 1942, ending seventy-three years of British rule, and for the remainder of the war formed the westernmost rampart of the Japanese empire of conquest. John Godfrey was a British admiral who had been head of naval intelligence at the Admiralty, assisted by Ian Fleming, until his outspokenness led Churchill to secure his removal. He was given command of the Royal Indian Navy, which by the end of the war had grown thirty-fold to number over 30,000 personnel manning more than 100 warships. This chapter argues that the Indian Ocean has been neglected as a theatre of war in its own right, a stunning omission because it was so important to both the imperial and the Allied war effort. It then considers the war experience of the Indian Ocean colonies of Ceylon and Mauritius.[71]

Admiral Godfrey visited the Andaman and Nicobar Islands and met the gin-loving queen on an official cruise after British rule had been re-established in 1945. The tour also took in the Andaman Islands, the Maldives, and the ports of Bombay, Calcutta, Cochin, Karachi, Madras, and Vizagapatam. All of these places came under Godfrey's purview as Flag Officer Commanding the Royal Indian Navy, a force that provided valuable support to the Royal Navy's Eastern Fleet during the war. The Eastern Fleet, which made extensive use of the Royal Indian Navy's bases and its communications network, was the Second World War's least heralded Royal Navy formation. Its neglect is surprising, because for much of the war it was the largest British fleet afloat and gave birth in 1944 to the British Pacific Fleet — the most powerful Royal Navy force ever assembled — which braved the *kamikazes* during the Okinawa campaign as part of the American armada closing in on the Japanese home islands. Its home was the colony of Ceylon with outlying bases in other colonies such as Aden, Kenya, and Mauritius.

The Eastern Fleet's primary task, assisted by the Royal Indian Navy and other imperial warships, was to secure the sea lanes of the Indian Ocean theatre, stretching from the Swahili coast to Malaya and Sumatra. It relied upon a network of colonial bases in order to do so. Upon these Indian Ocean sea lanes rested the ability of General Slim's 'forgotten' Fourteenth Army to beat back the Japanese from the gates of India. Upon these sea lanes also rested the ability of General Montgomery's Eighth Army's to hold Rommel in the Western Desert before winning victory at Alamein. Why? Because all of the reinforcements for Middle East Command in Egypt came around the Cape in armoured convoys and were escorted through the Indian Ocean to the Suez Canal. The same was also true in the East, where the defence of India and the build up of resources for the reconquest of Burma and Malaya depended utterly upon secure sea communications across the Indian Ocean. By March 1941 over 643,000 Empire troops had already passed through the waters patrolled by the warships of the East Indies Station.

In addition to this, the Indian Ocean sea lanes guarded by the Eastern Fleet and a host of RAF bases from Arabia to Mombasa and Calcutta carried the oil and aviation fuel from the wells and refineries of Iran and Iraq that kept British and Empire engines running all over the world. The Eastern Fleet was commanded by Admiral Sir James Somerville after his predecessor, Admiral Sir Tom Phillips, had died aboard the battleship *Prince of Wales* a matter of days after arriving from England to take command at Singapore and, as Churchill earnestly expected, outface the Japanese. After this shocking failure of British sea power, the fleet operated from Ceylon, the island stronghold that, after the fall of Singapore, became Britain's new Eastern headquarters as it sought to resist, and then slowly push back, the Japanese assault on Britain's Eastern Empire. Thus the Indian Ocean was a theatre of war that connected all of the British Empire's main fighting fronts, and that was crucial for the supply of fuel to British consumers, military and civilian, from the industrial heartlands of the north of England to the farms and cities of Australia.

A host of people, places, and military formations in the Indian Ocean region contributed to what amounts to a lost victory, won on the sea lanes of the world's third largest ocean and the British-dominated territories on its rim. It featured numerous British colonies, such as Aden, Ceylon, Kenya, Malaya, Mauritius, the Seychelles, Singapore, Tanganyika and tiny island colonies such as Diego Garcia and the Cocos-Keeling Islands. The Indian Ocean theatre stretched from Africa to the Malayan peninsula, from the Persian Gulf to Antarctica, and embraced a galaxy of islands and palm-fringed atolls over which the Union Flag flew. Here, in a forgotten heartland, Britain orchestrated the war effort of the Empire and its American, Dutch, and Free French allies in a breathtaking display of coalition warfare based upon three centuries of imperial growth and interaction, and the ability of proud, independent countries to overcome their differences and work towards a common goal. The struggle in this part of the world was vital to the outcome of the war, for without control of the sea lanes and resources of the Indian Ocean region the imperial war in the Middle East and South Asia could not have been sustained, nor the British Empire defended. The campaign in the Indian Ocean lasted from the earliest days of hostilities between Britain and Germany, when the pocket battleship *Graf Spee* nosed its way around the Cape, until long after the war had ended, as Japanese and imperial prisoners of war were repatriated from reconquered Allied colonies and British imperial divisions awaited the arrival of Dutch and French forces sent to re-establish control in Indo-China and the East Indies.

Despite the importance of the Indian Ocean, it is a theatre rarely given adequate prominence in the annals of the Second World War. This remarkable omission stems partly from the fact that history is usually written from the perspective of the land and not the sea, and so the interdependence of both environments is seldom fully grasped. It is also a result of the limited understanding and scholarly attention afforded the subject of logistics; historians prefer to concentrate on glorious battles and the 'teeth' end of military activity, not the 'tail' that supplies it. Neglect of the Indian Ocean theatre stems also from the fact that for none of the belligerents, vital though it was to the success of some of them, was it the theatre of primary focus. Finally, it is neglected because the war is not perceived in imperial terms due to a predominantly Eurocentric historiography and a general failure to see the Pacific war as anything more than

225

American revenge for Pearl Harbor. Even at the time, many failed to appreciate the imperial dimensions of the struggle, in striking contrast to the public understanding of the First World War.

In every theatre of military activity British imperial endeavour relied upon secure sea lanes. One look at a map of the world shows how significant the Indian Ocean was in linking Britain to its estates in Africa, Arabia, the Persian Gulf, South Asia, South-east Asia, Australasia, and the Far East, for it washed the shores of them all. The sprawling structure that was the British Empire was both a cause of war, because three aggressive dictators wanted to replace British rule with their own, and a target for their aggression when colonies and sea lanes from the Caribbean to the central Pacific came under attack as Hirohito, Hitler, and Mussolini pursued their imperial ambitions. In defending the Empire, America rose to power in many previously exclusive imperial domains, the price of an alliance in which Britain's position gradually waned. Because so much of the Empire was lost to the enemy during the war, and its existence gravely threatened, the war was by definition one of imperial reconquest and imperial survival. The battle to survive took place not just in the face of the enemy, but in the face of American politicians and generals seeking a post-war world in which European empires played a much diminished role.

Fighting the Axis in the Indian Ocean region

Aware of the British Empire's dependence upon sea lines of communication, the Germans showed a keen interest in severing them. Battleships and submarine packs were sent around the Cape to hunt athwart the major sea lanes, lurking in the Mozambique Channel, laying mines of South Africa's ports, operating from captured ports such as Batavia and Penang, and stalking tankers off the Arabian coast. Also dispatched from European ports to take up station in the Indian Ocean were armed merchant raiders such as the famous *Atlantis* and *Pinguin*, corsairs of the modern age whose deployment was inspired by the marauding voyage of the First World War raider *Emden*, which, as an earlier chapter has recounted, had sunk and captured dozens of Allied merchant ships in the Indian Ocean before being run to ground by an Australian cruiser escorting the first contingent of Anzacs to Europe. German and Italian ground and air forces attacked British colonies and British client states on the Indian Ocean rim, hundreds of thousands of Italian troops operated from Ethiopia and Somaliland, and Heinkels and Messerschmitts flew in the skies above Baghdad and the Euphrates. The Italian navy menaced British merchantmen and troopships delivering vital reinforcements through the Red Sea to Middle East Command and its manifold battle fronts from the Western Desert to Crete, Greece, and Iraq.

Dealing with the challenge of the Axis powers in the Indian Ocean before the Japanese onslaught was thus a difficult task for the British, preoccupied as they were with national survival and battles closer to home, but it was one that was within their capabilities. Victories in this region — and just as importantly, the avoidance of defeat — were unlikely to grab headlines with so much dramatic activity nearer to home and the bulk of the British Army overseas fighting in North Africa (the fact that this theatre was dependent on Indian Ocean supply routes was hardly likely to command much attention in the newspapers). Nevertheless, Britain's efforts in the Indian Ocean region were remarkable and demonstrated an extraordinary imperial awareness and strategic flexibility. This was manifest in several ways, key among them the introduction of a global convoy system, military operations launched to forestall enemy expansion, and the development of new fortified military bases. Italian forces were crushed in East Africa and the Red Sea, and Mussolini's dream of a new Roman Empire destroyed, the first blow in a series of reverses that were to lead to his downfall and execution later in the war. This conflict, affecting people in Ethiopia, Kenya, the Sudan and all colonies in the Horn of Africa, is usually seen as an adjunct to the war in the Middle East. But it also secured Britain's control of a crucial Indian Ocean supply line, and allowed American merchant vessels to conform with the Neutrality Act and begin funnelling supplies to the British through the 'non combat' area of the Red Sea, now dominated by British warships and maritime patrol aircraft. It also secured overland supply routes that took armoured cars, military supplies, troops, and food from Kenya, Northern and Southern Rhodesia, South Africa, Tangankiya, and Uganda to Middle East Command and its great Egyptian base. From East Africa, tens of thousands of East and West African troops were transported across the Indian Ocean to Burma and Ceylon.

British imperial forces fought in other lands on the Indian Ocean rim. Australian, British, and Indian troops and naval vessels were deployed to quell a serious rebellion in Iraq mounted in conjunction with the Luftwaffe, and a few months later invaded Iran in order to establish a secure overland route to Russia. The Royal Navy mounted a blockade to ensure that Vichy France struggled to maintain contact with its colonies in Africa, the Far East, and the Indian Ocean, preventing the exploitation of the French Empire by its Teutonic master. To further cripple France overseas, Britain launched an ambitious amphibious assault to seize Madagascar and the smaller French islands of the Indian Ocean (using the colonies of Kenya and Mauritius as bases, as well as Durban in South Africa). It was a strike urgently encouraged by the South African Prime Minister Jan Smuts in order to prevent the Japanese from dramatically extending their power in the western Indian Ocean with the collusion of a supine Vichy government. All of these campaigns were of great importance, because in the desperate days of 1941, before the battles of Midway, Alamein, and Stalingrad had begun to tip the balance in the Allies' favour, the enemy had to be held at every possible point if he were not to continue his rapid advances. These were resolute actions calculated to stymie Axis penetration of key regions, to secure vital oil supplies, and to establish a route for American and British aid to reach Russia via Iran, the one part of the world where the three great allies were in direct overland contact. Even Britain's friends in the Indian Ocean region harboured the enemy, and covert campaigns were waged in Portuguese East Africa and Goa in order to outwit Axis intelligence and save the lives of Allied sailors. In addition to these offensive campaigns, the British made defensive preparations, installing anti-aircraft guns, port defences, radar, and machine-gun nests across the Indian Ocean region. They developed the roads, pipelines, railways, aerodromes, and ports in Ceylon and India that would be the springboard for imperial reconquest, and began the transformation of Addu Atoll in the Maldives, where thousands of men prepared a fleet base in case Singapore should fall in a war against Japan. Finally, in order to safeguard the precious cargoes of imperial troops and to sustain the trade that kept the Empire nourished, a system of armoured convoys was organized to preserve secure communications, guarded by the warships of the Eastern Fleet.

1942: The most perilous year

All of this work to secure the sea lanes and to defeat German and Italian forces on the Indian Ocean rim early in the war was quickly overshadowed as 1941 drew to a close and the crucial year of 1942 dawned. Now the British Empire faced not only the German and Italian threat in the western Indian Ocean and the Middle East, spearheaded by General Erwin Rommel, but total collapse in Asia and the Far East. British colonies were in the front line, some conquered, some transformed into strategic redoubts, as for the first time in a century and a half it looked as if the system of imperial defence might actually fail. By March, the

Japanese had conquered Britain's Eastern Empire, along with those of America, France, and Holland. The loss of India became a distinct possibility for the first time since the struggles with France in the eighteenth century. The sea lanes of the Indian Ocean stood between defeat and survival in the Western Desert, and determined Britain's capacity to supply and hold on in India following the Japanese conquest of Burma. The enemy appeared at the gates of India just at the moment when Gandhi launched his 'Quit India' movement, requiring a period of British repression unprecedented since the Mutiny of 1857 following the rejection of Sir Stafford Cripps' offer of independence after the war. By March 1942 the flag of the Rising Sun had been run up in Hong Kong, Shanghai, the Solomon Islands, New Guinea, Borneo, the Philippines, the Dutch East Indies, Singapore, Malaya, Burma, Christmas Island, and the Andaman and Nicobar Islands, and the Imperial Japanese Navy was master of the Bay of Bengal and preparing its attack on Ceylon. With heavy losses of territory and the surrender of sea control to the Japanese, the Second World War in the East became, for the British, a war of imperial survival and of imperial reconquest.

Within weeks of entering the war in December 1941, therefore, Japan had wrested suzerainty of the eastern Indian Ocean from Britain's grasp, a startling imperial reverse ranking alongside the loss of the American colonies and a far-reaching disaster for British world power. After the fall of Singapore and Allied defeat at the Battle of the Java Sea, the sea lanes of the Indian Ocean — Transport Central of the British Empire and the key to imperial survival — lay at the tender mercies of Admiral Nagumo's carriers and battleships fresh from victory on the 'day of infamy'. The Japanese advance hit the Eastern Empire like a whirlwind. Colonies ruled for generations were lost in the twinkling of an eye. An entire imperial military command and the lion's share of its manpower was wiped out. A pioneering Allied command structure, American–British–Dutch –Australian Command led by General Sir Archibald Wavell, came into existence, fought forlornly, and was then disbanded, all within the few short weeks between the fall of Singapore and American surrender in the Philippines. In April 1942 the same aircraft carriers and battleships that had attacked Pearl Harbor raided Ceylon, led by the same men, in an attempt to extinguish Britain's naval power east of Suez. This strike was designed to complete the work that had begun with the sinking of HMS *Prince of Wales* and *Repulse* two days after the American Pacific Fleet was attacked at its moorings in Hawaii, thereby securing the new Japanese Empire's sea communications in the west. Over 130 dive bombers and Zero fighters flew in formation over the tea plantations, jungles, mountains, and harbours of the island, seeking out the warships of Admiral Sir James Somerville's Eastern Fleet, the composite naval force that stood between the Imperial Japanese Navy and mastery of the Empire's sea lanes. In this moment of high drama, the two massive fleets, the one modern, battle-hardened, and trained to the highest pitch, the other aged, inexperienced, and unpracticed, sought each other out in the waters to the south of Ceylon. Success for the enemy would have left the Indian Ocean open to Japanese domination, and, if Japan had taken the historic opportunity which presented itself, ended the imperial war effort and drawn the curtain upon Britain's position as a global power.

If the Japanese had struck true, and demonstrated a genuine understanding of the manner in which empires are made and empires are broken, Britain's last imperial war would have been a total loss. The major fighting fronts of the British Empire — in the Middle East (based on Egypt), in South Asia (based on Ceylon and India), and in the Southwest Pacific (based on Australia) — would have lost all connection, the convoys carrying troops and supplies would have been unable to sail; the galaxy of imperial territories, dependent upon the Merchant Navy for their sustenance, would have been left to wither on the imperial vine, their exports rotting in warehouses and godowns, their populations rapidly running out of food, kerosene, and soap, and praying to be spared the horrors of Japanese occupation that had been visited upon conquered cities in China.

Britain versus Japan after the fall of Singapore

There exists a hiatus in the historiography of Britain's involvement in the war against Japan, a breakdown in perception between the fall of Singapore and final victory in the Burma campaign. Britain's Eastern defeats, most famously symbolized by two photographs, one of men scrambling to abandon the battleship *Prince of Wales* as she foundered in the Gulf of Siam, the other showing the lanky figure of General Sir Arthur Percival and his surrender party, beneath a limp Union Flag in Singapore, have for long represented the sorry end of Britain's war in the East. Following this disaster, the Burma campaign is marooned in the popular memory of the war, a grim, jungle-bound, bloody but somewhat irrelevant struggle that had little to do with the final defeat of Japan and is rarely perceived in its true imperial context. After Britain's ignoble defeat in Malaya and its coastal waters, the war in the East becomes an all-American affair in standard histories, a testament to peerless industrial might and the grim determination of a rising superpower to make Japan pay for Pearl Harbor on every bloody Pacific atoll, to destroy its merchant marine, and to pulverize its homeland through strategic bombing, before grinding it into abject and atrocious defeat with atomic power.

But this picture does not fairly reflect the British Empire's participation in the Eastern war *and its continuation after the fall of Singapore*. Even after the famous island's surrender, the British Empire remained very much in the fight against Japan, a fight continued from a desperate defensive posture as the enemy threatened India itself and the forces of the Emperor reigned supreme. But the fight never ceased. After Singapore, British imperial forces, and those of its American and Dutch allies, remained to fight in Borneo, Java, the Philippines, Sumatra, and the forest of Dutch and Portuguese islands crowding the seas between Bali and New Guinea. The Australians provided the bulk of Allied troops attempting to stem the Japanese tide in New Guinea in the crucial early stages of fighting on that giant island. Following defeats in these lands and concomitant Allied retreat, the British fight continued, a rearguard fought from Ceylon, India, Kenya and a host of island bases supporting thousands of imperial servicemen and women. Britain shored up the defences of Ceylon and India and retained the capacity to wage war behind enemy lines in Japan's newly-conquered colonies. The Eastern Fleet protected convoys and hunted enemy raiders, and its submarines began a lengthy campaign against Japanese shipping in the Malacca Strait and the Bay of Bengal. Meanwhile the RAF built up its transport and bomber forces in Ceylon and India, and operated flying boats and bombers from airstrips and anchorages throughout the Indian Ocean.

Whilst the war could not have been won in the Indian Ocean region, it might have been lost, and here the forces of the British Empire, aided by luck and momentous military events elsewhere, held on and *avoided defeat*. This capacity to carry on was founded upon Britain's grip on infrastructure across the ocean, and its enormous naval resources that - even when Britain faced defeats around the world - enabled it to find the wherewithal to protect convoys and defend ports. It also managed against the odds to retain the ability to move military resources all around the world, the most telling benefit of the seapower that Britain had maintained for hundreds of years. Simply put, Britain *had* to hold on in its Indian Ocean demesne if it were not to be irrevocably defeated in the Middle East and South Asia, and if it were to stand any chance of regaining its lost colonies and ensuring that the defeat of Japan was not an exclusively American enterprise. This it did, with the grit and determination of a prize-fighter hanging on in the ring, desperately trying to hold on whilst summoning his strength for a final push against a fearsome opponent.

The tide turns

Having survived the hammer blows of 1941–42, the tide began to turn for the British Empire in 1943. Increasingly the Allies were able to take the offensive in the Indian Ocean, and the Eastern Fleet was able to break the routine of convoy escort work and begin to support army advances in Burma and conduct battleship and carrier strikes against Japanese-held territory. The combined American and British Chiefs of Staff sent Admiral Lord Louis Mountbatten to the theatre to lead a new South East Asia Command established to run the war against Japan in occupied territories from the China–Burma border through the Malayan peninsula and on to Sumatra and Borneo. Under him served Britain's great Eastern general, Sir William Slim, who had fought his way across the Indian Ocean, beginning the war in Kenya and Ethiopia before arriving to take over the shattered rump of Burma Corps by way of divisional commands in the Iran and Iraq campaigns. The turn around was achieved by Britain building up its forces in the East as and when it could, taking advantage of a turn of fortune in the Atlantic, or the surrender of Italy in the Mediterranean, to transfer resources to the Indian Ocean. It did so by wily tactics, by luck, and by alliance with America, which by 1944 was giving Japan so much to worry about closer to home that the Indian Ocean extremities of the Greater East Asian Co-Prosperity Sphere became strategic poor relations. In 1944 imperial and Allied forces went on the offensive throughout the Indian Ocean region, the Fourteenth Army in Burma and India, the Eastern Fleet in the waters of Malaya and the Dutch East Indies. The amphibious re-invasion of Malaya, Operation Zipper, went in just days after the atomic bombs were dropped, at the moment of Japan's catastrophic homeland defeat.

Mauritius at war

During the Second World War Mauritius contributed to the imperial war effort in many different ways, and was markedly affected on the home front. Its population was required to contribute to defensive measures as the island helped prosecute imperial campaigns in the region and reprised its original role as a strategic base athwart the Empire's communication and trade routes. On the political front, the Vichy sympathies of many of the island's Franco-Mauritians caused concern, and rioting on sugar estates in 1943 led to questions in both British houses of parliament. The British colonial administration had to tread carefully in mobilizing Mauritius for war and navigating its inter-racial sensitivities, because the Council of Government contained sophisticated politicians used to employing the media and maintaining links to British left-wing political organizations such as the Fabians.

Mauritius was used as a base for regional military operations, including those mounted against Réunion and Madagascar. This featured propaganda for the Allied and Free French cause broadcast to the Vichy territories from secret locations in Mauritius. SOE and other military operations against the islands were mounted from Mauritius. A Royal Naval Air Station was opened at Plaisance (like many wartime airfields in the colonies, it later became the island's international airport). A flying boat base opened at Tombeau Bay, and Hurricanes flew sorties from Mauritius collecting meteorological data. There were military facilities scattered across the island, including an armaments depot in Midlands, torpedo stores at Floreal, explosives stores at Rose Belle, and an Admiralty wireless station at Rose Bell. The colony was a base for Royal Navy warships and RAF aircraft involved in the search for enemy vessels, such as the much-hunted German submarine supply ships *Charlotte Schliemann* and *Brake*. Shipping losses in the waters around Mauritius and the wider Indian Ocean occurred throughout the war, the eventual tally of ships sunk reaching nearly 400. Sydney Moody, the Colonial Secretary of Mauritius (the Governor's number two) lost his daughter when the SS *Hoi How* was sunk on a journey from Port Louis to Tamatave in Madagascar. Miss Moody was travelling to East Africa to serve with the Women's Royal Naval Service when the ship was torpedoed on 2 July 1943, 105 miles west northwest of Mauritius. In February 1944, SS *Khedive Ismail*, part of the five-ship troop convoy KR8 sailing from Mombasa to Colombo, was sunk by the Japanese submarine *I-27*, commanded by Lieutenant Commander Toshiaki Fukumura. This cost the lives of 1,134 people, most of them members of 301st Field Regiment, East African Artillery, on their way to join the 11th East African Division in Ceylon. In addition to the 996 men of this regiment, others who lost their lives were 271 Royal Navy personnel, 178 crew members, fifty-three nurses, and nine members of the Women's Transport Service. The submarine was subsequently sunk by the destroyers HMS *Petard* and *Paladin*, sent from Colombo to escort the convoy on the final leg of its voyage.

Maurtius had a considerable role to play in the secret war of wireless interception. It was in a good position to intercept enemy wireless signals, and its location on the cable network meant that it was useful for censoring messages being sent all over the region, and for monitoring the traffic to and from the Vichy territories of Madagascar and Réunion. A considerable wireless, propaganda, and censorship organization developed on the island, and it was a useful addition to the worldwide coverage of Bletchley Park. SOE used Mauritius as a base for operations against neighbouring Vichy colonies, and developed a stay behind presence on the island in case of Japanese occupation. This meant embedding SOE agents who could conduct acts of sabotage as well as gather intelligence to be transmitted to the nearest British territory in the event of enemy occupation. This also involved recruiting pro-British civilians who could help the British cause under Japanese rule, even preparing prostitutes in Port Louis to act as informers. Scorched earth plans were devised to be put into effect should Japanese occupation look likely, destroying valuable industrial equipment and communications facilities. Meanwhile, the Mauritian home front was marked by the war in many different ways, beyond the obvious increase in the numbers serving in military formations and outfits such as the Red Cross. Food shortages meant dietary changes, and nutrition demonstration units toured the villages teaching people how to cook using unfamiliar ingredients, as staples such as rice were replaced by things like maize. Sugar estates had to make over large acreages to growing food for the population. Blackout and ARP facilities appeared in coastal towns. Nearly 2,000 Jewish internees who had been barred from entering Palestine were accommodated on the island from 1941.

There was a significant rise in the cost of living, and an excess profits tax was levied on businesses. Efforts were made to ensure that colonies were psychologically engaged with military forces during times of war, for example by the purchase of individual Spitfires or entire bomber squadrons (£100,000 was raised for Spitfires in Mauritius alone), fundraising for charities supporting sailors, prisoners of war, or bomb victims, and the sponsorship of naval vessels. Mauritius gifted its namesake cruiser a silver table centrepiece depicting the 1810 Battle of Grand Port fought in Mauritian waters, and a piano for the wardroom.

Meanwhile thousands of Mauritians served with the British Army overseas, including over 1,000 women who arrived in Egypt in 1945 as part of the Auxiliary Territorial Service. For service in Mauritius men were recruited into the Mauritian Home Guard, the Coastal Defence Squadron, the Mauritius Artillery, the Mauritius Signals Corps, the

Mauritian Volunteer Air Force, the Mauritius Territorial Force (which became the Mauritius Regiment), an air raid precaution outfit, and a Military Ambulance Service. These units aided the work of the Mauritius Garrison, and augmented the island's defensive capabilities. Over 8,000 men were also conscripted into the Civil Labour Corps, recruited for military construction work around the island. Recruitment was also undertaken in Mauritius for the East African Army Service Corps and units of the British Army, particularly the Pioneer Corps. Over 4,000 Mauritian soldiers served in the Middle East and Southern Europe.

Recruitment for the military, particularly the Pioneer Corps, solved dock unemployment, a phenomenon noted in other parts of the colonial empire where the war overcame the unemployment associated with the depression of the 1930s. Recruitment was undertaken through radio and press campaigns and through public meetings, in bars and on sugar estates. A Recruiting Centre and Training Camp opened at Bell Village south of the capital Port Louis, part of HQ Mauritius Garrison. Eateries and hawkers flourished around the bustling new camp, and a particular phenomenon was the 'Madames Pioneres', women hoping to marry soldiers in order to benefit from the generous allowances. Those who did marry soldiers contributed to price inflation because they were known by traders to be able to afford higher prices in the shops and markets.

The first contingent of Mauritian Pioneers left Port Louis aboard the *Tin How* on 19 August 1940, bound for Egypt. Thousands lined the streets and the Police Band played them onto the troopship. By the end of 1941 there were eight Mauritian Pioneer companies serving in the Middle East. The first unit to be recruited had been for the Royal Engineers — 741 Artizan Works Company. This company built dummy tanks, a hospital near Port Tewfik, repaired a Royal Navy torpedo boat at Mersa Matruh, built exercise targets for tanks, worked on a hospital and water pipe to Alamein, and a road from Kattara to Cairo. In Agouza 741 Company built a landmine factory; in Jisr el Majami it constructed fortifications to protect the Iraqi oil pipeline; in North Africa it repaired the runway at El Adem, and added two wings to a hospital at Tobruk.

Mauritian soldiers had a particular association with the much fought-over port of Tobruk, and suffered significant casualties there. 1501 and 1502 companies sailed into Tobruk just as German reconnaissance tanks reached its perimeters. Nine Axis aircraft spotted their ship and attacked it, killing twenty-six Mauritians and wounding forty-eight. An entire Mauritian company was captured by the Germans and became prisoners of war. Mauritian troops were involved in the more edifying events surrounding the imperial victory at Alamein later in 1942. Prior to the battle 1607 Mauritius Company and 1509 Seychelles Company constructed dummy Grant and Sherman tanks which on 20 October were sited on the spot where the Queen's Bays, the 10th and 11th Hussars, and the Yorkshire Dragoons had been. They lit fires and pretended to perform maintenance on the dummy tanks, all part of elaborate measures undertaken to deceive Axis intelligence. The headquarters of 1509 Mauritius Company, meanwhile, had taken up the previous position of HQ 1st Armoured Division. In March 1943, 1507 Rodrigues Company was sent to Malta to work on the Luca aerodrome, where it made blast pens out of tins and stone for the protection of RAF Spitfires and Hurricanes. When the Eighth Army invaded Italy in September 1943, 800 Mauritians landed with the infantry and started stockpiling supplies.

Ceylon, forgotten imperial battle base

Elsewhere in the Indian Ocean, the colony of Ceylon was transformed as it became a major military encampment, a surrogate Singapore once the island fortress had surrendered in February 1942. Departments of state led by Ceylonese politicians played a crucial role in bringing the island to war readiness, operating alongside British colonial and military officials. A dire food situation developed, caused by the Japanese conquest of import-supplying countries. Around the island propaganda and public information drives proliferated, aimed at ensuring local participation in the war effort. Indigenous labour was recruited for war-related tasks. There was some unrest caused by the influx of foreign soldiers, though the island made every provision for their welfare. The Ceylon Defence Force expanded to over 26,000 men, and Ceylon became the major base for the Royal Navy east of Suez.

Military disaster in the East upset imperial and Allied strategic calculations by conclusively disproving the belief that Singapore would deflect any threat to India and the British Indian Ocean empire. Its tragic surrender meant that Ceylon found itself unexpectedly thrust into the front line and threatened with invasion from powerful Japanese forces. As the Japanese conquered the colonies of America, Britain, France, and Holland one by one, thousands of troops and civilians arrived in Colombo as refugees. Despite calamitous defeats in the East, however, the convoy system connecting Britain and its distant battlefronts and imperial appendages still had to function. For this to happen, the Indian Ocean had to be held, and this is why Ceylon became strategically important. The waters of the Indian Ocean were vital for the defence of India and the Middle East, for imperial communications with Australasia, for oil exports from Iran and Iraq, and for Lend-Lease deliveries to Russia.

As well as being a pivotal strategic location for such defensive operations, Ceylon soon became a key springboard for Allied offensives intended to regain the lost colonies from Burma to Sumatra. With the Japanese in Burma, Malaya, and the Andaman and Nicobar Islands and dominating the Bay of Bengal, Ceylon was assailed from all around. In April 1942 the same Japanese fleet that had attacked Pearl Harbor steamed towards Ceylon and the coast of India. A large, but inferior, British fleet, commanded by Admiral Sir James Somerville, combed the waters south of Ceylon searching for Admiral Nagumo's force. An engagement would have led to the biggest sea battle since Jutland but, mercifully for the British, the opposing fleets failed to locate each other. Though calamity was avoided, the Japanese fleet attacked ports in India and Ceylon, causing panic and destroying many merchant vessels and sinking a British aircraft carrier, two heavy cruisers, and numerous other warships.

Ceylon buzzed with military activity and the multifarious construction projects that attended its rise to military prominence. Anti-aircraft guns, barrage balloons, and searchlights appeared around ports and towns and defensive trenches were dug in case the invader should come; air raid shelters, first aid posts, and cleared fields of fire appeared in coastal settlements; harbours were expanded to take more warships, defended by artillery and anti-torpedo booms; flying boat anchorages were established on inland lagoons, and airstrips and barracks sprouted across the country. Across the island land and buildings were requisitioned by the military. Offices and schools were shut down, areas of jungle and offshore islands were declared 'out of bounds' in order to become military practice grounds, swathes of coconut trees and bush were cleared for aerodromes and military camps, and lagoons and mangrove swamps became ideal training environments for troops destined to fight in Burma. Extended facilities at China Bay enabled fifty giant American B-29 Superfortresses to use Ceylon as a base for strikes on Sumatra in 1944.

Ceylon became a refugee camp, a haven for escaping ships and aircraft and the thousands of servicemen and civilians lucky enough to escape death or internment at Japanese hands. It also became a major Allied military base and headquarters facility, home to Mountbatten's Supreme Allied Command South East Asia and its staff of 7,000; the headquarters of the Eastern Fleet responsible for patrolling the 28,000,000 square miles of the Indian Ocean; and the headquarters of the RAF's Indian Ocean reconnaissance operations. It became the main base for Allied special forces operating behind enemy lines in Japanese-occupied territory, and headquarters of the Dutch and Free French forces operating in the East. It was home to Far East Combined Bureau, Bletchley Park's main eastern outstation, as well as the secret services of the Allies, including MI6 and the American Office of Strategic Services, forerunner of the CIA. During 1944 and early 1945 the huge British Pacific Fleet that was to take part in the final assault upon the Japanese home islands was built up in Ceylon's ports, and major raids against Japanese occupied territory, involving carriers and battleships, were launched from Trincomalee.

Because of Ceylon's escalating strategic importance, the British government decided to unify command under a military commander-in-chief, mindful of the disastrous civil–military disjuncture that had contributed to the downfall of Malaya and Singapore. Admiral Sir Geoffrey Layton was put in supreme command of Ceylon, and the Governor, Sir Andrew Caldecott, ceased to be the premier official on the island. This was an unprecedented move in the history of the modern colonial empire, and the first time that a unified command structure had been applied to an operational theatre. The Board of Ministers, which with the encouragement of the Colonial Office had become a quasi-Cabinet, was properly co-opted. In March 1942 a War Council was established under the presidency of Layton, of which the Governor, all the ministers, and the civil defence commissioner, Oliver Goonetilleke, were members. Thus was instituted an extremely effective political and administrative alliance that harnessed Ceylonese-run ministries and colonial administrators to the imperial war effort.

To augment these arrangements and present a credible deterrent, forces were rushed to the island in order to give it credibility as a defended base. By mid-1942 there were nearly three divisions of fighting troops and many more recruited locally. These ground forces included crack British and Australian brigades and Indian and East African divisions. Six squadrons of fighters (including Hurricanes), bombers, and reconnaissance aircraft were in place by March 1942, and by that date the Eastern Fleet that operated from Ceylon's ports comprised five battleships, three aircraft carriers, and dozens of cruisers and destroyers. It was the largest fleet that had sailed under a single commander in the war to date, and the unenviable task of Admiral Sir James Somerville was to search for Admiral Nagumo's mighty Japanese fleet in the waters south of Ceylon whilst continuing to safeguard the sea lanes of the Indian Ocean.

A daily train service known as the 'SEAC Special' provided regular transport between the network of military headquarters in Colombo and those in Kandy. The beautiful Royal Botanical Gardens at Peradeniya just outside of Kandy had been requisitioned in March 1942. There on the banks of the Mahaweli River Mountbatten's headquarters fanned out from colonial buildings with pillared verandahs and red-tiled roofs. Temporary buildings sprouted amidst giant Java figs and coconut avenues, overlooked by the mountain range known as the Knuckles. Kandy thus underwent a massive transformation as it became one of the most important military headquarters in the world.

In achieving the degree of civil–military cooperation that pertained, the supreme command of Layton was important, as was his formation of a War Council uniting British and Ceylonese officials. Goonetilleke's Department was a powerful war ministry responsible for preparing the island for attack and assisting the imperial military authorities in any way possible. It was also responsible for the National Food Campaign as the island faced major food shortages. Preparing Ceylon for war required more than just physical preparations; it required government to communicate with the people and prepare them for the novel and dangerous situation faced by the island. The Department unleashed a barrage of propaganda and information aimed at getting people to take the war seriously whilst avoiding panic and overreaction. One of the Department's main tasks was the organization of the island's extensive ARP programme, involving wardens, bomb shelters, first aid training, and the enforcement of blackout regulations. The Civil Defence Commissioner ordered the clearance of slums in Colombo as part of the fire-gap policy adopted so that fires caused by incendiary bombs would not spread. ARP and First Aid Posts were established throughout the city, and the Department built underground air raid shelters.

These preparations were in no way excessive. Throughout 1942 the Japanese threat was real, and everyone was mindful of the complete failure to make adequate civil defence preparations in Malaya and Singapore. The public worried about the prospect of invasion and tales of Japanese atrocities in captured cities from Shanghai to Singapore were common currency. In January the Governor noted that people were taking money out of savings banks and hoarding coinage and that Indians were returning to the subcontinent. When air raid sirens sounded in Colombo, stampedes occurred. In the State Council there were 'clamorous demands for evacuation' of the coastal towns of Batticaloa, Colombo, Galle, and Trincomalee, and well-to-do families moved inland. The Department of Civil Defence even prepared camps in case of the need for mass evacuations from coastal areas. The state of panic engendered by the Japanese raids on Colombo and Trincomalee in April 1942 caused thousands of people to flee inland, leading to steep rent rises.

239

Production for export was a most important calling as Ceylon, mirroring the military situation, found itself called upon to make good the loss of Malaya. The island became an important dollar-earning territory of the Sterling Area. After the loss of Malaya, Ceylon provided 60 percent of the Allies natural rubber. It produced over a quarter of the world's tea, and during the war the British Ministry of Supply contracted to buy the entire crop. Ceylon exported copra, and it became the Empire's most important source of graphite as enemy conquests robbed Britain of its traditional sources. In addition to the extensive war work of the Department of Civil Defence, other government departments contributed significantly. In December 1941 the Department of Development and Agricultural Marketing undertook to supply 16,000 charpoys to a newly-arrived Indian Army division. The Department also made 5,000 'donkey camp beds' of jute hessian for the Army, 23,000 bamboo telegraph poles, 2,500 latrine screen posts, 2,620 bivouac posts, and 700 camouflage nets. A Colombo-based company repaired 167 major warships, 332 minor warships and 1,932 merchant vessels during the course of the war, as well as producing over 39,000 article of furniture (mostly for use by the huge staff that followed in Mountbatten's wake), and dummy Hurricanes, Bofors guns, and wireless transmitters designed to foil Japanese aerial reconnaissance. Other important war work came under the purview of the Minister for Communications and Works, Sir John Kotalawala, in his role as Commander-in-Chief of the Essential Services Labour Corps (ESLC). This several-thousand-strong outfit was formed to provide mobile, disciplined, emergency labour. By 1945 83,500 civilians were employed on SEAC military works, and unemployment had plummeted to 4 percent of its 1939 level.

'The new theatre of war in the East' created by Japan's entry into the conflict meant that 'the outlook for food in Ceylon assumed a new gravity', as the prospect of food imports, on which the island depended, became 'very gloomy indeed' when Japan conquered Asia's rice bowl territories. Over 70 percent of Ceylon's rice had come from Burma before its conquest in March 1942. The Japanese raids on Ceylon and the attack on both coasts of India in the following month led to 'a very serious dislocation of the vital trade traffic with India'. People were exhorted to use new crops, particularly wheat and wheat flour, greens for iron and vitamins, chillies and French dwarf beans, and to rotate crops and prepare manure. Nutrition Demonstration Vans toured rural areas demonstrating how to cook with unfamiliar ingredients. There were also government farms producing food, tended by men recruited into the Agricultural Corps, a 'volunteer land army' comprising up to 15,000 labourers.

In attempting to avoid unsavoury incidents and in order to maintain discipline and morale, extensive efforts were made to entertain the thousands of service personnel stationed in Ceylon. These efforts involved the provision of rest camps as well as radio programmes, newspapers, welfare organizations, and sports competitions. Near to the well-known military rest camp at Diyatalawa in the hills was Nuwara Eliya, Ceylon's 'little England' hill station which during the war became the island's 'outstanding resort for servicemen'. Here, as in other parts of the island, hotels were requisitioned by the military, including the St Andrew's. The first arrivals were survivors from HMS *Hermes*, sunk off the east coast during the Japanese raids, who arrived in their oil-soaked clothes. All over Ceylon, rest camps and planters' bungalows hosted servicemen of all ranks.

As well as being Minister for Communications and Works and commanding the ESLC, the Honourable Lieutenant Colonel John Kotalawala ran the Services Welfare Organizing Committee (SWOC), dedicated to providing Ceylonese support for visiting imperial forces. SWOC's work was fully endorsed by the island's colonial government. As the Governor said in a broadcast, 'keep our defenders fit in mind as well as in body. We have now in our Island men come from all four corners of the earth to defend it. You have only to pass along our roads, streets, and lanes to see the British Commonwealth of Nations in microcosm'. The War Services League, a society of ex-servicemen who had served in imperial and local military forces in the past, supported the Governor's aims by making items to be sent to servicemen, producing 5,000 gifts and comforts in 1943 alone.

The Indian Ocean region, therefore, was a major theatre of British and Allied operations throughout the war. The entire Empire was mobilized for war using formal and informal networks of control and authority, and it is to these networks, and the role of colonial governors and proconsuls within them, that the final two chapters turn.

11

'A Prodigy of Skill and Organization'
British Imperial Networks and the Second World War

Red white and blue, what does it mean to you?
Surely you're proud, shout it out loud, Britons awake!
The Empire too, we can depend on you
Freedom remains, these are the chains, nothing can break.
> — *There'll always be an England*, composed by Ross
Parker and Harry Parr Davies, words by Hugh Charles (1940)

The chapters so far have considered the dynamics of imperial warfare and the role that colonies played in imperial defence and in aiding Britain during times of global war. The following two chapters consider the networks that enabled the Empire to be mobilized so successfully. As the above extract from a wartime song shows, colonies and imperial connections were often envisaged in terms of links in a chain of Britishness girding the globe. The nature of the chain, and of its interconnecting links, is the key to understanding the manner in which imperial mobilization was achieved, as London was connected to overseas military commands and political power centres, and beneath them to regional commands and the governments of individual colonies and the indigenous rulers through whom they ruled.

Physical and metaphysical networks — bonds both tangible and intangible — were vital to the functioning, understanding, and rhetoric of the British Empire. They were what made the Empire 'an interactive system, one vast interconnected whole'; they were what held it together, what made it something real. This chapter considers the nature of the networks that connected the British Empire and the manner in which they were activated in order to meet the extraordinary demands of the Second World War. The networks that connected and gave meaning to the Empire included networks of people, networks of institutions, and networks of physical infrastructure, the latter embracing overseas administrative and military headquarters which extended London's authority around the world. Between 1939 and 1945 these networks were activated in order to mobilize the empire to fight Britain's enemies and to ensure imperial survival.

During this latest in a line of global struggles dating back to the Seven Years War, the manifold 'chains of empire' that girded the globe were called to take up the strain in order to keep the British world together as it was assailed by three powers actively seeking the Empire's dismemberment. Taken as a whole, the improvisation involved was breathtaking. Imperial businessmen from the great eastern merchant houses and banks were transformed into Special Operations Executive (SOE) agents; planters left their verandas and gin slings to become suppliers of military labour to the military, as India Command's strategic gaze was prised from its historic watch on the Khyber Pass to focus anew upon Rangoon and the hilly borderlands of Assam; the Merchant Navy and the Royal Navy activated a far-flung network of ports and bases to link the world through a system of armoured convoys, the likes of which had never been seen before; missionaries extended their temporal and spiritual reach in order to keep servicemen in the Mediterranean in touch with their families in African villages as well as with their Christian God; and government houses and nawabs palaces hosted the itinerant rulers of empire as they journeyed to and fro between London and the centres of British overseas power.

A networked view of the world

To say that networks were important in the running of the British Empire is rather like saying that petrol is important for running a car. It almost goes without saying that the British Empire was governed and connected by innumerable networks; this is how humans and the structures that they create operate. But further elucidation is required so as to explain how decisions made in London — around the War Cabinet table, say — were passed to various administrative and military headquarters overseas and then translated into action. People born before the Second World War were familiar with the notion of multiple networks binding the Empire together, and the British knew all about forging physical and metaphysical networks based upon shared background and values, shared social and political rituals, and the well-known iconography of an imperial monarchy and its supporting honours system. The British were also past masters when it came to constructing physical networks that shrank the world and contributed to the 'annihilation of distance' — the famous 'All Red' cable route, railways spanning entire continents, ports, protected and well charted sea lanes for the use of Britain's huge merchant marine, and the ceaseless movement of people and of trade goods all around the world.

The Empire and its networks were among the most powerful vectors of what we now term globalization. The fact of imperial possession and the common employment of imperial rhetoric helped forge almost an innate — if often undeveloped — sense of imperial connectivity. Contemporary publications such as the *Web of Empire*, which documented the empire tour undertaken by the Duke and Duchess of Cornwall and York in 1901, took a sense of imperial community for granted, as did a great deal of popular and educational literature. A sense of shared imperial community was forged by the imperial media. Cultural references to empire were part of the tapestry of life for Britons all over the world, reading news syndicated by British agencies and published in papers such as the *Bombay Times*, the *Straits Echo*, the *Sydney Morning Herald*, and the *Times of Ceylon*. Such papers constructed cosmopolitan identities that could transcend ethnicity or nation. During the Second World War they carried daily war news from around the world as well as adverts for British products from Huntley and Palmer biscuits to Austin cars, whilst the Ministry of Information in London encouraged colonial governments to stimulate war awareness — by holding war picture competitions in Ceylon or praise poetry competitions in Bechuanaland — and by sending Mobile Cinema Vans to tour rural areas showing propaganda films. The standard themes of British home front posters — Join the Army, Careless Talk Costs Lives, and Dig for Victory — were localized and displayed with captions in English, Sinhalese, Swahili, and Urdu. The development of radio meant that people overseas could listen in on the news from Broadcasting House, concerts from the Royal Albert Hall, or (from the 1950s) to ball-by-ball test match commentary from Lord's as they sat on steamy verandas at sundown. During the war pre-existing radio stations, and new ones established for the military, such as Radio SEAC (South East Asia Command), broadcast a mixture of local and global programmes. Radio Ceylon was a pioneer broadcaster in South Asia, the then Governor, Sir William Manning, inaugurating the service in 1924. The radio listing for Radio Ceylon on 7 November 1942, for example, included programmes such as Arms for Russia, the Brain's Trust, a Talk in Tamil, a Tamil Concert, Sinhalese Folk Songs, Dvořák from the BBC, Sinhalese War Commentary, and British Forces Radio.

In Britain and its imperial domains the public learned of the networked nature of British imperial power through many common points of reference. It was an incidental part of childhood to see wall maps, atlases, and souvenir pull-outs that depicted the world in terms of British control and the linkages between land masses forged by British-dominated trade routes. Non-white children in the West Indies and elsewhere were taught to admire British literature and to view the world in imperial terms. The 1902 book *King Edward's Realm* made this connection between Britain and her distant appendages:

> A glance at the map of the world in which the parts of the British empire are coloured red may well fill us with astonishment that the little spot marked England has expanded into an empire that covers one sixth of the habitable globe . . . The British Empire looks like a sprawling giant with his limbs outstretched, having his head in one sea, and his arms and legs in as many others . . . the sundered portions of the British dominions are connected by the sea, and the sea offers a ready-made road to every ship that sails . . . We may rightly regard the seas that come between our shores and the rest of the Empire, not as separating but as connecting its several parts, and enabling the motherland to keep in constant touch with her daughter states in other lands.[72]

A networked imperial elite

Being able to visualize the Empire as a connected whole was second nature to the people who actually ran the Empire and were responsible for defending it. This was important when the Second World War became a truly global struggle, as was the experience gained by the British in previous world wars. Past experience meant that the arts of blockade and convoy, the importance of protecting merchant vessels and holding on to sea lines of communication, were understood, if sometimes imperfectly practiced; it meant that the British ruling elite had at least a clear *conception* of imperial unity and imperial preservation. This was in contrast to Britain's enemies, who displayed their *lack* of imperial experience in their attitudes to such techniques and strategic imperatives, the Japanese

245

in particular showing an infantile awareness of how maritime empires, once won, must be defended and succoured.

The British Empire was both governed and defended at the strategic, operational, and tactical levels by men steeped in the imperial tradition, from the highest reaches of the departments of state in Whitehall down to district commissioners and company commanders living in remote outposts and supervising the day-to-day business of imperial defence and administration. Governors and generals prepared whole regions for war whilst district commissioners and subalterns toured villages recruiting soldiers, supervising the clearance of new aerodromes and the construction of military camps. In this they were aided by indigenous rulers who themselves were a part of the imperial elite, often signified by the award of imperial honours and their position of precedence during local celebrations of imperial events such as coronations or Armistice Day commemorations.

At the summit of this sprawling system of global authority was the King-Emperor George VI, an imperial monarch whose image was known throughout the world, from Empire Day pageants linking Surrey to the Sudan, to the postage stamps that crossed the world and the pennies in people's pockets in Australia, Britain, and India alike. The symbolism of monarchy had developed under Queen Victoria and involved overseas durbars and Royal Tours, famously the 'warship tours' of the Prince of Wales in the early 1920s, undertaken in order to thank the Empire for its participation in the First World War. The future George VI had visited numerous parts of the empire whilst a young naval officer, including the Americas, the Caribbean, and the Mediterranean. In 1924 he visited Kenya, Uganda, and the Sudan with his new bride, the future Queen Mother, before undertaking his own 'warship tour' of the Empire in 1927, the centrepiece of which was the opening of the federal parliament in the new Australian capital at Canberra. As King George VI, he embarked upon a new empire tour in 1939, which included a tour of America. This was intended to sway American opinion in favour of Britain's cause as war clouds gathered over Europe. Given the deteriorating situation, however, the tour was postponed following the American and Canadian legs, to be taken up again in 1947 when George VI, Queen Elizabeth, and the two young princesses embarked on a tour of Africa which included a stop in Bechuanaland where the Royal Family was greeted by those two stalwart chiefs, Bathoen II and Tshekedi Khama, resplendent in uniforms modelled on those of the Life Guards, including elongated helmets plumed with horsetails.

Like their King, many of the men who served as His Majesty's ministers during the Second World War had direct experience of the Empire. Neville Chamberlain, Winston Churchill, Leo Amery, Clement Attlee, William Beaverbrook, Stafford Cripps, Anthony Eden, and Harold Macmillan all had experience of living and working in the Empire, or of holding political positions that gave them an intimate knowledge of its affairs. Politicians from the Dominions were also naturally experienced in the affairs of empire and the metropole, including men such as Jan Christian Smuts, Robert Menzies, William Mackenzie King and Peter Fraser, some of whom had actually sat in the Imperial War Cabinet in London during the First World War, and participated in Cabinet discussion on visits to London in the Second World War. Native chiefs and kings, meanwhile, often visited London during national commemorations, particularly coronations, reaffirming their position in the imperial hierarchy.

As with the politicians, Britain's senior soldiers, sailors, and airmen tended to be old Empire hands in one respect or another, or to actually be citizens of the Dominions. All of Britain's wartime chiefs of staff, for example, had extensive imperial experience, as did the majority of Britain's senior theatre commanders. Generals such as Brooke, Auchinleck, Montgomery, Slim, and Wavell had decades of imperial service between them, as had admirals Cunningham, Pound, and Somerville. The same was true of the RAF, in the shape of its most senior commanders, Tedder and Portal. At the operational level, many senior British commanders of the Second World War were from the Dominions, such as the Australian general Blamey, the New Zealand general Freyberg, and the New Zealand air marshals Coningham and Park.

An interconnected world

One of the striking aspects of the Second World War is the manner in which networks of empire, both well-established and ad hoc, were brought alive by the current of global mobilization and the enlivening prospect of defeat to a terrible enemy. The workings of a vast empire at war, and the movement of people and resources for war purposes on a scale never before witnessed, presents a dazzling spectacle and is what makes the Second World War a most revealing moment at which to study the British Empire. The drama and vitality of the empire's networks at war, the scale of global connections and inter-personal relationships, the *colour* of a now-dead imperial system, is difficult to capture in terms of cold historical fact. But the frequent comings and goings of diverse people engaged on war-related work, the chatter of cosmopolitan cities and the many people who knew each other or had mutual friends and acquaintances, is vividly captured in works of fiction. Such works include Evelyn Waugh's *Sword of Honour* trilogy (*Men at Arms, Officers and Gentlemen,* and *Unconditional Surrender*), Paul Scott's *Raj Quartet,* Anthony Powell's *A Dance to the Music of Time* cycle, which expertly shows 'how the military machine works at various levels' (the wartime volumes are *The Valley of Bônes, The Soldier's Art,* and *The Military Philosophers*), J. G. Farrell's novel *The Singapore Grip,* Noel Barber's Singapore and Malaya-based novel *Tanamera* and his Egyptian-based novel *A Woman of Cairo,* Olivia Manning's Cairo-centred Levant trilogy (*The Danger Tree, The Battle Lost and Won,* and *The Sum of Things*), and Artemis Cooper's study *Cairo 1939–1945.* The spirit is also captured in the diaries and letters of itinerant men such as General Sir Alan Brooke, Ian Fleming, Admiral Lord Louis Mountbatten, and Noel Coward, recording their various movements around the Empire and Britain's overseas power centres.

In London and the regional epicentres of the imperial war effort — places such as Accra, Brisbane, Cairo, Cape Town, Colombo, Durban, Freetown, Halifax, and Singapore — men gathered in clubs and residencies to plan, discuss, and speculate. The telegram traffic between Whitehall and the world increased dramatically as the imperial network upped its tempo of operations, the ether alive with reports, reprimands and requests for information. A thousand telegrams a day poured into the Ministry of War Transport from all over the world, whilst the Colonial Office tally rose from 15,500 in 1937 to 81,000 in 1944. Exiled governments and their agents, in London or these regional capitals, joined the fray, as did the discordant voices of allies, as American, Belgian, Chinese, Dutch, French, and Polish officers and diplomats came to be stationed in imperial power centres alongside senior politicians and servicemen from Britain's dominions. This was a living, breathing, British world in action, in which the networks of overseas businessmen, governors, indigenous notables, and military commanders worked from regional power centres which acted as miniature Londons, sharing the burdens of global mobilization. For the men involved in this cosmopolitan, sprawling arena of power and administration, it was a short step from the Savoy Grill to the terrace of Shepheard's Hotel in Cairo, from the Silver Faun night club at the Galle Face Hotel in Colombo to the Long Bar at Raffles in Singapore.

Frequent movement around the Empire was a common experience for British politicians, diplomats, administrators, and service personnel.

Imperial control during the war involved a merry-go-round of shuttle diplomacy, the business of running a war empire conducted by itinerant men moving from capital to capital and from headquarters to headquarters. This involved journeys over huge distances in noisy aircraft and aboard warships and converted liners as the Empire was brought to the highest pitch of war readiness. The exhaustive shuttle diplomacy of Winston Churchill provides the most famous example of this. In 1947 *Time and Tide* published a commemorative map entitled 'Dunkirk to Berlin: Journeys Undertaken by the Right Honourable Winston S. Churchill OM, CH, FRS, MP in Defence of the British Empire'. It showed the wartime journeys on a map, and the methods of travel, which included BOAC flying boat, RAF Skymaster, Liberator, and York aircraft, the converted liner *Queen Mary*, the sister battleships HMS *Duke of York*, *King George V*, and *Prince of Wales*, the battlecruiser HMS *Renown*, and the destroyer HMS *Kelvin*. He visited Newfoundland for the Atlantic Charter meeting with Roosevelt, went to Washington three times, Quebec twice, and Moscow three times (involving major conferences en route in Cairo and Tehran), Bermuda, Casablanca, Normandy, Italy and France during the invasion of Southern Europe, Greece and Malta and, after D-Day, made separate visits to Belgium and Holland, Normandy, Paris, and the Rhine, with a final appearance at Potsdam.

Churchill's peripatetic activity set the tone for subordinates such Sir Phillip Mitchell, Edward Twining and Admiral Lord Louis Mountbatten, who covered vast distances as he moved around South Asia and Southeast Asia from headquarters in Delhi and Kandy whilst regularly visiting the Middle East and London for high-level consultations. Networks of diplomacy, knowledge, and imperial and military authority also featured high commissioners, diplomats, and governors as well as secret agents, writers, and MPs. The war years even saw a proliferation of touring trades union advisers, health experts, cooperative advisers, and statistical surveyors as the managerial and the welfare state was exported from Britain to the colonies.

Millions of imperial servicemen and women shared the experience of passing through nodal points on the imperial communications network as troopships and aircraft conveyed them from A to B, usually via D, P and S. No overseas deployment was complete without a stop off at Gibraltar, passage through the Suez Canal (the 'Clapham Junction' or 'swing door' of the British Empire), and a stop at any one of a number of familiar ports of call — Gibraltar, Malta, Port Said, Suez, Aden, Cape Town, Colombo, Mombasa, or Singapore. The 'well trodden path' of imperial progression, as Admiral Godfrey called it, remembering his first journey overseas as a young subaltern sent to the China Station based in Hong Kong.

The dispersed nature of the British Empire meant that it was a common experience for servicemen and women to serve their time in the military in distant parts of the world as the rhythm of war dictated. It was a world of incredible movement, always involving colonies as way stations and as bases, as Indian soldiers or Rhodesian airmen found themselves alongside British WRNS and Mauritian ATS women stationed in Cairo, Colombo, or Mombasa. The war career of the subaltern and novelist John Masters gives a flavour of this world of movement. He was variously stationed during the war in Burma, India, Iraq, and Syria. Whilst he was shunted around the Indian Ocean rim his father soldiered with the Home Guard in Devon; his cousin and her RAF husband were killed by German bombs in London; and his brother was captured by the Japanese in Malaya. William Slim, the Fourteenth Army's pin-up general, progressed around the Indian Ocean theatre of war, moving through the ranks of command from brigade to division to corps to army, starting in East Africa and ending up in Burma and Malaya by way of Iran and Iraq. During the war Sir James Somerville commanded Force H based on the colony of Gibraltar and then the Eastern Fleet headquartered in the colonies of Ceylon and Kenya, before ending the war representing the Admiralty in Washington. Freddie Spencer Chapman, anxious for some fighting, removed himself from commando-style training in lonely parts of Scotland in order to get out to Australia, where he trained Australian and New Zealand forces in the black arts of 'ungentlemanly' warfare. From here he washed up in Singapore, destined to spend most of the war behind enemy lines in Japanese-occupied Malaya. Another typical imperial soldier was General Edward Quinan. Born in Calcutta, scion of the Indian Army, he had fought on the Western Front and in Mesopotamia during the First World War, before returning to India to develop his career on the busy North-West Frontier in the 1930s, commanding the campaign against the Fakir of Ipi in Waziristan. Appointed commander of the Indian Army Corps in the Persian Gulf in the Second World War, he successfully invaded Iran, Iraq, and Syria, all within a year. And so on. For many imperial servicemen and women, diverse geographical deployments were the norm during the war, as the needs of a sprawling empire dictated their movement and sent them hither and thither on its bidden business.

Churchill and his military, administrative, and diplomatic colleagues and subordinates travelled in the knowledge that it was a distinctly British world that they were traversing. The air journey to distant Singapore, for example, was made without ever leaving British airspace, stopping off along the way in countries where the Union Flag flew. This fact was remarked upon by many people, including the veteran American war correspondent, Cecil Brown. In August 1941 he took off from the waters of the Nile for a journey to Singapore. 'Before dawn, we took off and flew the entire way to Bahrein Island over the Persian Gulf at ten to eleven thousand feet altitude.' The following day the flying-boat 'paralleled the Ganges', and touched down at Calcutta before striking out across the Bay of Bengal for Akyab Island. Traversing South-east Asia, Brown mused in his journal that:

> It is impossible to conceive how any army could find its way down from Thailand to Singapore through this terrain. The jungle and disease would finish off any army which had to face even minor guerrilla operations . . . I think the monkeys down below are going to remain undisturbed by artillery fire. After I made that note I fell asleep and the steward woke me for tea to announce we would be in Singapore in twenty minutes. For five days of flying, from Suez to Singapore, at almost every stop we had touched on water under the protection of the British flag. It was a stunning reflection on empire.[73]

Knowing each other and keeping in touch: An imperial elite

The British Empire was run by politicians, administrators, businessmen, and soldiers who came from a shared social and educational background and formed a relatively narrow elite. People knew one another to a surprising extent or knew someone who did. This sense of a tight-knit elite was magnified in the colonial world where Europeans formed a tiny percentage of the population and where whites, be they civil or military, very often lived in close quarters, in cantonements, headquarters, suburbs, and civil lines. A significant amount of scholarly attention has been devoted to the study of the British/imperial elite and its support networks, including work on the 'gentlemanly capitalist' class, freemasonry, gentlemen's clubs, public schools and Oxbridge. Within the Empire informal and formal networks sprouted around certain people and regions. Thus in the British Army there were both African and Indian 'circles' revolving around generals who had served in one region or the other and developed links with brother officers. As High Commissioner to South Africa Sir Alfred Milner built a network of young administrators drawn from Oxford University, known as the Kindergarten. The Round Table formed a network of administrators, politicians, and scholars interested in closer imperial union which found an intellectual home at All Souls College, Oxford. So the Empire was peopled at all levels by men and women who to a large degree knew each other and came from similar backgrounds and whose world views were shaped by many common characteristics. Thus, for example, Britain's overseas governors had a great deal in common with Britain's overseas military representatives (as well as representatives of British business and finance), and the existence of networks enabled the civilian and military authorities to work successfully together in pursuit of British interests.

The Royal Navy furnishes useful examples of networks in action. Junior and senior ranks in the armed forces kept in touch with each other and kept their ears to the ground through writing letters and making visits. This had always been the case. During operations in the Indian Ocean in 1809–11 the Commander-in-Chief Bombay, Lieutenant-General Sir John Abercromby, was linked to all levels of the network of imperial authority through the medium of letter-writing. Correspondents ranged from commanders and governors on Indian Ocean islands to officers commanding ships afloat, and political and military authorities in Britain, India, and South Africa. In the space of only a few months a vigorous correspondence was maintained with, among others, the Governor-General of India (Lord Minto), the Honourable Robert Farquhar of the Madras Civil Service, sent to Mauritius as its first British governor; Lieutenant Colonel Henry Keating, commanding troops sent to conquer the French islands; Lieutenant-General George Grey, commanding British forces at the Cape of Good Hope; Vice Admiral Sir Albemarle Bertie, commander of the Cape of Good Hope Station; Lieutenant Colonel Fraser, commander of the 86th Regiment; the Right Honourable Robert Dundas, President of the Board of Control for India; General Sir George Hewitt, Commander-in-Chief India; the Earl of Liverpool, Secretary of State for War and the Colonies; Charles Grant, Chairman of the Court of Directors of the East India Company; and Sir George Barlow, Governor of Madras.

By the time of the Second World War, the advent of the telegraph and the telephone had changed things, though there was still a use for letter-writing. For instance, Vice-Admiral Algernon Willis, Commander-in-Chief South Atlantic in late 1941 and based at Freetown in the colony of Sierra Leone (the setting for Graham Greene's wartime novel *The Heart of the Matter*), was a frequent letter writer. This important naval command was responsible for shepherding British and Allied shipping through dangerous waters, part of a global network of merchant vessels, troopships, warships, ports, and naval commands responsible for protecting the trade of a maritime empire. Admiral Willis's correspondence indicates the manner in which the naval fraternity kept in touch. On 11 November 1941, for example, he wrote to his superior, the First Sea Lord Admiral Sir Dudley Pound:

> It was a great pleasure to have Tom Phillips through last week and I much enjoyed having a yarn with him . . . It's a fine strategical move — if I may say so — sending a strong force out there. From my little knowledge of our little yellow friends it's the one thing that will scare them.[74]

He was referring to Admiral Sir Tom Phillips, who a month later lay at the bottom of the Gulf of Siam along with his ships *Prince of Wales* and *Repulse*, whilst Willis's 'little yellow friends' remained, as yet, distinctly un-scared. A few days after this calamity Willis wrote to the Second Sea Lord, Vice-Admiral Sir W. J. Whitworth, with a hastily-revised appraisal of the strategic situation: 'I'm afraid the war in the Far East is going to strain the old Empire to the limit. It's devastating about the *Prince of Wales*, *Repulse*, and little Tom — awful. The little yellow devils seem to have some powerful bombs.' The correspondence illustrates the way in which news and opinion was transmitted, relationships forged, and superiors gently flattered.

Another senior naval commander visiting colonial bases as he moved from Britain to a posting overseas was Rear Admiral Ralph Edwards. He left Britain in December 1941 to take up an appointment aboard the battleship HMS *Prince of Wales* recently arrived at Singapore. Edwards stopped off at Malta on the voyage out and visited the Governor, General Dobbie, at Government House and consulted with several generals and with Sir Phillip Mitchell, a colonial governor responsible under Wavell for the administration of captured Italian colonies in Africa. Whilst in Malta Edwards heard the incredible news of the surprise Japanese attack on Pearl Harbor. The following day he was in Cairo, where he visited General Headquarters Middle East and the Naval Headquarters. Continuing his journey despite learning of the loss of the ship he was to join — *Prince of Wales* had been sunk alongside the battlecruiser *Repulse* on 10 December — he flew to Habbaniya in Iraq, visited the Senior Naval Officer Persian Gulf (Commodore Cosmo Graham) at Basra, and then flew via Bahrein to Karachi, where he met the Senior Naval Officer. He arrived in Ceylon via Bombay on 15 December 1941, to take up his position in the important Naval Headquarters located in that colony.

It was the practice of senior officers and ships captains to pay courtesy calls on their naval and military colleagues as they progressed from station to station, as well as local politicians and dignitaries. Thus as Admiral Phillips progressed eastwards to take up command of Force Z (HMS *Prince of Wales* and *Repulse* and their destroyer escorts) at Singapore, he stopped at Cape Town where he lunched with the Prime Minister Field Marshal Jan Smuts, and Colombo, where he lunched with Governor Sir Andrew Caldecott before flying on to Singapore. Admiral John Godfrey's wartime career also featured a great deal of movement between Britain and the major outposts of British power, as well as extensive travelling within India and the islands of the Indian Ocean.

Letters were commonly sent to congratulate colleagues on new appointments and promotions within the military fraternity. In February 1942, Admiral Algernon Willis was dispatched to the Indian Ocean as second in command of the Eastern Fleet, and spent much of his time based at Mombasa in the colony of Kenya, where the fleet's headquarters had been established since its retreat from Colombo following the Japanese raids on Ceylon in April 1942. He received congratulations from the military fraternity on his promotion, including letters from General William Platt, Commander-in-Chief East Africa (his 'neighbouring' army commander), and Admiral Chester Nimitz, America's commander in the Central Pacific. As well as his connection to a global military network, whilst stationed in East Africa Willis was able to plug into a regional imperial network and take advantage of the opportunities for official and social contact that were an integral part of British rule overseas. Thus whilst stationed in Mombasa he kept in touch with the Governor of Tanganyika and organized naval exercises off the Protectorate's coast, sometimes involving locally-recruited soldiers. Whilst on military business in Kenya Willis was the guest of the Governor, Sir Henry Monck-Mason Moore (who had been Governor of Sierra Leone at the start of the war and in 1944 became Governor of Ceylon). Willis stayed on several occasions with Moore and his wife, who was serving as chair of the joint Red Cross and St John committee and president of the Kenya's Women's Emergency Organization. Thus the civilian and military lynchpins in this region of the Empire worked together and dined together and helped prosecute Britain's global war effort.

The tight-knit nature of the networks responsible for directing the Empire's war effort is well illustrated by the names on the *Navy List*. The edition of the *List* issued in April 1945 was, effectively, the Britannia Royal Naval College class of 1902 writ large. Admiral John Godfrey (commander of the Royal Indian Navy at the time), one of that class and one whose name appeared on the list, remarked in his memoirs upon the fact that the *List* was crammed with the names of people, now in the Navy's most senior posts, who had been with him as cadets at Dartmouth between 1902 and 1904. The list of twenty-four names included Admiral Sir Bruce Fraser, Commander-in-Chief British Pacific Fleet; Admiral Sir Henry Rawlings, deputy Commander-in-Chief British Pacific Fleet; Admiral Sir Henry Moore, Commander-in-Chief Home Fleet; Admiral Sir Algernon Willis, 2nd Sea Lord; Admiral Sir William Wake-Walker, 3rd Sea Lord; Admiral Palliser, 4th Sea Lord; Admiral Sir Dennis Boyd, 5th Sea Lord; Admiral Burrough, naval Commander-in-Chief Expeditionary Force; Admiral Sir Henry Harwood, Assistant Chief of the Naval Staff; Admiral Sir Neville Syfret, Vice-Chief of the Naval Staff; Admiral Sir Bertram Ramsay, naval commander Normandy landings; Admiral Sir Tom Phillips, Commander-in-Chief Eastern Fleet; and Admiral Sir Arthur Power, Commander-in-Chief East Indies Station.

Institutions

Networks of people were given shape and directions by the institutions that they were a part of, from schools and universities to commercial companies, missionary societies, civil services, regiments and naval commands. Overseas civil services and the diplomatic and consular services formed vital imperial networks. The Colonial Administrative Service and Indian Civil Service were the most significant of the numerous civil services which ran the Empire. In the case of the former, the Corona Club provided a point of call for colonial officials' home on leave. Founded in 1900, it featured an annual dinner at the Connaught Rooms in Great Queen Street attended by up to 500 colonial servants on leave or working in the Colonial Office. The dinner was presided over by the Colonial Secretary himself, and the Club also provided a reading and meeting room in No. 2, Sanctuary Buildings, Great Smith Street for its membership of up to 4,000. Even during the war, when the annual dinner had to be suspended, Sir Thomas Southorn, Liaison Officer at the Colonial Office, managed to organize an annual tea-party.

Official publications helped to bind this community together, including the Corona Club *Bulletin*, the annual *Colonial Office List*, and the in-house journal of the Colonial Service, *Corona*, published monthly by HMSO. These publications helped maintain the shared vision of the service and contact among its disparate branches involved in ruling over fifty separate colonies and protectorates. They linked Britain to the network of alliances with indigenous leaders that was an important backbone of imperial power. The imperial honours system, clubs, masonic lodges, and old boy school and university networks provided important buttresses to imperial rule as indigenous rulers and politicians were given recognized status within the imperial hierarchy. A wartime innovation in the exercise of overseas military and civil authority was the creation of resident ministers, powerbrokers intended to coordinate regional networks and provide an interface with London. The resident ministers were senior political or diplomatic figures carrying Cabinet rank, installed in key regions to supervise the coordination of the local civil and military war efforts and act as a conduit for communications with Whitehall. The regions to which resident ministers were appointed were North West Africa, West Africa, the Middle East, and the Far East, and they included Richard Casey, Duff Cooper, Oliver Lyttelton, Harold Macmillan, and Viscount Swinton.

Institutions used to help mobilize the Empire for war included missionary societies such as the London Missionary Society (LMS). It was used by the British Army because its colonial networks were useful for keeping African soldiers in touch with their home communities, and by the colonial authorities because its spiritual authority could be used to bolster military discipline and welfare provisions. Thus LMS missionaries from Bechuanaland and Basutoland joined the army and toured amongst units stationed in the Mediterranean and Middle East, helping soldiers to keep in touch with their families back at home, whilst their colleagues who remained in the home territories encouraged letter writing and held special services. Reverend Arthur Sandilands, an LMS missionary in Southern Africa, was appointed Deputy Chaplain General in the Middle East to oversee this work.

Other institutions employed in support of the war effort included businesses with global interests and personnel and local companies in the colonies. Trading companies, shipping lines, and banks were part of the ready-to-hand network of empire that was turned to good effect during the war. Companies such as Unilever were able to provide expertise in the establishment of supply boards created to streamline the procurement of an entire region's crops by the Ministry of Supply. Shipping companies, such as Peninsular and Oriental and the Alfred Holt Line, were central to the mobilization of the Merchant Navy and the organization of a system of convoys connecting all imperial territories around the world, the government exercising its historic right to requisition ships and subject them to military command. In order to build an effective convoy network communication across Whitehall ministries had to be established — the Admiralty had to understand the Ministry of War Transport, and the Ministry of War Transport needed to understand the Ministry of Supply. Extending the convoy network overseas, major imperial ports such as Halifax, Freetown, and Colombo established local authority for convoy control. The wonder that was the British convoy system of the Second World War, which kept trade moving despite hostilities and enabled hundreds of thousands of soldiers to be moved across the seas — with few significant losses — was due not only to the skill and bravery of those involved, but to the fact that the networks and institutions necessary for such a feat already existed.

Special Operations Executive and the intelligence services in the Far East were to a considerable extent the great merchant houses 'in khaki', as employees of the Hongkong and Shanghai Banking Corporation, Jardin and Matheson, and Butterfield and Swire used their contacts and local knowledge to help fight the war against Japan. British businesses all over the world were called to arms. In Ceylon, Walker Sons and Company turned its tea and rubber expertise to military purposes, repairing and refitting hundreds of merchant marine and Royal Navy vessels in Colombo, making dummy aircraft and control towers to fool Japanese reconnaissance, and building tens of thousands of items of furniture as South East Asia Command and its 7,000-strong staff descended on Ceylon following the transfer of its headquarters from Delhi. SOE was extremely active in theatres beyond Europe. Two SOE missions were sent to the East initially (where the title 'Force 136' eventually became the general cover name for SOE). Valentine Killery, a businessman who worked for Imperial Chemical Industries (ICI), set up a headquarters in Singapore. Another imperial businessman, Colin Mackenzie of the firm J. and P. Coats, set up SOE's India Mission. Right at the summit of the SOE command structure, imperial businessmen were to the fore. Its first two directors, Sir Frank Nelson, a businessman with extensive Indian experience, and Sir Charles Hambro, a merchant banker, both understood that the war was a defence of the British Empire as a world wide financial and commercial entity.

Planters in Malaya and the employees of forestry companies operating in Burma joined watch-and-ward and spy/sabotage formations such as V-Force, and the Assam Tea Planters Association activated its labour power in order to build the Manipur Road, as India Command shifted its strategic focus in order to face the threatened Japanese invasion. South African mining houses were called upon to provide expertise in the Middle East when new railways were being constructed that required paths to be blasted through mountain ranges. The business houses of the Empire were also called upon to support the creation of wartime production and supply networks aimed at supplying fighting fronts and more efficiently connecting colonial resources to the war economies of Britain and America. These organizations included the Eastern Supply Group Council, the West African Supply Board, the Middle East Supply Centre, and the United Kingdom Commercial Corporation.

The military had its own regional organizations linked to the service ministries in Whitehall (Admiralty, Air Ministry, and War Office). In the case of the Royal Navy, these included stations such as the South Atlantic Station, the Mediterranean Fleet, the Home Fleet and Western Approaches Command, Force H (a Gibraltar-based fleet), the East Indies Station, China Station, and the Australia and New Zealand Station. Army commands included Middle East Command, Malaya Command, East Africa Command, and Persia and Iraq Command (PAIC). This last command was a wartime innovation formed on Churchill's initiative as he sought to relieve Middle East Command of some of its sprawling commitments in order to better meet the dire German threat to the empire's oil resources in Iran and Iraq. Its task was to channel tens of thousands of tons of Lend-Lease to Russia each month via conquered Persia, its Shah resting in uneasy exile in Mauritius, and to develop facilities for ten army divisions and thirty RAF squadrons for the defence of Northern Iraq against German forces.

Physical infrastructure

Besides the human and institutional networks described above, networks of physical infrastructure were of equal importance in mobilizing the Empire for war. A command group or colonial administration is of little use if it has nowhere to work and sleep or no means of travel and communication across the region in which it operates. A fleet is immobilized unless it has docks in which to repair, oil tanks from which to refuel, and defended anchorages in which to shelter and draw ammunition. Bringing an empire to war was all about the creation and use of infrastructure — using what already existed and hastily building new facilities, as colonies and dominions became major strategic bases and thoroughfares. The British Empire was fortunate in having major bases from which to prosecute war in all of the main theatres of operations — Egypt backing up the war in the Mediterranean and the Western Desert, India and Ceylon backing up the war against Japan in South-east Asia, and Australia backing

258

up the war in the Pacific (just as Britain backed up the war in North-western Europe). To make these major imperial strongholds ready to support huge numbers of service personnel and to withstand enemy attack, massive infrastructural work was required. In India, for example, millions of labourers were enlisted to transform the subcontinent's transport and fuel infrastructure as west coast ports were linked to an unforeseen eastern battlefront once the Japanese had conquered Burma and arrived at the borders of the Raj. Meanwhile in the Middle East, New Zealand and South African engineers, 2,000 Basotho Pioneers, and thousands of unskilled Arab labourers built a new military railway connecting Haifa to Beirut, extending a line from Cairo to Haifa built by General Sir Edmund Allenby in the First World War. In the Indian Ocean military installations were hastily built on remote islands in the Maldives, the Chagos Archipelago, and the Cocos-Keeling Islands, from where Liberator and Spitfire squadrons flew sorties over occupied Malaya and Singapore, in order to provide secret anchorages and aerodromes from which to prosecute the war against Japan. The Mediterranean fortress colonies of Gibraltar and Malta witnessed massive military construction work. By 1945 Air Headquarters Ceylon had a network of bases across the island, at China Bay, Kankesanterai, Vavuniya, Puttalam, Negombo, Minneriya, Sigiriya, Mawatagama, Colombo, Ratmalana, Katakurunda, Koggalla, and Kalamestya.

Roads, railways, underwater cables, wireless installations, subsidized shipping lines, and ports were the Empire's basic furniture, as were the ships of the Merchant Navy and the protected sea highways that connected Britain to the world. Thus dry docks, coastal artillery emplacements, wireless masts, anti-torpedo boom defences, port war signals stations, airstrips, and flying boat anchorages were vital to the Empire's development and prosperity and its survival in times of war as transport, communication, and defensive networks were forged around the world. These included stopping off points familiar to generations of Britons as liners or warships progressed from British ports to the Far East by way of the Mediterranean and the Suez Canal, as well as the colony-hopping air routes pioneered in the inter-war period. These included the air route running from Britain to Victoria Point in Singapore by way of Gibraltar, Malta, Egypt, Iraq, the Trucial States, India, and Burma. Another key strategic air route ran across the belt of Africa from the Gold Coast to Cairo. These routes required serious investment and forward planning, and their potential use as strategic highways in times of war was at least as important as their role in peacetime. In times of war, the Empire's physical network was vital to British strategy; thus Bletchley Park was

259

served by imperial outstations in Bermuda, Cairo, Colombo, Delhi, Hong Kong, Mauritius, Mombasa, Ottawa, and Singapore, whilst SOE was able to develop bases in many colonies to be used as springboards for regional operations against the enemy.

Communications and transport networks, therefore, were essential to waging war, as was the infrastructure of the built environment which created an overseas network of headquarters and administrative centres. Such facilities throughout the empire meant that colonies were able to act alongside London in bringing the Empire to war. Regional power centres such as Cairo, Cape Town, Colombo, and Delhi acted as overseas branch offices of imperial management. Colonies such as Ceylon, Sierra Leone, and Nigeria suddenly found themselves transformed from strategic backwaters into major strategic assets and threatened by enemy action. Nigeria, for example, was a regional command and communications hub, located on major air routes connected to Britain, Khartoum, the Congo, and Johannesburg, as well as a port of call for shipping heading for Britain or the East through the Atlantic. Colonies were pivotal in imperial defence calculations because they provided strategically located bases in an age where power projection relied upon local concentrations of troops, ports of call for warships, and airstrips. The extension of Britain's protective shield to distant dominions — the heart of imperial defence — depended upon this network of colonial bases.

Three centuries of imperial growth meant that Britain fought a uniquely imperial war between 1939 and 1945, the last in a line of global struggles stretching back to the Seven Years War and the struggles against Napoleon, made more deadly than any previous encounter by the enmity of Japan — an Eastern enemy — as well as Great Powers closer to hand in Europe and the Mediterranean. Though Britain is a European land, its greatest defeat of the Second World War occurred in a tropical peninsula seven thousand miles away, its greatest victory in an African desert. Incredibly, until Operation Overlord propelled Allied troops into occupied Europe in the summer of 1944, Britain's major fighting fronts on land were in Africa and Asia. This extraordinary state of affairs was a result of the fact that Britain was much more than just a European land; because of its history, it was an *imperial state*, which from 1939 faced destruction from the four corners of the globe. The need to hold history's largest empire together, and to sustain millions of troops on distant battlefields, required the projection of military, political, and economic power on an unprecedented scale. This required the utilization of organizational networks — of political and economic authority, military command, supply and logistics, and intelligence-gathering.

The scale of Britain's military, political, and economic operations during the war, and the fact that Britain, uniquely, had interests everywhere, necessitated the maintenance of armies and fleets overseas, the protection of the global trade that was the lifeblood of the British world's maritime economy, and the management of vast amounts of information. This required organizational genius in order to coordinate the activities of a state operating on a global scale. In announcing the fall of Singapore to the Commons in secret session, Churchill revealed that, since the start of hostilities with Japan, over 300,000 men had been moved from Britain and the Middle East to South-east Asia and South Asia, 'and we have over 100,000 on salt water at the present time'. This massive transfer of resources had been affected with little loss of life. As Churchill concluded: 'I regard this as a prodigy of skill and organization on the part of all those responsible for it.' This might stand as an epigram for the entire imperial war effort and Britain's unique ability to utilize global networks in order to bring to war a quarter of the earth's surface and the oceans in between. No other power could match this reach, and the German and Japanese war experiences eloquently illustrated the point that winning new territories can be relatively easily achieved, but that linking them, sustaining them, and exploiting them takes years, generations even, of practice in the arts of administration and the construction of social, political, military, and physical networks. The final chapter turns to an analysis of the role played in these networks by the governors in charge of Britain's colonies.

12

Colonial Governors and the Second World War

Breaking a lengthy journey in Lagos, capital of Nigeria, Admiral John Godfrey stayed in the 'fine, airy Government House, with its enormous bedrooms and a continual procession of people passing through'. The Admiral found the Governor of the colony less impressive than his regal abode. Godfrey thought Sir Bernard Bourdillon 'tall, pompous, and neither interesting or interested'. Bourdillon's apparent disinterest in his company piqued Godfrey who, as the Admiralty's ex-Chief of Naval Intelligence, was 'in a position to give him high grade news about the war'. But the Governor wasn't in the least bit inquisitive, though he cheered up, Godfrey noted, 'when he saw a bat-eating bustard'.

John Godfrey, the model for 'M' in the James Bond novels (Ian Fleming was his assistant at the Admiralty), was removed as Director of Naval Intelligence in 1942, largely because of his propensity for clashing with Churchill. Dispatched to become Flag Officer Commanding the Royal Indian Navy, Godfrey made his visit to Nigeria as he progressed eastwards to take up the reins in Delhi. The journey involved stop offs in numerous British and non-British countries, where he was invariably hosted by colonial administrators, diplomats, or military officers stationed at whichever capital city, port, or airbase he happened to alight. Leaving Bristol by flying boat on 23 February 1943, he stopped off in Lisbon, the Gambia, Lagos, the Congo, Khartoum, Cairo, and Baghdad before arriving in Karachi. 'The passengers are mostly service people', he noted, 'in plain clothes until Africa is reached, when they blossom with stars, crowns, and batons. One high grade scientist nurses a box full of mice'.

Admiral Godfrey's voyage illustrates the manner in which journeys were made in the wartime world, and the opportunities that travelling huge distances between overseas fighting fronts and British political and military strongholds afforded senior figures to meet their counterparts, all engaged in the business of administering and defending a vast Empire. As well as providing manpower and strategic raw materials for Britain's imperial wars, colonies were an important part of Britain's overseas networks of power and authority. Colonial governors were key players in these networks because the British Empire was an autocratic organization in which proconsuls were possessed of considerable authority. After considering the role of imperial networks in mobilizing the Empire for war in the last chapter, this chapter looks specifically at the important though neglected role played by colonial governors in the imperial war effort.

Governors were vital repositories of imperial power, directed by the Colonial Office in London and approached with respect and some caution by ministries that relied upon their good offices, such as the Admiralty and the War Office and the ministries of Economic Warfare, Food, and War Transport. Governors and their government houses, offices, secretariats, and field administrations were part of the Empire's physical infrastructure and its decision-making network. As generals, admirals, diplomats, politicians, and foreign dignitaries travelled around the world, government houses offered the basic requirements of shelter and hospitality, and the opportunities that this afforded for the transmission of information and opinion among influential people. During the Second World War the mammoth though unwieldy edifice that was the British Empire was mortally threatened, and with British forces engaged in fighting in, or from, colonies such as Bermuda, Burma, Borneo, British Somaliland, Ceylon, Fiji, Gibraltar, Hong Kong, Kenya, Malaya, Nigeria, Sierra Leone, and Trinidad, the cooperation of governors was essential to the imperial war effort. In a war where imperial battle zones and imperial resources featured so dramatically, good relations with the civil administrators of the Empire were essential. Where they failed, as in Malaya, disaster could result.

Given the importance of colonial resources and battlegrounds to the British war effort, colonial governors were instrumental in mobilizing the Empire for war and complimented the work of Britain's ambassadors and high commissioners overseas. A number of themes emerge from a consideration of the wartime service of the menagerie of British governors serving in Africa, the Caribbean, the Mediterranean, South-east Asia, and the Pacific. In many parts of the world governors had to work with military authorities based in their colonies, often suffering a reduction in their own power as military imperatives took precedence. In some colonies military officers were actually placed in authority above governors, as in Burma (where Governor Sir Reginald Dorman-Smith was subordinated to Admiral Lord Louis Mountbatten), Ceylon (where Governor Sir Andrew Caldecott was placed under the supreme command of Vice-Admiral Sir Geoffrey Layton as his colony became a 'military area'), and British Somaliland (where after the reconquest of the Protectorate from Italy, it became a supply line for imperial forces fighting in Ethiopia).

Some colonies assumed great strategic importance as military assets, logistical and manpower reservoirs and base camps, and as rallying points for regional assaults on enemy-held territory. Governors experienced the regionalization of colonial affairs — as war-related tasks and threats came to be viewed on a regional, rather than colony-by-colony basis — as well as their militarization. They often had to work alongside resident ministers appointed by the Cabinet and despatched to coordinate a region's war effort, as well as powerful military headquarters. Governors helped the military to administer colonies taken from vanquished enemies, such as Ethiopia, Burma, Libya, and Madagascar where British Military Administrations were established. Here governors were required to exercise diplomatic and political skills, as was also the case when duty called them to act at the interface between Britain and semi-autonomous territories such as Southern Rhodesia, and between Whitehall ministries such as the Dominions Office and the War Office in matter relating to the service of colonial troops in the British military. Some colonies became important focal points for the war efforts of conquered European powers such as Belgium, France, and Holland, and American forces became an important factor in British colonies in Africa, the Caribbean, and the Pacific, a process requiring delicate handling by experienced governors. As well as acting as mediators and brokers connecting Britain to the resources of its colonies and preparing them to defend themselves, governors needed to manage 'normal' colonial politics at a time when the functions of the state were deepening, demands for political advance growing louder, and the size of the colonial service shrinking as those who were able to join the armed forces did so.

Colonial governors, therefore, were instrumental in bringing the resources of the Empire to bear in support of Britain's overseas military commands, and were an integral feature of the global network of British power, as important in their own right as admirals, ambassadors, and generals. Governors were figureheads in their colonies, direct representatives of the King who 'yielded to none in precedence bar the sovereign himself'. Governors were heads of state and leaders of society, expected to rally and inspire their people through the hardships of war. They were not only involved in the affairs of their own colonies, but with the war effort in the surrounding region and further afield. The production of strategic raw materials gave a colony such as Malaya, for example, a level of importance that registered in Whitehall, as did Nigeria's contribution of tens of thousands of fighting troops for the Burma and East Africa campaigns.

The Second World War was both an exhilarating and exhausting period for colonial governors. Their workload went through the roof, but there was the knowledge that they were involved in a pivotal moment in the Empire's history. Their powers increased, as they were licensed to pull out all the stops in order to get their colonies to the maximum pitch of war readiness. Even backwater colonies could feel that they were taking part in something of fundamental importance to the future of the Empire and the world. Given the emergency situation — threats to colonial borders from enemy forces, disastrous imperial defeats, and the urgent need for all colonies to realize their highest war potential — governors had far more leeway than was usual. They were licensed to exert imperial authority in order to get things done, paying less heed than was considered prudent in peacetime to the slow and meandering ways in which business was usually conducted in the colonial world. For example, in Indian Ocean and Caribbean colonies governors were able by decree to order landowners to make over large sections of their property to the production of food crops for domestic consumption, cutting the acreage used to produce cash crops for export. The Governor of Ceylon permitted the slaughter tapping of rubber plants given Britain's desperate need for this commodity following the loss of Malaya. In some African colonies, most notably Nigeria, the Rhodesias, and Tanganyika, the Colonial Office reluctantly granted permission for the conscription of hundreds of thousands of civilians for agricultural and industrial war work.

Of course, such measures were hardly likely to be popular with colonial subjects. Nevertheless, their patriotic nature was appealed to and indigenous leaders enlisted in support of the war effort, as Britain's imperial alliance with chiefly rulers paid its richest dividend. Firm action was taken by governors with few qualms; dependent on food imports delivered by the hard-pressed British merchant fleet and often threatened by enemy action, colonies simply had to make every effort to feed and protect themselves. It wasn't a matter of choice, as Sir Bernard Bourdillon pointed out in a radio broadcast to the Nigerian people. 'You don't reward a man for failing to cut his own throat' was his response to nationalist demands for independence in return for cooperation with Britain during the war. With 100,000 American and British troops staging through West Africa during the war, over 10,000 military aircraft for Asia and the Middle East passing through, and the recruitment of over 200,000 African soldiers by West Africa Command, West Africa's governors were in no position to tarry.

Colonies as military bases

A key role for British colonies was to host British and Allied military commands, most notably the headquarters of Supreme Commanders and major military commands. In the former category, General Dwight Eisenhower used Gibraltar as his headquarters during the Allied invasion of North-West Africa, and Admiral Lord Louis Mountbatten, Supreme Allied Commander South East Asia, took up residence in Ceylon after leaving Delhi, constructing a mini military city in Kandy spreading out from his headquarters in the Peradeniya Botanical Gardens. There were numerous colonies in the latter category acting as hosts to large military command structures. Far East Command was based in Malaya, East Africa Command in Kenya, West Africa Command in the Gold Coast, the Eastern Fleet in Ceylon (and for over a year in Kenya after the Japanese had attacked Ceylon), the South Atlantic Station in Sierra Leone, and the Mediterranean Fleet in Malta. In the Pacific, Fiji was home to the 2nd New Zealand Expeditionary Force, and later in the war played host to thousands of Americans training for the Pacific campaigns and preparing Fiji as a link in the Allied defensive line.

It was the job of governors and their administrations to work alongside these British and Allied military commands and to do all that they could to facilitate their work as they sought to prosecute the war. This entailed the militarization of colonies as military personnel arrived in large numbers and defensive preparations were undertaken — anti-aircraft guns installed, barracks and roads constructed, ports expanded and fortified in order to support the global convoy system that underpinned the Empire's war, and aerodromes constructed. The political and particularly the economic impact of such rapid change were often profound. Military commanders relied on the cooperation of governors in their work, and did all that they could to maintain good relations.

As the Eastern Fleet's second in command and the commander of its 3rd Battle Squadron — a force of antiquated but powerful battleships representing over one-quarter of the Royal Navy's battleship strength — Sir Algernon Willis was based at Mombasa from April 1942 until September 1943. Here he developed the port of Kilindini and the naval shore establishment there (HMS *Tana*) in order for it to be able to accom-

266

modate and support a large fleet, building new barracks, instituting canteens in Nairobi, and sanctioning the development of a Sailors Rest Camp at a former Children's Holiday Camp (recommended to him by the Governor's wife, Lady Moore, during his stay at Government House in Nairobi). As well as developing Mombasa's naval facilities, Willis also needed the cooperation of East Africa's governors so that his warship could conduct exercises in the region. For example, in August and September 1942 a large Emergency Exercise was conducted throughout British East Africa and its coastal waters in order to test civil and military responses in the event of an enemy attack. This required the cooperation of the civil authorities and the calling up of the reserves of units such as the Kenya Defence Force. Out of courtesy Admiral Willis wrote to the Governor of Tanganyika, Sir Wilfrid Jackson, to reassure him, and anyone in his territory who was concerned, that the size of the naval force 'attacking' Dar-es-Salaam for Exercise Touchstone did not represent the size of a likely Japanese scale of attack. He explained that at that moment it was unlikely that the Japanese would attack with anything more than a single cruiser or armed merchant raider, but that the likely scale of attack would increase considerably if the Japanese managed to secure Ceylon or other islands in the western Indian Ocean.

Colonial governors and the prosecution of regional wars

As well as the recruitment of soldiers, military authorities required the support of governors in order to use their colonies as bases for operations and to install military facilities for their defence. As Governor of Nigeria, Sir Bernard Bourdillon had an advisory role in regional operations. He strongly recommended the seizure of Vichy Dakar in his communications with Whitehall and the regional military commanders, and was given authority by the War Cabinet to establish contact with the governors of neighbouring French colonies as part of the effort to secure their *ralliement* to the Free French cause. Thus Bourdillon played an important role in securing the switch of Chad and French Cameroon from Vichy allegiance to the Free French cause, and permitted the Free French to make extensive use of Lagos as a base for operations in West Africa.

In Mauritius Special Operations Executive (SOE) relied upon the cheerful and keen support of the wartime governors Sir Bede Clifford and Sir Donald Mackenzie Kennedy. This was because the island colony became an important base for political and military operations against the neighbouring Vichy territories of Madagascar and Réunion. SOE prepared for a possible Japanese occupation of the colony; naval communications and replenishment installations were developed throughout the island; the RAF used the island for flying boat operations; forces assembled there for an attack on Réunion and for naval operations against German vessels; and political, military, and propaganda operations against Madagascar were mounted from Mauritius. During his tenure as governor Clifford was very keen to get involved in the region's war effort, and as an officer on the Army's Reserve List offered his services in any capacity deemed fit during a leave period in Britain, though was told that governors needed to stay in post (during this visit to London early in the war he had meetings at the Colonial Office and was in the House of Commons to see Churchill become Prime Minister). In Mauritius Clifford offered his advice to anyone who would listen, and acted as gaoler to the deposed Shah of Iran, Reza Shah Pelavi. Pelavi had been 'requested' by the British to abdicate in favour of his son in September 1941, and subsequently sent into exile, in Mauritius until the spring of 1942, and then South Africa. He arrived off Port Louis and was met on board the ship by Clifford in full governor's regalia. As he left the ship a contingent of the Mauritius Territorial Force stood as a guard of honour. Whilst on the island he had three villas in the most exclusive areas, cars, and the best medical attention available.

Mauritius also played host to 1,500 Jewish internees who had been refused entry into Palestine. Clifford discussed the Indian Ocean strategic situation with visiting ships' captains, such as Admiral Willis, second-in-commander of the Eastern Fleet and Commander of the 3rd Battle Squadron, and Captain Richard Onslow of the aircraft carrier HMS *Hermes*. He was keen to offer advice on Vichy Madagascar, and on a visit to Durban was quizzed by Colonel Todd, head of the region's main SOE Mission, and Vice-Admiral Neville Syfret, commander of Gibraltar-based Force H which provided the naval component for the invasion of Madagascar in May 1942. Clifford's knowledge of the island from pre-war visits, and the intelligence efforts of his own administration in Mauritius, proved their worth.

Donald Mackenzie Kennedy continued Clifford's policy of engagement with the regional war effort, visiting military establishments in South Africa and aiding the development of military infrastructure in his colony. Mauritius continued to be a base for operations against Vichy territory and for intelligence initiatives which included the interception of enemy signals and cable traffic, and efforts to counter Axis spy networks in neutral Portuguese East Africa. Mauritius was important in all of this as a base for propaganda and military operations and as a secret intelligence interception site. This work was led by a member of Mackenzie Kennedy's administration, Edward Twining, who himself became a colonial governor during the war when he was sent as Administrator to St Lucia in 1944. In pursuit of his secret war work Twining sailed to India, Malaya, and Singapore aboard the Colony class cruiser HMS *Mauritius* in late 1941, and during the course of the war also visited the Belgian Congo, Ceylon, the Dutch East Indies, Egypt, Greece, Iran, Iraq, Madagascar, Mozambique, Nigeria, Palestine, South Africa, the Sudan, Tanganyika, Thailand, and Uganda. As he wrote to his wife from Durban in November 1941, 'sick to death of this continual travelling — 20,000 miles in eight weeks!!'.

Captain Michael Cadwallader Adams, SOE agent DZ11, worked for SOE's main mission in the region, based in Cape Town and commanded by Colonel Todd. The Mission's principal target was Vichy Madagascar, and Adams was appointed Director of Operations. The Mission was preparing for the large British invasion that was launched in May 1942 under the cover name 'Imperial Movement Control Intelligence Section', with an office at naval headquarters in Durban. Whilst in Durban Adams became friendly with Governor Mackenzie Kennedy, whose cooperation was needed by SOE. Adams sailed to Mauritius in July 1942 in the company of the Governor and Lady Mackenzie Kennedy, travelling on board SS *Carabao* 'under extremely uncomfortable conditions [with] virtually no passenger accommodation and a cargo of guano'. The governors of Mauritius and their staffs provided every facility for the military and intelligence officers and agents who sought to use the island for war purposes.

Sir Andrew Caldecott in Ceylon and Lord Gort in Gibraltar and Malta

Sir Andrew Caldecott's governorship in Ceylon illustrates the activities typical of governors during the war and the implications of a region's militarization for colonial authority. Caldecott's wartime speeches have been preserved in the archives by a diligent private secretary, and illustrate the extent of a governor's public involvement in a colony's war effort. A governor's professional duties were gruelling, including formal appearances at innumerable public functions at which, inevitably, he would be guest of honour and chief speechmaker. During the war years Caldecott addressed a diverse range of public and private bodies at all sorts of events, usually black tie dinners, ceremonial openings, and launches for public schemes and initiatives. During the war he gave speeches at the Oxford dinner, the Empire Day dinner, the Ceylon Planters' Association dinner, the Irish dinner, the Comrades dinner, and the Medico-Legal Society dinner. He opened the Bank of Ceylon, the Kandy Food Exhibition, the Ceylon Royal Naval Volunteer Force headquarters, the Harbour Lights carnival, and the London Calling festival, and inaugurated the Boy Scouts Messenger Service. He commemorated the thirteenth anniversary of the Ceylon Broadcasting Service, addressed the ARP at the Colombo Race Course, laid the foundation stone of the 2nd Anti-Aircraft Regiment's headquarters, and attended the Buddhist Theosophical Society's diamond jubilee and the Dutch Reformed Church's golden jubilee. He visited the Farm School and the Ceylon Society of Arts Exhibition, and made radio broadcasts on behalf of the Ceylon War Savings Scheme, the Ceylon War Loan, the Ceylon Food Week, and the Service Welfare Organization Ceylon.

No matter what the theme of his speeches, Governor Caldecott ensured that a war message was conveyed. When making his War Loans broadcast on 14 February 1941, for example, he said that 'if we lose the war we shall lose everything that makes life worth while. Give till it hurts!'. When addressing the Ceylon Planters' Association in the following month, he said:

> Our debt to the British Navy and the British Mercantile Marine is so vast that one hesitates perhaps to mention the debt we owe to our own little navy, the Ceylon Naval Volunteer Force, which day by day preserves our approaches from the danger of enemy mines. It is hard, unspectacular, but essential work that is being done.[75]

When talking about the expansion of Ceylon's own armed forces, Caldecott remarked that 'the Empire requires of Ceylon, as her first duty in the war, that she should keep her own defences up to requirements and man them fully and efficiently'. In December 1941 he inaugurated a weekly radio broadcast for Ceylonese servicemen overseas, numbered in their thousands and concentrated in the Middle East. Meanwhile, in the other direction came tens of thousands of imperial servicemen and women, responsible for defending Ceylon, transforming it into a major base, and using it as a platform for the war in Burma and occupied territories of South-east Asia. When introducing the new Services Welfare

Organization Ceylon, which comprised representatives of the British Soldiers and Sailors Institute, the Hospital Supply Association, the Salvation Army, the Troops Entertainment Committee, the United Services Hospitality Scheme, the War Services League, and the YMCA, Caldecott reminded his listeners of the need to:

> Keep our defenders fit in mind as well as in body. We have now in our Island men come from all four corners of the earth to defend it. You only have to pass along our roads, streets, and lanes to see the British Commonwealth of Nations in microcosm.

Ceylon had been transformed since the fall of Singapore into an imperial *place d'armes*, and it was the task of the Governor and his administration to continue to run the colony effectively, to increase its production of strategic raw materials, and to assist the military in any way possible. In order to do this, and as a result of the profound shock in Whitehall caused by the fall of Singapore and the hopeless civil–military relations that had pertained there, a novel arrangement was put in place. The Colonial Secretary, Lord Cranborne, cabled Caldecott to tell him that Ceylon and its dependencies were henceforth designated a 'military area' under a Commander-in-Chief Ceylon given the island's position as a vital communications link and military base now menaced by the Imperial Japanese Navy.

Thus Vice-Admiral Sir Geoffrey Layton, erstwhile Commander-in-Chief of the Eastern Fleet, was given control of Ceylon's civil government and granted almost dictatorial powers by the War Cabinet, as Ceylon's defence was considered so vitally important by the Cabinet and the Chiefs of Staff in London. This involved a loss of power for Caldecott, and cut through the delicate relations between the colonial administration and the Ceylonese political leadership in this, one of the Empire's most politically advanced colonies. Symbolic of this was the fact that Admiral Layton, with his notorious 'rough quarter-deck style', actually presided in the State Council. A colonial civil servant, John O'Regan, recalls his way of conducting business, recounting a Council meeting at which 'it was Layton's habit to review the past week's events. He would ask, for example, about the very slow progress with a road to the airport'.

'Kotalawala', he would demand.

'What the hell have you been doing in the last week?'

To which Kotalawala, then Minister of Communications and Works, replied: 'The head overseer is having a lot of trouble with supplies.'

'Then give him six on the backside', Layton would bark.[76]

271

In Layton's defence, he judged Ceylon to be completely unprepared to fulfil the major military role demanded of it once Singapore had fallen, and so extreme measures were required. Unfavourable reports to London about the state of preparations and the mindset of local civilian and military officers hit home, and the Eastern Fleet's Chief of Staff, Commodore Ralph Edwards, was present at a meeting in Colombo when a signal was received from the Colonial Office telling the Governor 'that Ceylon was falling below their expectations and that they must buckle to and prepare for the worst'. As a result of the war, therefore, the authority of the governor of Ceylon was eclipsed, and in the deliberations leading to the decision to appoint a Commission to consider Ceylonese self-government, the voices of military commanders such as Mountbatten counted for a great deal back in Whitehall. Caldecott nearly resigned over what amounted to an unceremonious diminution of the authority of his office, but to his credit saw the bigger picture and the need to pull in one direction at a moment of great peril both for his colony and the Empire as a whole.

Governors and their headquarters, as has been suggested, acted as important links in the communications network that governed the Empire and enabled full imperial mobilization for the war. As the example of Admiral Godfrey at the start of this chapter illustrates, senior British officers, when travelling by troopship, warship, flying boat, or transport aircraft to imperial headquarters and fighting fronts, would visit colonies along the way as their transport stopped for fuel or to disembark and embark passengers. When this happened, it was the custom to call upon the Governor, and this was one of the main ways in which the British overseas network of civil and military authority communicated. For the visitor, his stay with a governor enabled him to form impressions of the war's impact and direction from the local perspective, and his opinions would be passed on to colleagues in military headquarters and Whitehall ministries.

For governors, such visits afforded diplomatic opportunities, as they set about ensuring that their colonies got a hearing from visitors of importance whose voices counted in regional headquarters or Whitehall itself. Sir Andrew Caldecott welcomed the commander of Force Z, Admiral Sir Tom Phillips, when HMS *Prince of Wales* docked at Colombo on 28 November 1941, where the battlecruiser HMS *Repulse* already lay at anchor alongside the vintage battleship HMS *Revenge*. Admiral Phillips had stopped off at other imperial ports of call as he progressed east. He met with the Commander-in-Chief South Atlantic Station at Freetown in the colony of Sierra Leone and consulted with Jan Smuts, the South

African Prime Minister, when his ship called at Cape Town. After lunching with Caldecott at his official residence, Queen's House, Phillips 'promptly flew on to Singapore ahead of his force in order to confer with the civil and military authorities, leaving his battle force to await the arrival of two more destroyers from the Mediterranean, the *Encounter* and *Jupiter*'.

In August 1942 Field Marshal Lord Gort, Governor of Malta, hosted the Chief of the Imperial General Staff, General Sir Alan Brooke, as he travelled to Cairo for the Middle East conference at which Churchill shook up the command structure in the Middle East and Western Desert. Within the colonial Empire there were a number of colonies that were designated 'military colonies', acquired because of their strategic value. There were two such colonies in the Mediterranean, Gibraltar and Malta, both traditionally governed by senior military figures. During the Second World War both had periods under Lord Gort, one of Britain's most senior soldiers who before his appointments in the Mediterranean had served as Chief of the Imperial General Staff from 1937 until 1939 and Commander-in-Chief of the British Army in France at the time of Dunkirk. Whilst Governor of Gibraltar he oversaw an extensive programme of defence construction including massive excavation work inside the Rock in order to create barracks, storerooms, magazines, power stations, headquarters, hospitals, and offices. Later, as Governor of the besieged colony of Malta, Gort threw himself into the task of ensuring that the island held out against sustained Axis air attack. He helped to secure the arrival of sixty Spitfires and concentrated all available firepower to destroy the Stuka divebombers attacking HMS *Welshman* as she delivered a precious cargo. He also supervised the distribution of scarce food and water supplies so that even at the height of the crisis 200,000 people received rations each day.

General Brooke's visit gave Gort the chance to air his grievances about the beleaguered condition of his colony, to report his decision to surrender unless a relief convoy arrived, and to give Brooke a depressingly graphic impression of the shocking damage caused by Axis air raids. Brooke hadn't seen such devastation since Ypres. After his visit Brooke recorded in his diary that Gort was depressed, surviving on the meagre ration that the common people of Malta had to do with, and felt that he had been bundled into a sideshow and that the whole garrison might be abandoned without having the chance to give an account of itself. Alan Brooke's visit to Malta clearly strengthened his resolve to see the besieged island sustained when he returned to London.

Governors as diplomats and emergency administrators

Another theme in the study of colonial governors at war is their employment as trouble-shooters and emergency administrators in enemy occupied territory, and their role in devising and enacting imperial policy. Before taking up the governorship of the Gold Coast, for example, Sir Alan Burns spent the early years of the war in London as Assistant Under-Secretary of State at the Colonial Office, playing a key role in negotiating the destroyers-for-bases agreement that exchanged fifty old but precious American destroyers for extensive base rights in Britain's Caribbean colonies. Burns was subsequently appointed Governor of the Gold Coast, 'kissing hands' at Buckingham Palace in July 1941. He sailed for Africa in October in a convoy of over fifty vessels. His new territory, like so many others, was an important chain in the global war effort, for America as well as for Britain. It was surrounded by Vichy territory which required extensive defensive preparations, and became Headquarters of the General Officer Commanding West Africa as well as the Cabinet-ranking Resident Minister for West Africa, Lord Swinton (a previous Colonial Secretary). The port of Takoradi became extremely congested with shipping, and also formed part of the Anglo-American air route that delivered over 10,000 aircraft from the Americas to the Middle East and Asia.

As diplomats within the imperial system, governors had an important role in ensuring that colonial troops were treated correctly by the military authorities under whom they served, and that their service and demobilization was managed as smoothly and equitably as possible. Having been responsible for recruiting thousands of men for service in British military formations, governors felt morally bound to ensure that they received the best possible treatment, as illustrated by the activities of the resident commissioners of Basutoland, Bechuanaland, and Swaziland, as has been seen. They had been deeply involved in recruiting over 36,000 soldiers for the British Army and had toured their territories extensively during recruitment drives. Once the troops had departed for the Middle East, the resident commissioners regularly visited them, often in the company of chiefs, in order to check on their welfare and to keep them in touch with their homes. Charles Arden Clarke served as Resident Commissioner in both Bechuanaland and Basutoland during the war. As a well-regarded official destined for greater things, he was extensively employed by his superior, the High Commissioner to South

Africa, as a shuttle diplomat travelling between Southern Africa and the Middle East. He visited troops in the Western Desert and had meetings with the Adjutant General's Corps responsible for their welfare. If he considered that HCT troops were not being employed in the correct manner, Arden Clarke told the High Commissioner, who took the matter take up at the highest level, activating the Dominions Office back in London which would in turn contact the War Office. Thus governors were used to great effective in the recruitment of soldiers and the subsequent supervision of their employment, on the one hand in order to honour commitments made to them and their chiefs, and on the other to ensure that their war service caused as little disruption as possible when the legions returned.

Evelyn Baring's wartime career provides another good example of governors as diplomats within the imperial system. His background — son of Lord Cromer and previous employee of both the Indian Civil Service and the Foreign Office — qualified him well for this role. Although only thirty-five years of age when war broke out, he was deemed unfit for military service, and spent the early years of the war at the Egypt desk in the Foreign Office. In early 1942 he attended a dinner at which Clement Attlee, Deputy Prime Minister and Secretary of State for the Dominions, was present, and during the course of which he was informed that he had been chosen to go to Southern Rhodesia as governor. The award of a KCMG duly followed, bestowed by the King himself, before Baring departed with his young wife aboard the troopship *Athlone Castle*.

The position of governor in Southern Rhodesia was unique in the Empire. Though a colony it was not directly ruled from Whitehall, and though not a Dominion the white settlers' parliament dominated political affairs. Baring discovered that his three predecessors had seen it as their primary duty to maintain satisfactory relations with the Rhodesian Prime Minister, and, in pursuit of Whitehall's main interest in the territory, seeking to influence him 'against policies unfavourable to the Imperial government, especially in the field of native administration'. The Governor's role, therefore, was to act as a watchdog on the Rhodesian government. In addition to triangular diplomacy between the Prime Minister (Sir Godfrey Huggins) and the Dominions Office, there was a fair degree of ceremonial at Government House and touring in the African reserves. Baring's time in Southern Rhodesia illustrates the fact that, though there was a war on, normal politics continued, even though there was an attempt to shelve knotty political problems for the duration. The biggest issue in Central Africa at this time was the prospect of the 'amalgamation' or federation of Britain's Central African territories, an issue of profound local, regional, and imperial significance which absorbed Baring's energies both as Governor of Southern Rhodesia and, from 1944, as High Commissioner to South Africa.

The extremely varied wartime career of Sir Phillip Mitchell illustrates the manner in which colonial governors were employed as diplomats and emergency administrators. During the war he served as governor of no less than three separate colonies and as governor of conquered Italian colonies. He began the war as Governor of Uganda, though in June 1940 the Colonial Office asked him to go to Nairobi as Deputy Chairman of the Governors' Conference, a body responsible for moving the British East African territories along the path of federation. More importantly, this organization had from before the war been preparing East Africa to liaise effectively with the armed forces and prepare to meet their demands for supplies and manpower, as it was correctly forecast that the region would assume major strategic importance if Italy declared war. All across the globe, mobilizing an Empire for war was a feat that required detailed planning. In East Africa as elsewhere, an executive organization had to be put in place, and key directing posts and financial responsibilities worked out between the War Office, the East African colonial governments, and the South African government, which was heavily involved in the region's military affairs. Mitchell's task was to prepare East Africa for its designated role as a large military base centred on Kenya and dedicated to supporting Middle East Command and the war effort to the north. In doing this the region's food and raw materials were to be in great demand along with its transport infrastructure, ports, and manpower.

In September 1940 Mitchell travelled to Delhi to attend a conference of the Eastern Group Supply Council (a meeting of Australia, New Zealand, India, and Britain's eastern colonies which sought to coordinate military supplies in support of the Middle East war theatre). His exhausting journey, which had also taken him to Ceylon, brought him back to Nairobi by way of Baghdad and Cairo. Whilst in Cairo the Commander-in-Chief Middle East, General Sir Archibald Wavell, invited him to dine at the Turf Club, and Mitchell found himself seated at the Commander-in-Chief's side as he was entertained by the Dominions' generals Blamey, Freyberg and Duignan. Mitchell was to discover later that the dinner had been organized to deceive Italian intelligence, as it coincided with the British attack on Sidi Barrani. Shortly after returning to Nairobi, Mitchell was asked to become Chief Political Officer to oversee the administration of the ex-Italian colonies conquered by Wavell's forces. The Turf Club dinner had been an opportunity for Wavell to look over his man.

As Chief Political Officer for Occupied Enemy Territories Mitchell effectively became governor of ex-Italian Africa. He established his headquarters in Cairo before moving to Nairobi. In his new role he had to manage the competing interests of British ministries (the Colonial Office, the Foreign Office, and the War Office) as well as those of the Americans and of vocal individuals, such as Haile Selassie, the deposed Emperor of Ethiopia. He also had to consider the wishes of Somali nationalists and the thousands of Italians who remained in the occupied territories. Mitchell's position meant that he acted as British Plenipotentiary in negotiating an agreement with the Emperor of Ethiopia and conducted the preliminaries prior to his restoration. This did not take place until the end of January 1942, meaning that Mitchell and his officers governed Ethiopia by proclamation, subject to the Hague Convention which dealt with the occupation of enemy territory.

Soon after completing the transfer of power in Ethiopia, Mitchell received a telegram from Lord Cranborne, the Colonial Secretary, asking if he would become High Commissioner of the Western Pacific and Governor of Fiji, a sensitive front-line region where relations between American, British, Australian and New Zealand civil and military officials required expert coordination. The position made Mitchell governor of all British colonies in the region, from Fiji to the Gilbert and Ellice Islands. After visiting his wife at their orange farm near Grahamstown in South Africa, Mitchell duly flew off through Mombasa, Lagos, Liberia, Brazil, Trinidad and Puerto Rico, stopping off in Washington to have meetings with, amongst others, Lord Halifax, the British Ambassador, and General George Marshall, the US Army's Chief of Staff. He received briefings from the Foreign Office and the State Department, and read files at the British Embassy relating to Anglo-American relations in the region. After an intense ten-day period Mitchell flew across America and the Pacific to take up residence in Government House, Suva.

Mitchell's task in the Western Pacific was delicate indeed. He needed to protect British interests in a region under an American supreme commander that was an *operational* theatre of war. As in the West Indies, the problems in the Anglo-American alliance did not lie at the highest levels of authority, where Mitchell soon established very cordial relations with the American commander, Admiral Chester Nimitz, based at Pearl Harbor. Problems tended to occur further down the chain of command. Not only did he have to mediate Anglo-American differences and sensitivities, he also had to take into account the Australians and New

Zealanders, who felt minimized by American commanders and sought British imperial assistance in fighting their corners. As well as looking north to Pearl Harbor and south to the Pacific Dominions, Mitchell needed to consider the plight of the people of the Solomon Islands and the Gilbert and Ellice Islands, parts of the British colonial empire engulfed by intense fighting. The stationing of large numbers of American (and Empire) troops in the Pacific territories had profound economic and social ramifications, from the trauma of fighting and occupation and the requirement of both sides for local labour. As well as dealing with the war situation, Mitchell struggled with Fiji's communal divisions, and developed self-government plans for the colony's future. Indicating the success with which he managed Anglo-American relations, he was awarded the American Legion of Merit. In 1944 the peripatetic Mitchell became Governor of Kenya.

Just as Sir Phillip Mitchell was beamed into the Fiji Islands to become High Commissioner for the Western Pacific in order to smooth troubled intra-Allied waters, Sir Bede Clifford was transferred in the opposite direction on a similar mission, moving from Mauritius to Trinidad. As in the Pacific, at issue in the Caribbean was British juridical responsibility in a region where America had come to dominate because of the war. Trinidad had become the southern hinge of the Caribbean Sea Frontier, the American military command responsible for security in the region. The destroyer-for-bases agreement of September 1940 had already witnessed an increase in American power in Britain's West Indian colonies.

Before Clifford's arrival in Trinidad, Governor Sir Hubert Young and Admiral Sir Michael Hodges, the Naval Officer-in-Charge, had not enjoyed cordial relations with their American counterparts. They were keen to assert British paramountcy in the local command system, which angered the Americans and led to pressure being brought to bear in London for their removal. Sir Bede Clifford was brought in from Mauritius to replace Young as Governor and smooth troubled waters. He was urbane, had served as Governor of the Bahamas before the war, had an American wife and knew the American President socially; in short, just the man to take hold of the situation and improve relations between Britain and America. After leaving Mauritius to take up his new appointment, Clifford sailed from Durban to Simonstown and then to North America on board the *Queen Elizabeth*, still being employed as a troopship and carrying 4,000 Afrika Korps prisoners of war. In Washington Clifford visited President Roosevelt and discussed the situation in Trinidad. The colony came within an American naval zone, and the admiral in charge, Admiral Hoover (based in Puerto Rico), was at odds with the local British commander, Admiral Hodges, Flag Officer in Charge Trinidad and the West Indies. Hoover was close to the US Navy's chief, Admiral Ernest King, and was thus deemed unsackable. Instead, Hodges was relieved of his duties. To ensure no future doubts about the scheme of things, it was made clear that America would exercise paramountcy in command relations in Trinidad and throughout the Caribbean Sea Frontier region and the Western Hemisphere.

As well as dealing with these difficult matters caused by war on a global scale, governors such as Sir Bede Clifford had to deal with the 'normal' affairs of their colonies. In the West Indies as elsewhere political and economic changes were afoot that were to have long-term ramifications for the Empire after the war. Nationalism was rising and leading to demands for political advancement, and the Colonial Development and Welfare acts of 1940 and 1945 were about to transform relations between Britain and the colonies. During his time as Governor of Trinidad earlier in the war Sir Arthur Richards had had to deal with the internal politics of the island and its leading nationalists, Alexander Bustamante and Norman Manley, gaoling them both as the colony was turned to war and political issues shelved for the duration. Later in the war, whilst serving as Acting Governor Jack Huggins was able to be more forward-looking as the war situation stabilized and more attention was paid to the colonial situation in the post-war years. In 1944 he was appointed to the British Colonies Supply Mission, a 'miniature Whitehall' in Washington, and became co-chairman of the Anglo-American Caribbean Commission. Whilst there a cable arrived from the Colonial Secretary, Colonel Oliver Stanley, offering him the governorship of Jamaica and a knighthood. One of Huggins' achievements whilst governing Jamaica was to introduce universal suffrage in 1944.

The war was manifest in Trinidad in other ways. German submarines appeared in the area, initially enjoying great success, one even penetrating Port of Spain harbour and attacking a merchant vessel. 'Grow More Food' campaigns were launched and the French fleet visited Trinidad before the surrender of May 1940. Trinidad was the convoy assembly point for all oil shipments from Venezuela, Aruba, and Gulf refineries to Europe and North Africa, as well as a staging post for thousands of aircraft being sent to help formations in the Middle East and North Africa, primarily the Eighth Army. Its status as a regional hub was augmented by the fact that all ships and aircraft en route to North America and trans-Atlantic destinations from South America had to report to Trinidad for clearance, and this contributed to a vigorous traffic in VIPs at

Government House (doubtless a pleasure for the aristocratic socialite Clifford) as the colony played its part in the diplomatic and administrative networks of an empire at war. In December 1943 Richards was appointed Governor of Nigeria, succeeding Bernard Bourdillon. Here he focused on planning the post-war settlement in the colony, with a new constitution as the centrepiece. Whilst Bourdillon had been in post when war was the main focus of the governor's attention, Richards' stewardship coincided with a period in which planning for the post-war world became the main task in hand.

Conquered colonies

For some governors the war was the worst period of their professional lives, as they were forced to surrender colonies to the enemy and endure internment for upwards of three years. Sir Shenton Thomas, Governor of the Straits Settlement and High Commissioner of the Federated and Unfederated Malay States, was incarcerated in Tokyo while his wife endured the privations of Changi gaol in Singapore. Sir Mark Young experienced a similar fate after surrendering Hong Kong on Christmas Day 1941. Some governors escaped capture by the enemy though nonetheless spent the war without a territory to govern, as their colonies were wrested from British control. Thus Sir Reginald Dorman-Smith, governor of Burma, spent the war with his government in exile in the Indian hill station of Simla.

Before the Japanese invasion of Malaya, Sir Shenton Thomas followed the instructions that he received from the Colonial Office, which in effect ordered him to keep Malaya's production of tin and rubber up, and not to worry about Japanese invasion. Set on this course, the Governor was not in step with the requirements of the military authorities based in his colony, represented by the General Officer Commanding Malaya, General Sir Arthur Percival, and the Commander-in-Chief Far East, Air Chief Marshal Sir Robert Brooke-Popham (a former Governor of Kenya). He also had difficult relations with the Resident Minister despatched to Singapore shortly before it fell, Duff Cooper. The debate about who was responsible for the mess in Singapore is unlikely to abate, though Shenton Thomas has come in for more criticism than is his due. Suffice to say here that the British in Singapore were badly let down by the strategic assessment and tone of Whitehall, by a frankly racist view of the Japanese, and by two decades of complacency and bluff in British relations with Japan, symbolized by the faith placed in what was inaccurately described as the 'Singapore strategy'. The intensity of the debate, however, sheds light on the central importance of colonial governors to the success or otherwise of a colony's war preparations.

Controversy also surrounds the governorship of wartime Burma. Much of the country was conquered by the Japanese, though slivers remained under British administration, in the hills and mountains on the border with India and in the coastal Arakan region. This rump was still there to be governed, though the man in charge, Sir Reginald Dorman-Smith, had to struggle in exile to accomplish this in the shadow of supreme military authority, whilst also planning for the return of British rule to the rest of the country. Burma was not 'supposed' to have been attacked, considered safe behind Singapore's shield, and so the Governor and his administration, not to say the Burmese people, were badly let down by the British government's faulty strategic assessment of the Far East situation and by the inadequate military preparations for their defence. As the surprise Japanese attack materialized and then became a rapid advance, the Governor did what he could to prepare for occupation and resistance. Frontier Service officers such as Henry Stevenson were sent into remote regions of the country to coordinate guerrilla units in the hills. Thus began a period in which the Governor sought to manage affairs in the inaccessible, unoccupied parts of the country, and to facilitate the work of behind-enemy-lines organizations such as SOE (known as Force 136 in Asia).

In attempting to keep in touch with and influence Burmese affairs ready for the day when British rule would be restored, Dorman-Smith had great difficulties in coordinating his policies with those of the Supreme Allied Commander South East Asia, Admiral Lord Louis Mountbatten. Despite still being Governor, Dorman-Smith was not in a position to do much more than paper planning, as the loudest voices in Burma belonged to the military. In late 1943 Dorman-Smith was officially subordinated to Mountbatten. As the latter recorded in his diary:

This week I signed the most unusual document which has so far fallen to my lot to sign. This was a proclamation by which I am taking over on 1st January the Government of unoccupied Burma from the Governor of Burma. Apparently I am empowered to do this without even consulting the Governor, merely by signing a proclamation. This proclamation also places this part of Burma under martial law.[77]

Military imperatives, and the personal assessments of Mountbatten, outweighed those of Dorman-Smith as he planned Britain's return, leading to disagreements, particularly regarding the position of Aung San and the Japanese-supporting Burma National Army. Nevertheless, Dorman-Smith remained an influential figure, and was destined to retain his position at the end of the war. In October 1944 Mountbatten had a houseful at his official residence, the King's Pavilion in Kandy, high in Ceylon's central mountains. His guests included Dorman-Smith, General Sir George Giffard, commander of the 11th Army Group (which included General Slim's Fourteenth Army), and the 'French Mission to my Staff, under General Blaizot'. Mountbatten and Dorman-Smith had a stormy relationship because the latter deplored Mountbatten's policy of backing Aung San and the Burma National Army when they switched sides from the Japanese to the British. Despite his objections, Mountbatten's will prevailed. As he wrote in his diary in May 1945 after a spat with Dorman-Smith, 'damn it all, I'm governing Burma, not he, whatever his title'. Though Mountbatten portrayed Dorman-Smith as a hidebound colonialist, the Governor's concern was that Burma be brought to self-government more gradually in order to give the post-colonial Burmese state a better chance of survival.

Nigeria

The wartime activities of the Governor of Nigeria, Sir Bernard Bourdillon, provide a useful summary of the colonial governor's role in wartime. With war a matter of days away, the Governor and his wife, Lady Violet, were away from the capital, *in communicado* on a tour of the Eastern and Western Provinces of Britain's most populous African colony. Given the gloomy news from London his deputy, Chief Secretary Charles Woolley, decided to recall the Governor to Lagos. Finding him and the *Valiant* in the vastness of the Niger Delta, however, presented a problem, because the vessel didn't possess a radio. This was solved by sending an aircraft with a pilot instructed to fly low over the maze of channels and lagoons. 'On spotting the tall pyjama-clad figure of Sir Bernard on board the craft he dropped a message in a "tennis ball tin", a device with a flag tied to the top and a weight to the bottom'. Thus the Governor was summoned back to his capital.

Nigeria's huge wartime mobilization included the recruitment of more than 120,000 soldiers and the colony was an important staging post for the Allied war effort. Bourdillon recognized the need to 'keep the war in the forefront of everyone's thinking'. In increasing the tempo of the colony's war effort, he had to face the eloquent and forceful nationalism of men such as Nnamdi Azikiwe, given wide publicity by Nigeria's outspoken and vigorous press. Bourdillon firmly believed in the need for greater cooperation and coordination of the war effort of the four British West African colonies, particularly in the spheres of civil and military relations, civil and political intelligence, military supplies, and political and economic relations. This was a constant theme in his communications with the Colonial Office. One of the fruits of his endeavours was the establishment of the West African Supply Council after he had decided that the 'civil and military requirements of British West African could best be met if West Africa was regarded as one economic unit'. He helped overturn Colonial Office complacency regarding the region, arguing that the unexpected should be expected. This indeed occurred when Malaya fell and Nigeria's tin deposits became crucial to the Empire's economy.

Nigeria, like other colonies such as Ceylon, Gibraltar, and Trinidad, was a regional communications hub, located on major air routes connected to Britain, Khartoum, the Congo, and Johannesburg, as well as a port of call for shipping heading across the Bay of Biscay for Britain or the around the Cape to the East. Therefore Government House, 'an imposing three-storey structure built in 1894 on the Lagos Marina', often acted as a hotel for travelling dignitaries. Elaborate dinners were the norm here, and Government House staff had to be prepared to meet flying boats first thing in the morning as well as to run around after eminent guests. A typically busy night occurred in March 1942. Bourdillon was hosting a dinner for the Nigerian Legislative Council, involving fifty guests plus their wives. Simultaneously, his residence was playing host to numerous birds of passage. Upstairs, King George of Greece and his Prime Minister, Mr Tsouderos, were dining separately. As if this wasn't enough, Bourdillon's hard-pressed ADC lamented, 'unluckily, Sir Stafford Cripps arrived on his way to India'. He insisted on joining the Legislative Council dinner, and asked for a poached egg on spinach to be prepared as his vegan repast.

Guests at Government House during the war included, in addition to maharajahs, generals, and admirals (like John Godfrey): King Peter of Yugoslavia and his entire Cabinet; Princess Olga of Yugoslavia; King George and Prince Peter of Greece; the prime ministers of Australia and New Zealand; Henry, Duke of Gloucester; the imperial historian Sir Reginald Coupland; General Charles de Gaulle; Lord Swinton, Resident Minister for West Africa; Lord Moyne, Secretary of State for the

Colonies; Sir Kinahan Cornwallis, British Ambassador to Iraq; Captain James Roosevelt; and Lord Louis Mountbatten.

It has been seen that governors were essential mediators and brokers of imperial power, and that their participation in the imperial war effort was a crucial aspect of the worldwide mobilization achieved by the British state. The war was in so many ways an imperial war, and naturally therefore the colonies and their resources were integral to the prosecution of that war. The war was also the swansong of gubernatorial autonomy, a tradition of British colonial administration. In the post-war years, central direction and Whitehall control of the colonial agenda increasingly became the norm, and this was to a large extent due to the manner in which colonies had been used and authority dispensed during the Second World War, and the profound economic and political impact of the last global war of empire.

In his short story, *Quantum of Solace*, Ian Fleming offered an insightful summary of the colonial governor type. James Bond had been sent on a routine mission to the colony of the Bahamas, and was having an after dinner drink with the governor in his Nassau residence.

> He belonged to a routine type that Bond had often encountered around the world, solid, loyal, competent, sober, and just. The best type of colonial civil servant. Solidly, competently, loyally, he would have filled the minor posts for thirty years while the Empire crumbled around him and now, just in time, by sticking to the ladders and avoiding the snakes, he had got to the top. In a year or two it would be the GCB and out, out to Godalming or Cheltenham or Tunbridge Wells, with a pension and a small packet of memories of places like the Trucial Oman, the Leeward Islands, British Guiana, that no one at the local golf club would have heard of or would care about.[78]

But during the Second World War these men had been instrumental in bringing the British Empire to full mobilization, demonstrating once again the vital role performed by colonies in British Imperial warfare.

13

Conclusion

The Continued Role of Colonies
in Post-Imperial Defence

As the preceding chapters have shown, the colonial empire's role in the Second World War was profound. In his foreword to the official report on the colonial empire at war, Arthur Creech Jones, Secretary of State for the Colonies, wrote that the war had been a 'time of intense strain and difficulty everywhere'.[79] Creech Jones presided over the 1,168-strong staff of the Colonial Office located in Downing Street and five other London sites, served overseas by the members of the Colonial Administrative Service who ran things on the ground in Malta, Malaya, Mauritius and dozens of other territories.* The contribution of the colonial empire in terms of manpower and resources was huge. It was a war effort rendered even more impressive because so many things — such as the expansion of colonial military forces and raw materials production capacity— were achieved almost from scratch, so unexpected had been the waves of reverses that the early years of war had yielded.

As the official report noted, the colonies 'have never kept large standing armies', and what forces existed were intended 'primarily for internal security'. All the more remarkable then that the armed forces of the colonial empire rose from 42,800 in 1939 to a staggering 510,000 in 1945.[80] And even this figure represents a conservative estimate, for it didn't include the many thousands of colonial empire subjects who served in wartime labour and agriculture corps', or in British (as opposed to

---

* During the war there was also a substantial Colonial Office presence in America. In 1941 the Colonial Supply Liaison office opened in Washington, its name soon changed to the British Colonies Supply Board. Its task was to ensure access to Lend-Lease and cash-bought supplies for the colonies, and it employed 200 members of staff.

colonial) military formations. There were, in addition, an officially esti-mated 15,000 colonial empire subjects in the Merchant Navy. The Colonial Office believed that, of the 30,000 merchant seamen to lose their lives during the war, 5,000 haled from the colonies. This extremely high proportion — meaning that one in three colonial empire merchant seamen lost their lives — was because most of them worked 'in the engine room of coal-burning ships', a veritable death trap should the dread moment come when a torpedo or a mine made contact with the hull.[81]

All colonies had been affected by the war, from the demands of infla-tion, food shortages, and manpower recruitment to the trials of bombing, ground combat, and enemy occupation. West Indian colonies experi-enced the U-boat war, Barbados even having a ship attacked in its harbour. The Mediterranean colonies were in the front-line for most of the conflict, Gibraltar having its entire population of 14,500 removed to Britain and Northern Ireland as their home became an exclusive military base. Malta took over 16,000 tons of Axis bombs, which killed 5,000 civilians and destroyed or damaged 28,000 buildings. Palestine and Trans-Jordan were important bases, for war in the eastern Mediterranean as well as in Iraq, and as a fall back in case Egypt was lost. Borneo, Hong Kong, Malaya, and islands of the Western Pacific experienced catastrophic imperial defeat, enemy occupation, and re-invasion. Some colonies felt the strain of war through becoming major Allied military bases, such as the East African colonies, Ceylon, and Fiji.

As well as sending their men and often giving their lives, the people of the colonial empire donated huge sums of money and gifts in kind to the British war effort. Women across the world knitted comforts for servicemen; donations of sugar, rum, molasses, and citrus fruit poured into British kitchens; mobile canteens sponsored by colonial girl guides toured bombed-out British streets; interest-free loans to the British government were a commonplace, as were the ubiquitous bomber and Spitfire funds and subscriptions to a galaxy of British-based charities such as the Red Cross, St Dunstan's Fund for Blind Soldiers and Sailors, the Belgium Relief Fund, and Aid to Russia. Beyond this, there were gifts of sterling to the British government, and those 'monetary gifts' seen by the Secretary of State (i.e. not including those made directly to British organizations or gifts in kind), amounted to over £24,000,000.

In the decades following the Second World War, colonies moved to the centre of Britain's imperial defence planning. (They emerged as more valued sources of manpower, particularly once the Indian Army had ceased to exist, and as providers of bases as new technology meant that the footprint of overseas forces could be reduced. Carrier battle groups, strategic air lift, and jet fighters replaced the need for large garrison forces, and were supported by colonial bases. The colonies also moved to the centre stage as consumers of imperial defence resources in this period. Though the 'turbulent frontier' may have become calmer as the twentieth century progressed, during the terminal decades of empire the colonies made huge demands on imperial military resources, as primary resistance matured into political opposition to British rule, often operating alongside insurgencies. Colonial territories such as Aden, Borneo, Cyprus, Kenya, and Malaya featured prominently in the post-Second World War experience of the British military. Empire was not to be had on the cheap anymore, and this was one of the main reasons why it subsided, though even into the twenty first century, colonies with military utility remained, including the British sovereign base areas on Cyprus, Gibraltar, Ascension, the Falklands, and British Indian Ocean Territory.

After the Second World War the colonial empire became more important in British imperial defence planning and Cold War security. The war had proved the huge value of the colonial empire as a source of human and material resources, and in the penurious years that were to come its produce, particularly its dollar-earning exports, became invaluable. India had gone; now the jewels in the imperial crown were to be found in the rubber and tin-rich colonies of South-east Asia, with other valuable gems, such as the Northern Rhodesian copperbelt, located in the colonies of tropical Africa. It was expected that the colonies would become more of a feature in the provision of imperial defence, matching their increased significance in the economic affairs of the British Empire. The Dominions were behaving with much greater autonomy and could not be automatically relied upon to support British military causes, and India had become an independent state showing little inclination to play the role the British had in mind (that of a loyal Commonwealth ally following Britain's lead).

So during the twentieth century colonies moved from the peripheries of imperial defence thinking to the very core as Britain came to rely more heavily on colonial bases and manpower resources as traditional suppliers — particularly Egypt and India — gained independence and ceased to be at Britain's beck and call. Britain retained a large global base infrastructure well into the 1960s, and there was plenty of work to be done to support military activities overseas. Thus, for example, a 3,600-strong High Commission Territories Corps was recruited from Basutoland, Bechuanaland, and Swaziland in 1946, serving in the Middle East until 1949. Similarly, the Indian Ocean colonies of Mauritius and the

Seychelles formed the backbone of the British Army's pioneer support in the Middle East, maintaining over 10,000 men attached to Middle East Land Forces until the time of the Suez crisis in 1956. When the Anglo-Egyptian Treaty was abrogated by the Egyptian government in 1951, over 40,000 Egyptians left the employment of the British military. Over 20,000 men from East Africa, and colonies such as Cyprus and Mauritius, were taken on to fill the gap. In the 1950s the British Army still included over 80,000 colonial service personnel, reflecting the centrality of the colonies to imperial defence in the changing post-war world.

The colonial empire also became important as a new base for Middle East Command as the Middle East itself became increasingly untenable. Though the emergency in the Suez Canal Zone between 1951 and 1955 saw a huge build up of British military resources in Egypt, including colonial troops, Britain's days in Egypt were numbered. The colonial empire was considered as an alternative to the Middle East as a home for Middle East Command for various reasons. First, Britain's withdrawal from Palestine in 1948 ruled out a location that had once been considered a strategic reserve supporting the Egypt base. Secondly, Britain's increasingly controversial position in Egypt and the future of the massive military encampment that was the Suez Canal Base Area spurred the search for alternatives. Thirdly, Britain's failure to persuade the United Nations to grant it a mandate over Libya, where Britain retained significant military facilities until Colonel Gaddafi's take over in 1969, ruled out that country as a new home for Middle East Command. As a result of these three factors, the strategic stock of Kenya colony rocketed. Millions of pounds were spent on military facilities there. The Royal Engineers, for example, cleared 1,600 acres of land and built nine miles of road at the Mackinnon Road base area north of Mombasa, along with facilities including aircraft hangars and a 600-bed hospital. But changing circumstances, including the Mau Mau rebellion, meant that the Kenya plan was eventually aborted.

Yet it was nevertheless a part of the colonial empire that stepped in to counter Britain's withdrawal from Egypt when in 1961 Aden became the new home of Middle East Command. Along with the strategic base in the colony of Singapore, Aden formed the mainstay of Britain's east of Suez military presence until the late 1960s. Small colonies also became important in this period as military staging posts supporting key aspects of Britain's strategic and military system. They acted as stepping stones for the RAF's island strategy for power projection in the Indian Ocean region, for example, with Masirah, Socotra, the Seychelles, the Maldives, and the Cocos Islands all involved in the RAF's staging system connecting

Britain and the Mediterranean to South-east Asia and Australia, the very core of imperial defence planning in the 1960s.

Unfortunately for British strategic planners, the colonial empire was not immune from nationalism and political activity that compromised its strategic value. This was a growing problem in the twentieth century. Malta, for example, grew in importance as a naval base for the Mediterranean Fleet and warships detailed to reinforce the Far East just when Maltese nationalism and the influence of fascist Italy were becoming a problem in the 1930s; Cyprus and Kenya, both viewed as strategic bastions with imperial and Cold War utility, became less attractive when nationalism and insurgency marred their internal affairs; and in the 1960s the value of Aden, one of only two remaining imperial strongholds east of Suez, was undermined by Arab nationalism. Despite these difficulties, colonies continued to play an important role in helping Britain remain a power with global military reach, and to this day Ascension, Cyprus, Diego Garcia, and Gibraltar support British operations overseas.

Even the British government's resolve from the late 1950s to severely prune imperial commitments was largely a result of an assessment of how best to *preserve* British influence in the world, how to secure Britain's continued leadership of a global Commonwealth that, whilst not quite imperial red on the map, would remain cheerfully pink. In particular, it did not denote a lessening of commitment to the vast Indian Ocean region; in fact, quite the reverse. The 1962 Defence Review confirmed that Britain would tighten its grip in this region, the last great imperial redoubt. Moreover, in terms of imperial defence, the British government saw no reason why a *post-imperial* state could not still form part of British plans to project power. Ceylon provided a good example of this; becoming independent in 1948, the new government was willing to remain a Commonwealth member, whilst granting the Royal Navy the continued use of Trincomalee, from which the navy's East Indies Station continued to police the Indian Ocean from the Malacca Straits to the Swahili coast, and from the Southern Ocean to the Persian Gulf.

In the decades following the Second World War, imperial defence continued to be a key element in Britain's strategic posture, though commitments in this direction slowly contracted, and the word 'imperial' was dropped as the British Empire disappeared and Britain's relative power declined. Despite this, Britain's appetite for a global military stance and the defence of overseas territories and interests — main features of imperial defence — never ended. In this light, the *Strategic Defence Review* of 1998 was not a departure in British defence policy so much as a refocusing on wider world commitments in an age where, not for the first time, Britain's investment in European security could be scaled down. Before that, from the 1960s to the 1990s, despite insistent calls in other strategic directions from NATO and the European Economic Community — and the urgent pleas of the British economy for strategic austerity - Britain never lost the ardent desire to remain a world policeman, even if its historic role of Chief Constable had been usurped by the Anglo-Saxon power on the other side of the Atlantic. Even when scaling down its territorial possessions or defence establishment, the British time and again evinced a desire to stay on, to never withdraw completely, to retain a strategic culture associated with a global presence and global intervention. The former American Secretary of State, Dean Acheson, once said — to be paraphrased by many thereafter — that 'Great Britain has lost an empire and has not yet found a role'. On the contrary, in substance as well as in policy, Britain never in fact entirely lost that empire, and certainly never lost the appetite and capacity to perform a world role, despite the turn towards Europe that Acheson approvingly discerned, and the relative contraction of British economic, political, and military power in the post-war decades.[82]

So the British Empire never entirely disappeared, and even today Britain has as one of its core defence missions the protection of overseas colonies, and retains overseas military bases. Even when colonies gained their independence, the British remained reluctant to abandon military commitments in the surrounding region, and often the transfer of power to an independent government was the cause of a new defence attachment between fledgling nation and erstwhile colonial power. The British 'non-withdrawal' from East of Suez commitments remains much in evidence to this day.

The focus on post-imperial decline and contraction has concealed an obvious continuum of extra-European British defence interests, facilities, and deployments running from the 1960s to the present day. Similarly, the focus upon the end of empire has blinded many to the numerous imperial legacies — not to say imperial commitments — that survived the 1960s. Though the major territories that had formed the British Empire — located in Africa, South Asia, and South-east Asia — had gained independence by the late 1960s, Britain's empire in fact remained sizeable, and certainly global, well into the 1990s. The remaining islands and enclaves of empire still represented a significant global footprint, and many did not gain their independence until the years after Africa, South Asia, and South-East Asia had witnessed the end of British rule. Between

1968 and 1971, for example, independence came to Aden, Mauritius, Swaziland, Nauru, Tonga, Fiji, Bahrain, Qatar, and the United Arab Emirates. Between 1973 and 1984 independence was granted to the Bahamas, Grenada, the Seychelles, Dominica, the Solomon Islands, the Gilbert and Ellice Islands, St Vincent and the Grenadines, St Lucia, the New Hebrides, Belize, Antigua and Barbuda, St Kitts and Nevis, and Brunei. Hong Kong remained a British possession, and military base, until 1997.

Part of the British Empire still exists today, and the fact that the defence of these colonies remains a primary British military commitment has helped preserve the global posture of Britain's armed forces. The remaining British colonies, known today as Overseas Territories, are Anguilla, Ascension Island, Bermuda, British Antarctic Territory, British Indian Ocean Territory, the British Virgin Islands, the Cayman Islands, the Falkland Islands, Gibraltar, Montserrat, Pitcairn, Henderson, Ducie, and Oeno Islands, St Helena, South Georgia and the South Sandwich Islands, Tristan da Cunha, and the Turks and Caicos Islands. Some of these territories have a military use for Britain and its allies, or require garrison forces, such Ascension Island, British Indian Ocean Territory, the Falklands, and Gibraltar. Britain also has two Sovereign Base Areas in Cyprus, which support permanent British military establishments. The retention of some of Britain's imperial base infrastructure represents another important continuum with the era of classic imperial defence, and Britain also enjoys base rights and military facilities in numerous independent countries, such as Belize, Brunei, Canada, Kenya, Oman, and Singapore, as well as supplying defence and security expertize to scores of countries around the world and being a signatory to numerous defence alliances. Today, British forces are committed in Africa, the Caribbean, Central Asia, the Mediterranean, and the Middle East, as well as in European locations such as the Balkans, several former Soviet states, Germany, and Northern Ireland. According to the Chief of the Defence Staff, General Sir Michael Walker, in addition to British warships, air squadrons, and regiments serving in Afghanistan, the Balkans, Brunei, Cyprus, the Falklands, Gibraltar, Iraq and Sierra Leone, in 2005 Britain had small detachments of service personnel in seventy-four different countries and eighty-four defence attaché sections around the world. The fact of Britain's continuing commitment to a global military presence and global military deployments — irrespective of the Cold War and the downsizing of the armed forces — should come as no surprise; for the defence of British overseas interests and overseas territories has always been a priority for British foreign and defence policy. Furthermore, despite relative decline and imperial contraction, its financial, commercial, diplomatic, and cultural links with the wider world remained substantial.

Notes

Chapter 1

1 From *Israel in East Africa*, BBC Radio 4, 30 July 2003.
2 Michael Howard, 'A Brief Vision', review of Ashley Jackson, *The British Empire and the Second World War*, in the *Times Literary Supplement*, 1 September 2006.

Chapter 2

3 David Niven, *The Moon's a Balloon* (London: Penguin, 1994), p. 71.
4 Raymond D'Unienville (ed.), *Letters of Sir John Abercromby September 1810–April 1811* (Quatre Bornes, Mauritius: Michel Robert, 1969).
5 Gerald Graham, *Great Britain in the Indian Ocean* (Oxford: Clarendon Press, 1967).

Chapter 3

6 Michael Pearson, *The Indian Ocean* (London: Routledge, 2003), p. 127.
7 N. A. M. Rodger, *The Command of the Ocean: A Naval History of Britain, 1649–1815* (London: Penguin, 2004), p. 436.
8 Ian Hernon, *Britain's Forgotten Wars: Colonial Campaigns of the Nineteenth Century* (Stroud, Gloucestershire: Sutton, 2003), p. 22.
9 Michael Ondaatje, *Running in the Family* (London: Picador, 1984), p. 150.
10 Christopher Bayly, *Imperial Meridian: The British Empire and the World, 1780–1830* (Harlow: Longman, 1989), pp. 191–92.
11 M. Pearson, *The Indian Ocean*, p. 216.
12 Donald Mackenzie Wallace, *The Web of Empire: A Diary of the Imperial Tour of Their Royal Highnesses the Duke and Duchess of Cornwall and York* (London: Macmillan, 1902).
13 Ronald Hyam, *Empire and Sexuality: The British Experience* (Manchester: Manchester University Press, 1990), p. 34.
14 Wilfred Nunn, *Tigris Gunboats: The Forgotten War in Iraq, 1914–1917* (London: Chatham Publishing, 2007), p. 155.
15 *The Prince of Wales' Eastern Book: A Pictorial Record of the Voyages of HMS Renown, 1921–1922* (London: Hodder and Stoughton, n.d.).
16 Gerald Graham, *The Politics of Naval Supremacy: Studies in British Maritime Ascendancy* (Cambridge: Cambridge University Press, 1965).

17 Peter Relf to A. Jackson, 6 September 2005 and 15 October 2005.

18 Michael Hutton, 'Royal Marines Band East Indies Station: Reflections of HMS *Gambia*, 1957–58', <http://www.royalmarinesband.co.uk/history/eastindies.htm>, found on 13/7/05.

19 Ibid.

20 A. Cecil Hampshire, *The Royal Navy Since 1945: Its Transition to the Nuclear Age* (London: William Kimber, 1975), p. 140.

Chapter 4

21 Gerald Graham, *The Politics of Naval Supremacy: Studies in British Maritime Ascendancy* (Cambridge: Cambridge University Press, 1965).

22 Edwin Hoyt, *The Last Cruise of the* Emden (London: Andre Deutsch, 1967), p. 7. Also see Prince Franz of Hohenzoller, *Emden: My Experiences in SMS* Emden (London: Herbert Jenkins, 1928) and 'The Cruise of the *Emden*' in Jacques Mordal, *Twenty-Five Centuries of Sea Warfare* (London: Abbey Library, 1970).

23 E. Hoyt, *The Last Cruise of the* Emden, p. 14.

24 Ibid., p. 103.

25 Ibid., p. 133.

26 Ibid., p. 133.

27 Ibid., p. 150.

28 Ibid., p. 150.

29 Kevin Patience, Konigsberg: *A German East African Raider* (Bahrain: Dar Akhbar, 1994).

30 John Morrow, *The Great War: An Imperial History* (London: Routledge, 2004), p. 60.

31 John Godfrey, 'The Naval Memoirs of Admiral J. H. Godfrey, Volume I, 1902–1915', typed manuscript (1964), p. 110.

32 Ibid.

33 John Godfrey, 'The Naval Memoirs of Admiral J. H. Godfrey, volume II, 1915–1919', typed manuscript (1964).

34 Ibid.

35 Wilfred Nunn, *Tigris Gunboats: The Forgotten War in Iraq, 1914–1917*, preface.

36 John Godfrey, 'The Naval Memoirs of Admiral J. H. Godfrey, volume II, 1915–1919'.

37 Admiralty 167/57 quoted in Eric Grove, *The Royal Navy since 1815: A New Short History* (Basingstoke: Palgrave Macmillan, 2005).

Chapter 5

38 Botswana National Archives (hereafter BNA), BNB 14. Jules Ellenberger, Acting Government Secretary, 'Bechuanaland Protectorate Annual Report, 1916–17'.

39 The National Archives, Kew. DO 119/889. Resident Commissioner to High Commissioner, 17 August 1914.

40 BNA, S. 28/2. Resident Magistrate Tsau to Resident Commissioner Mafeking, 11 December 1914.

41 BNA, DCS 43/11. Resident Commissioner to Chief Khama III, 22 June 1917. For the fame of Khama, see Neil Parsons, *King Khama, Emperor Joe, and the Great White Queen: Victorian Britain Through African Eyes* (London: University of Chicago Press, 1998).

42 Rhodes House Library, Oxford. Mss. Afr. S. 1568 (1). Jules Ellenberger, 'Early Days in the Bechuanaland Protectorate' (1966), volume II, p. 221.

43 Sir Charles Lucas, *The Empire at War*, volume IV, *Africa* (London: Oxford University Press, 1924), p. 354.

44 BNA, BNB 16. 'Bechuanaland Protectorate Annual Report, 1918–19'.

Chapter 6

45 Interview with Selogwe Pilane, Mochudi, 1994. The oral history used in this chapter was recorded in Botswana between June 1994 and June 1995.

46 All archival material is drawn from the Botswana National Archives.

47 Neil Parsons, Willie Henderson, and Tom Tlou, *Seretse Khama, 1921–1980* (The Botswana Society/Macmillan, 1995).

Chapter 7

48 E. R. Elliott, *Royal Pioneers, 1945–1993* (Hanley Swan, Worcestershire: SPA, 1993), p. 32. See also E. H. Rhodes-Wood, *War History of the Royal Pioneer Corps, 1939–1945* (Aldershot: Gale and Polden, 1960).

49 W. H. Walton, 'Colonel Herbert Johnson OBE, MC, TD, Leader of the Swazi Pioneers, 1941–1945: A Memoir', unpublished paper (1993), p. 5.

50 BNA, S. 133/2/1. Sergeant Samson to Resident Commissioner, 13 June 1943.

51 B. Gray, *Basuto Soldiers in Hitler's War* (Maseru: Basutoland Government Press, 1953), p. 79.

52 Ibid., p. 72.

53 Ibid., p. 77–78.

54 Royal Logistics Corps Museum, Deepcut. 1991 Swazi Company War Diary, entries from 13 and 16 September 1943.

Chapter 8

55 The National Archives, Kew. WO 253/1. Colonel H. G. L. Prynne to Colonel F. J. Scott, 2 July 1945. See Prynne's attached 'History of Pioneers and Labour in the Middle East, 1940–1945'.

56 W. H. Walton, 'Colonel Herbert Johnson', p. 14. Unsigned memorandum, 11 November 1942.

57 Botswana National Archives, Bangwato Tribal Administration 9/2.

58 The National Archives, Kew. DO 35/1184 (Y1069/1/2). Major Germond report, April 1945.
59 The National Archives, Kew. DO 35/1183 (Y1069/1/1). Lieutenant Colonel Charnock report, 9 January 1944.
60 Botswana National Archives. BNA, S. 142/1/1. Bechuanaland Administraton memorandum, 1944.

Chapter 9

61 Material in this chapter is drawn from The National Archives at Kew, the Imperial War Museum, Rhodes House Library Oxford, and from oral and archival material gathered during a research trip to Mauritius in 1999.
62 Timothy Parsons, *The African Rank and File: The Social Implications of Colonial Military Service in the King's African Rifles, 1902–1964* (Oxford: James Currey, 1999), p. 41.
63 The Diary of Alfred North-Coombes, in possession of Monica Maurel. Entry, 3 February 1944.
64 Imperial War Museum Sound Archive. Colonel Yeldham interview, accession 3960.
65 Rex Woods, *Cambridge Doctor* (London, 1962), p. 167.
66 The National Archives, Kew. WO 169/18285. War Diary. Quarterly Morale Report.
67 Interview with J. F. C. Harrison, Cheltenham, 22 January 1999. See his book *Scholarship Boy: A Personal History of the Mid-Twentieth Century* (London, 1995).
68 Alfred North-Coombes' Diary, p. 156.
69 Guy Sauzier, 'The Events Which Marked the Arrival of the Mauritian Battalion at Diego Suarez in 1943', Mauritius Historical Society lecture (1995), pp. 4–5.
70 T. Higginson, 'Mutiny in Madagscar', *Rhino Link*, 15 (1998).

Chapter 10

71 This chapter is based upon Ashley Jackson, *War and Empire in Mauritius and the Indian Ocean* (Basingstoke: Palgrave Macmillan, 2001); Jackson, '"Defend Lanka Your Home": War on the Home Front in Ceylon, 1939–1945', *War in Society*, 16, 2 (April 2009); Jackson, 'The British Empire in the Indian Ocean' in S. Chaturvedi and D. Rumley (eds), *Geopolitical Orientations in the Indian Ocean* (New Delhi: South Asian Publishers, 2002); Jackson, 'The Indian Ocean' and 'The Islands of the Indian Ocean', in Jackson, *The British Empire and the Second World War* (London: Continuum, 2006); and Jackson, *Ocean Victory: Britain's War from Suez to Sumatra* (forthcoming). A visit to Sri Lanka in 2007 was sponsored by the British Academy.

Chapter 11

72 Reverend C. S. Dawe, *King Edward's Realm: Story of the Making of the Empire* (London: The Educational Supply Association, 1902).

73 Richard Aldrich, *The Faraway War: Personal Diaries of the Second World War in Asia and the Pacific* (London: Corgi, 2006), p. 83.

74 Churchill Archives Centre, Churchill College, Cambridge. 2WLLS 5/4. Willis to Admiral Sir Dudley Pound, 11 November 1941.

Chapter 12

75 Rhodes House Library, Oxford. Mss Ind. Ocn s. 235, 'Speeches of His Excellency the Governor of Ceylon, Sir Andrew Caldecott'.

76 John O'Regan, *From Empire to Commonwealth: Reflections on a Career in Britain's Overseas Service* (London: Radcliffe Press, 1994).

77 Philip Zeigler (ed.), *Personal Diaries of Admiral the Lord Louis Mountbatten, Supreme Commander South-East Asia, 1943–1946* (London: Collins, 1988). Entry 21 December 1943.

78 Ian Fleming, 'Quantum of Solace', first published in *Modern Woman* magazine, then in Fleming's 1960 collection *For Your Eyes Only* (London: Jonathan Cape).

Chapter 13

79 Command 7167, *The Colonial Empire (1939–1947)* (London: HMSO, 1947). This 115 page report covers the whole Colonial Empire, making much use of material provided by Sir John Shuckburgh, a Narrator in the Historical Section of the Cabinet Office then compiling his civil history of the war in the colonial empire, which was completed in 1949 but never published.

80 Command 7167, *The Colonial Empire (1939–1947)*, Appendix III 'Comparative Strengths of Military Forces in Various Colonial Territories, 1939 and 1945'.

	1939	1945
East Africa	11,000	228,000
West Africa	8,000	146,000
Caribbean/Bermuda	4,000	10,000
Falklands	250	200
St Helena		250
Gibraltar		700
Malta	1,400	8,200
Cyprus		9,000
Palestine/Transjordan	1,500	25,000
Aden	700	1,800
Mauritius	250	3,500
Seychelles		1,500

Ceylon	3,500	26,000
Malaya/Borneo	10,000	
Sarawak		
Hong Kong	1,500	
Fiji	650	7,000
Tonga		2,000
New Hebrides		100
Gilbert/Ellice/Ocean	50	2,000
Solomons		2,000
Total:	42,800	473,250

NB: This excludes the 36,000 from Basutoland, Bechuanaland, and Swaziland (because, though run like colonies and staffed by the Colonial Administrative Service, they formally came under the Dominions Office and not the Colonial Office) as well as some of the less formal home guard units and colonial civil labour units such as the Mauritius Civil Labour Corps and the Ceylon Essential Services Labour Corps, both many thousands strong, and units such as the Ceylon Agriculture Corps. It also omits colonial personnel serving in *non colonial* services, thus the thousand-plus Mauritian women in the ATS or the 6,800 Mauritians in the Royal Pioneer Corps, are not captured by this picture.

81 Ibid., p. 116.
82 The arguments made in this conclusion are further developed in A. Jackson, 'Imperial Defence in the Post Imperial Era', in Greg Kennedy (ed.), *Imperial Defence: The Old World Order, 1856–1956* (London: Routledge, 2008) and Jackson, 'Empire and Beyond: The Pursuit of Overseas National Interests in the Late Twentieth Century', review article, *English Historical Review*, cxxii, 499 (2007). For a recent account of one of Britain's numerous 'Post Imperial' colonial escapades, see Rowland White, *Phoenix Squadron: HMS Ark Royal, Britain's Last Top Guns, and the Untold Story of their Most Dramatic Mission* (London: Bantam, 2009). This is the story of the 1972 defence of British Honduras from Guatemalan aggression.

Bibliography

Extensive archival research has been conducted in the Bodleian Library and Rhodes House Library, Oxford, The National Archives, Kew, Churchill Archives Centre, Churchill College, Cambridge, the Imperial War Museum, London, the Royal Logistics Corps Museum, Deepcut, the Botswana National Archives, the Mauritius Archives, and the Sri Lanka National Archives. Lengthy bibliographies appear in Ashley Jackson, *Botswana 1939–1945: An African Country at War*; Jackson, *War and Empire in Mauritius and the Indian Ocean*; *The British Empire and the Second World War*; and 'Supplying War: The High Commission Territories Military-Logistical Contribution in the Second World War', *Journal of Military History*, 66 (2002).

Oscar M Abey'ratna, *The History of the Ceylon Light Infantry* (Colombo: Ceylon Daily News, 1945).

Richard Aldrich, *Intelligence and the War against Japan: Britain, America, and the Politics of Secret Service* (Cambridge: Cambridge University Press, 2000).

——, *The Faraway War: Personal Diaries of the Second World War in Asia and the Pacific* (London: Corgi, 2006).

Ray Alexander, *The Cruise of the Raider* Wolf (New Haven: Yale University Press, 1939).

D. T. Aponso-Sariffodeen, 'How D. S. Saved Ceylon from a Food Crisis', *The Sunday Times* (Colombo), 24 March 2002.

Douglas Austin, *Malta and British Strategic Policy, 1925–1943* (London: Frank Cass, 2004).

John Bach, *The Australia Station: A History of the Royal Navy in the Southwest Pacific, 1821–1913* (Kensington, New South Wales: New South Wales University Press, 1985).

Arthur Banks, Wings of the Dawning: The Battle for the Indian Ocean, 1939–1945 (Malvern Wells: Images Publishing, 1996).

Michael Barber, *Anthony Powell: A Life* (London: Duckworth, 2005).

Fitzroy André Baptiste, *War, Co-operation, and Conflict: The European Possessions in the Caribbean, 1939–1945* (New York: Greenwood Press, 1988).

Terry Barringer, *Administering Empire: An Annotated Checklist of Personal Memoirs and Related Studies* (London: Institute of Commonwealth Studies, 2004).

Darrel Bates, *A Gust of Plumes: A Biography of Lord Twining of Godalming and Tanganyika* (London: Hodder and Stoughton, 1972).

Christopher Bayly, *Imperial Meridian: The British Empire and the World, 1780–1830* (Harlow: Longman, 1989).

—— and Tim Harper, *Forgotten Wars: The End of Britain's Asian Empire* (London: Allen Lane, 2007).

R. A. R. Bent, *Ten Thousand Men of Africa: The Story of the Bechuana Pioneers and Gunners, 1941–1946* (London: HMSO, 1952).

Patrick Beesly, *Very Special Admiral: The Life of Admiral J. H. Godfrey, C.B.* (London: Hamish Hamilton, 1980).

Michael Bloch, *The Duke of Windsor's War* (London: Weidenfeld and Nicolson, 1982).

Robert Blyth, *The Empire of the Raj: India, Eastern Africa, and the Middle East, 1858–1947* (Basingstoke: Palgrave, 2003).

Elleke Boehmer, 'Global and Textual Webs in an Age of Transnational Capitalism; or, What Isn't New About Empire', *Postcolonial Studies*, 7, 1 (2004).

Andrea Bosco and Alex May (eds), *The Round Table: The Empire-Commonwealth and British Foreign Policy* (London: The Lothian Foundation Press, 1997).

A. G. Boycott, *The Elements of Imperial Defence: A Study in the Geographical Features, Natural Resources, Communications, and Organization of the British Empire* (Aldershot: Gale and Polden, 1931).

Martin Brice, *The Royal Navy and the Sino-Japanese Incident, 1937–1941* (London: Allan, 1973).

Damon Bristow, 'The Five Power Defence Arrangements: Southeast Asia's Unknown Regional Security Organization', *Contemporary Southeast Asia: A Journal of International Strategic Affairs*, 27, 1 (2005).

Richard Brohier, 'The Boer Prisoners of War in Ceylon', *Journal of the Dutch Burgher Union in Ceylon*, 36, 1 (July 1946).

J. H. Brown, 'Admiralty House and the Royal Navy at Trincomalee, 1810–1957', Naval Historical Branch (1980).

Neville Brown, *Arms without Empire* (Harmondsworth: Penguin, 1967).

Alan Burns, *Colonial Civil Servant* (London: George Allen and Unwin, 1949).

B. C. Busch, *Britain and the Persian Gulf, 1894–1914* (Berkeley, California: University of California Press, 1967).

Peter Burroughs, 'Defence and Imperial Disunity', in Andrew Porter (ed.), *The Oxford History of the British Empire, volume III, The Nineteenth Century* (Oxford: Oxford University Press, 1999).

P. J. Cain and A. G. Hopkins, *British Imperialism, 1688–2000* (Harlow: Longman, 2001).

David Cannadine, *Ornamentalism: How the British Saw Their Empire* (London: Allen Lane, 2001).

Dennis Castillo, *The Maltese Cross: A Strategic History of Malta* (Westport, Connecticut: Praeger, 2006).

A. Cecil Hampshire, *The Royal Navy Since 1945: Its Transition to the Nuclear Age* (London: William Kimber, 1975).

John Cell, *Hailey: A Study of British Imperialism, 1872–1969* (Cambridge: Cambridge University Press, 2002).

John Charmley, *Duff Cooper: The Authorized Biography* (London: Weidenfeld and Nicolson, 1986).

Martin Charnock, *Unconsummated Union: Britain, Rhodesia, and South Africa, 1900–1945* (Manchester: Manchester University Press, 1977).

Warren Chin, 'Operations in a War Zone: The Royal Navy in the Persian Gulf in the 1980s', in Ian Speller (ed.), *The Royal Navy and Maritime Power in the Twentieth Century* (London: Frank Cass, 2005).

Anthony Clayton, *The British Empire as a Superpower, 1919–1939* (London: Macmillan, 1986).

——, '"Deceptive Might": Imperial Defence and Security, 1900–1968', in Judith Brown and William Roger Louis (eds), *The Oxford History of the British Empire*, volume IV, *The Twentieth Century* (Oxford: Oxford University Press, 1999).

—— and David Killingray, *Khaki and Blue: Military and Police in British Colonial Africa* (Athens, Ohio: Ohio Center for International Studies, 1989).

Bede Clifford, *Proconsul: Being Incidents in the Life and Career of The Honourable Sir Bede Clifford* (London: Evans Brothers, 1964).

Norman Clothier, *Black Valour: The South African Native Labour Contingent, 1916–1918 and the Sinking of the* Mendi (Pietermaritzburg: University of Natal, 1987).

D. H. Cole, *Imperial Military Geography: General Characteristics in Relation to Defence* (London: Sifton Praed, 1928).

H. A. Colgate, 'Trincomalee and the East Indies Squadron, 1754–1844', MA Thesis (University of London, 1959).

——, 'The Royal Navy in Trincomalee', *The Ceylon Journal of Historical and Social Studies*, vii, 1 (1964).

Robert Collins, 'The Sudan Political Service: A Portrait of the "Imperialists"', *African Affairs*, 71, 284 (1972).

John Collyer, *The Campaign in German South-West Africa, 1914–1915* (Pretoria: Government Printers, 1937).

Command 7176, *The Colonial Empire (1939–1947)* (London: HMSO, 1947).

Dudley Cowderoy and Roy Nesbit, *War in the Air: Rhodesian Air Force, 1935–1980* (Alberton, Zimbabwe: Galago, 1987).

Michael Crowder, 'The First World War and Africa', in Adu Boahen (ed.), *UNESCO General History of Africa*, volume VII, *Africa Under Colonial Domination, 1880–1935* (London: James Currey, 1990).

Alex Danchev and Daniel Todman (eds), *War Diaries, 1939–1945: Field Marshal Lord Alanbrooke* (London: Weidenfeld and Nicolson, 2001).

Edmund Dane, *British Campaigns in Africa and the Pacific, 1914–1918* (London: Hodder and Stoughton, 1919).

Philip Darby, *British Defence Policy East of Suez, 1947–1968* (London: Oxford University Press for the Royal Institute of International Affairs, 1973).

C. S. Dawe, *King Edward's Realm: Story of the Making of the Empire* (London: The Educational Supply Association, 1902).

Peter Day, 'Bureaucratic Blunders Ambushed Malta Ships', *BBC History Magazine*, 9, 8 (August 2008).

A. de Moor and H. L. Wesseling (eds), *Imperialism and War: Essays on Colonial Wars in Asia and Africa* (Leiden: Brill, 1989).

T. Dent and D. Will, 'The Boer War as Seen from Gaborone', *Botswana Notes and Records*, 4 (1972).

K. M. de Silva, *History of Ceylon*, volume III, *From the Beginning of the Nineteenth-Century to 1948* (Colombo: University of Ceylon, 1973).

——, (ed.), *Sri Lanka, Part One: The Second World War and the Soulbury Commission, 1939–1945,* British Documents on the End of Empire Series (London: Stationery Office, 1997).

——, 'Ceylon (Sri Lanka)', in Robin Winks (ed.), *The Oxford History of the British Empire, Volume V: Historiography* (Oxford: Oxford University Press, 1999).

Charles Douglas-Home, *Evelyn Baring: The Last Proconsul* (London: Collins, 1978).

Klaus Dodds, *Pink Ice: Britain and the South Atlantic Empire* (London: I. B. Tauris, 2002).

Athalie Ducrotoy, *Air Raid Sirens and Fire Buckets: Wartime in Seychelles, 1939–1945* (Kent: Rawlings Publications, 1997).

Raymond Dumett, 'Africa's Strategic Minerals during World War Two', *Journal of African History*, 26 (1985).

Raymond D'Unienville (ed.), *Letters of Sir John Abercromby September 1810–April 1811* (Quatre Bornes, Mauritius: Michel Robert, 1969).

Brian Dyde, *The Empty Sleeve: The Story of The West India Regiments of the British Army* (St John's, Antigua: Hansib Caribbean, 1997).

Charles Eade (ed.), *Secret Session Speeches by the Right Honourable Winston S. Churchill* (London: Cassell, 1946).

Robert Edgar, 'Lesotho and the First World War: Recruiting, Resistance, and the South African Native Labour Contingent', *Mohlomi: Journal of Southern African History*, 3, 4, 5 (1979–1981).

Robert Edgerton, *The Fall of the Asante Empire: the One Hundred Years War for Africa's Gold Coast* (New York: The Free Press, 1995).

——, *Africa's Armies: From Honour to Infamy — A History from 1791 to the Present* (Boulder, Colorado: Westview, 2002).

——, *Like Lions They Fought: The Zulu War and the Last Black Empire in South Africa* (London: Weidenfeld and Nicolson, 1988).

'Egypt Gets a Railway Line to Europe', *Picture Post*, 20 March 1943.

Jules Ellenberger, 'The Bechuanaland Protectorate and the Boer War, 1899–1902', *Rhodesiana*, 11 (1964).

Byron Farwell, *Queen Victoria's Little Wars* (London: Penguin, 1973).

Kent Fedorowich, *Unfit for Heroes: Reconstruction and Soldier Settlement in the Empire between the Wars* (Manchester: Manchester University Press, 1995).

A. G. Field, 'The Expedition to Mauritius in 1810 and the Establishment of British Control', MA Thesis (University of London, 1931).

Karen Fields, *Revival and Rebellion in Colonial Central Africa* (Princeton: Princeton University Press, 1985).

John Flint and Glyndwr Williams (eds), *Crown and Charter: The Early Years of the British South Africa Company* (Berkeley, California: University of California Press, 1974).

Giles Foden, *Mimi and Toutou Go Forth: The Bizarre Battle of Lake Tanganyika* (London: Penguin, 2005).

Richard Frost, *Enigmatic Proconsul: Sir Philip Mitchell and the Twilight of Empire* (London: The Radcliffe Press, 1992).

Vivian Fuchs, *Of Ice and Men: The Story of the British Antarctic Survey, 1943–73* (Oswestry, Shropshire: A. Nelson, 1982).

John Galbraith, 'The "Turbulent Frontier" as a Factor in British Expansion', *Comparative Studies in Society and History*, 11 (1960).

Immanuel Geiss, *War and Empire in the Twentieth Century* (Aberdeen: Aberdeen University Press, 1983).

Peter Gibbs, *The History of the British South Africa Police*, volume I, *The First Line of Defence, 1899–1903* (Salisbury, Rhodesia: British South Africa Police, 1972).

——, *The History of the British South Africa Police*, volume II, *The Right of the Line, 1903–1939* (Salisbury, Rhodesia: British South Africa Police, 1974).

N. H. Gibbs, *Origins of Imperial Defence: An Inaugural Lecture Delivered at the University of Oxford, 8 June 1955* (London, 1955).

——, 'The Origins of Imperial Defence', in John Hattendorf and R. Jordan (eds), *Maritime Strategy and the Balance of Power: Britain and America in the Twentieth Century* (Basingstoke: St Antony's/Macmillan Series, 1989).

J. H. Godfrey, 'The Naval Memoirs of Admiral J. H. Godfrey, volume I, 1902–1915', typed manuscript (1964).

Philip Goodhart, *Fifty Ships That Saved the World: The Foundation of the Anglo-American Alliance* (London: Heinemann, 1965).

Donald Gordon, *The Dominion Partnership in Imperial Defense, 1870–1914* (Baltimore, Maryland: Johns Hopkins Press, 1965).

Chris Goss, *It's Suicide But its Fun: The Story of 102 (Ceylon) Squadron, 1917–1956* (London: Crécy Books, 1995).

Barry Gough, *The Royal Navy and the Northwest Coast of North America, 1810–1914: A Study of British Maritime Ascendancy* (Vancouver, British Columbia: University of British Columbia Press, 1971).

Gerald Graham, 'The Indian Ocean: From the Cape to Canton' in Graham, *The Politics of Naval Supremacy: Studies in British Maritime Ascendancy* (Cambridge: Cambridge University Press, 1965).

——, *Great Britain in the Indian Ocean, 1810–1850: A Study in Maritime Enterprise* (Oxford: Clarendon Press, 1967).

——, *The China Station, 1830–1860* (Oxford: Oxford University Press, 1967).

R. L. Greaves, *Persia and the Defence of India, 1884–1902: A Study in the Foreign Policy of the Third Marquis of Salisbury* (London: Athlone Press, 1959).

Albert Grundlingh, *Fighting Their Own War: South African Blacks and the First World War* (Johannesburg: Ravan Press, 1987).

Gregory Haines, *Gunboats on the Great River* (London: Macdonald's and Jane's, 1976).

Jessica Harland-Jacobs, *Builders of Empire: Freemasons and British Imperialism, 1717–1927* (Chapel Hill, N. C: University of North Carolina Press, 2007).

Philip Haythornthwaite, *The Colonial Wars Source Book* (London: Caxton Editions, 2000).

Robert Heussler, *Yesterday's Rulers: The Making the British Colonial Service* (Oxford: Oxford University Press, 1963).

Ian Hernon, *Britain's Forgotten Wars: Colonial Campaigns of the Nineteenth Century* (Stroud: Sutton, 2003).

Robin Higham, *Britain's Imperial Air Routes, 1918–1939: The Story of Britain's Overseas Airlines* (London: G. T. Foulis, 1960).

History of the Ceylon Garrison Artillery, Formerly Ceylon Artillery Volunteers (Colombo: *Times of Ceylon* c. 1924).

Geoffrey Hodges, *The Carrier Corps: Military Labour in the East African Campaign, 1914–1918* (New York: Greenwood, 1966).

——, 'African Manpower Statistics for the British Forces in East Africa, 1914–1918', *Journal of African History*, 19, 1 (1978).

Prince Franz of Hohenzoller, *Emden: My Experiences in SMS Emden* (London: Herbert Jenkins, 1928).

Rob Holland, 'The Imperial Factor in British Strategies from Attlee to Macmillan, 1945–1963', *Journal of Imperial and Commonwealth History*, 12 (1984).

David Hollett, *The Conquest of the Niger by Land and Sea: From the Early Explorers and Pioneer Steamships to Elder Dempster and Company* (Gwent: P. M. Heaton, 1995).

Richard Hough, *The Hunting of Force Z: The Sinking of the* Prince of Wales *and the* Repulse (London: Collins, 1963).

Raymond Howell, *The Royal Navy and the Slave Trade* (London: Croom Helm, 1987).

Edwin Hoyt, *The Last Cruise of the* Emden (London: André Deutsch, 1976).

Molly Huggins, *Too Much to Tell* (London: Heinemann, 1967).

Archibald Hurd, *The Merchant Navy* (London: John Murray, 1921), volume i.

Michael Hutton, 'Royal Marines Band East Indies Station: Reflections of HMS *Gambia*, 1957–58', <http://www.royalmarinesband.co.uk/history/eastindies.htm>, found on 13/7/05.

Ronald Hyam, *The Failure of South African Expansion, 1908–1948* (London: Macmillan, 1972).

——, *Britain's Imperial Century, 1815–1914: A Study in Empire and Expansion,* 3rd edition (Basingstoke: Palgrave, 2003).

——, *Empire and Sexuality: The British Experience* (Manchester: Manchester University Press, 1990).

Illustrated Programme of the Royal Jubilee Procession (London: Prince of Wales Hospital Fund for London, 1897).

Hamish Ion, 'The Idea of Naval Imperialism: The China Squadron and the Boxer Uprising', in Greg Kennedy (ed.), *British Naval Strategy East of Suez, 1900–2000* (London: Frank Cass, 2005).

Charles Jeffries, *Whitehall and the Colonial Service: An Administrative Memoir, 1939–1956* (London: Athlone Press, 1972).

Ashley Jackson, Tswana War Poetry', *Botswana Notes and Records* (1995).

——, '"Bad Chiefs" and Sub-Tribes: Aspects of Recruitment for the British Army in the Bechuanaland Protectorate', *Botswana Notes and Records* (1996).

——, 'Motivation and Mobilization for War: Recruitment for the British Army in the Bechuanaland Protectorate, 1941–42', *African Affairs*, 96, 384 (1997).

——, *Botswana 1939–1945: An African Country at War* (Oxford: Clarendon Press, 1999).

——, 'African Soldiers and Imperial Authorities: Tensions and Unrest during the Service of High Commission Territories Soldiers in the British Army, 1941–46', *Journal of Southern African Studies*, 25, 4 (1999).

——, 'Tshekedi Khama, Bechuanaland, and the Central African Federation', *South African Historical Journal*, 40 (1999).

——, *War and Empire in Mauritius and the Indian Ocean* (Basingstoke: Palgrave Macmillan, 2001).

——, 'Bechuanaland, the Caprivi Strip, and the First World War', *War and Society* 19, 2 (2001).

——, 'Refitting the Fleet in Ceylon: The War Record of Walker Sons and Company', *Journal of Indian Ocean Studies*, 10 (2002).

——, 'The Military-Logistic Contribution of the High Commission Territories during the Second World War', *Journal of Military History* 66, (2002).

——, 'The British Empire in the Indian Ocean' in Sanjay Chaturvedi and Dennis Rumley (eds), *Geopolitical and Regional Orientations in the Indian Ocean* (Delhi: South Asian Publishers, 2002).

——, *The British Empire and the Second World War* (London: Hambledon Continuum, 2006).

'The Royal Navy and the Indian Ocean Region since 1945', *RUSI Journal*, 151, 6 (2006).

——, 'The British Empire and the Second World War', *World War Two Quarterly*, 4, 1 (2007).

——, 'The Colonial Empire and Imperial Defence' in Greg Kennedy (ed.), *Imperial Defence: The Old World Order, 1856–1956* (London: Routledge, 2008).

——, 'Imperial Defence in the Post-Imperial Era', in Greg Kennedy (ed.),

305

Imperial Defence: The Old World Order, 1856–1956 (London: Routledge, 2008).

——, '"Defence Lanka Your Home": The Home Front in Ceylon, 1939–1945', *War in History*, 16, 2 (2009).

——, *Mad Dogs and Englishmen: A Grand Tour of the British Empire at its Height* (London: Quercus, 2009).

Robert Jackson, *The Malayan Emergency and Indonesian Confrontation: The Commonwealth's Wars, 1948–1966* (London: Routledge, 1991).

Lawrence James, *The Savage Wars: Campaigns in Africa, 1870–1920* (London: Hale, 1985).

Ivor Jennings, *The Constitution of Ceylon* (Oxford: Oxford University Press, 1949).

Cedric Joseph, 'The British West Indies Regiment, 1914–1918', *Journal of Caribbean History*, 2 (1971).

Nihal Karunaratna, *Kandy Past and Present, 1474–1998* (Government Printing: Central Cultural Fund, 1999).

Chandrika Kaul (ed.), *Media and the British Empire* (Basingstoke: Palgrave, 2006).

J. B. Kelly, *Britain and the Persian Gulf, 1795–1880* (Oxford: Oxford University Press, 1968).

Greg Kennedy, (ed.), *Imperial Defence: The Old World Order, 1856–1956* (London: Routledge, 2008).

Paul Kennedy, 'Imperial Cable Communications and Strategy, 1870–1914', *English Historical Review*, 86 (October 1971).

——, *The Rise and Fall of British Naval Mastery* (London: Allen Lane, 1976).

V. G. Kiernan, *Colonial Empires and Armies, 1815–1960* (Stroud: Sutton, 1998).

David Killingray, 'The Ideal of A British Imperial African Army', *Journal of African History* 20 (1979).

——, '"A Swift Agent of Government": Air Power in British Colonial Africa, 1916–1939', *Journal of African History*, 20 (1984).

—— and Richard Rathbone (eds), *Africa and the Second World War* (Basingstoke: Macmillan, 1986).

——, 'Labour Exploitation for Military Campaigns in British Colonial Africa, 1870–1945', *Journal of Contemporary History*, 24, 3 (1989).

—— and David Omissi (eds), *Guardians of Empire: The Armed Forces of the Colonial Powers, c. 1700–1964* (Manchester: Manchester University Press, 1999).

—— and David Anderson (eds), *Policing and Decolonization: Politics, Nationalism, and the Police, 1917–65* (Manchester: Manchester University Press, 1991).

—— and —— (eds), *Policing the Empire: Government, Authority, and Control, 1830–1940* (Manchester: Manchester University Press, 1992).

Robin Kilson, 'Calling up the Empire: The British Military Use of Non-White Labour in France, 1916–1920', Ph.D. Thesis (Harvard University, 1990).

Clifford Kinvig, *Scapegoat: General Percival of Singapore* (London: Brasseys, 1996).

A. H. M. Kirk-Greene, *The Corona Club, 1900–1990: An Introductory History* (London, 1990).

——, *On Crown Service: The History of H. M. Overseas Civil Service* (London: Tauris, 1999).

——, *Britain's Imperial Administrators* (London: Macmillan, 2001).

——, (ed.), *Glimpses of Empire: A Corona Anthology* (London: I. B. Tauris, 2001).

J. M. Lee, "'Forward Thinking" and War: The Colonial Office during the 1940s', *Journal of Imperial and Commonwealth History*, 6 (1977).

—— and Martin Petter, *The Colonial Office, War and Development Policy: Organization and Planning of a Metropolitan Initiative, 1939–1945* (London: Institute of Commonwealth Studies/Maurice Temple Smith, 1982).

J. Lee Ready, *Forgotten Allies: The Military Contribution of the Colonies, Exiled Governments, and Lesser Powers to the Allied Victory in World War Two*, two volumes (Jefferson, NC: McFarland and Company, 1985).

Alan Lester, 'Imperial Circuits and Networks: Geographies of the British Empire', *History Compass*, 4, 1 (2006).

Julian Lewis, *Changing Direction: British Military Planning for Post-War Strategic Defence, 1942–1947* (London: Sherwood, 1988).

Charles Lucas (ed.), *The Empire at War*, five volumes (London: Oxford University Press, 1924).

James Lunt, *Imperial Sunset: Frontier Soldiering in the Twentieth Century* (London: Futura, 1981).

J. F. Macdonald, *The War History of Southern Rhodesia, 1939–45*, 2 volumes (Salisbury: Government Printers, 1947 and 1950).

Donald Mackenzie Wallace, *The Web of Empire: A Diary of the Imperial Tour of Their Royal Highnesses the Duke and Duchess of Cornwall and York in 1901* (London: Macmillan and Company, Limited, 1902).

John Mackenzie (ed.) *Popular Imperialism and the Military, 1850–1950* (Manchester: Manchester University Press, 1992).

Harold Macmillan, *The Blast of War, 1939–45* (London: Macmillan, 1967).

J. A. Mangan (ed.), *'Benefits Bestowed'? Education and British Imperialism* (Manchester: Manchester University Press, 1988).

Arthur Marder, *Old Friends, New Enemies: The Royal Navy and the Imperial Japanese Navy - Strategic Illusions, 1936–1941* (Oxford: Clarendon Press, 1981).

——, *Old Friends, New Enemies: The Royal Navy and the Imperial Japanese Navy — The Pacific War, 1942–1945* (Oxford: Clarendon Press, 1990).

T. E. Marston, *Britain's Imperial Role in the Red Sea Area, 1800–1878* (Hamden, Connecticut: Shoe String Press, 1961).

John Masters, *The Road Past Mandalay* (London: Michael Joseph, 1961).

David McIntyre, *The Imperial Frontier in the Tropics, 1865–1875: A Study of British Colonial Policy in West Africa, Malaya, and the South Pacific in the Age of Gladstone and Disraeli* (London: Macmillan, 1967).

'Mauritius: A Brief Communications History', <http://www.rnca.org.uk/ditty /art-7a.htm, found on 31/3/06>.

David McLean, *Britain and Her Buffer State: The Collapse of the Persian Empire, 1890–1914* (London: Royal Historical Society, 1979).

G. C. Mendis, *Ceylon under the British, 1795–1832* (Colombo, Colombo Apothecaries, 1944).

Lennox Mills, *Ceylon under British Rule, 1795–1932* (Oxford: Oxford University Press, 1933).

Philip Mitchell, *African Afterthoughts* (London: Hutchinson, 1954).

K. W. Mitchinson, *Pioneer Battalions of the Great War: Organized and Intelligent Labour* (London: Leo Cooper, 1997).

Paul Mmegha, *British Military and Naval Forces in West African History, 1807–1874* (New York: NOK Publishers, 1978).

Thomas Mockaitis, *British Counterinsurgency in the Post-Imperial Era* (Manchester: Manchester University Press, 1995).

Brian Montgomery, *Shenton of Singapore: Governor and Prisoner of War* (London: Leo Cooper, 1984).

Barry Morton, 'Linchwe I and the Kgatla Campaign in the South African War, 1899–1902', *Journal of African History*, 26, 2 (1985).

Archie Munro, *The Winston Specials: Troopships Via the Cape, 1940–1943* (Liskeard: Maritime Books, 2006).

Michael Murfett, John Miksic, Brian Farrell, and Chiang Ming Shun, *Between Two Oceans: A Military History of Singapore from the First Settlements to Final British Withdrawal* (Oxford: Oxford University Press, 1999).

Wesley Muthiah and Sydney Wanasinghe, *Britain, World War Two and the Sama Samajists* (Colombo: Young Socialist Publication, 1996).

George Simeon Mwase, *Strike a Blow and Die: The Classic Story of the Chilembwe Rising* (London: Heinemann, 1975).

Robin Neillands, *A Fighting Retreat: The British Empire, 1947–1997* (London: Coronet, 1997).

Keith Neilson and Thomas Otte (eds.), *Railways and International Politics: Paths of Empire, 1848–1945* (London: Routledge, 2006).

Walter Nimocks, *Milner's Young Men: The 'Kindergarten' in Edwardian Imperial Affairs* (London: Hodder and Stoughton, 1970).

C. Northcote Parkinson, *War in the Eastern Seas, 1793–1815* (London: Allen & Unwin, 1954).

Mary Ntabeni, 'Military Labour Mobilization in Colonial Lesotho during World War II, 1940–1943', *Scientia Militaria: The South African Journal of Military Studies*, 36, 2 (2008).

Wilfred Nunn, *Tigris Gunboats: The Forgotten War in Iraq, 1914–1917* (London: Chatham Publishing, 2007).

David Omissi, *Air Power and Colonial Control: The Royal Air Force, 1919–1939* (Manchester: Manchester University Press, 1990).

——, *The Sepoy and the Raj: The Indian Army, 1860–1940* (Basingstoke: Macmillan, 1994).

H. C. O'Neill, *The War in Africa, 1914–1917 and in the Far East 1914* (London: Longmans, 1919).

John O'Regan, *From Empire to Commonwealth: Reflections on a Career in Britain's Overseas Service* (London: Radcliffe Press, 1994).

Ritchie Ovendale (ed.), *British Defence Policy since 1945* (Manchester: Manchester University Press, 1994).

Christopher Owen, *The Rhodesia African Rifles* (London: Leo Cooper, 1970).

Melvin Page (ed.), *Africa and the First World War* (London: Macmillan, 1987).

Ed Paice, *Tip and Run: The Untold Tragedy of the Great War in Africa* (London: Weidenfeld and Nicolson, 2007).

K. M. Pannikar, *India in the Indian Ocean: An Essay on the Influence of Sea Power on Indian History* (London: Allen & Unwin, 1951).

Neil Parsons, 'Colonel Rey and the Colonial Rulers of Botswana: Mercenary and Missionary Traditions in Administration, 1884–1955', in J. F. Ade Ajayi and J. D. Y. Peel (eds), *People and Empires in African History: Essays in Memory of Michael Crowder* (London: Longman, 1992).

——, *King Khama, Emperor Joe, and the Great White Queen: Victorian Britain Through African Eyes* (London: Chicago University Press, 1998).

Timothy Parsons, *The African Rank-and-File: Social Implications of Colonial Military Service in the King's African Rifles, 1902–1964* (Oxford: James Currey, 1999).

Kevin Patience, *Konigsberg: A German East African Raider* (Bahrain: Dar Akhbar, 1994.

——, *Zanzibar and the Shortest War in History* (Bahrain: Dar Akhbar, 1995).

——, *Zanzibar and the Loss of HMS* Pegasus, *20 September 1914* (Bahrain: Dar Akhbar, 1996).

K. David Patterson, 'The Demographic Impact of the 1918–1919 Influenza Pandemic in sub-Saharan Africa: A Preliminary Assessment', in Christopher Fyfe and David McMaster (eds), *African Historical Demography*, volume II (Edinburgh: University of Edinburgh Centre of African Studies, 1981).

Robert Pearce, *Sir Bernard Bourdillon: The Biography of a Twentieth Century Colonialist* (Oxford: The Kensall Press, 1987).

Michael Pearson, *The Indian Ocean* (London: Routledge, 2003).

Richard Peel, *Old Sinister: A Memoir of Sir Arthur Richards* (Cambridge: The Author, 1986).

Roger Perkins, *Regiments and Corps of the British Empire and Commonwealth, 1758–1993* (Newton Abbot: The Author, 1994).

Louis Picard, 'Recruitment in the Civil Service: The Oxbridge Model, Localization, and the Protectorate', in Louis Picard, *The Politics of Development in Botswana: A Model for Success?* (London: Lynne Reinner, 1987).

Howard Philips, *Black October: The Impact of the Spanish Influenza Epidemic of 1918 on South Africa* (Pretoria: Government Printer, 1984).

Jonathan Pittaway and Craig Fourie, *LRDG Rhodesia: Rhodesians in the Long Range Desert Group* (Durban: Dandy Agencies, 2002).

Douglas Porch, *Wars of Empire* (London: Cassell, 2000).

G. Powell, *The Kandyan Wars: The British Army in Ceylon, 1803–1818* (London: Leo Cooper, 1973).

Michael Pye, *The King Over the Water: The Windsors in the Bahamas, 1940–45* (London: Hutchinson, 1981).

P. J. Rich, *Chains of Empire: English Public Schools, Masonic Cabalism, Historical Causality, and Imperial Clubdom* (London: The Regency Press, 1991).

——, *Elixir of Empire: English Public Schools, Ritualism, Freemasonry, and Imperialism* (London: The Regency Press, 1993).

Adrian Preston (ed.), *In Relief of Gordon: Lord Wolseley's Campaign Journal of the Khartoum Relief Expedition, 1884–1885* (London: Hutchinson, 1967).

Richard Preston, *Canada and Imperial Defense: A Study of the Origins of the British Commonwealth's Defence Organization, 1967–1919* (Durham, North Carolina: Duke University Press, 1967).

Richard Rathbone (ed.), 'Special Edition: Africa and the First World War', *Journal of African History*, 19, 1 (1978).

Report by the Chiefs of Staff, 'Future Defence Policy' (May 1947).

Al Richardson and Bob Pitt (eds), *Blows Against the Empire: Trotskyism in Ceylon: The Lanka Sama Samajist Party, 1935–1964* (London: Porcupine Books/Socialist Platform, 1997).

Colin Richardson, *Masirah: Tales from a Desert Island* (Lancaster: Scotforth Books, 2003).

Andrew Roberts, 'Lord Mountbatten and the Perils of Adrenalin' in Andrew Roberts, *Eminent Churchillians* (London, 1994).

Nini Rodgers, 'The Abyssinian Expedition of 1867–68: Disraeli's Imperialism or John Murray's War?', *Historical Journal*, 27 (1984).

William Roger Louis, *Great Britain and Germany's Lost Colonies* (Oxford: Oxford University Press, 1967).

——, 'The South West African Origins of the "Sacred Trust", 1914–1919', *African Affairs*, 66, 262 (1967).

——, *In the Name of God Go! Leo Amery and the British Empire in the Age of Churchill* (London: I. B. Tauris, 1991).

William Roger Louis (ed.), *The Oxford History of the British Empire*, 5 volumes (Oxford: Oxford University Press, 1999).

David Rooney, *Sir Charles Arden Clarke* (London: R. Collins, 1982).

Stephen Roskill, *A Merchant Fleet in War, 1939–1945* (London: Collins, 1962).

Robert Rotberg, *Rebellion in Black Africa* (Oxford: Oxford University Press, 1971).

Fred Rowe, 'Royal Navy Shore Bases UK and Overseas Stations', <http://www.gwpda.org/naval/rnshore.htm>, found on 13/7/05.

Jane Russell, *Communal Politics under the Donoughmore Commission, 1931–1947* (Colombo: Tisara Press, 1983).

Beryl Salt, *A Pride of Eagles: The Definitive History of the Rhodesian Air Force, 1920–1980* (Johannesburg: Coros-Day, 2001).

Glen St J. Barlcay, *The Empire is Marching: A Study of the Military Effort of the British Empire, 1900–1945* (London: Weidenfeld and Nicolson, 1976).

Celia Sandys, *Chasing Churchill: The Travels of Winston Churchill* (London: HarperCollins, 2004).

D. C. Savage and J. Forbes Munro, 'Carrier Recruitment in the British East Africa Protectorate, 1914–1918', *Journal of African History*, 7, 2 (1966).

Isaac Schapera, *Migrant Labour and Tribal Life: A Study of Conditions in the Bechuanaland Protectorate* (Oxford: Oxford University Press, 1947).

Deborah Schmitt, *The Bechuanaland Pioneers and Gunners* (Westport, Connecticut: Praeger, 2006).

Sir John Shuckburgh, 'Civil History of the Colonial Empire at War' (1949).

Regi Siriwardena, *Working Underground: The LSSP in Wartime — A Memory of Happenings and Personalities* (Colombo: International Centre for Ethic Studies, 1999).

Herbert Sloley, 'The South African Native Labour Contingent and the Welfare Committee', *Journal of the African Society*, LXIII, XVII (1918).

Michael Smith, *The Emperor's Codes: Bletchley Park and the Breaking of Japan's Secret Ciphers* (London: Bantam, 2000).

Richard Smith, *Jamaican Volunteers in the First World War: Race, Masculinity, and the Development of National Consciousness* (Manchester: Manchester University Press, 2004).

Ian Speller, '"A Splutter of Musketry?": The British Military Response to the Anglo-Iranian Oil Dispute, 1951', *Contemporary British History*, 17, 1 (2003).

C. P. Stacey, *Canada and the British Army, 1846–1971: A Study in the Practice of Responsible Government* (London: Royal Empire Society/Longmans, 1936).

Andrew Stewart, *Empire Lost: Britain, the Dominions, and the Second World War* (London: Continuum, 2008).

—— and Chris Baxter (eds), *Diplomats at War: British and Commonwealth Diplomacy in Wartime* (Leiden, Netherlands: Brill, 2008).

Michael Summerskill, *China on the Western Front: Britain's Chinese Work Force in the First World War* (London: Michael Summerskill, 1982).

Lord Swinton, *I Remember* (London: Hutchinson, 1948).

Richard Symonds, *Oxford and Empire: The Last Lost Cause?* (Oxford: Clarendon Press, 1986).

David Thomas, *Battle of the Java Sea* (London: André Deutsch, 1968).

Martin Thomas, Bob Moore, and L. J. Butler, *Crises of Empire: Decolonization and Europe's Imperial States, 1918–1975* (London: Hodder Education, 2008).

A. P. Thornton, *The Imperial Idea and its Enemies: A Study in British Power* (London: Macmillan, 1959).

Hugh Tracey, 'Basutoland's Gift to Britain: A Broadcast', *African Affairs* (April 1941).

'Transport: Key to Our War Effort', *Picture Post*, 26 September 1942.

Michael Tomlinson, *The Most Dangerous Moment* (London: William Kimber, 1976).

L. W. Trushel, Nation-Building and the Kgatla: The Role of the Anglo-Boer War', *Botswana Notes and Records*, 4 (1972).

L. C. F. Turner, H. R. Gordon-Cummings, and J. E. Betzler, *War in the Southern Oceans, 1939–1945* (Cape Town: Oxford University Press, 1961).

G. Tylden, 'The Ceylon Regiments, 1796 to 1874', *Journal of the Society for Army Historical Research*, 30 (1952) and 32 (1954).

Jonathan Walker, *Aden Insurgency: The Savage War in South Arabia, 1962–1967* (Staplehurst: Spellmount, 2005).

Richard Waller, 'The Maasai and the British, 1895–1905: The Origins of an Alliance', *Journal of African History*, 17, 4 (1976).

Ben Warlow, *Shore Establishments of the Royal Navy: Being a List of the Static Ships and Establishments of the Royal Navy* (Liskeard: Maritime Books, 1992).

Philip Warner, *Dervish: The Rise and Fall of an African Empire* (London: Macdonald, 1973).

Bernard Wasserstein, *Secret War in Shanghai: Treachery, Subversion and Collaboration in the Second World War* (London: Profile Books, 1998).

Nira Wickramasinghe, *Sri Lanka in the Modern Age: A History of Contested Identities* (Sri Lanka: Vijitha Yapa, 2006).

Brian Willan, 'The South African Native Labour Contingent, 1916–1918', *Journal of African History*, 19, 1 (1978).

Michael Wilson, *A Submariner's War in the Indian Ocean, 1939–1945* (Stroud, Gloucestershire: Tempus, 2000).

John Winton, *The Forgotten Fleet: The British Navy in the Pacific, 1944–45* (London: Michael Joseph, 1969).

W. H. Walton, 'Colonel Herbert Johnson, OBE, MC, TD Leader of the Swazi Pioneers, 1941–45: A Memoir', unpublished paper (1993).

Rhodri Williams, *Defending the Empire: The Conservative Party and British Defence Policy, 1899–1915* (London: Yale University Press, 1991).

Suki Wolton, The Loss of White Prestige: Lord Hailey, the Colonial Office and the Politics of Race and Empire in the Second World War (Basingstoke: Macmillan, 2000).

Philip Ziegler, *Personal Diaries of Admiral the Lord Louis Mountbatten, Supreme Allied Commander South East Asia, 1943–1946* (London: Collins, 1988).

Index